C000276689

Explorer
Australia

Michael Ivory

 Publishing

Front cover (a): Kata Tjuta (The Olgas), Northern Territory
(b): Windsurfer
(c): Ritual and ceremony are central to Aboriginal culture
Spine: Australian cricketer
Back cover: Diving on the Great Barrier Reef
Page 2: The Pinnacles, Nambung National Park
Page 3: Sydney Harbour Bridge and Opera House
Page 4: Parade at Victoria Barracks, Sydney
Page 5 (top): Surfing Australia
Page 6: Sunset at Uluru (Ayers Rock)
Page 7 (top): Building façades at Maldon, Victoria
Page 8: Uluru (Ayers Rock)
Page 9: Kalbarri Gorge, Western Australia
Page 33: Sydney Opera House and Circular Quay
Page 39: Sydney Tower
Page 251: Clock Tower Square Shopping Centre, Sydney

Written by Michael Ivory
Revision verified by Anne Matthews
Original photography by Adrian Baker

Reprinted with new cover 1999
Revised third edition 1998
Reprinted 1994, Oct 1998
First published 1994
Edited, designed, produced and distributed by AA Publishing, Norfolk House, Priestley Road, Basingstoke, Hampshire, RG24 9NY 1996.
Maps © The Automobile Association 1994, 1996, 1998.

The contents of this publication are believed correct at the time of printing. Nevertheless, the publishers cannot be held responsible for any errors or omissions or for changes in the details given in this guide or for the consequences of any reliance on the information provided by the same. Assessments of attractions, hotels, restaurants and so forth are based upon the author's own personal experience and, therefore, descriptions given in this guide necessarily contain an element of subjective opinion which may not reflect the publishers' opinion or dictate a reader's own experiences on another occasion. We have tried to ensure accuracy in this guide, but things do change and we would be grateful if readers would advise us of any inaccuracies they may encounter.

A CIP catalogue record for this book is available from the British Library.

ISBN 0 7495 1597 X
Published by AA Publishing (a trading name of Automobile Association Developments Limited, whose registered office is Norfolk House, Priestley Road, Basingstoke, Hampshire RG24 9NY. Registered number 1878835).

Colour separation: Fotographics Ltd
Printed and bound in Italy by Printer Trento srl

Titles in the Explorer series:
Boston & New England • Britain • Brittany • California
Caribbean • China • Costa Rica • Crete • Cyprus • Egypt
Florence & Tuscany • Florida • France • Germany • Greek Islands
Hawaii • Indonesia • Ireland • Israel • Italy • Japan • London
Mexico • Moscow & St Petersburg • New York
New Zealand • Paris • Portugal • Prague • Provence
Rome • San Francisco • Scotland • Singapore & Malaysia
South Africa • Spain • Thailand • Turkey • Venice• Vietnam

AA World Travel Guides publish nearly 300 guidebooks to a full range of cities, countries and regions across the world. Find out more about AA Publishing and the wide range of services the AA provides by visiting our Web site at www.theaa.co.uk.

How to use this book

This book is divided into five main sections:

❏ Section 1: *Australia Is*
discusses various aspects of life and living today, from landscape to culture

❏ Section 2: *Australia Was*
places the country in its historical context and explores those past events whose influences are felt to this day

❏ Section 3: *A to Z Section*
is broken down into regional chapters, and covers places to visit, including walks and drives. Within this section fall the Focus-on articles, which consider a variety of subjects in greater detail

❏ Section 4: *Travel Facts*
contains the strictly practical information vital for a successful trip

❏ Section 5: *Hotels and Restaurants*
lists recommended establishments throughout Australia, giving a brief résumé of their attractions

How to use the star rating
Most of the places described in this book have been given a separate rating:

▶▶▶ **Do not miss**

▶▶ **Highly recommended**

▶ **Worth seeing**

Not essential viewing

Map references
To make the location of a particular place easier to find, every main entry in this book has a map reference to the right of its name. This comprises a number, followed by a letter, followed by another number, such as 176B3. The first number (176) refers to the page on which the map can be found, the letter (B) and the second number (3) pinpoint the square in which the main entry is located. The maps on the inside front cover and inside back cover are referred to as IFC and IBC respectively.

Contents

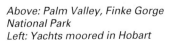

*Above: Palm Valley, Finke Gorge
National Park
Left: Yachts moored in Hobart*

Quick reference

This quick-reference guide high-lights the features of the book you will use most often: the maps; the introductory features; the Focus on articles; the walks and the drives.

7

Bright flowers of the bottlebrush

My Australia by Michael Ivory

Crossing the interminable Nullarbor Plain aboard the Indian Pacific train, I made the Englishman's mistake of heading for an empty table in the dining car. The steward was shocked: 'Hold on a minute, mate! Why don't you sit over here with these folk? I'm sure you'll have plenty to talk about'. He was right of course. Australia is a place where human contact is easy. Indeed, Australian friendliness is proverbial; first names are used freely and 'mates' are easily made, especially if you show yourself ready to muck in, say what a wonderful country it is (not difficult!), and refrain from invidious comparisons with wherever you come from.

I won't forget that train ride eastward from Kalgoorlie across the Nullarbor Plain, where the scenery doesn't change from one day to the next and it was a real relief to have entertaining companions at the dining table. Australians have long since overcome what one of them called the 'tyranny of distance', the impossibly vast spaces which faced early explorers and travellers. Nowadays half the enjoyment of Australia lies in the many different ways there are of getting around. It was a special thrill to get up into the cab of the big diesel heading towards the Indian Pacific to marvel at the aching emptiness of the scene and at the single track heading ruler-straight to the far horizon. In utter contrast was the bumpy ride up the Broomfield Track in Far North Queensland, with rain forest to either side. Rather more relaxing was a trip through the same kind of landscape aboard an amphibious DUKW, which took jungle, rivers and snake-filled pools in its stride. I joined bushwalkers in their wanderings among the beautiful bush country and eucalyptus forest which surrounds most of the big cities. Here, perhaps more than anywhere else, flying comes into its own. Not by comfortable airliner, but in a light plane, tossed around by the thermals bubbling upwards from the hot surface of Ayers Rock, or in a little seaplane skimming the surface of Tasmania's Gordon River gorge. And the most sublime moment of all? Not in the air, but whizzing across the waters of Sydney Harbour in a powerboat, 'tinnie' in hand, at the moment when the Opera House came into sight beneath the great span of the Harbour Bridge, and I felt I'd really arrived 'Down Under'.

Michael Ivory has written extensively about the lands of Eastern Europe – his books for AA Publishing include AA *Essential Hungary*, AA *Essential Czech Republic*, AA *Explorer Prague* and AA *CityPack Prague*. He welcomed the chance to write a guide to Australia, a place which has always intrigued him. AA *Explorer Australia* reveals something of his pleasure in experiencing this fascinating, diverse country.

AUSTRALIA IS

■ **Australia occupies a lonely place on the globe. Apart from the frozen Antarctic, it is the only continent to lie wholly within the southern hemisphere; though Papua New Guinea is only just over the horizon on the far side of the shallow Timor Sea, New Zealand is more than 2,000km away across the Tasman Sea and the Asian mainland at Singapore is nearly 3,000km distant.** ■

Girded by nearly 37,000km of coast-line, the 'island continent' has a simple threefold structure which is a gift to the teacher of geography.

The Western Plateau Almost two-thirds of the land surface belongs to the Western Plateau, a vast and arid tableland covering most of Western Australia, South Australia, the Northern Territory and part of Queensland. Mostly flat and low-lying, it is interrupted by spectacular

10

Mount Warning National Park, New South Wales

individual features like Ayers Rock (Uluru) and the Olgas (Kata Tjuta), by rocky strongholds like the Kimberley and Arnhem Land, and by rugged ridges like those of the MacDonnell, Flinders and Hamersley Ranges.

The plateau is an ancient land whose fertility was leached away by rains which fell millions of years ago, leaving arid wastes with evocative names like the Nullarbor Plain or the Sturt Stony Desert. Similarly, winds which ceased to blow long ago left achingly repetitive patterns of sand dunes. Except in the tropics, rainfall is not only minimal but also irregular; none may fall for years, then sudden downpours will fill the normally vacant river beds, only to peter out in the great salt lakes.

Much of the area is uninhabited or very thinly settled, with a population measured in hundreds of square kilometres per person. Only to the west of the Darling Ranges, on the relatively fertile coastal plains around the great city of Perth, are there extensive farmlands and a network of settlements linked by roads and railways. Elsewhere, settlements exist in isolation as ports, mining towns and staging posts along an interminable highway, or, increasingly, as centres for Outback tourism.

The Great Dividing Range Running down the whole of Australia's eastern coastline from Cape York in the far north to the hills and highlands of New South Wales and Victoria in the south, the Great Dividing Range leaps Bass Strait to reappear in the mountains of Tasmania. It is here that the continent's highest peaks are found: Mount Kosciuszko in New

South Wales (2,228m), Mount Bogong in Victoria (1,986m) and Mount Ossa (1,617m) in Tasmania.

However, much of the area is not made up of mountains but instead of high plateaux, from which rivers run eastward across the coastal plain. The bulk of the country's population lives here, clustering for the most part in the metropolitan areas around the great coastal state capitals of Sydney (New South Wales), Melbourne (Victoria), Adelaide (South Australia) and Brisbane (Queensland). Rural settlement is quite dense in the valleys between the uplands and all along the fertile strip extending into the tropics along the Queensland coast. The only inland city of any size is Canberra, the artificially implanted federal capital.

Central Eastern Lowlands Between these two great geographical divisions run the Central Eastern Lowlands, sloping down gradually from the east towards the interior. A series of broad basins succeed one another, from the southern rim of the Gulf of Carpentaria through Queensland's Channel Country to the area drained by the country's greatest river system, the Murray/ Darling/Murrumbidgee. Here in the Outback, grazing animals outnumber people by a factor of several hundred to one, and rural life depends as much on unreliable rainfall as on the state of world markets. Mineral wealth has created a small number of towns like Broken Hill and Mount Isa, linked by interminably long roads and railways to the coast.

South Australian opals

❏ In view of its size, the world's driest continent after Antarctica has a surprisingly small range of climates. The highest rainfall is in the tropical or subtropical north, where temperatures stay high all year round (29°C in summer and 24°C in winter). Unlike the north, where the rain falls during the summer, temperate southern Australia experiences its highest rainfall in winter and spring, and there is more variation in average temperatures (24°C in summer to 10°C in winter when snow falls on the higher peaks). Much of the interior is arid, with little rain (none at all in some years), and temperatures here soar to scorching heights – a maximum of 53.1°C was recorded at Cloncurry in Queensland in 1889 – although nights can be cold. ❏

■ The uniqueness of Australia's plants and animals is the result of the continent's 40 million years of isolation from the rest of the world. Over this long period, both fauna and flora evolved in response to local conditions quite independently of developments elsewhere, resulting in the array of strange creatures and plants which so surprised and delighted Joseph Banks as he accompanied Captain Cook aboard the *Endeavour* in 1770. Despite subsequent development that had little regard for environmental side effects, Australia was quick to create national parks, some 2,000 of which await today's visitor. ■

Forests The richest habitat in Australia is that of the rain forest. Tropical rain forest is best seen in northern Queensland (see page 222), but occurs in parts of the northern coastlands in the Northern Territory and Western Australia. Temperate rain forest, of equal fascination and beauty, spreads over much of the wild country of southwestern Tasmania. This is the domain of the **southern beech** and of one of the longest-lived trees on earth, the **Huon pine**.

Great forests still cloak some of the less accessible areas of the south-east and southwest, but all of Australia's woodland has suffered grievously at the hands of the timber-getters. The majority of the country's trees are variations on the theme of **eucalyptus** (also referred to as eucalypts and gum trees); they include some of the tallest trees on earth, like the mountain ash of the Victorian coastal forests or the karri of south-western Western Australia.

Scrubland and desert Away from the coast, the pioneers found impenetrable **mallee** (a dense scrub of low-growing eucalyptus) or more open, park-like woodland. Most of these original plant communities have been cleared for grazing land, while native grasses and herbs have given way to exotic, high-yielding varieties. The desert is perhaps the most intriguing

The rainbow lorikeet

of all Australian ecosystems, where **saltbush**, **spinifex** and the occasional **desert oak** provide shelter for creatures like scorpions and spiders, themselves food for snakes, lizards and **goannas**. The seeds of many small plants lie in wait for the sparse rain, flowering spectacularly when thus nourished.

From pouches to platypuses Of all the marsupials that inhabit the island continent the macropods – **kangaroos** and **wallabies** – seem to need little introduction, having long been

The kangaroo – one of Australia's best-known marsupials

familiar as one of the country's best-known emblems. But there's a whole world of roos and wallabies out there; in addition to the red kangaroo (reaching over 2m), there are some 50 other varieties, ranging from the equally large Forester kangaroos to the quokkas (mistaken for rats by early explorers) and brush-tailed bettongs. Kangaroos live in most parts of the country, even occasionally on the fringe of towns.

After the kangaroo, it is the endearing **koala** that every visitor wants to see and, if possible, hug. Koalas spend most of their time asleep and the rest chewing on the leaves of certain eucalyptuses. The population is recovering after being hunted for its fur, but it is still subject to disease and loss of habitat. As a result, you're more likely to see them in one of the country's excellent wildlife parks than in the wild. Here you may also see **wombats**, burrowing marsupials, and **possums**, some of which are able to glide from tree to tree thanks to their flight membrane.

Another creature that you are more likely to see in an artificial environment is the **platypus**. This shy, egg-laying mammal with its soft bill was thought to be a hoax when a specimen was first sent to Britain for examination. The spiny ant eater, or **echidna**, is less timid, being well defended by its ability to burrow below ground or present an attacker with its array of sharp spines.

National parks Australia declared its first national park (**Royal National Park**) as early as 1879. Today more than 2,000 such areas are protected and managed in order to conserve their natural beauty, protect their wildlife, and make them accessible to visitors. The outstanding quality and global importance of the country's natural treasures has also been recognised by the designation of no fewer than 11 World Heritage areas. Visitors to national parks in Australia will usually find a high standard of management in evidence, with good provision of information and encouragement to explore by means of walking trails. Always seek the advice of wardens and rangers if you are at all unfamiliar with local conditions.

■ It's quite possible you'll meet a stereo-typical Australian male while Down Under. You've probably imagined him already: tall, sunburnt, probably blond and blue-eyed, short on words but long on ability to sink the stubbies (get drunk) with his mates, unhurried, an enemy of pretentiousness, and unreconstructed in his male chauvin-ism. The stereotype exists, of course, but today's Australians are much less easy to categorise. ■

The story of Australia's earliest European settlement is bizarre, to say the least. Some years after James Cook's 1770 voyage of discovery, the British government came up with a highly ambitious – some would say outrageous – solution to the 'disposal' of its felons and criminals, large numbers of whom had been sent to the American colonies prior to the 1776 revolution. In May 1787, 11 ships carrying over 1,400 people, including 759 male and female convicts and their keepers, set sail from Portsmouth, England for

A classic Aussie 'character'

❏ An old cartoon shows hopeful British immigrants disembarking beneath a quayside banner bearing the cryptic message: 'Welcome Pommie Bastards!' Among the derogatory terms for non-Australians, the one describing the British is the most venerable and, surprisingly, the most obscure in origin. The name has a variety of explanations, none of them really convincing. Could Pom really come from 'Prisoner of Motherland'? or 'pomegranate' (which, like Poms, turn red in the sun)? ❏

a long and arduous voyage to the virtually unknown southern continent. On their arrival in Sydney in January 1788, this motley crew of Britons became Australia's first, albeit unwilling, immigrants.

The 19th- and early 20th-century non-British migrants to Australia were very conspicuous and were often resented, although the pious and hard-working Germans who helped settle South Australia fitted in well enough. Gold strikes brought in thousands of Chinese, against whom there existed prejudice of almost paranoid proportions, and South Sea Islanders known as Kanakas worked the sugar plantations of Queensland, until they were sent back home in order to preserve 'white jobs'.

War refugees Until World War II, the flow of British migrants was sufficient to satisfy Australian needs.

But the post-war boom demanded more workers than Britain could supply, and the country opened its gates to a Europe crowded with 'reffos' (refugees) and displaced persons. Without asking too many questions of the 'what did you do in the war?' variety, Australia accepted hundreds of thousands of migrants from northern and central Europe, the Netherlands, Germany, Scandinavia, Czechoslovakia and the Baltic states.

When this source began to dry up, the emphasis changed to southern Europe, and the next wave of 'New Australians' consisted of Italians, Greeks, Maltese, Croats and Serbs. A tacit 'White Australia' policy was followed; non-Europeans were rarely admitted, excluded sometimes by means of the infamous dictation test which allowed an immigration officer to give the would-be migrant a test in a language of his (the immigration officer's) choice. An undesirable applicant of Chinese origin could thus have been examined on his knowledge of Gaelic, and, not surprisingly, fail.

A multi-cultural society A continuing though fluctuating demand for labour, coupled with an increasing

Greek delicatessen in Melbourne

awareness of Australia's geo-political position and social ties with Asia, made a continuation of this policy unsustainable – a fact instantly verifiable on the streets of any of the state capitals, where plenty of faces belonging to recent Cambodian, Vietnamese, Filipino and other Asian immigrants may be seen.

Total assimilation has been abandoned in favour of preserving migrant cultures; one TV channel (SBS) even specialises in programmes in a variety of different languages. For a country which pursued a policy of racial purity for much of its life and which still has a rich repertoire of seemingly abusive (but actually fairly harmless) terms for anyone who isn't a 'fair dinkum' Aussie, to have accomplished such a transition in so short a space of time without serious social repercussions is a remarkable achievement.

In the midst of all this multi-culturalism, the Aborigines – who are, after all, the only Australians who are neither recent settlers nor descended from migrants – strive hard to retain their traditions and culture.

■ 'No worries' seems to sum up much of the average Australian's attitude to life. Work doesn't play the central role here that it does in some societies around the Pacific Rim or even in Europe. Life is to be made the most of, preferably out in the open, enjoying food and drink, watching sports with passionate intensity, or swimming, surfing, bushwalking, and simply lazing around in the great outdoors of the 'best country in the world'. ■

16

Celebrating at the Melbourne Cup

Once a source of shame, the founding period of convictism is now looked back on with pride, and can be seen as contributing positive factors to the way Australians are today. Australian 'mateship' has its roots in shared oppression and in the importance of comrades in making a life in a harsh and empty land. The land posed a tough physical challenge, in which the conventional qualities of 'manliness' were directly related to success or even survival. Work was originally performed under duress and for someone else, after which you were free to lead your own life. Authority was exercised by prison warders and governors, and consequently resented, but there was no old ruling class or complicated code of manners. Strangers were seldom seen, but if they needed help they could be sure of getting it.

Everyone is equal So Australia has long been a land where people feel themselves to be basically equal and as good as the next person. Money and the making of it are admired, but this does not mean that the monied become beings apart. There is an openness about social contacts that is surprising to many visitors. When Australians say 'How are you?' there's a good chance that they actually mean it, and will enjoy hearing your answer (especially if you reveal to them how much you like their country). If you expect to be deferred to, you could be in for an unpleasant surprise; Australians don't like pretension, least of all the British variety, and will prickle if they detect it.

The outdoor life Given the character of the country, with its space, climate, the grandeur of its natural landscapes and the fact that the vast majority of the population lives close to a beach, it's hardly surprising that people seem obsessed with outdoor life and sport. Everyone loves a 'barbie' and a session on the beach, whether sunbathing or surfing. Though the great days of lifesaving clubs and parades may be over, the life of the beach certainly isn't; surfing is indeed a way of life for quite a number of people.

Gambling is also a national passion, taking place indoors in front of endless ranks of 'pokies', at the casino or outdoors at the racetrack. On the

Lifeguard at Bondi Beach

❏ Even though women got the vote in Australia at an early date, Australia was always a man's country. The male-female ratio among the transportees brought by the First Fleet was hardly a balanced one, and the scenes that took place when the first cargo of women was discharged were said by some to be 'indescribable'. 'Sheilas' were kept in their place longer here than in most other countries, both at home and behind the bar, where they filled the glasses while the men on the other side got on with the serious business of drinking. Big changes came during World War II, however, and then later with the growth of feminism, one of the key works of which, *The Female Eunuch*, was by the Australian writer Germaine Greer. ❏

first Tuesday in November life stops across the nation for the big horse race, the Melbourne Cup.

Sport Most Australians have a favourite sport, to watch if not to play. A passion for cricket is shared with the English and some other members of the British Commonwealth, and has been made less stuffy by innovations like one-day matches, floodlighting and the wearing of coloured clothing. Rugby Union exists and Rugby League is played in NSW and Queensland. The really big football game, however, and certainly in its Melbourne stronghold, is that known as Australian Rules. It originated on the goldfields, a crude version of Gaelic football played by prospectors taking time off from the diggings, and has been described as 'a kind of organised mayhem remarkable for its lack of obvious rules'. Up to 120,000 spectators gather to watch the grand final at the MCG (Melbourne Cricket Ground) every September.

The year 2000, however, is set to place Australia squarely on the world's sporting map, when Sydney plays host to the XXVII Olympiad.

■ **Australian culture goes back far longer than the 200 years of white settlement, and visitors will be fascinated by the evidence of at least 40,000 years of uninterrupted civilisation in the dot and x-ray style rock- and cave-paintings, and in the haunting stories of the creation legends of the Aboriginal Dreamtime.** ■

The 'cultural cringe' which once caused Australians to defer to the supposed superiority of the artistic and intellectual life of Europe has now vanished. Throughout Australian society there is a high regard for culture and talent, and pride in the international success of Australian artists, film-makers and writers. Most Aussies cannot resist a good performance, and visitors who are aware of this and who let themselves go a bit are bound to get a warm welcome.

Literature and films Drama has developed from such elegies for lost youth as Ray Lawlor's *Summer of the Seventeenth Doll* to the tautly constructed plays of David Williamson, exploring many aspects of Australian life including politics, business, crime, retirement and 'mateship'. His *Emerald City* is a must for anyone who wants to understand modern Sydney.

Tongue-in-cheek Crocodile Dundee

In literature, Judith Wright and Gwen Harwood are poets of world stature, weaving together the personal and the public, and capturing the elusive character of the Australian environment. Patrick White's *Voss* and *The Tree of Man* evoke the spirit of the land, while the younger generation of writers such as Thomas Keneally, David Malouf and Peter Carey explores more universal problems of the human condition. Films have also moved from the tongue-in-cheek stereotypes of *Crocodile Dundee* to the more sensitive social commentary of *Strictly Ballroom, Muriel's Wedding* and *The Last Days of Chez Nous.*

Painters Marvellous light and scenery have contributed to a tradition of outstanding painting. The early dreamy landscapes of McCubbin and the Heidelberg School, lending the Australian scenery a European beauty, gave way to the more distinctively Australian works of painters like Sidney Nolan with his series of pictures depicting the fatal defiance of Ned Kelly. Arthur Boyd's and Brett Whiteley's enlargements of their own dreams and obsessions sometimes achieve a vast scale, and Fred Williams' wonderful evocations of the arid Australian landscape rival the originality of Aboriginal art.

Music Australia also has much to offer musically. The golden voice of Joan Carden makes her a worthy successor to Dame Nellie Melba and Dame Joan Sutherland ('La Stupenda'). Each state capital boasts an Australian Broadcasting Commission symphony orchestra of

The Sidney Nolan painting Dog and Duck Hotel

❏ Born in Melbourne in 1917, Sir Sidney Nolan was one of the 'Angry Penguins', a group of young and radical artists who, in the early 1940s, wanted to shake Australian painting out of what they saw as its complacency. Nolan brought the strangeness of the Australian landscape to the attention of the world as well as elevating the status of near-mythical episodes such as Kelly's exploits or the ill-fated expedition of Burke and Wills. Given a British knighthood, Nolan lived the latter part of his life in England, where he died in 1992. ❏

world standard, with internationally recognised conductors and repertoires including music by contemporary Australian composers such as Colin Brumby, John Antill and Peter Sculthorpe. Aboriginal music is increasingly entering the mainstream of the country's culture, and the growing international reputation of Yothu Yindi, the Aboriginal rock band, was recognised by the 1992 'Australian of the Year' award given to its lead singer, Mandawuy Yunupingu. The country is also a hotbed of good jazz (James Morrison), folk (Kev Carmody), and country and western (John Williamson), all competing for listeners.

The media By contrast, most Australian newspapers and TV channels are owned by three media moguls – Murdoch, Packer and Black. Their content is dominated by personality trivia, sports, sentimental 'bushwhacker' pap and investigations into the private lives of public figures, making the Australian press as sensationalist as any in the world.

The Australian Broadcasting Commission's radio and television programmes, on the other hand, gain many international awards for quality and interest, particularly in the fields of science, environment and religion. Especially outstanding is the current-affairs weekly *Four Corners*, which for 20 years has exposed big business and government scandals that have been ignored by the commercial media.

■ The six states which came together on the first day of the 20th century to create the nation of Australia had all developed outwards from the isolated footholds of their port-of-entry capital cities, with very different characteristics and cultures. The evolution of a national consciousness has been slow, and states still maintain vigorous political and economic competition with each other and with the Federal Government. ■

Since 1940 Commonwealth control of tax revenues and appointment of Supreme Court judges has guaranteed the Federal Government victory in most disputes. This included the 1983 prohibition of damming of the World Heritage-listed Franklin River in Tasmania (where British botanist David Bellamy joined young Australian protesters in front of the bulldozers) and the 1990 exclusion of logging from the unique tropical rain forests of northern Queensland. In these matters, the Commonwealth Government has been influenced by a Green movement which commands a disciplined voting block – generally estimated at between eight per cent and 15 per cent of the electorate.

The political parties After 13 years in power (an unprecedented six terms of office), Australia's Federal Labor Government was heavily defeated by the coalition of the Liberal Party (representing the urban middle classes and employers) and National Party (the traditional voice of rural interests) in the March 1996 elections. The new Liberal Party Prime Minister is John Howard, best known for his self-righteous and extremely conservative approach.

Although a large proportion of the population is delighted by this transfer of power after Labor's long, and perhaps increasingly complacent, rule, many Australians now wonder, for example, what will become of the push for a new and more appropriate flag and an Australian republic, free of obeisance to the Queen and Great Britain, by the Olympics year of 2000. Aboriginal, Asian immigration and arts policies have also changed, with John Howard and his supporters expressing little interest in these issues.

Until at least 1999, the challenge to the Liberal/National Party coalition will be spearheaded by the Leader of the Opposition, formerly the Deputy Prime Minister, Kim Beazley.

Economic development There is little genuine debate about changing current economic policies. The 'Lucky Country' cannot now find enough markets for its wool, wheat, beef or mineral exports to pay for its insatiable appetite for expensive imports. The tariffs that previously protected small local industries from being swamped by European and Asian manufacturers have been drastically cut in the interests of economic rationalism, unemployment is approaching nine per cent and the overseas debt increases each year. Governments hope that growth in international tourism will help save the economy.

There is now bi-partisan political agreement on the need to develop manufactured goods for export, though current government policy of reducing tariff barriers has had the opposite result and has caused massive unemployment. However, there can be no argument about the need to integrate better with the economies of the demographic and economic giants of Southeast Asia and the Pacific Rim – Australia's closest neighbours.

AUSTRALIA WAS

■ In some parts of the globe vigorous land-shaping processes are obviously hard at work. Ice and snow attacks alpine peaks, glaciers grind through valleys, torrents and waterfalls erode, while elsewhere geysers boil and lava pours from beneath the earth. By contrast, Australia is a quiet continent, much of whose active geological history ended long ago. ■

Ancient tectonics Some 50 million years ago Australia was part of Gondwanaland, the great southern supercontinent that slowly split into the separate fragments we know today as Antarctica, South America, Africa and India, as well as Australia and New Zealand. But its geological evolution goes back much further than this time of continental drift; Precambrian rocks more than 600 million years old are exposed over much of the continent, among them the ancient iron ore deposits of the Pilbara in Western Australia. Subsequently, much of the heart of the continent was periodically submerged beneath the sea, leaving deposits of sands, shells and grits, or the limestone of the Nullarbor Plain. Great coral reefs were also formed which, when uplifted, became the basis of the extensive cave systems

The Great Dividing Range

of New South Wales and Queensland, or the great bastion which today guards the southern rim of the Kimberley. The Great Artesian Basin came into being at this time too, its pumped waters still supporting life in much of the Outback.

More recent changes About 2 million years ago, what is now the arid Red Centre of the continent enjoyed a far higher rainfall and carried a rich vegetation of tropical forest, traces of which can still be seen in the palms and other plants which live in the gorges penetrating the area's harsh ranges. In the east, the Great Dividing Range was thrown up as the result of convulsive earth movements; its southern, alpine area, together with the Tasmanian highlands, is the only part of the continent to have been subjected to glaciation in the last Ice Age (10,000 years ago). As the ice melted, the sea level rose, creating a wonderful natural harbour for the future city of Sydney. At the same time, the land bridges with Tasmania and New Guinea were cut. Later still (some 5,000 years ago), an outburst of volcanic activity covered the plains of southwestern Victoria with lava, leaving a legacy of cones and crater lakes and of deep fertile soil.

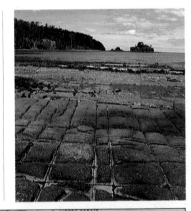

Right: Tesselated pavement on the Tasman Peninsula
Below: Australia in 1848 – note the dearth of information on the unexplored interior of the continent

■ **European explorers and educated early settlers tended to romanticise the black people they encountered on the shores of the unknown continent. Aborigines were seen by some as typifying the 'Noble Savage' dreamt up by the imaginative powers of 18th-century thinkers; an endlessly fascinating subject for artists and draughtsmen, the first Australians were sometimes depicted in the heroic poses of ancient Greek statuary.** ■

Victims of the white man The Aborigines failed to correspond to the European stereotypes; in what now seems an entirely appropriate response, albeit one doomed to failure, some groups put up a vigorous resistance to the encroachment of white settlement on the lands which had formed the basis of their lives since time immemorial. Others fell

Ritual and ceremony are central to Aboriginal culture

easy victim to the diseases and vices of their conquerors. Only a few decades after the arrival of the First Fleet, the Aborigines of the Sydney region had been decimated by drink and influenza, and before the 19th century had run its course, the Tasmanians had virtually disappeared. For much of this century Aborigines have been seen as unreliable farm hands, 'welfare bludgers', or, huddled on a few remaining reserves, as ripe material for conversion to Christianity.

It is only in relatively recent times that white Australians have begun to appreciate the richness and subtlety of the life that their appropriation of the continent all but destroyed, but which sustained the first Australians in material and spiritual harmony with the Australian environment for at least 40,000 years.

Dreamtime Aboriginals inhabited the land in a way remote from European concepts of ownership and property. They believed not only that the landscape had been created by ancestral beings during the Dreamtime, but that these very ancestors were incorporated in landscape features. The land itself was part of the spiritual realm of the whole of creation, in which all creatures, animals as well as men, and the dead as well as the living, had their being. The landscape was therefore venerated by individuals, large family groups or clans, with certain places – 'sacred sites' – having a particularly intense meaning.

A deep understanding of the spiritual significance of the land was

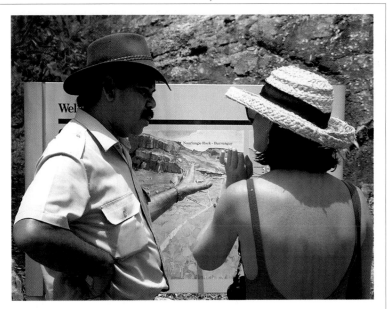

passed on by highly refined and diversified traditions of song and dance. Never codified in writing, many of these oral traditions have tragically been lost. Ritual gatherings, sometimes known as *corroborees*, took up large amounts of time, with men and women often having rigorously separate ceremonies. Visual arts, like cave- or wall-paintings, or designs executed on the ground had a ceremonial or story-telling role, and were ephemeral or subject to periodic renewal.

Lifestyle Virtually all Aboriginal groups were nomads, living a Stone-Age lifestyle of hunting, gathering and fishing based on seasonal availability of game, seeds and fruits. Controlled burning of the bush took place in order to encourage regrowth and thus attract animals to the area. Material impedimenta were kept to an absolute minimum: baskets and nets, digging sticks, shelters of brushwood, weapons of carved wood and sharpened bone, canoes of bark and boomerangs. Clothes were minimal, except in the colder, wetter areas of the southeast, where skins and furs were worn.

Each clan had its own distinct territory, defined orally by song rather

Aboriginal rangers are happy to share their knowledge of the land

than marked out on the ground. For another group to cross such an invisible but nevertheless definite boundary might have involved complex negotiation. The whole of Australia can now be mapped in terms of these traditional territories, but at the time of European settlement no such map existed except in the hearts of its inhabitants. This allowed legalistic Europeans to appropriate the land with a more or less clear conscience.

❏ Some 200 Aboriginal languages existed, related to one another but not necessarily mutually intelligible. Most people were multilingual, speaking perhaps five or six tongues. The language of the Aborigines around the future site of Sydney was, of course, unknown to Europeans, and the cry of '*Warra! Warra!*' they were greeted with was not understood. Even if it had been, would they have taken any notice? '*Warra! Warra!*' means 'Go away!' ❏

■ **The first people to explore Australia were the ancestors of today's Aborigines, who may have crossed the still intact land-bridge linking the continent to New Guinea well over 40,000 years ago. Living at first along the coasts and in other areas where food was easily obtainable, they eventually spread all over the country, learning to live even in those regions where survival seemed all but impossible to later explorers.** ■

Portuguese and Dutch explorers

The European discovery of the island continent began in a tentative, almost accidental way in the 16th century, as Portuguese mariners looked for routes to the eastern Spice Islands. But the first definite landfall was made in 1606 by the Dutch ship *Duyfken* ('Little Dove') sailing out of the Dutch colony of Batavia (now Jakarta). Her captain, Willem Jansz, was unimpressed by what he saw of the desolate western coast of Cape York and its 'wild, cruel black savages'.

A little later, Dutch skippers on their way to Java found that they could cut weeks off their journey by making use of the Roaring Forties until they made a northward turn well short of the coast of western Australia. Some sailed straight on, like Dirk Hartog in 1616 (who left an inscribed pewter plate nailed to a post on the island which bears his name), and Frederik de Houtman, who landed on the Houtman Abrolhos islands in 1619.

Under the command of a captain whose name is unrecorded, the *Leeuwin* ('Lioness') sighted the southwestern tip of the continent in 1622. Subsequently, more systematic attempts were made by the Dutch East India Company to survey the coastline. The most famous of them was the voyage of Abel Tasman in 1642–3 in the *Heemskerck* and *Zeehaan*; put ashore on Tasmania's Blackman Bay, his pilot heard voices coming from the bush, but the natives failed to show themselves. Tasman had the flag run up, and named the island after the Governor

W R Stott's painting shows William Dampier being attacked by Aborigines when he landed in 1699

of the Dutch East Indies, Van Diemen, a name only changed to honour the actual discoverer in 1855.

In the course of a second voyage, Tasman failed (as had all his predecessors) to find the gap between New Guinea and Australia, subsequently called the Torres Strait, but mapped 3,000km of the north coast instead. By this time, the coast had been explored by Dutchmen from the tip of Cape York around Western Australia to the archipelago in the Great Australian Bight. Although the Dutch did not take the continent under their control, they did name it – New Holland.

Early settlers – Captain Phillip arriving at Sydney Cove in 1788

The British arrive The first Englishman to set foot on the shores of New Holland was the adventurer William Dampier, who landed twice on its northwestern coast, first in 1688, then again in 1699. It was Captain Cook, however, who not only found the unknown east coast, but sailed the length of it and identified the spot where British settlement was to take place. He completed his mission in spite of the fact that his ship the *Endeavour* ran aground on the Barrier Reef (see page 214). The name he gave to the land he claimed for the British Crown was New South Wales.

Even after British settlement had been well and truly established around Sydney Harbour (by Captain Phillip in 1788), many uncertainties remained as to whether the three known fragments added up to a continent. Part of the answer was provided by two truly intrepid men, George Bass and Matthew Flinders, who by 1798 had posited the existence of a channel between the mainland and Van Diemen's Land, now named Bass Strait.

Aboard the *Investigator*, Flinders went on to explore the south coast with great thoroughness, meeting the French survey ship *Geographe* in what came to be known as Encounter Bay. The master of the *Geographe*, Nicolas Baudin, behaved impeccably, though Flinders, not unnaturally, was suspicious of the intentions of a servant of France, a country with which Britain had recently been at war. A lack of comparable wariness was Flinders' later undoing; having sailed right round Australia in 1802–3, he was arrested by the Governor of French Mauritius on his way back to England, unaware that war had broken out again. Held for six years by the French, he returned to England a prematurely aged 40-year-old, barely able to complete his *A Voyage to Terra Australis* before dying in 1814.

❏ Non-Europeans also made contact with Australia. Chinese junks seem to have sailed as far south as Australia's northern coast, possibly as early as the 15th century, and there were exchanges between the Aborigines and the warlike inhabitants of New Guinea. From about 1700 onwards, fishermen from Macassar in the Celebes frequented the north coast in search of trepang (sea-cucumbers), an activity which only ended quite recently. ❏

■ **The map of Australia is scattered with surnames attached to natural features or to settlements, honouring governors or similar worthies. But there are others like the Sturt Stony Desert, which are memorials to a different kind of fame – that earned by the inland explorers, a breed of men who set out with varying degrees of success to explore the new country's uncharted interior.** ■

Straightforward curiosity may have impelled some adventures into the interior, but another factor was the hunger for land as the colony grew and needed to be fed. In addition, industrial England had developed an insatiable appetite for wool, which the merino cross-breeds so successfully developed by John Macarthur could satisfy if only enough pastures could be found. For many years, the Blue Mountains seemed to bar the way from Sydney to the interior, but in 1813 this obstacle was overcome by William Lawson, William Charles Wentworth and Gregory Blaxland. Governor Macquarie had a road built across the mountains in record time, and settlers rushed into the rich grazing lands beyond.

Sturt's journey For many years the puzzle of what became of the rivers flowing westward from the moun-

Many lost their lives in the exploration of Australia's interior

tains perplexed authorities and explorers alike. Did they perhaps feed a great inland sea? A partial answer – no! – was given in 1829–30, when Charles Sturt hauled a whaling boat over the hills and sailed down the Murrumbidgee to its confluence with the Murray. From there he continued downstream to wide Lake Alexandrina and the river mouth, which had thus far been concealed from maritime explorers behind a sand bar. Sturt's return, rowing upstream against a swelling current, was an epic of endurance, and one which nearly ended in disaster as food for his party ran out and their strength ebbed.

❏ Not all those who braved the unknown were of British descent. In 1839–40 a Polish adventurer, self-styled 'Count' Paul Strzelecki, underwent hardships almost equal to those suffered by Sturt as he traversed the uplands to which he gave the name Gippsland, and from which he was only extracted by the skills of his Aboriginal guide. An impetuous and quarrelsome Prussian, Ludwig Leichhardt, was less lucky, though in 1844 his first journey succeeded in covering an amazing 4,800km from Brisbane to Arnhem Land. An even more ambitious foray which was intended to carry him right across the centre from Sydney to Perth failed. Leichhardt and his companions simply disappeared into the void. ❏

Above: Burke and Wills leave Melbourne in August 1860

Burke's expedition Another great failure, but a fully documented one, was the expedition which set out from Melbourne in 1860 under the impatient leadership of Robert O'Hara Burke. This did reach its objective, the mangrove swamps of the Gulf of Carpentaria, but when the party returned to base camp at Cooper Creek, they found it had been abandoned a mere seven hours previously by their support group. Both Burke and his deputy Wills perished, though another man, John King, was fed roots and fish by the Aborigines and survived to tell the tale.

Before successfully crossing Australia's centre, Stuart had reached Alice Springs

Eyre and Stuart The names of highways spanning the great emptiness of the centre and the west commemorate the epic treks undertaken by two explorers whose persistence has an almost legendary quality. In 1840–1, with the loyal support of his Aboriginal guide Wylie, Edward Eyre reached Albany, having crossed the waterless desert across the top of the Great Australian Bight. In 1862, John McDouall Stuart, almost blind and with hair turned white, finally reached the coast near what was to become Darwin. His previous attempts to cross the centre from south to north had been frustrated by spinifex, scurvy and native hostility, though he had planted the Union Jack on a hilltop near Alice Springs. His return to Adelaide, where he was mobbed by the ladies of the city, was made partly on a stretcher.

■ **In the first half of the 19th century Australia developed at a steady but unspectacular pace. Free settlers soon outnumbered convicts, and each colony won its right to a separate existence from New South Wales. But it was the discovery of gold that transformed the country, drawing in a mass of enterprising folk who helped lay the foundation of Australia's essentially urban civilisation. ■**

Gold fever The news of early gold finds was suppressed by the authorities, fearful of the disruption they might cause. But there was no stopping Edward Hargraves, a veteran of the Californian gold rush of 1849, who made a strike near Bathurst in NSW in February 1851. The rush began, draining the cities of population and making Melbourne so fearful for its prosperity that it offered a prize to whoever found gold within a certain distance of the city. One James Esmond obliged, and his find at Clunes in July 1851 was followed by others at Castlemaine, Bendigo and Ballarat. Melbourne was emptied of able-bodied men and ships stood

Prospectors in the mid-19th century

crewless in the harbour as sailors hurried inland to make their fortune.

Life in the goldfields was raw enough, but with nothing like the violence of the North American finds. Many of the prospectors longed for nothing more than solid respectability, founding farms and businesses after striking lucky, or returning to seek their fortune among the seemingly limitless opportunities offered by 'Marvellous Melbourne'.

More rebellious spirits made their stand at the Eureka stockade (see page 110), and even though they failed, their gesture helped create a new atmosphere in which representative government was to thrive. Victoria's population rose in ten years from less than 100,000 to more than half a million, and the whole country received an injection of energy which carried it through a boom lasting until the 1890s.

Fortune-seekers Prospectors came from all over the world, but mainly arrived from Britain. The largest minority were the Chinese, many of whom disembarked in South Australia and walked overland to the Victorian goldfields rather than pay the £10 landing tax at Melbourne. They were much resented by other settlers for their willingness to work hard, for keeping themselves to themselves, and for their sheer numbers. At the time of the Palmer River gold rush in the 1870s in North Queensland, Chinese diggers formed a majority of men in the state, notwithstanding the rumour at the time which claimed that the local Aborigines had a taste for Asian flesh!

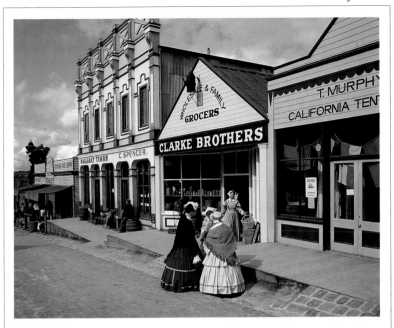

From boom town to ghost town In Victoria, the rip-roaring days were soon over. By the late 1850s most of the gold available on the surface or by shallow diggings had been worked out. Individual miners could not afford the equipment needed for the excavation and maintenance of deeper mines, and the initiative passed from the self-sufficient pioneer to companies able to raise the necessary capital. Ballarat ceased being a muddy chaos and turned itself into the most respectable of Victorian cities.

In the second half of the 19th century gold strikes were made all over Australia, many of them ephemeral and leaving a legacy of strangely poignant ghost towns. The last great rush was to the Eastern Goldfields of Coolgardie and Kalgoorlie-Boulder in Western Australia in 1892–3. This gave a similar boost to the languid economy of the colony, and transformed Perth into a real city. Large-scale operations continue in this area today, based on vast open-cast pits worked by huge machines, a method which is in total contrast to the primitive hand tools and hard manual labour of the prospectors of early days.

Sovereign Hill at Ballarat in Victoria is a re-creation of gold-rush days

❏ Highway robbery had been practised in the colony for as long as highways had existed, and increased in appeal as the wealth created by the gold rush was moved around. Australia's bushrangers were adept at 'bailing up', their dash and daring sometimes giving them legendary status among a population none too enamoured of the law. The most notorious of them all, and a symbol of Australian defiance and sheer cussedness, was of course Edward 'Ned' Kelly, son of an Irish ex-convict. After a series of exploits, which included holding up whole towns, the Kelly gang was cornered in June 1880 at Glenrowan, a small town in northeastern Victoria. The wounded Kelly emerged wearing his famous home-made suit of armour, but was shot in the legs, brought to trial and hanged in Melbourne on 11 November 1880. ❏

■ The Australian landscapes the early European settlers first cast eyes upon lacked the ordered character of the scenes they had left behind. Much of the European effort in Australia was to impose a rational and productive discipline on this unfamiliar and seemingly chaotic scene, sometimes at a cost which only now is being calculated in terms of destruction of habitat and loss of beauty. ■

In Europe, the conversion of the forest into farmland began in neolithic times and took some 5,000 years to complete. In the wooded southeastern and western areas of Australia, the same process was virtually complete after a single century. The replacement of the bush by productive fields was one motive, but in many areas the timber itself was highly valuable and logging quickly developed into a major industry.

The removal of the native forest or its replacement by exotic tree species like radiata pines continued into the 20th century, but a partial halt has now been called, and no visitor should miss seeing such glories of the Australian landscape as the tropical rain forest of Queensland, its temperate equivalent in the southeast and in Tasmania, the blue gums which have given their name to the Blue Mountains, or the splendid karri forests of Western Australia.

The farmers move in Once the bush had been cleared, squatters and graziers parcelled out their land, erecting fences, planting European trees to give the place a more homely look, and building themselves homesteads with whatever degree of architectural elaboration they could afford. Australian country properties cover a range which extends from elegant stone mansions to tin shacks of decidedly temporary appearance.

This attempt to impose order often faltered in the face of the capricious nature of the land. Rainless years ruined many a farmer who had tried to push the frontier of agriculture too far inland, and Australia has as many forgotten farmsteads as it has ghost towns abandoned by prospectors when mineral wealth ran out.

As settlement advanced, native animals retreated, displaced in many cases by myriads of sheep grazing on the imported grass species sown by farmers. Often shot as pests, kangaroos and other animals sometimes profited by the irrigation of otherwise arid landscapes, and became a greater nuisance than ever.

Conflicts of interest The effect of the other changes was to convert a seemingly formless scene into one which made economic and visual sense to the Europeans, and which could be controlled and managed. It also meant that the landscape became uninhabitable by the Aborigines in any traditional way. Such basic differences of viewpoint probably contributed more than anything else to conflict between settlers and natives, a conflict in which the latter were the inevitable losers.

❑ Rabbits were imported as game in the 1850s. Within a few years, the population exploded, and rabbits advanced at the rate of 100km a year, destroying much of the native herbage for ever. Supposedly rabbit-proof fences were built, one running 2,000km across a large part of Western Australia. But the rabbits found ways round them, and were only defeated when myxomatosis spread among them in the 1950s. ❑

How to tackle Australia

Many visitors to Australia will already have a good idea of what they want to do once there. For those whose plans are less definite, however, the first thing to remember about Australia is that it is a continent. Planning a holiday here is like visiting Europe or the United States – Australia is a comparable size to the USA, excluding Alaska, and approximately 24 times as big as the British Isles. You could get an overall idea of the country in one trip, but you need several months and quite a lot of money (though not as much as elsewhere) if you want to get to know it really well.

The extended visit An absolute minimum for an extended trip which takes in all major sights would be three months. In this time it would be feasible to visit all the states, including Tasmania, and cover most of the three-star attractions of this guide, especially if you were able to do most of your travelling – and some of your sightseeing – by plane. If you have more time, so much the better; you could then stay in some places and absorb their atmosphere in a relaxed way rather than just ticking off the principal sights. Now that it is feasible to drive right around the continent on asphalted roads, many retired Australians are discovering the pleasures of getting to know their own country in a leisurely way, usually on board a camper-van.

The shorter trip Most visitors to Australia will have less than limited time at their disposal, and choices will have to be made. As well as seeing something of city life, if you want to enjoy what Australia has to offer you will need to

How far?
Before you head off into the Outback in your rented car or camper-van, contemplate the distances involved. Remember that Cairns is 2,546km from Sydney, Alice Springs is 2,644km distant, Darwin 3,999km and Perth a staggering 4,144km from Sydney – no short hop!

Camper-vans are ideal for exploring the country, particularly for those on a tight budget

get out into the country, drive along the unsurfaced roads of the Outback, leave your car behind and walk through the bush or along the beach, potter around an old gold rush township, sit at the bar of an Outback pub, or let yourself be persuaded that diving and snorkelling are not just for the experts.

Australians are exceptionally good at inviting you to join in; you can take part in all kinds of activities, from riding a camel in the desert to digging for witchetty grubs in the company of an Aboriginal ranger. Not only are there probably more museums per head than anywhere else in the world (from the impeccably professional to the endearingly amateur), but all kinds of industries and enterprises open their gates to visitors. Wineries without tastings are unheard of, fruit and animal farms make you welcome and there is plenty of accommodation on country properties with the chance to take part in rural activities.

Planning an itinerary Within the confines imposed by a conventional holiday of a few weeks, setting definite limits on what you can reasonably undertake is very important. Though vast, nearly all the Australian states are dominated by their capital city, each with its own character and wealth of attractions. This is where colonial life began and where its traces are thickest on the ground. Wild landscapes start just beyond the suburbs; no big city lies out of sight of the hills or mountains of a national park. One solution therefore would be to stay in a single centre and then make excursions, some involving overnight stays in order to appreciate the extraordinary contrasts between city and rural life that are such a feature of Australia. An overland trip by hire car, train, coach or organised tour beginning in one centre and taking your time to reach another is a good way of getting the feel of the country; your return air-line ticket from abroad can usually be arranged to accommodate this. It would be a pity to miss the Outback, but remember that you don't have to go all the way out and back overland; if time is short, you can fly to one of the many bases for Outback tours and start from there.

Australia now has a well-developed and very varied tourist infrastructure, mostly staffed by people who will go out of their way to be helpful, particularly if you are prepared to treat them as human beings and not just dispensers of information. Apart from accommodation and restaurants to suit all pockets, there are also many travel operators standing by to take you on trips. It is, however, always worth while checking that the trips on offer are exactly what you want; the ingredients of a package may have been put together to suit the operator's convenience rather than yours.

But if you want to go somewhere really badly, you're bound to find an Australian who will help you get there!

Drivers: beware of camels!

Australian islands
Far out in the Pacific, Lord Howe Island (over 700km northeast of Sydney) and Norfolk Island (another 1,000km further on) don't feature in the itineraries of most visitors to Australia, though both are favourites with Australians in search of something different. Some 40 sq km in size, Norfolk was a prison island where unrepentant offenders from Sydney were sent to suffer under a notoriously brutal regime, and the remains of convict-era buildings give it something of the atmosphere of Port Arthur. The climate is subtropical and as well as rain forest, there are stands of the famous Norfolk pines and rolling pasturelands. Lord Howe Island is less than half the size of Norfolk Island and is dominated by mountain peaks, with unique vegetation and birdlife which has led to its designation as a World Heritage Area. There are hardly any cars, and when not snorkelling you will have to get around by bike.

35

RI

Melville
Island

Bathurst
Island

DARWIN ✈ Jabiru

Arnhem

Cape
Londonderry

*Joseph
Bonaparte
Gulf*

Daly

Katherine ✈

Bonaparte
Archipelago

Wyndham ✈

Kununurra

Daly Waters

Kimberley

N O R T

Broome ✈

Derby

Halls
Creek ✈

Fitzroy
Crossing

Tanami

Desert

T E R R I

Port
Hedland ✈

*Great Sandy
Desert*

*Lake
Mackay*

MacDonnell

Dampier

Barrow Island

95

Pilbara

1

Ashburton

Newman

*Lake
Disappointment*

*Lake
Mackay*

Ayers Rock
Resort ✈
Uluru (Ayers Rock)

87

Gibson Desert

*Lake
MacLeod*

W E S T E R N

Musgrave Ranges

Carnarvon ✈

Gascoyne

*Lake
Carnegie*

Meekatharra ✈

A U S T R A L I A

Great Victoria Desert

S O U T H

1

95

*Lake
Barlee*

Geraldton ✈

Kalgoorlie ✈

Nullarbor Plain

1

Great Australian Bight

PERTH ✈

94

Norseman

Bunbury

Esperance ✈

1

Augusta

Cape Leeuwin

Albany ✈

| 0 | 200 | 400 | 600 | 800 km |

SYDNEY

0   500 m

E

Dawes Point

Pier One

Sydney Harbour Bridge

Bennelong Point

SYDNEY HARBOUR TUNNEL

DAWES POINT

Millers Point

The Merchants' House

Sydney Opera House

Garrison Church (Holy Trinity)

Sydney Visitor Centre

Overseas Passenger Terminal

Government House

MILLERS POINT

ARGYLE PLACE

Argyle Centre

Cadman's Cottage
Sydney Cove

Museum of Contemporary Art

Ferry Terminal
Circular Quay Station

Observatory Hill & Sydney Observatory

THE ROCKS

CAHILL EXPRESSWAY

Justice & Police Museum

Sydney Conservatorium of Music

D

National Trust Centre
SH Ervin Gallery

Darling Harbour

Jones Bay

BRADFIELD HIGHWAY

Customs House

MACQUARIE PLACE

BRIDGE STREET

GROSVENOR STREET

Australia Square

Museum of Sydney

State Library of NSW

State Parliament House

WESTERN DISTRIBUTOR

Wynyard Station

GEORGE STREET

YORK STREET

CLARENCE STREET

PITT ST

PHILLIP ST

MACQUARIE STREET

CAHILL EXPRESSWAY

Sydney Hospital

ERSKINE STREET

MLC Centre

GPO

Martin Place Station

Martin Place

St James Church

Sydney Hospital

C

Sydney Harbour Casino

Sydney Light Rail

Pyrmont Bay

Australian National Maritime Museum

KING STREET

Strand Arcade

AMP Tower

QUEENS SQUARE

Hyde Park Barracks

PYRMONT

Sydney Aquarium

YORK STREET

MARKET STREET

State Theatre

St James Station

Hyde Park

HARRIS STREET

Pyrmont Bridge

Harbourside

Queen Victoria Building

Great Synagogue

ELIZABETH STREET

COLLEGE STREET

Monorail

DRUITT STREET

PARK STREET

B

Harris Street Motor Museum

Sydney Convention Centre

DARLING HARBOUR

Imax Theatre

Sydney Town Hall

Town Hall Station

St Andrews Cathedral

Museum Station

BRIDGE ROAD

WATTLE STREET

Sega World

BATHURST STREET

Anzac Memorial

Sydney Exhibition Centre

Tumbalong (Park)

Chinese Garden

Monorail

DIXON ST

GEORGE STREET

LIVERPOOL STREET

WENTWORTH AVENUE

GOULBURN

WENTWORTH PARK RD

Wentworth Park

PIER STREET

GOULBURN STREET

ELIZABETH STREET

CAMPBELL

A

WILLIAM HENRY ST

Sydney Entertainment Centre

Chinatown

HARBOUR ST

SURRY HILLS

Powerhouse Museum

Paddy's Markets & Market City

HAYMARKET

GEORGE STREET

RAWSON PLACE

Belmore Park

ALBION

MARY ANN STREET

HARRIS STREET

EDDY AVE

Central Railway Station

FOVEAUX ST

ULTIMO

Harbourside and History Walk

City Centre and Darling Harbour Walk

1   2   3

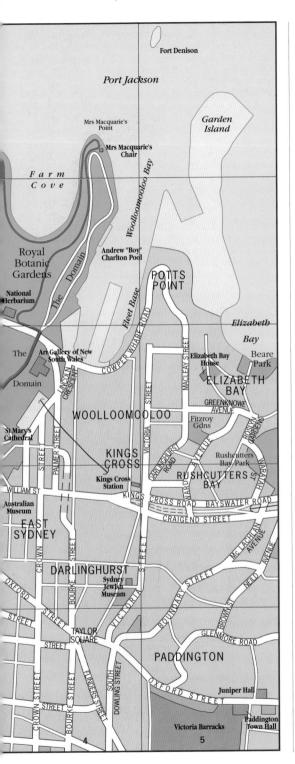

Fort Denison

Port Jackson

Garden Island

Mrs Macquarie's Point

Mrs Macquarie's Chair

Farm Cove

Royal Botanic Gardens

Andrew "Boy" Charlton Pool

POTTS POINT

National Herbarium

The Domain

Fleet Base

Elizabeth Bay

Beare Park

The Domain

Art Gallery of New South Wales

Elizabeth Bay House

ELIZABETH BAY

COWPER WHARF ROAD

LINCOLN CRESCENT

MACLEAY STREET

GREENKNOWE AVENUE

St Mary's Cathedral

WOOLLOOMOOLOO

VICTORIA STREET

Fitzroy Gdns

ROSLYN GARDENS

KINGS CROSS

PALMER STREET

Kings Cross Station

DARLINGHURST ROAD

RUSHCUTTERS BAY

Rushcutters Bay Park

WARATAH ST

WILLIAM ST

KINGS CROSS ROAD

BAYSWATER ROAD

Australian Museum

CRAIGEND STREET

EAST SYDNEY

CROWN STREET

MCLACHLAN AVENUE

NEILD AVENUE

DARLINGHURST

BOURKE STREET

Sydney Jewish Museum

VICTORIA STREET

BROWNS

OXFORD STREET

STREET

TAYLOR SQUARE

BOUNDARY STREET

GLENMORE ROAD

PADDINGTON

CROWN STREET

BOURKE STREET

FLINDERS STREET

SOUTH DOWLING STREET

VICTORIA STREET

OXFORD STREET

Juniper Hall

Victoria Barracks

Paddington Town Hall

4

5

SYDNEY

39

The first Sydneysiders
Three main Aboriginal groups, numbering several thousand people, seem to have inhabited the area around the future city as the First Fleet sailed in. Large numbers of their carvings survive in the sandstone plateaux to the north and south. The Aborigines' response to the invaders was a mixture of indifference, resentment and curiosity, but they were in no position to resist and by the early 1800s those who remained in the area had been reduced to a pitiful state of drunkenness and beggary.

40

Sydney Curling lasciviously around its sparkling harbour, Sydney's wretched beginnings as a penal colony are forgotten in sheer enjoyment of its good luck in being so alive in such a superb setting. One of the world's great cities, with nearly a quarter of the population of the continent in its metropolitan area, it seems still in the first flush of youth – enthusiastic, welcoming, vibrant, open to growth and change. Two of its landmarks, the Harbour Bridge and Opera House, became icons the day they were completed. Seen from across the water, the improvements to the city centre add a further element of drama and excitement, while all around the 240km of harbour foreshore, waterfront suburbs of dream homes mingle with the remains of wild bushland.

Sydney, then, is beautiful, almost extravagantly so. There is also a fair measure of what has been called 'the Australian ugliness'. The skyscrapers make no attempt to harmonize with their immediate surroundings; close up, much of the city centre appears chaotic. Beyond the often charming Victorian suburbs sprawls an almost horizon-less sea of red-roofed bungalow suburbs. But the monotony of this urban sprawl is compensated for by magnificent natural surroundings: the heaths and forests of **Ku-ring-gai Chase** and **Royal National Park**, the high wall of the **Blue Mountains** and the string of beaches along many miles of Pacific coastline. One's enjoyment is enhanced by a climate that, despite a fair amount of rain, gives hot summers and bright winter days.

Early days In January 1788, a favourable climate played no part in Captain Phillip's choice of Port Jackson as a landing place for his motley cargo of convicts. It was simply that the area around today's Circular Quay seemed more promising than the bleak expanses around Botany Bay where the First Fleet had originally anchored. The flag was run up and the name given to the landing place, Sydney Cove (after the British Home Secretary of the time), was soon transferred to the not very orderly settlement that grew up around its shore.

As the colony became more firmly established, free settlers moved in, and the population of the city increased sharply when gold was found to the west of the Blue Mountains in the 1850s. Handsome villas were built in the outskirts, while in the later years of the 19th century middle- and working-class suburbs like Balmain and Paddington unrolled their streets of humble cottages and superior terraces over the countryside near by, leaving areas like The Rocks to a life of drink, vice and violence. By the time the population of the city had reached the million mark in the late 1920s, Sydney was a confident, swaggering sort of place, where a strong trade union movement helped ensure one of the highest living standards in the world for its members.

Up to date World War II brought the city into abrupt contact with a wider world, which came even closer in the postwar period, when Sydney became the recipient of waves of New Australians, firstly from devastated Europe and later from Lebanon, Vietnam, China, the Philippines and countless other Asian countries. Once resolutely Anglo-Celtic, it is now a thoroughly multicultural city.

Sydney is a great tourist destination: its charms are not hidden away, but put boldly on display; its intriguing convict and other history is accessible; and it has all the museums, galleries, shops, restaurants and entertainment you would expect in a metropolis.

Penetrating the defences
Sydney's first fortification, on Observatory Hill, was built to protect the colony's Establishment against a possible convict uprising; later, it was potential foreign invaders who became the worry, and by the mid-19th century virtually every promontory had been fortified. In World War II, despite a boom across the Harbour mouth, a Japanese midget submarine crept up as far as Garden Island. Here it launched its torpedoes at the cruiser USS *Chicago*; they missed. Depth-charges dealt with the brave and ingenious submariners; their vessel was recovered and is on display in the National Maritime Museum.

41

Many consider Sydney to be 'the best address on earth'

Lovely homes

Not all Sydney's early houses were as unassuming as Cadman's Cottage, though the first Government House (see page 45) was damp and suffered from inexplicable smells. The aspirations of successful citizens were expressed in such delightful dwellings as Elizabeth Bay House, a splendid classical mansion in white stucco which turns its back on its sleazy neighbours in adjacent Kings Cross (see page 59). Further to the east is another highly desirable residence, Vaucluse House, whose battlements and verandas were added for the explorer William Charles Wentworth in the 1830s.

The Australian Museum houses ethnographic displays from all over the world

▶▶▶ Art Gallery of New South Wales 39C4

Art Gallery Road

This dignified classical sandstone edifice was opened in 1887 and extended several times over the years, most recently and lavishly to mark the 1988 Bicentennial. Its generous interior houses what can fairly be described as the country's greatest art collection, even though the national collection is now at Canberra. It covers the evolution of Australian art up to the present day, and has major sections on Aboriginal (in the exciting new Yiribana Gallery), Asian, American and European art; the collection of British 20th-century painting is outstanding. In addition the gallery hosts world-class visiting exhibitions. But it is the painters of Australia and their response to the people and places of the strange new land who most fascinate; they are all here, from John Glover's Tasmanian landscapes to Grace Cossington Smith's metamorphosis of the Harbour Bridge and Sidney Nolan's interpretation of the Ned Kelly saga.

▶▶▶ Australian Museum 38B3

Corner of College Street and William Street

Australia's largest natural history museum is a lively place, extended and altered in recent years so that its Victorian architecture almost becomes part of the intriguing displays on earth history, animals, insects and birds, and the life of the sea. Human rituals of the present as well as of the past are presented in a challenging way, as is the evolution of Aboriginal culture over tens of thousands of years. There are also sections on Indonesia, Papua New Guinea and the Pacific, as well as the 'Planet of Minerals', featuring Australia's extraordinary mineral wealth. There are stuffed animals, but they are always shown in context rather than as lifeless specimens, and there are plenty of 'hands-on' computer displays.

▶ Cadman's Cottage 38E3

George Street

This modest two-storey Georgian house has the distinction of being the city's oldest surviving building. It was erected in 1816, getting its name from the pardoned convict John Cadman who lived in it from 1827 to 1845. A lintel carries the initials GR for England's King George III in immaculately carved lettering. Cadman's home once gave directly on to the beach, but now stands some 50m inland and houses an information centre of the National Parks and Wildlife Service.

▶ Chinatown 38B2

Migrants from China first arrived as part of the gold rush and took up residence in The Rocks or around Botany Bay. Sydney's Chinese citizens are now scattered around the suburbs, but the city's Chinese heart beats strongest along Dixon Street, behind whose ornamental gateways is an array of exotic shops, food centres and restaurants. A few steps away is the **Chinese Garden▶▶**, part of the redevelopment of Darling Harbour. Laid out by landscape architects from Sydney's sister city of Guangzhou in southern China, the gardens are a calm retreat of sensitively designed planting, lakes, bridges and waterfalls, with a traditional tea house overlooking a lily pond.

▶▶▶ Circular Quay   38D3

Sydney's 'chief people-watching site' (Jan Morris) is also one of the city's most historic places, since it was here at Sydney Cove that the First Fleet dropped anchor on 26 January 1788. It is still the epicentre of daily life, with a continuous stream of people pouring between railway station, taxis, buses and the busy ferries that bustle in and out of the quays. Trains and traffic roar by overhead, ignored by those with time enough on their hands to stop and listen to the street performers on the broad promenade. Landward are the cliff-like buildings of the city centre, while towards the water are alluring and ever-changing glimpses of the Harbour Bridge and Opera House. A map on the quayside shows the colony as it appeared in 1808.

Two hundred years on, Sydney Cove, the First Fleet's landing site, would be unrecognisable to those early pioneers

▶▶▶ Darling Harbour   38D1

The deep inlet on the western side of the city centre was called Cockle Bay by the early colonists. Like so many docklands of its kind around the world, it eventually lost its commercial functions but is now enjoying a vigorous new lease on life as a tourist centre, with major exhibition and entertainment facilities.

The Harbour is an exciting place, an extraordinary medley of old and new, defined to the east by glittering office towers, with expanses of water and paving framing some of the city's most stimulating new buildings. The parkland at the southern end seems none the worse for its overhead expressways, while the whole area is linked to the centre of Sydney by a controversial monorail which glides over Pyrmont Bridge, the oldest swing bridge of its kind in the world.

For details on attractions in the area other than the National Maritime Museum (covered on page 45), see the adjacent panel.

Darling Harbour attractions
Apart from the Pumphouse Brewery Tavern and the splendid Sydney Aquarium there are the IMAX theatre, a 'virtual-reality' Sega World centre, outdoor entertainments of all kinds, cruises on the harbour, the 200 shops, boutiques and bazaars of the Harbourside complex, a major convention centre and the Sydney Exhibition Centre hosting events like the Motor Show. The Harris Street Motor Museum and the vast Saturday and Sunday Paddy's Market are just a step away. The vast Sydney Harbour Casino is also in this region.

Unknown soldier

The Anzac Memorial in Hyde Park was designed by the Sydney architect Bruce Dellit 'to give an impression, not of the glory of war, but of its tragedy and horror'. It is a masterpiece of its kind. The external sculptures depicting the different branches of the services (including nursing) are by British-born Rayner Hoff. Inside, the dramatic central figure of the dead soldier can only be observed properly by bowing one's head. The vault above is pierced by 120,000 stars, each one representing a World War I volunteer.

Observatory Hill and Sydney Observatory

With commanding views over the harbour, Millers Point was the site of a citadel, a windmill, and then an observatory. The latter survives, established in 1858 to survey the hitherto unknown southern skies, and functioned until 1982. With its time-ball tower and domes, the observatory building has now been renovated as a museum of astronomy with plenty of intriguing hands-on features.

▶▶ **The Domain** *39D4*

The Domain extends inland from Mrs Macquarie's Point to the large green space fringed by fig trees which serves as one of the city centre's most important parks. This is where orators challenge their audiences along the lines of London's Speaker's Corner, where joggers jog and office workers eat their sandwiches. Open-air opera and classical music concerts are also held here, particularly during the January Festival of Sydney. The Domain has, however, suffered from the incursions of the Cahill Expressway, the Eastern Suburbs Railway and the construction of an underground parking garage.

▶ **Garrison Church** *38E2*
Millers Point

Hacked through the central ridge of The Rocks area, **Argyle Cut** was one of the colony's early engineering feats. It leads to **Argyle Place**, frequently described as Sydney's sole village green, though not many village greens benefit from such close proximity to a multiple-lane expressway (the Harbour Bridge approach). Nevertheless, it is a pleasant enough place, lined with attractive mid 19th-century cottages. Holy Trinity Church, near the entrance to the Cut, was given the name Garrison Church because of its use by the redcoats manning Dawes Point Battery. Built from the stone quarried from the Cut, its squat appearance isn't helped by its lack of a spire, but it has a spacious interior and some of the city's finest stained-glass windows.

▶ **Hyde Park** *38C3*

Like its London namesake, this fine park once marked the very edge of town, but today has become one of those central city oases where people retreat from the heat, fumes and noise of the street. Its avenue of majestic Moreton Bay fig trees is particularly fine, and there is a splendid imitation-baroque fountain, but the park's centrepiece is undoubtedly the **Anzac Memorial**▶▶ (see panel). This solemn but sumptuous essay in art deco forms the focal point of the Anzac Day march on 25th April.

▶▶ **Hyde Park Barracks** *38C3*
Queens Square

This splendid three-storey edifice with pediment and pilasters is one of the city's finest classical buildings. Standing in dignified seclusion behind its grand gates, it was designed on Governor Macquarie's orders by the brilliant ex-convict Francis Greenway, whose architectural skills transformed Sydney. It provided accommodation for up to 1,000 convicts, who until then had had to find their own lodgings. It is now a museum of social history, with excellent displays on the early history of the colony and the life-style led by its former inmates.

▶▶ **Museum of Contemporary Art** *38D3*
Circular Quay West

The rather forbidding-looking brown sandstone building facing Circular Quay used to be the offices of the Maritime Services Board. Designed at the very end of the art deco period, it is an incongruous setting for the country's major collection of contemporary art.

▶▶ Museum of Sydney   38D3

Corner of Bridge and Phillip streets

Built on the site of the first (1788) Government House, this museum offers an evocative portrayal of life in colonial Australia. The house was demolished in 1846, but excavations have revealed the foundations, part of which can be viewed through the paving. Using state-of-the-art technology such as computer displays and a vast video wall, the museum takes you on a journey of discovery – from the story of the local Aborigines to the relatively sophisticated Sydney of the 1850s. One of the museum's highlights is outside – in the forecourt. The unusual 'Edge of the Trees' sculpture consists of poles, some of which 'speak', that represent both Sydney's original inhabitants and the early settlers.

▶▶▶ National Maritime Museum   38C1

Darling Harbour

Looking more like a ship of the future than anything so conventional as a museum, this extraordinary structure houses an equally extraordinary array of objects that tell the story of the island continent's intimate relationship with the seas surrounding it.

There are many real vessels in the museum's huge and strangely shaped interior, from Aboriginal canoes to hi-tech yachts, but the emphasis is as much on people as on things. There are displays on explorers, convicts, settlers, refugees and other migrants, on whalers and wharfies who made their living from the sea, on swimmers and surfers who simply enjoyed it, and on maritime 'neighbours' like the Americans and Japanese. Tied up at the dock outside are more boats, including the *Tu Do* which arrived in Darwin in 1977 overloaded with Vietnamese boat people, a Russian submarine, and the destroyer HMAS *Vampire*.

Playground of the Pacific

This was the name originally given to Bondi Beach, and the early days of Australia's exuberant beach culture are celebrated with gusto in the National Maritime Museum. Within living memory, the sands were scoured by eagle-eyed inspectors who ensured that no male swimmer went topless, but what emerges from the posters, photos and videos here is the sheer joy young Australians have always had in stripping off and letting sea and sun work on their bodies. A sombre note is struck by recalling Black Sunday, 6 February 1938, when what was described as an avalanche of waves took five lives in spite of the efforts of 60 lifesavers.

45

The Observatory, a colonial building constructed from the local sandstone

■ One of the great privileges of life in Sydney is access to the beaches of the Harbour and the Pacific Ocean. Astonishing as it might seem, until the early years of this century bathing was prohibited by law during daylight hours; finally, the flamboyant editor of a Manly newspaper strolled fully clad into the surf in the middle of the day, defying the prosecution which, in fact, was never made. ■

Check before you swim
Few big cities are entirely free of water pollution problems, and some of Sydney's beaches occasionally suffer contamination by sewage. Measures are taken to remedy the situation, and conditions can be checked locally.

46

The Harbour beaches
These hardly compare with those on the ocean, but there are plenty of good spots for picnicking and sunbathing. On the south shore at Vaucluse are Nielsen Park and Parsley Bay; the north shore has beaches around Manly, as well as Mosman's Obelisk and Balmoral.

Surfers and surfboat crews make good use of Sydney's beaches

To the north, **Manly** is the city's seaside resort *par excellence*, 'seven miles from Sydney, but a thousand miles from care'. Lined with shops, take-aways, cafés and pubs, a broad concourse called the Corso channels you from the ferry landing to the curving sandy beach with its double line of Norfolk pines facing the ocean. It was here, in 1915, that the art of surfing was born in Australia, and a big surf competition is held here every year. Manly has many other attractions, including the Oceanworld aquarium and the interesting old Quarantine station, once used to protect Sydney from contagious diseases, but now open daily for tours.

World-famous **Bondi**, to the south, has an even more magnificent beach, stretching between two headlands, though its setting of cafés, pubs and apartment blocks has a tatty look about it. Bondi is suburban and popular, once connected to the centre by a famous tramway whose cars would make the final descent to the beach at breakneck speed, giving rise to the expression 'to go like a Bondi tram'.

Eighteen other beaches, equally fine if less famous, stretch north from Manly up the Warringah Peninsula to delightful Palm Beach. Some, like Narrabeen, are urban in character, while others, like Freshwater and Whale beaches, are still largely undeveloped. Similarly, a string of beaches runs south from Bondi, ending at 10km-long Cronulla, the only beach accessible by suburban train.

▶ **Parliament House** 38C3

Macquarie Street
Like the Mint, the home of the New South Wales legislature was once part of the 'Rum' Hospital that was built in 1816. The Legislative Council Chamber is a prefabricated iron structure, originally sent out from England to serve as a goldfields church. Parliament House is open to the public, even when in session.

▶▶▶ **Powerhouse Museum** 38A2

Harris Street, Ultimo
The cavernous boiler halls and other generous interior spaces of the old power station and tram depot on the edge of Darling Harbour are now home to the vast collections of Sydney's Museum of Applied Arts and Sciences. The array of objects in what is Australia's largest museum is quite astonishing. The decorative arts are strongly represented, as is social history, with stimulating displays on the life of the local Aborigines, traditional women's work and brewing. There are many hands-on features as well as audio-visual presentations, sound effects and holograms–ideal for kids.

The highly entertaining Powerhouse Museum is one of the best places for kids to visit

▶▶ **Queen Victoria Building** 38C2

George Street
This many-domed late-Victorian shopping gallery occupying an entire city block was completed in 1898; in recent years a thoroughgoing renovation has restored it to its former glory. With its many levels, stained glass and mosaics, it is a cathedral to conspicuous consumption.

▶▶▶ **The Rocks** 38D2

Named after the sandstone ridge ending in Dawes Point, this is the site of Australia's first European settlement. For many years, it had a reputation as a place of brawling, hard drinking, whoring and villainy of all kinds, but this murky past does no harm whatsoever to The Rocks' present status as a tourist mecca (see panel). In fact, the area has long since been tamed, first by wholesale demolition of many of its unsanitary dwellings after the outbreak of bubonic plague in 1900, and then by another swathe of destruction preceding construction of the Harbour Bridge.

▶▶▶ **Royal Botanic Gardens** 39D4

These luxuriantly planted 30-hectare gardens are the perfect counterpoint to the high-rise buildings and bustle of the city centre. They benefit enormously from their proximity to the harbour, looking on to the long curving promenade of Farm Cove, which is set between twin promontories, one crowned by the Opera House and the other by Mrs Macquarie's Point. Once the site of the first government farm, the gardens contain a visitor centre, the National Herbarium (with more than a million plant specimens), a new fernery under a slatted steel dome, and the extraordinary shapes of the Pyramid and Arc glasshouses, which shelter tropical plants from many countries.

The Rocks today
The area is now a place to wander at leisure and savour the almost medieval atmosphere – quite absent elsewhere in Australia. You may wish to start your visit at the informativeSydney Visitor Centre at The Rocks, at 106 George Street.

▶▶▶ **Sydney Harbour Bridge** 38E3

Not just a symbol of Sydney but of Australia itself, the Harbour Bridge leaps in a great arch between its granite pylons to span the narrows between Dawes Point and

SYDNEY

De Groot's dark deed
The opening of the Harbour
Bridge on 19 March 1932
was the excuse for the
biggest carnival Sydney
had yet known, attended
by one million people. As
the crowds waited for the
Labor Premier of NSW,
Jack Lang, to cut the tape,
a uniformed horseman
darted forward and
slashed the tape with his
sword. Irishman Francis de
Groot couldn't bear the
thought of a socialist politi-
cian getting all this glory.

AMP Tower
The view from the observation deck of this 305-m-
high structure – Sydney's
tallest building – is nothing
short of spectacular. With
a 360-degree vista that
takes in the entire
Metropolitan area, it's the
ideal place to familiarise
yourself with Sydney's layout.

A drama of an opera
In spite of the brilliance of
its design, the Sydney
Opera House is not an
ideal building for opera,
with acoustics inferior to
those of Melbourne's Arts
Centre. A local joke has it
that Australia has the
world's best opera house,
the outside in Sydney, the
inside in Melbourne.

Milsons Point to the north. The bridge was opened in
1932, after almost nine years of complicated construction, and carries eight traffic lanes, a double-track railway,
a cycleway and a footpath. Its broad deck is the widest in
the world and rises 134m above water level. Since the
early 1990s, the congestion-prone bridge has been supplemented by the Sydney Harbour tunnel, which passes
beneath the harbour.

The footway leading across the bridge (access is via
Cumberland Street in The Rocks) gives stupendous
views, and you can climb the southeastern pylon to a
small museum and an observation platform.

▶▶▶ Sydney Opera House
38E3

Bennelong Point
Once the site of a ramshackle tram terminus, since 1973
Bennelong Point has been crowned by this spectacular
building, which is the inspired and outstanding creation of
Danish architect Joern Utzon, born in 1918 and educated
at the Royal Danish Academy. Though construction of the
Opera House was plagued by both technical and political
problems, leading Utzon to resign from the project before
the building's completion, the complex curving shapes of
the exterior are quite spectacular and have been compared to billowing sails, shells, or the hoods of nuns'
habits. The elegant, soaring roofs are covered in over a
million Swedish ceramic tiles. The interior houses not just
the auditorium of the opera, but also a concert hall and
two conventional theatres, plus restaurants, bars, gift
shops and a library. Outside are huge steps and a promenade around the point.

Guided one-hour tours of the interior are available on
most days, generally between 9–4, but times vary according to rehearsal schedules.

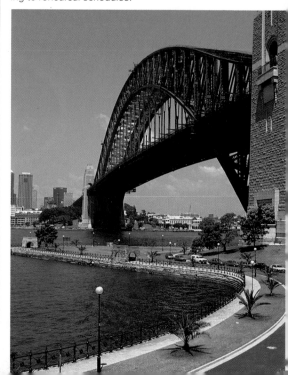

*The Sydney Harbour
Bridge, completed in
1932, still functions
as a major link
between north and
south*

Walk **Harbourside and history**

See map on pages 38–9.

This 5km walk gives magnificent harbourside views, leads through the splendid botanical gardens, and then returns to Circular Quay past many fine early buildings.

The landward approach to the **Opera House** may lack some of the drama of the waterside approach but is still impressive, made part of the way underneath a canopy, then up gigantically scaled flights of steps. The fine trees of the **Royal Botanic Gardens** and Government House sweep down to the footpath leading around Farm Cove to the promontory of Mrs Macquarie's Point, a deservedly popular harbourside viewpoint. Do not miss the Botanic Gardens Tropical Centre with its 'Arc' and 'Pyramid' greenhouses.

The bridge leading to the **Art Gallery of New South Wales** over the Cahill Expressway gives good views over city and eastern suburbs. Macquarie Street leads northward back towards the harbour, bounded to the west by mostly modern structures, and to the east by an unparallelled sequence of fine historic buildings. Bridge Street penetrates west, modern buildings, including the Museum of Sydney, vying with old. Macquarie Place makes a green interlude before the 1885 Customs House and the quayside.

Walk **Sydney city centre and Darling Harbour**

See map on pages 38–9.

A walk through tightly built-up streets to revitalised Darling Harbour and back through the calm and dignity of Hyde Park.

From Martin Place Station, walk to Martin Place, Strand Arcade and Pitt Street Mall, pedestrian-friendly in their different ways. As you cross Pyrmont Bridge look up to see the monorail – a costly and unpopular initiative – and back to enjoy the city skyline.

An amazing array of new and varied facilities clusters around **Darling Harbour**. A rest in the **Chinese Garden** could precede the final leg of this walk: across Dixon Street leading to **Chinatown**, then up into **Hyde Park**, with its splendid avenues of fig trees and the imposing **Anzac Memorial**.

The Chinese Garden, designed by landscape architects from China

Accommodation

Where to stay?
In many ways it's an advantage to be right in the city centre, but Sydney's suburbs offer some excellent, and often cheaper, alternatives. Kings Cross has a wide range of hotels and price brackets, and is just one train stop from the city centre. You can stay on the beach at Bondi, Coogee and Manly, and the inner east suburb of Double Bay offers sophisticated surroundings – albeit at a price.

A tremendous variety of accommodation is available in the Sydney area, though the city is not renowned for being cheap, except in the area of backpacker-style lodges. Hotels range from top-rate – like the superb Inter-Continental or The Observatory – to modest, and there are serviced apartments, motels, backpackers' lodges, campsites, and bed and breakfast accommodation. An important factor is location; it's a good idea to have the *Sydney Transport Map* to hand before making your choice, since there are places that are extremely remote unless you have a car, and others whose distance from the sights is compensated for by good public transport links. Advance reservation is advisable for peak periods like Christmas and January.

Hotels The city centre has an excellent range of top-class hotels, as do a number of inner suburbs like Manly, Kings Cross and North Sydney. Whatever your price bracket, Manly is worth considering for its holiday atmosphere and its link to the centre – by conventional ferry in 30 minutes or in about half that time by JetCat. The heart of town also has medium-priced and budget hotels, with a particular concentration around the Central Railway Station; Kings Cross also has a variety of such places, many of them in streets of relative tranquillity.

Budget Kings Cross is a backpacker's paradise, with many lodges in Victoria Street. The scene here is in constant flux, so it is as well to check at the time whether a particular establishment is for you. Demand is often heavy, and it might be a good idea to start your tour of inspection early in the day. There is another cluster of accommodation at Bondi – an intriguing temporary address! The emphasis here is on affordable lodgings, with plenty of places offering rooms with cooking facilities. Bed and breakfast establishments are scattered all over the city. Details are obtainable from a number of agencies (see also Hotels and Restaurants on pages 268–81), and again, accessibility is a key factor. Camping sites, not surprisingly, are a long way out of the city.

Luxury epitomised – one of the city's best hotels

Food and drink

Eating out Even more so than in the rest of Australia, eating in Sydney has been revolutionised in recent years, largely because of the huge influx of migrants. *The Sydney Morning Herald*'s *Good Food Guide* has no less than 50 categories of cooking in its index, beginning with African and ending with Vietnamese. In spite of recession, new restaurants continue to open, ingredients are good and chefs are increasingly skilled, particularly in the popular, internationally acclaimed style of cooking known as 'Modern Australian' (or 'Mod Oz' for short) – a fusion of culinary styles and ingredients. Prices are extremely reasonable, particularly in pubs. Gourmet restaurants often offer a set-price lunchtime menu at a considerable saving over their evening prices. Prices are kept even lower because of the Bring Your Own (booze) or BYO phenomenon. Remember that a small corkage charge may be made. The highest prices are charged for restaurants that offer something extra, like a harbourside setting or a panoramic view.

Ethnic restaurants These are scattered all over the city, though there are concentrations in particular neighbourhoods that have been settled by different nationalities. Thus **Greek** restaurants cluster around Elizabeth and Liverpool Streets, **Chinese** restaurants are found in Chinatown, **Italian** in Leichhardt and Newtown, and **Vietnamese** in the southwestern suburb of Cabramatta. Restaurants of many different kinds keep each other company in certain parts of town, along Darlinghurst's Oxford Street and on Stanley and Crown Streets in East Sydney, or to the west of the centre, along Glebe Point Road, in King Street, Newtown, or Darling Street, Balmain. The eating establishments at Double Bay are as kosher as their designer boutiques, while Manly has an array of cafés, 'chippers', take-aways and more conventional restaurants.

Drink There is no shortage of places to drink in Sydney. The basic 'hotel' or pub is still much in evidence, while other pubs have been renovated and offer a more varied experience, which might well extend to food and entertainment. Further up the scale of sophistication are the many hotel and cocktail bars; the locally famous **Marble Bar** of Adams' Hotel has found a new home at the Hilton.

Sydney's excellent brasseries and bistros are deservedly popular

Exclusive eating
Given Sydney's extensive shoreline, there are plenty of expensive restaurants with harbourside settings, from The Rocks to Watsons Bay near South Head. The most stunning view is from the two restaurants on top of the AMP Tower.

Refreshments
Sydney has plenty of cafés featuring excellent Italian-style coffee. The tourist may also be pleasantly surprised at the quality of food and refreshments available at the various museums and galleries.

Shopping

The Rocks Market
A visit to The Rocks on a Saturday or Sunday has the added bonus of the lively market – held in Upper George Street. In addition to the 100 or so stalls that sell jewellery, homewares and unusual gifts, you'll find free entertainment and a carnival atmosphere.

52

Duty free
Duty- and tax-free merchandise is available to those with an international air ticket, with substantial discounts on electrical goods, jewellery and watches, drink and perfume. City centre outlets are likely to be cheaper than those at the airport.

Browsers Welcome

Sydney's CBD (Central Business District) has all the temptations a shopper might reasonably expect in the centre of a metropolitan city. There are department stores like **David Jones** and elegant 19th-century galleries like the **Strand Arcade**, or its modern equivalent, the shopping complex inserted into the lower floors of an office block. With its 200 boutiques and cafés on several levels, the immaculately restored **Queen Victoria Building** (see page 47) is a visitor attraction in its own right.

Souvenir hunting In places where tourists congregate like The Rocks or Darling Harbour, souvenirs are plentiful. Faced with the problem of what to bring home from Australia in addition to the inevitable cuddly koala or kangaroo (often made in Taiwan), you might consider a stylish Akubra hat or tough outdoor clothing to go with it, like a bush shirt or an oilskin coat. Sheepskin products, opals, or surfing gear are other possibilities. Australians are great readers, and bookshops are well stocked with a good range of Australiana, albeit quite expensive, while newsagents sell an almost incredible range of periodicals catering to every possible taste.

First-rate maps are difficult to come by in Australia; a visit to the **Travel Bookshop** (Bridge Street) could be helpful here.

Aboriginal artefacts of varying quality – paintings, carvings, boomerangs, didgeridoos and fabrics – are widely available, better bought from a specialist shop than from a souvenir stall. The best souvenir shops are probably those run by the main museums and galleries; the **Australian Museum**'s platypus actually looks like the real thing!

Markets Outside the centre, the shopping streets of the more colourful suburbs such as Paddington and Balmain are good places to browse for something special, while Sydney's markets offer a colourful shopping experience. Usually held on a Saturday or Sunday, they take place in The Rocks, Bondi Beach, Balmain, Glebe, Manly and in Paddington. The famous **Paddy's Market** in the Chinatown area is good for fresh produce, but otherwise full of rather cheap and nasty goods, but the vast and lively fish market at Pyrmont is a daily spectacle well worth watching.

Nightlife

Sydneysiders' main evening activity is probably eating and drinking, which can be combined with an enormous range of entertainments, from opera to jazz, from discos to drag acts – everything you would expect to find in a city of this size with a population whose main aim in life seems to be to enjoy itself.

Concerts and theatre With several auditoriums, the **Opera House** is also a major venue for classical concerts, ballet and drama. Classical music can also be heard at the **Town Hall** and, performed by student musicians, at the **Conservatorium of Music**. Some 20 theatres offer a choice of musicals, mainstream or fringe plays in a variety of locations, some – like the **Wharf Theatre** (near The Rocks) or **Ensemble Theatre** (on the north shore) – in an attractive waterside setting. A visit to the beautifully restored 1928 Capitol Theatre in the Haymarket area is highly recommended. The exciting **Sydney Dance Company** and the **Aboriginal and Islander Dance Theatre** frequent various venues.

Cinema City centre cinemas show the latest block-busters, and there are a number of houses specialising in second runs and foreign films in Paddington (Academy Twin) as well as in the centre (the two Dendy cinemas, Mandolin). The **State Theatre**, with its extravagant décor, is the home of the city's June Film Festival.

Music The Sydney jazz scene has a lot going for it, with numerous venues; the best being the long-running Basement, near Circular Quay. Rock is also well represented, with mammoth concerts held in the **Entertainment Centre** and a legion of other performers in pubs and clubs. Discos, cabarets and nightclubs abound, catering to all tastes and pockets. There are probably more gays in Sydney than in the rest of Australia put together, with the many bars, clubs and pubs of Darlinghurst's Oxford Street as the main focus.

Information
The wealth of distractions available in this exhilarating city can be found in the Friday edition of *The Sydney Morning Herald*, while several giveaway publications also provide comprehensive entertainment listings. A good way of sampling Sydney's nightlife is to take one of the several guided tours on offer, although these can be tourist traps.

Sydney Harbour Casino
Sydney's first, temporary, casino opened in the mid-1990s, and has now moved to its permanent site to the west of Darling Harbour. This vast complex includes a hotel and theatre, as well as restaurants, bars, 1,500 poker machines, and 200 gaming tables that offer roulette, blackjack, baccarat, Asian games such as *pai gow*, and the Australian favourite – two-up (which is essentially betting on which way two coins will fall).

53

Studebaker's night-club, Kings Cross

Practical points

The SydneyPass

This combined ticket gives unlimited bus (including Airport Express, Sydney Explorer and Bondi Bay Explorer) and ferry travel for three, five or seven days, and is a bargain well worth thinking about.

Taxis are numerous, and can be hailed on the street, picked up at a cab rank or ordered by telephone. Don't get worried if the driver has to consult his street directory!

Sydney Light Rail

Sydney's latest tranportation system recreates the days of trams. The Light Rail track runs from Central Station to Chinatown, Darling Harbour, the casino and the Sydney Fish Markets, covering the major city attractions. At peak times, trams are expected to run every five minutes.

The Monorail

Tourist information The following centres will provide all the help you need: **Sydney Visitor Centre, 106 George Street, The Rocks** (tel: 9255 1788); **Sydney Visitors' Information Centre**, Martin Place (tel: 9235 2424); **Transport Infoline** (tel: 13 1500) for all metropolitan bus, rail and ferry inquiries.

Getting around Probably the best way of familiarising yourself with the layout of the city and its main sights is to take a guided coach tour, most of which pick up and drop off at central hotels. Alternatives are the very reasonably priced bright red Sydney Explorer, which trundles round a 20km circuit of the principal attractions, allowing you to get on and off at will for a flat fare, and the blue Bondi & Bay Explorer, which travels to the harbourside eastern suburbs, Bondi, Bronte and Coogee beaches, and Paddington on the same basis.

Buses run a comprehensive scheduled service in the city centre and suburbs, and with patience it's possible to get almost anywhere. They connect with ferries and trains at Circular Quay and with trains at Wynyard and Central Stations. A shuttle bus links The Rocks with Darling Harbour, while the Airport Express runs from Circular Quay and a few stops in the centre as well as from Potts Point, Kings Cross and Oxford Street.

Ferries travel at frequent intervals between Circular Quay and a number of destinations like Manly and Taronga Zoo on the north shore, or Balmain, Hunters Hill and Meadowbank upriver. There are also daily ferries east to Double Bay, Rose Bay and Watsons Bay.

Double-decker electrified trains run on an extensive network of suburban lines as well as on a City Circle linking a number of stations in the CBD. There's a useful spur from Central Station and Town Hall to Kings Cross and Bondi Junction (continue by bus to the beach). The line to North Sydney includes a trip over the Harbour Bridge. A novelty is the overhead **Monorail**, which runs between the southwestern part of the city centre and Darling Harbour.

Sydney Harbour

■ **The glorious stretch of water running inland from the twin heads *is* Sydney, the reason for the city's existence, the source of its distinct identity and special glamour. What Captain Cook named Port Jackson and Captain Phillip called 'one of the finest harbours in the world' is still alive with freighters, ferries and pleasure craft.** ■

One of the world's largest harbours Sydney Harbour has a complex outline of inlets, tributary rivers, bays, coves and promontories, so that a good proportion of the city's residents has some sight of the water from where they live, though competition is fierce and prices astronomical for dwellings enjoying what are considered to be the best views. Not that the entire 240km of shoreline is built up; much of it, like the headlands near its mouth, has been preserved as national park land. Added interest is given by an array of islands, including Fort Denison, where the skeletons of the executed once swung, and Goat Island with its old shipyards west of the Harbour Bridge.

How to explore To board your rich friend's luxury ocean yacht, then take all day to cruise past the sights in total comfort would be an offer not to be refused. Water taxis would do the same kind of job, albeit expensively, while realistic alternatives include a variety of commercial cruises. But perhaps the most authentic way, enjoyed by the city's inhabitants as a matter of course, is the ferry. Now that the tramcar has vanished from the streets, the ferry is the city's only traditional means of conveyance.

An assortment of vessels plies between any number of points, of which the multiple piers of Circular Quay form the hub. In a matter of minutes you can slip across the water in the shadow of the Harbour Bridge to Kirribilli or chug upstream in the afternoon with uniformed schoolchildren returning to their pleasant suburban homes on the promontory of Hunters Hill. Another recommended trip is the 50-minute journey by Rivercat upriver, past Sydney Olympic Park, to the historic city of Parramatta (see page 61).

The magnificent harbour and its twin symbols of Sydney – and Australia

A stroll around The Rocks
The Museum of Contemporary Art contrasts with Cadman's Cottage of 1816 and the other old buildings above it in well-restored George Street where the visitor centre dispenses useful information. Old and new come together around Campbells Cove, while Dawes Point Park, crouching at the feet of the Harbour Bridge, was the first fortified position in Australia. The way back is via the high-level Gloucester Walk and Argyle Street.

The Blue Mountains Drive
Palm Beach and West Head Drive

E

Ebenezer

Cattai National Park

Cattai

Australian Pioneer Village

Freemans Reach

Wilberforce

Hawkesbury

Marayla

Glenorie

Arcadia

North Richmond

Butterfly Farm

Pitt Town

Richmond

Galstor

Windsor

Mulgrave

Box Hill

Agnes Banks

John Tebutt Observatories

Vineyard

Rouse Hill

Round Corner

D

South Creek

Schofields

Kellyville

Castle Hill

Castlereagh

Marsden Park

Quakers Hill

Baulkham Hills

Lucas

56

Doonside

Featherdale Wildlife Park

Seven Hills

Emu Plains

Penrith

St Marys

Rooty Hill

Eastern Creek

Blacktown

Northmead

Panthers World of Entertainment

GREAT WESTERN

HIGHWAY

Pendle Hill

Old Government House

C

Blue Mountains, Wentworth Falls, Cliff Drive, Echo Point, Govett's Leap Lookout

4

WESTERN MOTORWAY

Australia's Wonderland

Prospect Reservoir

Parramatta

Experiment Farm Cottage and Elizabeth Farm

Merrylands

The Australian Wildlife Park

Prospect Creek

Guildford

Erskine Park

Smithfield

Fairfield

Chest Hill

Cecil Park

31

Kemps Creek

Cabramatta

B

Wallacia

Bonnyrigg

Warwick Farm Racecourse

Warragamba

Luddenham

Badgerys Creek

Milperra

Liverpool

Hoxton Park

SOUTH WESTERN

East Hills

Nepean

Bringelly

Rossmore

Glenfield

Harris Creek

George

Ingleburn

Military Reserve

A

HUME HIGHWAY

Gledswood Homestead

Australiana Park

31

Minto

Minto Heights

Lucas Heights

0   5   10   15 km

1

2

Southern Highlands

Campbelltown

3

Drive The Blue Mountains

The famous Three Sisters pillars

See map on pages 56–7.

The truly spectacular cliffs, canyons and forests of the Blue Mountains can be sampled in a day trip.

The exit from Sydney via Route 40 gives good views of the upper harbour from Gladesville Bridge. The route joins the Western Motorway near Parramatta and crosses the plain past Penrith to begin the climb up into the mountains, running parallel to the railway. Several places of interest are signposted off the freeway; these are described below.

Wentworth Falls are probably the grandest waterfalls in the region. Pretty little Leura marks the start of the **Cliff Drive**, which skirts the 300m drop into the valley below. **Echo Point** is, deservedly, the most famous viewpoint in the mountains. Not far from the visitor centre, viewing platforms offer panoramas over cliffs, eucalyptus forest and the Three Sisters sandstone columns. There are signposted walks from here, or you can ride the Scenic Railway or Scenic Skyway further along the Cliff Drive.

Stops can be made at Katoomba, 'capital' of the Blue Mountains, and northeast of Blackheath at the Blue Mountains Heritage Centre. **Govett's Leap Lookout** offers amazing views of the canyon.

Return on the Western Motorway, via Parramatta and the Sydney Olympic Park (the main venue for the Sydney 2000 Olympics), which you can tour.

Drive Palm Beach and West Head

This drive goes from Sydney to the splendid northern beaches and headlands. See map on pages 56–7.

Beyond the Harbour Bridge, Route 14 (Military Road) leads northeastwards, crossing Middle Harbour by the Spit Bridge. A detour can be made to Manly (better visited by ferry from Circular Quay), or continue north past the fine beaches and splendid resorts of Long Reef, Collaroy, Narrabeen and Whale Beach.

The road narrows and winds, rises and descends past desirable homes and holiday retreats as it approaches **Palm Beach**. To the west are fine views over the calm waters of the Pittwater inlet, a contrast to the crashing surf of the ocean beach to the east. On its headland to the north, the **Barrenjoey Lighthouse** beckons. Return to Mona Vale and follow the road around the southern end of Pittwater, turning right through the trees and wildflowers of the **Ku-ring-gai Chase National Park** to **West Head**. The head offers a completely different but equally spectacular view over Pittwater and Broken Bay.

Return via Mona Vale Road (Route 3) and the Pacific Highway.

The suburbs

There is a great deal to see and do in the various historic inner suburbs of the city; these are covered below.

Sydneysiders seem proud of the red-light district of **Kings Cross▶▶** which has its fair share of hookers, strip joints and adult bookshops. But there are also lots of places to eat and drink and plenty of shops for the local community. A stroll along Darlinghurst Road between Kings Cross Station and Fitzroy Gardens with its El Alamein Fountain is sure to entertain day or night. The neighbouring, rather more genteel, suburb of Elizabeth Bay holds another, contrasting attraction – 1830s **Elizabeth Bay House▶**. This elegant mansion, built for the NSW Colonial Secretary, stands as a reminder of the area's former glory.

Bourgeois in its origins, then proletarian and now gentrified, **Paddington▶▶**, or 'Paddo', has had a chequered career as it has passed in and out of favour. Its glory is its delicious terrace houses with their fine ironwork and their subtle adaptation to the contours of the slopes falling northwards to the harbour. Built between the 1860s and 1890s, most of them have been carefully restored by sensitive owners. Also here are **Juniper Hall** (1824), the **post office** (1885), and **Paddington Town Hall** (1891). Laid out to mark Sydney's 100th birthday, **Centennial Park** supports a varied birdlife as well as a whole range of human activities.

The population of **Balmain▶** used to work in its shipyards, but its delightful terraces and little detached weatherboard cottages have been colonised by a middle-class population with Paddington-style aspirations, but not the means to realise them. It too has a richly varied shopping street.

Detached from the common folk on its pleasantly wooded peninsula, **Hunters Hill▶** is a tranquil place of expensive, fine stone houses and humbler cottages. Many of the former were built in French style in the 1850s, while one of the 19th-century tradesmen's abodes, **Vienna Cottage**, has been restored by the National Trust and houses a local museum.

Sydney Jewish Museum
A short stroll from Kings Cross brings a very different experience. The excellent Sydney Jewish Museum (corner of Darlinghurst Road and Burton Street, Darlinghurst) traces Australia's Jewish connections, from First Fleet convicts to post World War II arrivals, and serves as a poignant memorial to the millions of Jews who perished in the Holocaust.

Eastern suburbs
Sydney's eastern suburbs are nothing if not monied, and at Double Bay it shows, with plenty of designer labels and a discreet lack of price tags in its exclusive shops. There are lots of pleasant cafés too, where the shoppers can be seen relaxing after making their difficult choices.

See how the other half lives in exclusive Hunters Hill

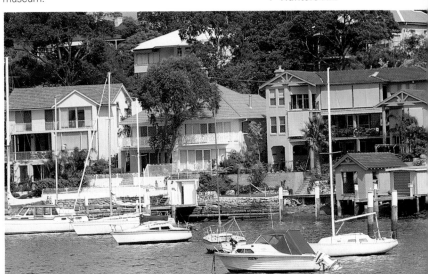

Excursions

Up the Hawkesbury
The area around Richmond and Windsor along the upper reaches of the easily navigable Hawkesbury River was settled within a few years of the arrival of the First Fleet. The winding lower river is best explored in a leisurely way; a unique experience is to board the mail boat at Brooklyn and accompany the letters, parcels and much more on their journey to isolated little places situated along the tranquil river.

The loss of La Perouse
Jean-François de Galaup, Comte de La Perouse had brushed with the British before his meeting in Botany Bay with Captain Phillip. He was taken prisoner after the battle of Quiberon Bay in 1759 and later fought in the American wars. His ships *Astrolabe* and *Boussole* had reached Australia after a long search for the elusive North West Passage. On quitting Botany Bay La Perouse disappeared for ever, though wreckage assumed to be that of his ships was discovered off the New Hebrides in 1826.

Captain Cook's landing place memorial

Easy-to-reach sights from Sydney are covered alphabetically on these two pages.

Broad **Botany Bay▶** (12km south of the centre) where Captain Cook's *Endeavour* dropped anchor on 28 April 1770, was given its name in recognition of the array of Antipodean plants collected here by Joseph Banks. Oil installations and industry now dominate the scene, but to commemorate Cook's historic landing on the Kurnell Peninsula, the national park contains monuments, a visitor centre and a museum. At the northern edge of the bay, La Perouse, named after the commander of the French expedition that arrived just after the First Fleet, is the site of an interesting museum and Sydney's principal Aboriginal settlement.

With splendid coastal and river scenery, **Brisbane Water National Park▶** (75km north) resembles Ku-ring-gai Chase, its sandstone foundation supporting the same spectacular range of flowers and wildlife. There are woodlands of eucalyptus and pockets of rain forest, and Aboriginal carvings can be viewed at the Bulgandry site.

A visit to Parramatta (by road – see page 61) can easily encompass a tour of **Homebush Bay▶▶** and Sydney Olympic Park – the main site for the 2000 Olympic Games. Much of the site is still under construction, but you can visit the Aquatic Centre and other facilities.

Kuring-gai Chase National Park▶▶ (30km north of Sydney) remains in its wild state thanks to its designation as a national park as far back as 1894. The rugged sandstone plateau of which it consists is deeply incised by the deep sheltered waterways running inland from the Hawkesbury River. From West Head there are spectacular views across Broken Bay and the broad expanse of Pittwater. The Kuring-gai (Guringai) Aborigines who once lived here traced many carvings in the sandstone. There is a useful visitor centre at Bobbin Head, with displays on the area's varied animal and bird populations.

A short train ride away from today's glittering metropolis is the meticulously researched reconstruction of **Old Sydney Town▶▶** (stop at Gosford Station), showing what life might have been like as the city struggled to establish itself. Among buildings which faithfully re-create the atmosphere of the pre-1810 period, convincing-looking characters in authentic costume ply their trades, fight duels, or endure the barbaric punishments prescribed by harsh judges and sadistic floggers.

At the very tip of the Warringah peninsula, 40km north of the city centre, is the exclusive residential area of **Palm Beach▶▶**. To the east, the ocean surf crashes on the beach, and to the west the tranquil surface of the **Pittwater** inlet is a paradise for boat lovers and windsurfers. A lighthouse crowns the Barrenjoey headland, offering a terrific view over Broken Bay and up the drowned valley of the Hawkesbury River.

Founded only a matter of months after Sydney itself because of the fertility of the surrounding area, **Parramatta▶▶** might have become the colony's capital. Now the focal point of the sprawling western suburbs 24km from the city centre, it has been much redeveloped, but many traces remain of early days, including some of the nation's very first buildings.

Beyond the mock-Tudor gatehouse to Parramatta Park stands Australia's most venerable public edifice, **Old Government House**, which was built in 1799 though much extended early in the 19th century. For many years the official Vice-Regal residence, it contains early Australian furniture. **Elizabeth Farm** in Alice Street is even older, begun in 1793 by the agricultural pioneers John and Elizabeth Macarthur. Its veranda is the prototype of countless others that adorn dwellings all over Australia. It too has been refurnished in the style of that period, as has the interior of **Experiment Farm Cottage** in Ruse Street. The land on which this house stands belonged to one of the few convicts with any farming experience; in 1789, James Ruse was the first man in Australia to sow a crop of wheat successfully.

Australia's first national park, proclaimed as early as 1879, the **Royal National Park▶▶** consists mostly of a rugged sandstone plateau with a varied vegetation of heathland (a brilliant show of wildflowers in spring), fine forests of blue gum and patches of rain forest. Eaten into by the sea, it has a coastline of spectacular cliffs interspersed with sandy coves. About 35km from Sydney, it has long been a favourite of serious bushwalkers, and is now a popular place for weekend outings of all kinds.

The splendid **Taronga Zoo▶▶** benefits from its superb site almost directly opposite the city centre and is worth visiting for the view alone, particularly if you take the cable-car ride (ferry from Circular Quay). Taronga doesn't limit itself to native animals, but it is the Australian fauna that most visitors will want to see.

A room inside 1835 Experiment Farm Cottage, Parramatta

The road to Parramatta
A road was built from Sydney to Parramatta as early as 1794, but for years it was easier to bring people and goods up the river than along the highway. Partly superseded by a motorway, today's Parramatta Road is neither lovely nor efficient, though a trip along it reveals a cross-section of Australian suburbia. In spite of interminable traffic lights and shabby shopping centres, there remains something indefinably romantic about it, a whiff of the days when it alone pointed to the interior of the unknown continent.

NEW SOUTH WALES

Sunset on Black Mountain, Canberra, capped by the Telstra Tower

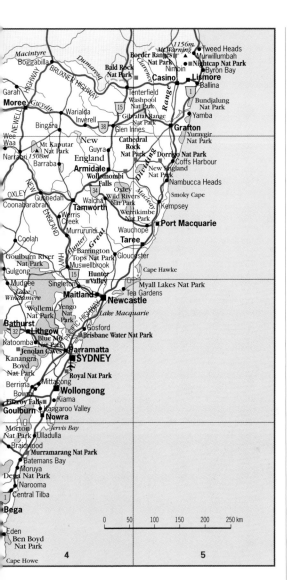

New South Wales

New South Wales This state *was* Australia in the early days of European settlement. Today it is still the country's most populous state, and its capital, Sydney, is the country's greatest city. If time is short, tourists are sometimes advised to concentrate on this state alone; and it is true that a holiday spent entirely within New South Wales' far-flung borders can be very rewarding, regardless of whether the visitor comes in search of urban pleasures or the delights of wild nature.

The Coastal Lowlands The 'Premier State' can be divided into four regions, between them encompassing much that is typical of the country as a whole. Most of the population lives in the Coastal Lowlands, a fertile strip of country of varying width running some 1,400km from Victoria

NEW SOUTH WALES

Clinging to the coast
Between them, the cities of Sydney, Newcastle and Wollongong are home to almost 4.5 million people – a very large proportion of the state's 6.2 million. The remainder of the population lives mostly in coastal towns – far from the often inhospitable interior.

What's in a name?
Between 1768 when he set out for Tahiti, and 1779 when he was hacked to pieces on a Hawaiian beach, Captain Cook probably named more places than anyone else in history. Some recall people (Port Jackson), some are a lively evocation of events (Cape Tribulation), some characterise a quirk of topography (Mount Dromedary in Tasmania has two humps). Inspiration seems to have failed him when confronted with the task of finding a suitable name for the whole of the eastern coast of Australia, even given the supposed resemblance of part of it to the coastline of southern Wales. But perhaps New South Wales, as a name, is one up on such masterpieces of inventiveness as South Australia.

to Queensland. Apart from glamorous Sydney, the region is home to the industrial cities of **Newcastle** and **Wollongong**, as well as a glorious chain of little ports and seaside settlements like Ulladulla (directly east of Canberra). White Australia's history began here, when Captain Cook's charts led the First Fleet to Botany Bay, and where, after a shaky start, the process of colonisation gradually got under way with the founding of townships and the clearing of the bush for farmland.

The area has also been the focus of much of the country's modern history, its industrial heartland and stronghold of the Labor movement which has played an often decisive role in Australian government and politics. It is here that the foundation was laid for Australian beach culture, as love of the sun, surf and sheer physical well-being overcame the remnants of Victorian prudery in the early decades of this century, the process owing not a little to the incomparable beaches which are still the state's main tourist attraction.

The Great Dividing Range Providing a constant backdrop to the coast, with its hills, peaks and tablelands also running the length of the state, in places the Great Dividing Range drops almost directly into the sea, elsewhere withdrawing to a distant but always visible horizon. It formed a puzzling and frustrating barrier in the early years of the colony, until 1813 when the spectacular **Blue Mountains** were successfully crossed.

The highlands are as wonderfully varied as the coast: to the south, in the **Snowy Mountains**, they include the country's highest peaks and most extensive snowfields; to the north lies the high-level plateau of **New England**, named after the old country for its misty coolness and vivid green. In places, as in the **Southern Highlands**, the ranges are interspersed with broad plains which were converted early on into attractive farmland. Here there is a wealth of old buildings in town and country, as well as a 2,500-sq km tract carved out of the state to form the Australian Capital Territory (ACT), the site of the nation's capital, Canberra. Most of the rivers of southeastern Australia have their source in the uplands, with their relatively abundant rain and snowfall. Some, like the Hawkesbury and Hunter, are quite short, running east to the Pacific; others, much longer, form part of the huge Murray/Darling system, flowing slowly westward.

The Western Slopes Beyond the mountains and tablelands, the Western Slopes fall gradually towards the interior. Opened for settlement once the way across the Blue Mountains had been established, the area today consists mostly of unspectacular wheat and wool country, and there are several substantial towns and even small cities in this region – including Moree, Dubbo, Orange, Wellington, Bathurst and Wagga Wagga. To the south, in the Riverina, the waters of the Murray and Murrumbidgee have been used to create huge irrigated areas that now support a variety of crops.

The Western Plains This area stretches to the borders with South Australia and Queensland. It is the New South Wales Outback, with vastly more sheep than people and where the unfortunate township of **Bourke** has given its name ('back of Bourke') to utter remoteness, the Outback beyond the Outback. In the harsh landscape, the city of **Broken Hill** has grown up based on the world's richest lode of silver, lead and zinc; it is a place that attracts many visitors for its sheer strangeness.

65

Attractive Canberra, a modern planned city that is like nowhere else in Australia

The home of foreign embassies

Canberra

Framed by glorious mountain scenery, Australia's capital comprises the prestigious buildings housing the nation's central institutions, all in a setting of broad boulevards and cosy neighbourhoods. As well as being the country's only major inland city, Canberra is unique in having been planned in every detail from its very beginnings.

At the time of Federation, in 1901, the bitter dispute between Sydney and Melbourne about which should become the country's capital was finally resolved by choosing neither. Instead, the new Constitution stipulated that a site should be found in New South Wales, no closer than 100 miles (160km) to Sydney. After much debate the present location was chosen, and in 1911 some 2,500sq km of land south of the Goulburn Plains became the Australian Capital Territory. Over 130 hopefuls took part in the international competition for the design of the new city, the American landscape architect Walter Burley Griffin emerging as winner.

Griffin had never seen Canberra when he drew up his plans for a new city thousands of miles from his Chicago base, but his experience enabled him to interpret maps and diagrams, and to appreciate the potential of the chosen location. His design is very much of his period, a combination of great vistas framing noble buildings, and self-contained residential neighbourhoods providing a setting for everyday life.

The target population for the country's capital was 25,000, but Canberra's growth was painfully slow and this total was only reached in the years following World War II. Growth took off in the 1960s, and today the city is home to over 300,000 people. Around half of its workforce has always consisted of public employees, not necessarily a sound basis for a satisfactory social balance. In its infancy and adolescence, the city was seen as a place of exile, populated by bored civil servants longing for the fleshpots of Sydney or Melbourne. Nor is its contemporary image among Australians a particularly happy one; many think of it as a privileged place of parasitic politicians and cosseted bureaucrats, although Canberra has improved greatly in recent years, with a far more lively dining, entertainment and nightlife scene.

Canberra has been described with some truth as a collection of suburbs in search of a city, but what it lacks in urbanity it more than makes up for with convenience (no traffic jams!), easy access to superb countryside and sheer spacious beauty. It certainly is nothing like any other city and is well worth visiting for that reason alone, with an array of splendid modern buildings in the immaculately landscaped setting planned for them in the early years of the nation's foundation.

The extraordinary new Parliament House (built in 1988) is rich in national symbolism

The 81-m flagpole on top of Parliament House and Capital Hill

A capital museum
The National Museum of Australia is still in the early stages of development. Its ambitious plans are presented in a visitor centre on Lady Denman Drive, Yarralumla, and some exhibitions are now being held in Old Parliament House.

An Aussie 'digger' (soldier) runs up the flag outside the Australian War Memorial

▶▶ **Australian National Botanic Gardens**   *66C1*

These attractive gardens on the lower slopes of Black Mountain present a wonderful range of native Australian plants – some 6,000 species in all. A network of paths leads through a series of contrasting environments, each with its fully labelled array of trees, shrubs and other plants. This is one of the best places to appreciate Australia's unique flora.

▶▶▶ **Australian War Memorial**   *66C3*

Limestone Avenue, Campbell

Flanked by massive stone pylons, the dome of the War Memorial stares sombrely from the lower slopes of Mount Ainslie down Anzac Parade towards Capital Hill on the far shore of Lake Burley Griffin. With its great courtyard containing the Roll of Honour and the Eternal Flame, it was officially opened in 1941.

It is not just a great monument, but a world-class museum that attempts to make some sense of the senselessness of war. Beyond the carefully crafted symbolism of the exterior are extensive galleries and displays evoking the many conflicts in which the country has been involved, from the Maori Wars of the 1860s to 1970s Vietnam. As well as the hardware of war-like guns and aeroplanes, there are superb paintings, photographs, huge dioramas, film and sound recordings, and documents and papers. This is not a museum to be visited casually or in a hurry.

▶▶ **Diplomatic Missions**   *66B2*

One of the most fascinating tours in Canberra is to the suburb of Yarralumla. Here many foreign countries have built their embassies, free from any of the constraints of fitting into a long-established city. National self-expression takes a variety of forms: America occupies the most space, Greece has classical columns, Papua New Guinea has an exuberantly gabled longhouse and Indonesia has a Balinese temple.

▶▶ **Lake Burley Griffin**   *66B2*

Burley Griffin included a lake in his visionary plan for the new city, but it was not until 1964 that the great body of water bearing his name finally came into being, with an area of more than 7 square km and a highly varied shoreline stretching some 35km long. A number of islands enliven the scene, which is further enhanced by lakeside landscaping, as in the recently completed and award-winning **Commonwealth Park**. The **Captain Cook Memorial Jet** waterspout is capable of reaching a spectacular 140m in calm weather.

Dating from 1860, **Blundell's Farmhouse** near the lakeshore is one of the few remaining old buildings in Canberra. Rising over the weeping willows on Aspen Island are the crisp white concrete shafts of the **National Carillon**, a gift from Britain to mark Canberra's 50th anniversary in 1963. Its 53 bells play Australian melodies as well as a medley of tunes from the old country. Designed to be the focal point of this extraordinary city, the lake makes a splendid setting for many of its most prominent buildings. A trip on one of the cruise boats is a pleasant way to make the most of it.

69

▶ National Aquarium and Australian Wildlife Sanctuary   66C1

In a fine setting by Scrivener Dam, the aquarium is a reminder that Australia owes much to the sea, whose myriad creatures can be observed here in a spectacular walk-through environment.

▶▶ National Capital Exhibition   66C2

Regatta Point, Commonwealth Park

Boasting 'the best view of the national capital', this is a good place for appreciating the meticulous and sometimes controversial planning of the new city. The exhibition features models, plans, photographs and audiovisuals.

▶ National Film and Sound Archive   66C2

McCoy Circuit, Acton

Australia was one of the first in the field as the movie age developed, and this centre presents an intriguing selection from the nation's contribution to the delights of the silver screen, including a short film of the 1896 Melbourne Cup. Radio and TV are also represented.

▶▶▶ National Gallery of Australia   66B3

Parkes Place

The national art collections are housed in an imposing structure of sandblasted concrete that opened in 1982. Its neighbours on the banks of Lake Burley Griffin are also of national significance. The National Gallery has an excellent array of Australian art, beginning with Aboriginal artefacts and ending with canvases on which the paint seems hardly dry. There is much else besides, displayed to

The Botanic Gardens are renowned for their splendid collection of Australian native plants

Capital views

Canberra's ring of uplands provides several splendid viewpoints over the carefully planned city in its superb setting. The spike of Telstra Tower sticks up from the top of Black Mountain (812m), giving panoramic vistas from its viewing galleries. Mount Ainslie (842m), rising through bushland behind the War Memorial, has equally spectacular views, as does Red Hill, 2km south of Parliament House.

Parliament House is one of Canberra's most popular attractions

Capital coinage
As well as a gallery enabling visitors to see the country's money being made, the Royal Australian Mint has a public coining press where you can mint your own coins or tokens.

Capital punishment
Justice has moved on in Australia since the early days when the gaol was sometimes the most prominent building in town. But modern Australians are second only to Americans in their fondness for litigation, and many interesting cases end up in the imposing High Court, with its exhibition explaining the workings of the country's legal system.

A sporting capital
Sports fans shouldn't miss a tour of the Australian Institue of Sport (AIS) in the northern suburb of Bruce. The institute, set up in 1980, features top-class facilities and an interesting visitor centre with displays and entertaining hands-on exhibits. Tours are conducted by the AIS's élite athletes.

advantage in well-lit and highly varied spaces, including a good selection of European and American art – particularly of the 20th century – as well as works from Asia and the Pacific. Sculpture benefits from the attractive setting of the Sculpture Garden, which also serves as a venue for outdoor events.

►   **National Library of Australia**   *66B2*
Parkes Place
In addition to several million books, this rather severe neo-classical building houses other unique collections relating to the history and evolution of Australia – paintings, films, maps, photographs and newspapers. The interior is adorned with fine tapestries and stained glass.

►►►   **Parliament House**   *66B2*
Capital Hill
The truly spectacular structure of Parliament House was completed in time for Australia's Bicentenary in 1988. Not just home to the House of Representatives and the Senate, it has become a major visitor attraction in its own right, rich in artworks and national symbolism. A million cubic metres of soil was removed from the top of Capital Hill to make way for the new building, then replaced to form its green roof. This superb viewpoint over the city is topped by an 81m flagstaff of stainless steel flying what must be the biggest flag in the world. Below is a complex of beautifully designed internal spaces, adorned with the creations of Australian artists like Arthur Boyd, whose gloriously colourful tapestry graces the far wall of the Great Hall. The 48 marble columns of the foyer recall the country's eucalyptus trees, whose cool green colour appears again in the chamber of the House of Representatives, intended perhaps to calm the often inflamed tempers of its occupants.

►►   **Questacon**   *66B2*
King Edward Terrace
The recently completed National Science and Technology Centre in its exciting modern building has around 200 hands-on displays in six different galleries. This informative and interactive centre brings the world of science alive – even to the most non-technical – and is worth an extended visit.

How to travel

By air A comprehensive network of international and domestic air services operates from Sydney's Kingsford Smith Airport, 12km south of the city centre on Botany Bay. The separate domestic and international terminals are linked by bus and taxi, and the frequent Airport Express bus takes 30 minutes to the city centre or Kings Cross (20 minutes to Central Railway Station). There are flights to the NSW Outback and many coastal resorts, to Cooma (for the Snowy Mountains) and to Canberra.

By bus and coach The network of long-distance coach services is a far-flung one, although timings can be inconvenient in the case of remote townships. On the main routes there is likely to be a choice of operator and times. Organised coach tours are very popular, and many places can be visited in this way from Sydney. Most major towns have a well-developed network of local bus services.

By rail Of all the Australian states, NSW has kept the most widespread rail network, and of those towns which have lost their train service, many are connected to a railhead by Countrylink buses operated by the State Rail Authority (Countrylink). Multiple-unit express trains (XPTs and XPLORERS) ply between many major centres (Canberra, Tamworth, the North Coast, Hunter Valley, Dubbo). Luxurious interstate trains run to Brisbane and Melbourne. Broken Hill is visited by the *Indian Pacific* on its way to and from Western Australia, and has its own weekly XPT link to Sydney. The Greater Sydney region is particularly well served by frequent CityRail services which extend as far as Newcastle and Dungog in the north, the Blue Mountains in the west, Goulburn and the Southern Highlands, and Nowra on the south coast.

By car Driving is not recommended in the Sydney area, unless you are heading out of town to places like Palm Beach or the Royal National Park. Here, public transport and the occasional taxi should get you anywhere you are likely to want to go. However, many remote parts of the state are only accessible if you have your own vehicle.

Save time and fly
Unless you have plenty of time and are happy to drive, flying to the more distant parts of the state is highly recommended. Quantas, Ansett and their subsidiaries cover most major NSW destinations.

A long way by car
New South Wales is comprehensively criss-crossed by a web of named highways, very helpful in planning an itinerary, though they tend to be of variable quality. Driving the Pacific Highway north along the coast can get tedious, and many prefer the inland New England Highway.

71

Renting a 4WD makes sense if you plan to go off road

72

One of the grand old buildings in the pleasant city of Bathurst

The way to the west
Just visible from the area around Sydney, the dark escarpment of the Blue Mountains rises abruptly some 600m from the Sydney plains, a formidable barrier blocking the way westward to the early colonists. Some convict escapees were convinced that China lay just beyond the mountains as they headed towards what they hoped would be freedom. The puzzle of how to cross the mountains, by keeping to the ridges rather than to the valleys, was solved by Blaxland, Lawson and Wentworth in 1813, and within two years Governor Macquarie had a road built by convict labour on the alignment still followed by the modern road and railway. This marked a great leap forward in the development of the colony, promising an opening up of the immense potential of the still unknown interior.

▶▶ **Armidale**   *63C4*

Unofficial capital of the cool uplands of New England in the northeast of the state, Armidale is the nearest thing Australia has to a university city, with a number of higher education colleges and several private schools as well as the University of New England in its parkland campus. A couple of cathedrals, plus a number of venerable public buildings and delightful old houses further enhance the refined atmosphere. The modern **New England Regional Art Museum▶** has a reputation as the best provincial collection of Australian art, and there is a good Folk Museum housed in a building dating from 1863.

Armidale makes a good base for exploring this part of New England (whose Scottish settlers tried and failed to make the name New Caledonia stick); within easy reach are a number of spectacular waterfalls, including the highest in Australia, **Wollomombi Falls▶** in the Oxley Wild Rivers National Park.

▶ **Batemans Bay**   *63A4*

This fishing port and popular tourist resort on the estuary of the Clyde River is conveniently situated for the citizens of Canberra, only 150km away over the mountains. There are fine oysters and lobsters, and a penguin colony on the Tollgate Islands Nature Reserve.

▶▶ **Bathurst**   *63B4*

At the end of the Great Western Highway from Sydney, Bathurst was founded by Governor Macquarie in 1815, making it the country's oldest inland settlement. It was the point of departure for many expeditions further into the interior, and in 1851 this area was the scene of Australia's first gold rush. Those days are re-created in the open-air museum called Bathurst Goldfields, and the town itself is full of interest. The scenic drive around Mount Panorama forms part of what is considered to be Australia's finest motor-racing circuit.

▶▶▶ **Blue Mountains National Park**   *63B4*

Sheer cliffs dropping into deep canyons and glorious eucalyptus forests make up some of the most spectacular landscapes to be seen in Australia. The grandeur of the natural scene is all the more impressive because of the proximity of the manicured residential and retirement areas clustered along the main road and railway from Sydney, 90 minutes away.

The Blue Mountains are not really mountains, but a vast sandstone tableland, deeply incised by watercourses like the Nepean and Cox's rivers. Their colour is real, however, as a vaporous emanation from the leaves of the eucalyptus hangs in the air as a blue haze. Since the early part of this century the mountains have attracted serious bushwalkers as well as sightseers, and they offer all kinds of pleasures today, from antique hunting in sophisticated little townships, to real escape into wild country for those who are prepared to abandon their cars. The following main sights could just about be seen in the course of a day trip from Sydney, but it would be far better to stay at least a couple of days.

A good place to start is at the excellent **National Parks and Wildlife Service's Heritage Centre▶** 2km to the

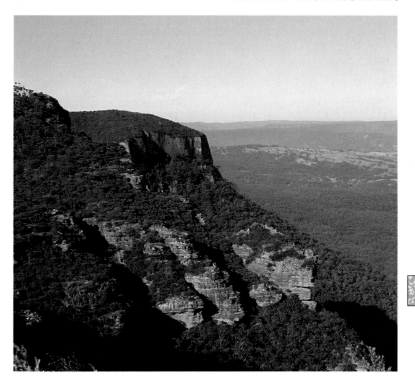

east of the main highway at Blackheath. A short distance away is one of the most spectacular lookouts in the whole national park, **Govett's Leap►►**, with breathtaking views of the Grose Valley and Bridal Veil Falls. A panoramic walk leads along the clifftop to various other vantage points, while a steep track descends into the superb forest of blue gums far below – this is a particularly scenic walk for experienced hikers.

The other great viewpoint in the park is **Echo Point►►** just to the south of **Katoomba**, the 'capital' of the municipality known as City of the Blue Mountains. Here there is another visitor centre whose glass wall looks straight out into the treetops, while projecting platforms give giddy views of the famous sandstone pillars of **The Three Sisters**. A number of popular walks fringe the clifftop or descend into the valley. Just to the west are two exciting forms of tourist transport, the Skyway, a cable car, and the Scenic Railway, a modernised inclined plane dropping steeply into the valley bottom.

To the east are the famous **Wentworth Falls►►**, the highest in the area with a drop of 270m. Wentworth Falls village is the location of the charming 1888 house, Yester Grange, now containing tearooms and period antiques, and nearby Faulconbridge is the home of the **Norman Lindsay Gallery and Museum►**, which commemorates this well-known artist and writer. Westward are the truly spectacular **Jenolan Caves►►** and the charming late-Victorian guesthouse associated with them, while one of the country's great feats of railway engineering, the **Zig Zag Railway►** (see panel) can be enjoyed near Lithgow.

Dramatic sandstone cliffs and densely forested valleys around Katoomba

The great Zig Zag
In 1866, the engineers building the railway line to the west were confronted with the problem of how to lower it from the top of the Blue Mountains down the sheer cliff face into Lithgow. Their solution was to construct a line in the form of a letter Z down the cliff face, with reversing stations at two points. This was eventually replaced by the present main line which takes a long way round but eliminates the need for reversing. The Zig Zag has been restored as a tourist railway, an impressive spectacle as powerful engines haul their coaches up the steep slope.

74

Wentworth Falls lookout in the Blue Mountains

World Heritage sites
Three of Australia's World Heritage listed sites lie within New South Wales. The most accessible includes the lush rain forest of Dorrigo National Park, inland from Coffs Harbour, while the others are more remote – Lord Howe Island and the Willandra Lakes region in the state's far southwest.

Not just parks
The NSW National Parks and Wildlife Service manages a number of sites whose interest is primarily human, rather than natural. These include places like Mootwingee Historic Site, with its wealth of mysterious Aboriginal relics, and sites of significance in the early European settlement of the country like Captain Cook's Landing Place at Botany Bay. Sydney's oldest dwelling, Cadman's Cottage, is a National Parks and Wildlife Service shop and resource centre.

With its long coastline, mountains and extensive Outback, New South Wales has wonderful examples of many of the continent's characteristic natural landscapes.

In the far west On the fringes of Australia's Red Centre and well over 1,000km from Sydney are two superb arid wildernesses. In **Sturt National Park** summer temperatures can reach 50°C for days on end; grassy plains alternate with claypans and pebbly desert from which rise flat-topped mesas (rocky tableland). In the extreme west are the ruddy-coloured sand dunes of the Strzelecki Desert. **Kinchega National Park** has vast plains of red sand as well as the strange saucer-shaped overflow lakes of the Darling River. Both areas are home to emus and the large red kangaroo.

To the east The land gradually rises through the western slopes of the Great Dividing Range to the range itself, the backbone of the state. On the border with Victoria is one of the world's great national parks, centred on Australia's highest peak, **Mount Kosciuszko**, after which the park itself is named. Glacial lakes, wild heathlands, alpine flowers and glorious forests of snow gums make a superb setting for summer walking, while the area becomes the nation's winter playground during the ski season – from early June to early Octobrer each year. The forested highlands that extend from near Newcastle through New England to the Queensland border have a rich vegetation which includes much undisturbed rain forest; here 16 separate parks and reserves have been grouped together to form one of Australia's World Heritage areas, the **Australian East Coast Temperate and Subtropical Rain Forest Parks**. Old volcanoes give rise to dramatic landforms here and at **Warrumbungle National Park** further inland, a weird world of rocky crags and natural skyscrapers. **Bald Rock National Park**, near the Queensland border in the far north, is another extraordinary landform, a great granite dome which rises 200m out of the surrounding bush.

*Mount Kosciuszko:
good walking country*

What to see 'outback'
From Broken Hill you can travel to many interesting Outback locations. Lying within the relatively small distance of 200km are the opal-mining village of White Cliffs and Mootwingee National Park and the Menindee Lakes, and Wilcannia, a quiet Darling River town.

► Bourke   62C2

This Outback town 800km northwest of Sydney seems utterly remote. It is the centre of a vast and semi-arid area supporting large numbers of sheep and cattle as well as some crops on land irrigated with water from the Darling River. Originating in a wooden stockade built in 1835 against Aboriginal attack, Bourke has a number of buildings dating from the latter part of the 19th century. Its main attraction, however, lies in its very remoteness and as a base for penetrating further into the New South Wales Outback.

►► Broken Hill   62C1

Founded on a 7km lode of silver, lead and zinc, the richest of its kind in the world, the unique 'Silver City' faces an uncertain future as rationalisation takes place against a background of low world prices for its products.

Thanks to the water piped in from its recreational reservoir at Lake Menindee 110km away, Broken Hill is a surprisingly green and leafy spot in what is one of the world's harshest environments: bitterly cold in winter, intolerably hot in summer, with a negligible rainfall that is only a tiny fraction of the evaporation rate. Nearly dead from thirst, the explorer Sturt gave the hump-backed ridge its name in 1844, but it was not until the 1880s that a German-born boundary rider, Charles Rasp, founded the Broken Hill Proprietary Company (see panel) which exploited the underground wealth in uneasy partnership with the workforce for many years. A great strike of 1919 ended in a historic compromise; the companies were ensured their profits and the workers granted conditions far in advance of the time, like a 35-hour week. A confederation of trade unions effectively ran the town, not always on what today would be regarded as progressive lines.

Broken Hill has always been a long way from the government in Sydney, and its ties are closer to South Australia, with smelters at Port Pirie, union beaches at Adelaide, clocks that keep South Australian time – half an hour behind that of Sydney – and a South Australian region telephone prefix code.

Broken Hill Proprietary Company
BHP, as it is universally known, had its roots in Charles Rasp's discovery in 1883 of the immensely rich silver, lead and zinc lode at Broken Hill. It is now Australia's largest company, having long since diversified into iron and coal, gas and oil, and steel-making. Its profits are taken by many as an index of the prosperity of the country as a whole.

75

Continued on page 78.

■ Born the son of a farm labourer at Marston in Yorkshire in 1728, James Cook became the greatest explorer of his age. He was educated at the expense of his father's generous-minded employer, then learned seamanship aboard a Whitby collier. In 1755 he joined the Royal Navy, where he refined his navigational and other skills in the course of the Seven Years War. His charts of the St Lawrence River helped Wolfe in the conquest of Quebec. But the achievement for which Lieutenant (as he then was) Cook is best remembered is his masterly voyage of exploration along the wholly unknown east coast of Australia in 1770. ■

Ahead of his time

Cook was well in advance of his time in seeing beyond his own culture and background to the deeper harmony of Aborigines' way of life. He wrote: 'In reality they are far more happy than we Europeans, being wholly (*sic*) unacquainted not only with the superfluous but the necessary Conveniences so much sought after in Europe, they are happy in not knowing the use of them. They live in a Tranquillity which is not disturbed by the Inequality of Condition: the Earth and sea of their own accord furnishes them with all things necessary for life.'

As Cook had documented an eclipse of the sun off the coast of Newfoundland, he was a natural choice when the Royal Society wished for an accurate observation to be made from Tahiti of the transit of Venus across the face of the sun. Accompanying him on this mission aboard the barque *Endeavour* was an astronomer, Charles Green, together with two eminent botanists, Daniel Solander and Joseph Banks, still a young man of 25.

East coast sighting On 3 July 1769, the transit of Venus was duly observed and Cook opened the sealed orders given him by the Admiralty. These instructed him to investigate the existence or otherwise of a great southern continent and to survey and take possession of New Zealand. Having completed a thorough exploration of the New Zealand coast, Cook decided to return via the hypothetical 'East Coast of New Holland'. This was sighted on 19 April 1770, when Cape Everard (originally called Cape Hicks in honour of Cook's sharp-eyed second in command) came into view.

1770: Cook takes possession of NSW for Britain...

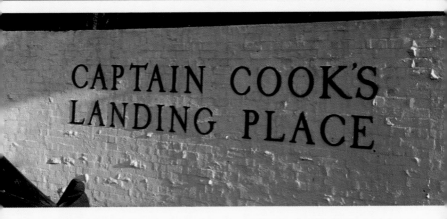

CAPTAIN COOK'S LANDING PLACE

Sailing northward along the coast, Cook found a convenient harbour to drop anchor and investigate local conditions. The crew feasted on fresh fish, and the delighted botanists discovered an extraordinary array of plants, birds and animals previously unknown to science. In deference to their serious purpose, Cook altered his original name for the anchorage, Stingray Harbour, to Botany Bay.

Grounded on the Barrier Reef Further north, Cook noted in passing the existence of what seemed to be a fine natural harbour and named it Port Jackson. The wonderful setting for the future city of Sydney had to await full discovery until the arrival of the First Fleet 18 years later. Feeling his way into 'the labyrinth of coral islands, shoals, rocks and lee shores' of the Barrier Reef, even Cook's superb seamanship couldn't fend off a grounding, and the *Endeavour* struck a reef.

Although it floated off thanks to all kinds of impedimenta being jettisoned (a cannon is now in the National Library in Canberra), the barque needed repairs and was beached for a month near today's Cooktown at the base of Cape York. Once more the scientists had a field day, making their first acquaintance with kangaroos and turtles. When the *Endeavour* was seaworthy again, Cook sailed north to the tip of the cape where, on Possession Island, he hoisted the flag and formally declared the whole of eastern Australia to be British, giving it the unremarkable name of New South Wales.

The end of the road Promoted to captain, Cook went on in 1772–5 to become the first to sail within the Antarctic Circle, finally putting paid to the idea of the great southern continent. In the course of an attempt in 1779 to find the elusive northern passage between the Atlantic and Pacific, he landed on Hawaii. As he was mediating in his usual calm and dignified way in a relatively trivial dispute with the islanders, one of his men stupidly discharged his firearm; enraged, the islanders fell upon Cook, who had turned his back on them to restore order, and he collapsed beneath blows from clubs and daggers.

Banks the botanist
Australia's 73 species of *Banksia* commemorate the rich young scientist who sailed with Cook and who has been described as 'the father of Australian botany'. On the voyage out he listed 230 plant species at Madeira, 316 at Rio, 104 at Tierra del Fuego and 400 in New Zealand. Later, Banks was president of the Royal Society for 32 years, continuing to take an interest in all things Australian.

77

...having made his mark in Botany Bay

Guess what grows at this Coffs Harbour plantation!

Silver screen Silverton
About 25km west of Broken Hill is the ghost town of Silverton, whose population moved to the bigger town when mining became unprofitable here in the late 1880s. With its restored buildings seeming to typify the spirit of the Outback, it has taken on a new lease of life as a stage set for a number of films, including *A Town Like Alice* and one in the *Mad Max* series.

Our banana's the biggest
The improbably oversized fruit known as the Big Banana dominates the scene on the Pacific Highway just to the north of Coffs Harbour. Made of concrete rather than skin and starch, it marks the entrance to a banana plantation that welcomes visitors. Here you can see bananas growing, eat bananas in every imaginable form, buy banana-shaped souvenirs, and find out everything you always wanted to know about bananas – but never dared to ask.

Continued from page 75.

Protected from dust storms by extensive tree belts, Broken Hill is laid out on a grid of streets with names like Chloride, Mica and Cobalt. The excellent Tourist Information Centre is close to the old Sulphide Street Station, now a mineral and train museum. The Gladstone Mining Museum has interesting exhibits, but it's more exciting to go down a former mine, like Delprat's Mine or Day Dream Mine. The town is also the base for the **Royal Flying Doctor Service** and the **School of the Air**, both of which are open to the public. The strange environment of the city and its surroundings seems to have acted as a stimulant to a number of artists, and there are several galleries, of which the best known is that run by Pro Hart.

▶▶ Byron Bay   63D5

Cape Byron is the easternmost point of the Australian mainland, capped with a powerful lighthouse. Byron Bay itself, with wonderful beaches and a gloriously scenic hinterland of forests and mountains, has been a focal point of alternative lifestyles since the late 1960s. A major attraction here is the Byron Bay Whale Centre, which documents the town's whaling history and its position on the whale migration route.The beaches to either side of the headland vary in character, from secluded coves to great stretches of sand. Surfing is well established; the first life-saving club was founded here as early as 1907.

▶ Cobar   62C2

This copper-mining town on the fringe of the Outback straddles the Barrier Highway on its way west to Broken Hill. Founded in the early 1870s as a typical mining city of tents and huts, it soon reached its peak population of some 10,000. That time has left a legacy of buildings like the Great Western Hotel with its extraordinarily long veranda and the mining company's office, which is now the excellent Cabar Regional Museum. After a long decline, the place prospered again from the 1960s.

► **Cockington Green, ACT**   *66D3*

The original Cockington in the southwest of England, a picture-postcard village with thatched cottages, a pub, a forge and other assorted items of rusticity, is reproduced here on the outskirts of Canberra in miniature form. There are also scaled-down versions of Stonehenge and other quaint features of the country Australians used to refer to as 'home'.

►► **Coffs Harbour**   *63C5*

Roughly halfway between Sydney and Brisbane, this old timber port is famous for its beaches and banana plantations (see panel opposite). A string of fine beaches runs northwards from the town's Park Beach, some with good surf. There is rafting on nearby rivers, while man-made attractions for holidaymakers include the Pet Porpoise Pool, with seals, penguins and sharks as well as amiable porpoises. The harbour is protected by a headland to the south, and by Muttonbird Island (reached by the old timber jetty) where there really are muttonbirds. The town centre, with its Historical Museum and Bicentennial Botanical Garden, is some distance inland. It is a popular place for craftsmen and handicraft shops.

► **Dubbo**   *62C3*

At the junction of the Newell and Mitchell Highways, Dubbo is the flourishing centre for a large part of NSW's Central West area. First settled in the 1840s, it became a stopping point for those in search of 'better land, farther out'. Overlanders driving their cattle southwards to the markets of SA and Victoria used to cross the Macquarie River near here. There are a number of fine old buildings in the town centre, among them the 1876 bank, which now houses a good local museum and the gaol, complete with gibbet. But most visitors come here for the **Western Plains Zoo►**, the biggest of its kind in the country, with animals from all over the world roaming its parkland.

► **Eden**   *63A4*

The last place of any size on the NSW coast before the border with Victoria, this little port and resort began life as a whaling station, recalled in the **Killer Whale Museum►**. On Twofold Bay are the remains of Boydtown, begun in the 1840s by the English entrepreneur Benjamin Boyd and vaingloriously intended to rival Sydney as the colony's capital. More recently, Eden has been the focus of the battle to save Australia's forests from the wood-chip industry.

► **Forbes**   *62B3*

Almost deserted after the gold rush of the 1860s, this western town survived as the centre for a rich agricultural area. Some fine late 19th-century buildings like the imposing Town Hall still grace the wide streets. Just outside town is a re-created settlement of pioneer days, **Lachlan Vintage Village►**, where you can pan for gold or watch sheep being shorn. The bushranger Ben Hall met his end in Forbes in 1865, an event recalled in some detail in the old music hall which houses the town's museum.

Whale and chips
The first whaling station on the Australian mainland was established at Eden in 1818, and whaling continued to be based here until the 1930s. A revival of Eden's economy took place in the late 1960s with the building of the Harris Daishowa mill, designed to turn the forests of the area (some of the finest in the state) into woodchips for the Japanese paper industry. The project aroused the ire of the growing Australian conservation movement, whose members saw in it the export of part of the country's irreplaceable natural heritage. The other side of the story is presented in the chip-mill's visitor centre.

These days, whale-watching is popular at Eden's Twofold Bay

Watering the wilderness
The explorer John Oxley reckoned no white man would ever want to take up residence in the 'barren and desolate' country he glimpsed from Mount Binya in 1817. But in the early 1900s, the NSW government, enthused by private successes with irrigation experiments, built the Burrinjuck Dam and encouraged settlement in the Murrumbidgee Irrigation area. Many settlers were out-of-work miners from Broken Hill; later, returned servicemen and Italian immigrants with important agricultural skills moved in, and in spite of many disappointments and technical difficulties, the area produces a variety of crops. Together with similar projects, a total of 6,000sq km of near desert has been made to bloom.

All of the 50 or so wineries in the Hunter Valley welcome visitors; most are around Cessnock and Pokolbin

► **Glen Innes**   63D4

This high-altitude town in northern NSW is at the centre of a prosperous farming area, once named the 'Land of the Beardies' after two pioneers. The region is well known for the sapphires and other gemstones which are extracted commercially (amateur fossicking is also possible). The town centre has several well-cared-for late 19th-century buildings; the old hospital houses the **Land of the Beardies History House Museum►**, one of Australia's most interesting small museums.

► **Goulburn**   63B4

The second oldest inland town in Australia straddles the Hume Highway some 200km southwest of Sydney and is the focal point of the well-tended farmlands all around, whose speciality is proclaimed by another one of those Australian 'big ones'; 15m high, the Big Merino guards the town's western approach. Goulburn is a 'real' city, with two cathedrals, a long main street and a number of imposing 19th-century buildings. On the edge of town is Riversdale, a coaching inn dating from the late 1830s, authentically restored and furnished.

► **Grafton**   63D5

Centre of the Clarence River district, Grafton was 'green' before its time. The town council initiated a policy of tree-planting as early as the 1860s, and today's citizens are benefiting from the many jacarandas and other flowering species that grace its broad streets. The bend of the Clarence was only bridged in 1932, when the present double-decker structure was built. Grafton is a good base for tours, with several national parks within easy reach.

► **Griffith**   62B2

Designed by Walter Burley Griffin, the architect responsible for the planning of Canberra, this model township was built to act as the main urban centre for the

Murrumbidgee Irrigation Area. Its conception on the drawing board can be seen in its radial street pattern and in the decorative use of irrigation water in its gardens.

▶ Gundagai 62B3

The name of this township along the Hume Highway is derived from an Aboriginal word meaning 'up-river'; in spite of warnings from the local Aborigines, the first settlers built their houses on the floodplain of the Murrumbidgee, and were duly swept away when the river broke its banks in 1852, causing the country's worst-ever flood disaster. The Murrumbidgee is crossed here by the longest timber viaduct in Australia.

▶▶ Hunter Valley 63C4

The broad valley of the Hunter River, which ends in the sea at Newcastle, has contrasting landscapes created by mines and wines. The coalfield has been exploited for a century and a half, and has been the making of the city of Newcastle. The vineyards were first planted here in the 1830s and, after periods of decline, are flourishing once more. A day trip or, better still, one lasting a couple of days is a favourite outing for Sydneysiders, not least because of the excellent food on offer in the area.

The landscape of the Hunter is one of its attractions, in its framework of wooded hills running down from the Brokenback Range to the southwest of the valley. Grapevines benefit from the rich soil which has its origin in the outpourings of ancient volcanoes. The wineries range from family-sized concerns to large-scale commercial enterprises. Australia's oldest wine-press is on display at the **Golden Grape Estate**. The vineyards of the Wyndham and Rothbury Estates are well worth visiting, while the McGuigan Hunter Village has a complex of attractions including restaurants, playgrounds, shops and carriage rides. Other wineries are situated in the Upper Hunter Valley, some 90km further on.

A dog's life
The teamsters travelling along the rough roads of early Australia were inevitably accompanied by various breeds of dog, one of which seems to have committed an unspeakable act while sitting (*sic*) on his master's tuckerbox by the side of the road. This and other deeds were recorded in the crude ballads of the time, refined somewhat in a version by the poet Jack Moses, and commemorated in a sculpture just outside Gundagai. This is the work of one Frank Rusconi, who was also responsible for the amazing model cathedral of marble on show in the Tourist Information Centre.

81

■ **This part of the Great Dividing Range is the roof of Australia, much of it a highland plateau from which rise a number of peaks more than 2,000m high. Parts of it make up the country's most popular winter sports area, with several well-equipped ski resorts. But the mountains are glorious in summer too; a carpet of alpine wildflowers is unrolled as the snow retreats, and there are superb paths and trails offering some of the most exhilarating walking in Australia. ■**

The region is popular with winter sports enthusiasts

82

The Snowy Mountains Scheme
This was a visionary project to alter the course of rivers to irrigate the parched agricultural areas further west and generate hydro-electric power in the process. Many dams were built, of which the largest, at Lake Eucumbene, holds back more water than is contained in Sydney Harbour. There are 80km of aqueducts, 150km of tunnels and seven power stations, the latter providing a good proportion of the electricity consumed in southeast Australia. Some of the impressive installations (like Murray No 1 on the Alpine Way, or Tumut 2 north of Cabramurra) are open to the public.

KOALA BEAR
CONTENTS 50
SAFETY MATCHES

History Aboriginal interest in the mountains was more recent than in many parts of Australia, dating only from the end of the last Ice Age some 10,000 years ago. This is one of the few Australian landscapes with glacial lakes, cirques and moraines, all the result of the action of the ice sheets that were absent throughout most of the country.

The mountains attracted graziers from early on in the days after White settlement, and a few determined bushwalkers between the two world wars, but it was only after the start of the Snowy Mountains Scheme in the late 1940s, when roads were driven through the wilderness and many other facilities created, that the area became accessible and visitors were able to come here in large numbers.

A popular starting point for exploring the mountains is the town of **Cooma** at the junction of the Monaro and Snowy Mountains highways. It was from here that the Snowy Mountains Authority oversaw what was to become one of the greatest 20th-century engineering projects in the world. Two centres provide all conceivable kinds of information about the mountains and the great project which so transformed them: the visitor's information centre in town and the Snowy Information Centre on the Canberra road.

The resort town of **Jindabyne** on its lake provides plenty of accommodation for winter sports enthusiasts heading for the snowfields further west. The National Parks and Wildlife Service has a useful visitor centre here, at Kusciuszko Road, before visitors head for the skiing areas in the heart of the mountains. These include the delighful alpine-style village of Thredbo on the southern side of the range, and the mega-resort of Perisher Blue, which encompasses the ski regions of Smiggin Holes, Mount Blue Cow, Guthega and Perisher Valley – the latter reached by the underground railway known as the Ski Tube. At the end of the northern road is Charlotte Pass, with superb views of the mountain peaks. This is the starting point for a number of wonderful walks, including the Summit Walk to the top of **Mount Kosciuszko**, at 2,228m the highest peak in Australia.

Jindabyne is also the terminus of the **Alpine Way**, the splendid scenic highway that leads to the 1,582m-pass at Dead Horse Gap. From here the (partly unmade) road descends into the valley of the Murray River and on to Khancoban. This is the starting point for a fair-weather highway leading to **Mount Selwyn**, a winter sports resort on the north side of the peaks, and to the remains of the old gold-mining township of Kiandra. Further north still are **Yarrangobilly Caves**; of the 60 caves so far discovered, four are open to the public.

Skiing

Although the snow isn't always as abundant as resort operators would like, the Snowy Mountains offer ideal conditions for cross-country skiing and some excellent downhill facilities. The main resorts are the vast Perisher Blue region, which incorporates four ski areas and offers 50 lifts and T-bars, and the smaller and more charming alpine village of Thredbo. The ski season runs from early June to early October.

Murray No 1 hydro-electric power station

NEW SOUTH WALES

A souvenir of your visit to Kangaroo Valley

The Kiama Coast
Kiama's beaches are pleasant enough – and excellent for surfing – but further south lie Gerroa and Gerringong, and then the spectacular, wave-pounded expanse of Seven Mile Beach, part of a national park.

Black is beautiful
The Lightning Ridge black opals are not quite unique, but this is the only place in the world where this unusual stone occurs in quantity. It has been described as combining 'the iridescence of the dewdrop with the colour of the rainbow, set in the blackness of night'. Its allure is certainly enough to maintain interest in its extraction. The biggest stone ever found was given the name 'Queen of the Earth'.

Mootwingee Historic Site
Located within the national park, this extraordinary site represents one of the state's greatest collections of Aboriginal art and cultural relics. Some of the 20 rock-shelters and 15 engraving sites can be visited in the company of an Aboriginal ranger.

▶ **Kangaroo Valley** 63B4

This is a delightful old settlement tucked away in an upland valley on the beautiful scenic road leading inland from Nowra, 100km south of Sydney. Apart from being the starting point for bushwalks, its main attraction is the **Pioneer Farm Museum**, a faithful reconstruction of a dairy farm of the 19th century.

▶ **Kiama** 63B4

The most famous feature of this pleasantly situated little port and resort on the 'Kiama Coast' south of Wollongong is the **Blowhole**, through which rough seas send a 60m spout high into the air. With its rocky headlands and fine beaches, Kiama has long been popular with visitors. To the west is the Minnamurra Rain forest Reserve, with its palms, ferns, fig trees and other rain forest plants; rare red cedars; and exquisite lyrebirds. The reserve can be explored via its two marked and interpreted walking tracks.

▶▶▶ **Kosciuszko National Park** 62A3

See pages 74 and 83.

▶▶ **Lanyon Homestead, ACT** 66A3

This fine building on the Murrumbidgee River near Canberra was built in 1859 and added to around the turn of the century. Now in the care of the National Trust, both buildings and gardens have been restored with care. There is a gallery housing a collection of the works of Sidney Nolan, one of the best places to get to know this idiosyncratic Australian artist.

▶▶ **Lightning Ridge** 62D3

Just off the Castlereagh Highway before it quits NSW for Queensland, this far northwestern township is famed for its black opals, mined here since 1902, in recent years by machine rather than by hand. Amateur fossickers are welcome, provided they don't trespass on professionals' rights, and there are many old mines to visit and demonstrations of cutting to watch, as well as artesian baths to relax in.

▶▶ **Mootwingee National Park** 62C1

Beyond Broken Hill, in NSW's furthest northwest, are the rugged sandstone ranges of this remote national park, which is nevertheless accessible on gravel roads. Arid sandy plains and pebble deserts contrast with pools and watercourses fringed with river red gums and other lush vegetation. Aborigines occupied the area for countless years, leaving a wealth of rock paintings and engravings.

▶▶ Mount Warning National Park   63D5

This 1,157m peak is the plug of an ancient volcano, given its name by Captain Cook to mark the reefs off Point Danger, on which the *Endeavour* almost came to grief. It is the first place on the Australian mainland to receive the rays of the rising sun, and the view from the top is well worth the 750m climb from the car park and visitor centre. The steep but well made path rises through splendid woodlands that change from subtropical rain forest to temperate rain forest and finally to open bush.

▶▶ Myall Lakes National Park   63B4

These tranquil lakes (60km north of Newcastle), separated from the Pacific Ocean by windswept sand dunes, are best reached from the township of Tea Gardens by boat up the Myall River. There is little development along the shores of the lakes, though the fishing village of Seal Rocks on the coast at the eastern end of the park is popular with visitors, who come here to get away from it all. Boating is a popular activity on the lakes, and it is possible to hire everything from canoes to live-on-board houseboats to explore this magnificent region.

▶ Nambucca Heads   63C5

Subtropical crops now grow here (50km south of Coffs Harbour) where the cedar forests were cleared last century, making this an attractive and popular resort with fantastic views from various lookout points, of which Yarrahapini is the most spectacular. You can take trips inland to the rugged ridges and deep forested valleys of the New England and Dorrigo national parks.

Myall Lakes flora and fauna
The Myall Lakes make up the largest such lake system in the state, and are fringed by splendid forest, which includes rain forest species like cabbage palms. The lakes are also famous for the prawns that breed in them. Waterbirds abound, as well as sea eagles, and the area is rich in other wildlife too.

85

Swim or surf from the beach at Nambucca Heads

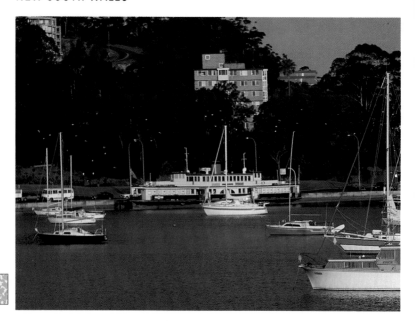

Attractive Lake Macquarie, Australia's largest saltwater lake, near Newcastle

Australian country
Far inland from Port Macquarie, halfway between Sydney and Brisbane on the New England Highway, is the town of Tamworth. This sizeable place claims fame as the capital of Australian country music. An annual festival, held in January, draws thousands of fans to hundreds of performances; other attractions are the Gallery of Stars (waxworks), and the Hands of Fame Corner Stone (handprints). More enduring stars can be contemplated at the Pyramid Planetarium to the north of town, where the solar system is reproduced in miniature.

▶ **Newcastle**　　　　　　　　　　*63B4*

Dominated by the BHP steelworks, industrial Newcastle is the largest city in Australia not to be the capital of a state. It began as the convict colony of a convict colony, but its later fortunes were founded on the abundant coal reserves of the Hunter Valley; Newcastle coal constituted the country's first export.

But there's much more to Newcastle than trade and industry. The Foreshore Park, Queen's Wharf and Customs House Plaza make a fine setting for festive occasions. **Fort Scratchley▶** is one of the few such places in Australia to have fired its guns in anger – at a Japanese submarine in 1942. The old stronghold gives a good panorama over the city in its setting, and houses the **Maritime Museum** and **Military Museum**. The city centre has some imposing 19th-century buildings and more museums and galleries. The 'Bogey Hole' on the city beach below beautiful King Edward Park was built as a saltwater bath in convict days. To the south of the city is the country's largest saltwater lake, popular **Lake Macquarie▶**, offering all kinds of watersports. The lake, four times the size of Sydney Harbour, is also the home of a koala colony, and a delightful flora and fauna reserve.

▶ **Nimbin**　　　　　　　　　　　*63D5*

Set among the natural splendours of northern NSW, Nimbin developed from the early 1970s as a centre for artists and bohemians. Today, its craftshops and cafés attract the curious as well. It is on the way to **Nightcap National Park▶▶**, whose 900m peaks form part of the outer walls of the huge extinct volcano of which Mount Warning is the core. The park, with its glorious rain forest and diverse wildlife, is now part of NSW's World Heritage Area protecting the temperate and subtropical forests of the north.

▶ Nowra 63B4

Nowra is located just upstream from the mouth of the Shoalhaven River. It is an extremely busy tourist resort, largely because of the beaches that extend north and south along the coast, one of them (Hyams Beach on Jervis Bay) boasting the whitest sand in the world.

▶ Orange 62B3

Lava flows from the extinct volcano of Mount Canobolas – the highest point between the Great Dividing Range and the Indian Ocean – have broken down over the milleniums into fertile soils which today support great tracts of orchards growing apples, pears, cherries – but no oranges! The town of Orange has prospered from the fertility of its surroundings and is a busy but pleasant place, leafy with parks and trees. The first goldfield to be exploited in Australia was at nearby **Ophir**, where two prospectors made a sizeable strike in 1851. You can try your luck at fossicking today in picturesque surroundings along Summer Hill Creek.

▶ Port Macquarie 63C5

At the mouth of the Hastings River, Port Macquarie has turned from trade and commerce to tourism and retirement with considerable success. **St Thomas' Church** is a reminder of these early days; one of the very first churches to be built in Australia (1824), it has box pews and a view from its tower. The **Hastings District Historical Museum▶** has exceptionally good displays on the evolution of the town and its hinterland, and nature is on show at **Sea Acres Rain forest Centre▶** with a long boardwalk through the rain forest. A series of good beaches stretches southwards from the town.

▶▶ Southern Highlands 56A2

Easily accessible by rail and by the Hume Highway, this is one of the great rural playgrounds of Sydneysiders. The district was opened up early in the colony's history, in the 1820s, and much of it has a pleasant air of maturity, with lush landscapes recalling those of Tasmania. Recreational facilities cater for every possible desire of the weary city weekender.

Among the towns in the area, Bowral is a leafy place with a number of fine old buildings along its main street. **Berrima▶▶** retains even more of its past; founded in the 1830s, it still has many sandstone buildings dating from that period, though the inns have dwindled in number from the original 13. The Surveyor General Inn is one of those that claim to be the oldest licensed premises in the country. Popular **Bundanoon** acts as the gateway to the Morton National Park, a starting point for energetic bushwalks or casual strolls up Glow Worm Glen.

▶▶ Tidbinbilla, ACT 66A1

There are two important visitor attractions at Tidbinbilla, 40km southwest of Canberra. The **Canberra Deep Space Communications Complex▶** is a combined US/Australian tracking station; it is open to the public, with multi-media displays and model spacecraft. Back on earth, **Tidbinbilla Nature Reserve▶** is a vast tract of countryside with bushwalks and an array of Australian wildlife.

Morton National Park
This high sandstone plateau into which rivers have cut deep gorges is one of the great attractions of the Southern Highlands. Waterfalls pour into the depths from high cliffs, as at Fitzroy Falls, where there is a visitor centre. Scenic highways connect the area to the coast (one of them goes via Kangaroo Valley), making an interesting round trip from Sydney possible.

Rugged Morton National Park is popular with Sydneysiders

■ **The list of Australian creatures able to cause you harm, in some cases of a fatal kind, is an impressive one. Do bear in mind, however, that you are much more likely to come to grief at the hands of a local driver, or suffer heatstroke, than you are to fall victim to any of the following.** ■

CROCODILES

88

Marine hazards Of the 85 species of **sharks** around the coast of Australia, only some are man-eaters. Attacks are rare, and the average number of fatalities per year is just one person. The highest risk occurs in summer when the water temperature is in excess of 22°C, and during this time it might be advisable to swim only from one of the many beaches protected by systems of netting. More dangerous are **saltwater crocodiles** (salties – see page 183), and on no account should you swim (or stand close to the water's edge) in the northern areas frequented by these formidable creatures. Their numbers are also on the increase as they have been given the status of protected species.

Box jellyfish breed in river estuaries and infest the coastal waters of Queensland and the NT from October to May. Practically invisible, they deliver a sting which can be fatal. Stay out of the sea at this time! Some of the beautiful corals can also be unpleasantly poisonous, as is the crown-of-thorns starfish which is attacking the Barrier Reef. Much worse, however, is the **stonefish**, which looks like a rock as its name suggests; wear shoes when walking on a reef, and avoid rooting around in rockpools. There are also sea snakes, which become active at the same time as the box jellies.

Terrestrial hazards Snakes also inhabit the land, and there are some 170 species, the venomous ones outnumbering the harmless. Rangers and bush folk are fond of detailing their degree of poisonousness in terms of the number of mice a bite could kill; this can get into the hundreds of thousands, and is quite enough to see you off. However, even the most lethal of snakes – like the taipan, tiger snake, death adder or brown snake – will get out of your way if it possibly can.

Spiders and insects
Spiders can reach an alarming size, and their bite can be unpleasant. Avoid the redback (or black widow), a small, black spider with red patches on its back, and the larger funnel-web, at all costs – tourist information centres can give further information on how to recognise them. The funnel-web, unlike most of its kind, is aggressive and rears up for the attack. It's also a Sydneysider, so don't think you are safe in that city. Insects abound in Australia, but flies, mosquitoes, wasps, ants and even scorpions are more of a nuisance than a real hazard.

Steer clear of the deadly taipan

▶ Wauchope 63C5

Among the forests of the Hastings River district, Wauchope has long been a centre of the timber industry, a fact made much of in **Timbertown**▶▶. This ambitious re-creation of a late 19th-century pioneer settlement has a whole range of buildings (shops, houses, church and sawmill), demonstrations of all the activities associated with timber-getting and processing, as well as rides round the area aboard a cart or a steam train.

Kempsey▶, 25km north of Wauchope, is home to the world-famous Akubra hat. Akubras (believed to be an Aboriginal word for hat) are made from rabbit pelts – a good use for the skins of these imported agricultural and environmental pests.

▶ West Wyalong 62B3

In the harsh countryside at the junction of the Mid-Western and Newell highways, West Wyalong was NSW's busiest goldfield at the turn of the century. Now the centre for an extensive wheat-growing area, it also produces and exports that quintessential Australian fluid, eucalyptus oil. However, visitors may be more interested in the model of a gold mine in the District Museum.

▶ White Cliffs 62C1

This old opal-mining settlement more than 1,000km northwest of Sydney is a place to experience life in the Australian Outback. A small, highly individual population of opal miners lives here, some of them underground, so avoiding the need for air-conditioning, otherwise a must in the sometimes intolerable climate. There are plenty of opportunities to see opals in their various states, as well as a real oddity, the opalised skeleton of a plesiosaur.

▶ Wollongong 63B4

The life of New South Wales' third largest city is based on heavy industry and there are few conventional tourist attractions. But, as always in Australia, you are never far away from natural beauty, and the rugged Illawarra Coast has wonderful beaches while inland there are splendid hills and forests. There are fantastic views from the **Illawarra State Recreation Area**▶.

Australia's famous Akubra hats are made in Kempsey, near Wauchope

89

Wagga Wagga or Wogga Wogga?
More famous for its name (pronounced Wogga) than for its touristic amenities, Wagga (240km south of West Wyalong) is a fair-sized town which has profited from its location on the Murrumbidgee River and Sydney–Melbourne railway line to become the thriving centre of NSW's Riverina district.

The Dandenong Ranges harbour a rich profusion of native flora

Victoria The Garden State is the smallest of Australia's mainland states. However, it is comparatively densely populated and highly industrialised, with something like a quarter of the country's inhabitants living on what only amounts to 3 per cent of its land surface, a good proportion of which is agriculturally productive. Out of the state's total of 4½ or so million people, just over 3 million live in the metropolitan area of Melbourne, whose area of more than 6,000sq km makes it one of the largest cities in the world.

Beyond the metropolis, Victorians live in a variety of settlements, many of them of considerable charm and historic interest. There are delightful little ports and well-established resorts along the 1,200km coastline, a multitude of places founded in the mid 19th-century rush for gold such as charming Yackandandah, old river ports along the Murray and prosperous agricultural centres quietly getting on with their own lives.

Old Victorian building in Melbourne

The state's landscapes are diverse; with varied and spectacular coastal scenery, high mountains and extensive forested uplands, rich farmlands and near desert, Victoria has been described as a microcosm of Australia, though true Outback lies beyond its border. Agriculture takes many forms. The rolling hills of Gippsland feed dairy cattle, sheep graze on the vast pastures of the plains stretching to the west, and fruit grows in profusion along the Goulburn River and by the Murray too, thanks to irrigation works carried out on a huge scale at the turn of the century.

For the tourist, the presence of such variety in close proximity to the state capital makes a stay particularly rewarding; few places are more than half a day's comfortable drive from Melbourne.

As it was Victoria belonged to the second, or even third phase of European colonisation of the new continent. The coast had been sighted from aboard the *Endeavour* in the course of Captain Cook's 1770 voyage; in 1803, Lieutenant David Collins attempted to found a settlement on the shores of Port Phillip Bay but gave up and went on to Tasmania instead. For decades, only whalers and sealers landed along the coast. Then, in 1835, one John Batman from Tasmania sailed into the bay again and signed a treaty of dubious legality with the local Aborigines which gave him title to 600,000 acres (243,000 hectares) of land. In spite of official attempts from Sydney to discourage settlement on the bay, Batman and others persisted; his famous phrase 'This will be the place for a village' marked the founding of Melbourne.

Buckley's chance

One of the members of Lieutenant Collins' party, which tried and failed to establish a settlement at Sorrento on the Mornington Peninsula in 1803, was the Cheshire-born convict William Buckley. Taking a chance he decamped and fled right round Port Phillip Bay to the Barwon area, where he lived with the local Aborigines. Decades later, in 1835, some of John Batman's associates were amazed at the emergence of 'a wild white man' at their encampment, hardly able to speak English any more. Buckley earned a pardon, a government pension and a place in the language ('Buckley's chance' means no chance at all).

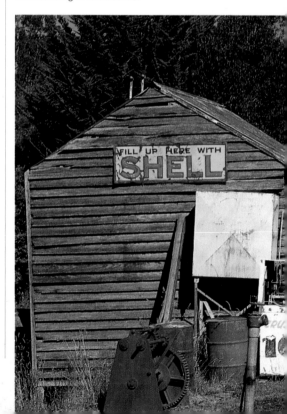

The new settlers wanted nothing to do with the convict system, sending any ships that arrived with prisoners on to Sydney, and petitioning for separation from New South Wales. This was granted in 1851, and the new colony was given the Queen's name. Only weeks after this event, gold was found near Ballarat and at Clunes; other finds followed, the rush was on, and Melbourne and Victoria changed utterly in the process. Handsome new towns arose from the tent cities erected by the prospectors, and Melbourne boomed, fitting itself out with fine new buildings paid for by the profits made from the precious metal.

In spite of periodic slumps, the state has remained the financial and industrial powerhouse of the nation, boosted by massive immigration in the early 20th century from the British Isles, and after World War II from Europe and elsewhere. Melbourne is now perhaps the most cosmopolitan of all Australia's major cities, while other places within the state retain a pleasing atmosphere of bygone days.

Outdoor Victorians In spite of (or is it because of?) their unpredictable weather, the people of Victoria are great outdoor types, igniting the barbecue or flocking to the beaches at the slightest opportunity. *The* event in the racing calendar is the Melbourne Cup, which takes place on the first Tuesday of November, when not only Victoria but the whole country seems to come to a stop. Australian Rules football is followed with passion by people of all ages and both sexes. The accessibility of fine scenery brings out the bushwalkers in summer, while in winter the roads to the snowfields of the Alps are crowded with the cars of skiers.

Skiing in Victoria
Skiing began in the 1930s, when the first lift started taking people up to the high plateau country beneath Mount Buffalo. Nowadays Mount Donna Buang and Mount Baw Baw are even accessible to day-trippers from Melbourne. Mount Buller, further on in the Alps, is Australia's most popular winter resort; that at Mount Hotham is the highest in the country, with an award-winning, environmentally friendly complex at Dinner Plain, while Falls Creek in its sheltered bowl in the Alpine National Park has slopes catering for every kind of skier.

93

Morning Star Creek, still with one foot in the past

Queen Victoria Market

Moomba
The Melburnians' ability to let their hair down is demonstrated every March in the huge carnival known as Moomba, an Aboriginal word which can be translated as 'let's get together and have fun'. Ten days of festivities culminate in a monster multicultural procession.

Batman's bargain
In exchange for 600,000 acres (243,000 hectares) of Aboriginal land, John Batman delivered 40 blankets, 30 tomahawks, 100 knives, 50 pairs of scissors, 30 mirrors, 200 handkerchiefs, 100lb of flour and 6 shirts. The understanding that a similar quantity of useful items would be handed over annually was soon consigned to oblivion.

Outside the 1856 Parliament House

Melbourne

Australia's second great metropolitan city sprawls around the head of Port Phillip Bay at the outlet of the muddy Yarra River. Hardly a generation ago, Melbourne was almost a synonym for dull respectability of a peculiarly British flavour, but since the 1960s Melbourne and its inhabitants have undergone a startling transformation. Much of the city centre has been redeveloped with glittering office towers, to which the remaining treasures of 19th-century architecture act as a wonderful foil. Massive immigration, principally but by no means wholly from southern Europe, has enlivened the city's social scene. In addition to countless galleries, museums, theatres and cinemas, the city has a thriving nightlife not only of bars and discos but also of cabaret and comedians, jazz and rock and a casino. And whatever Sydney says, Melbourne is the gastronomic capital of Australia, with a multitude of different types of cuisine on offer, from 'Mod-Oz' to Vietnamese. The shopping is excellent too.

The early years Once John Batman's illegal treaty of 1835, by which he acquired 600,000 acres (243,000 hectares) of land, had been accepted as a *fait accompli* by the authorities in Sydney, his 'village' above the Yarra soon became an incipient city laid out on the usual grid pattern by an army surveyor. Within a few years, the wealthy were buying estates to the south-east of the river where they could set themselves up as country gentlemen and build elegant houses. Thanks to gold and land speculation, Melbourne boomed for most of the second half of the 19th century, leading a roistering kind of life characterised as 'American' in contrast to Sydney's staid 'Britishness'. A great slump in the 1890s brought the era of 'Marvellous Melbourne' to an end, and the city entered the long period of gloom from which its recent renaissance has so triumphantly rescued it.

Attractions today Melbourne is a wonderfully green metropolis of parks and trees, but it is also renowned for its excellent 19th-century architecture. The best view of the city – and one of the finest panoramas in Australia – is from the south bank of the Yarra.

The city's inner suburbs have a strong and varied identity which makes them well worth exploring.

Just north of the city centre, **Carlton** is home to the University of Melbourne and many examples of the terrace houses so characteristic of late 19th-century Melbourne. The suburb's largest landmark is the huge 1870s Royal Exhibition Building, which will house the new Museum of Victoria (see page 100).

Once decidedly 'rough', **Fitzroy** has now turned Bohemian, its original inhabitants supplemented by students and trendies. Brunswick Street is a fascinating mixture of cheap restaurants and alternative bookshops.

East Melbourne is a charming enclave of carefully restored terrace houses within walking distance of the city centre via Fitzroy Gardens.

The suburb of **St Kilda** became Melbourne's seaside in the 1880s, when the pier and the substantial villas of the rich were built. These days it is very colourful, and Acland and Fitzroy Streets are hard to beat as restaurant strips. The beaches stretching from here round to Port Melbourne are still popular, though the water is not always the cleanest. The fun palace of Luna Park has been here since 1912. On Sundays, St Kilda hosts a big arts and crafts market.

South Melbourne has one of the most attractive of all inner city residential areas; in St Vincent's Square, fine houses in a variety of styles were laid out around central gardens from the 1860s onwards.

One of the richest inner suburbs east along the Yarra, **Toorak** is synonymous with a certain kind of trendiness, and neighbouring South Yarra, the location of the historic Como house, is famous for its restaurants, fashion shopping and nightlife.

Beyond the Yarra to the west, **Williamstown** has a superb view of the city centre across the water. A stroll along the Strand is well worthwhile, and rail fans will enjoy the Railway Museum. On the way here, at Spotswood on the western side of the Westgate Bridge, is the highly entertaining Scienceworks, an outstation of the Museum of Victoria. It has an amazing array of interactive exhibits on the theme of science and technology.

Melbourne is the only Australian city with an extensive system of tramways

Melbourne's trams
One of the emblems of the city, the network of green and yellow trams covers much of the Melbourne metropolitan area. The older trams are classified by the National Trust, while a new line speeds commuters and workers between the city centre and Port Melbourne. Visitors can make good use of the free City Circle Tram Service, and you can even dine aboard a vintage model; the Colonial Tramcar Restaurant is fitted with specially smooth suspension to keep your Yarra Valley red in its glass and has one-way windows to maintain your privacy while you glide through the streets.

*The gateway to
Chinatown*

►► ANZ (Australia and New Zealand) Bank — 94C2

386 Collins Street

One of the finest examples of Gothic revival architecture in the country, the building of what used to be the English, Scottish and Australian Bank is more Venetian than the Doges Palace in Venice, with a magnificently elaborate interior whose blue décor is enhanced by lavish use of gold leaf.

The ANZ Banking Museum has changing exhibitions on the history of Australian banking.

► Chinatown — 94D3

Centred on Little Bourke Street, Melbourne's Chinatown has existed ever since Chinese prospectors joined the rush to the goldfields in the 1850s. It expanded later in the 19th century as the goldfields contracted and miners drifted back to the big city. Today it still flourishes as a centre for the Chinese community and for diners in search of cheap and excellent food and groceries, and has been fitted out with the usual archways which boldly proclaim its identity.

An interesting addition to the area is the **Museum of Chinese Australian History►►** in an old warehouse in Cohen Place, just off Little Bourke Street. Its displays bring alive the whole of the considerable Chinese contribution to Australian history. Star exhibits include a life-size replica of a warrior-general of the 2nd century BC and Dai Loong, the 100m 100-legged dragon that emerges once a year for the Chinese New Year parade. Fascinating guided heritage walks of the old Chinatown area depart from the museum daily.

►► Como — 95A6

Como Avenue, South Yarra

Begun in 1847, this delicious white mansion crowning the rise in the middle of its richly landscaped gardens is a wonderful example of the gracious buildings of Melbourne's pre-boom period. Behind the nicely proportioned façade in South Yarra are a series of furnished rooms evoking the comfortable and very sociable life lived here in the 19th century; to the side are outbuildings containing the original laundry. Como's unselfconscious elegance was not imitated by the nouveau riche owners of the next generation of villas to be built in the suburb of Toorak; they preferred something altogether more ostentatious, usually combining a number of architectural styles. Most of these pompous residences have now given way to blocks of flats, but Como, thankfully, passed into the hands of the National Trust in 1959.

►► Fitzroy Gardens 95E5

Just to the east of the city centre and consequently a favourite place for lunchtime sandwiches and assignations are the sweeping lawns and splendid trees of these 19th-century gardens, complementing the spires of St Patrick's Cathedral in the background. Towards the southern end of the park is **Cooks' Cottage►►**. A modest stone building of the mid-18th century with the characteristic Yorkshire pantiled roof, this was the home of the great navigator's parents; it was dismantled and brought here in 1934 to mark the centenary of the founding of Melbourne. It is open to the public, as is another reminder of Anglo-Australian ties, the miniature Tudor Village, a gift from the citizens of the London borough of Lambeth in thanks for World War II food parcels.

►► Kings Domain 95B5

A splendid tract of parkland sweeps southeast along the Yarra from the city centre through Victoria and Alexandra Gardens to the Kings Domain and beyond to the Royal Botanic Gardens (see page 101). Alexandra Gardens has a fine riverside view of the city centre, and Queen Victoria Gardens has an elaborate floral clock. Altogether more functional is the **Sidney Myer Music Bowl**, whose soaring canopy shelters all kinds of open-air musical events. Crowning the higher ground in the Domain is the great white pile of **Government House**, the fourth to be built on this site (see panel). Its square tower rises above the trees and is a well-known city landmark. In contrast to this magnificence is the very first Government House, **La Trobe's Cottage**, a prefabricated two-storey cottage brought out from England, erected in Jolimont in 1839, and moved here in 1963.

► Melbourne Cricket Ground 95C6

Jolimont Terrace, Jolimont

To the southeast of the city centre at Jolimont, divided up by roads and railway tracks, are sports grounds of all kinds, many of them laid out for the 1956 Olympics. The central venue for the games was the great MCG – the Melbourne Cricket Ground – a vast stadium with a capacity well in excess of 100,000, just as much associated with football ('Aussie Rules') as with cricket. Here too is the MCC Cricket Museum, the Australian Gallery of Sport, and the Olympic Museum, recalling the triumphs and disappointments that have attended the modern games since their revival in 1896.

Government House
Built appropriately enough by government architect William Wardell in the 1870s, the present Government House was modelled on Queen Victoria's Osborne House on England's Isle of Wight. That monarch is supposed to have been rather miffed that Melbourne's ballroom was twice as big as the one in Buckingham Palace.

One of the world's greatest stadiums, the Melbourne Cricket Ground at Jolimont creates an incredible atmosphere

VICTORIA

The Sydney sneer
The rivalry between Sydney and Melbourne is long-standing and will probably never go away, though these days the tone of exchanges between Sydneysiders and Melburnians is bantering rather than bitter. The 1955 painting by John Brack entitled *Collins Street, 5 o'clock,* showing grim-faced commuters marching along Melbourne's main artery, has given much pleasure to Sydneysiders by confirming their view of Melburnians as archetypal wowsers.

The carefully restored barque Polly Woodside *at the Maritime Museum*

The National Gallery is also the venue for international travelling exhibitions

►► **Melbourne Zoo**   94E2
Elliott Avenue, Parkville
This vast zoo with its progressive approach to introducing visitors and animals to each other is located in Royal Park, just 4km from the city centre and the city's largest tract of open space. Most of the old cages have been done away with, and visitors move easily through large enclosures simulating the native habitat of the creatures within. The internationally acclaimed zoo features an African rain forest, a butterfly house and creatures from all over the world. The whole range of Australian fauna is also on show, from birds in their giant aviary, to fur seals in their tank and platypuses in their platypusary.

►► **Museum of Victoria**
Other than its science and technological sections, now located at Scienceworks (see page 97), Melbourne's premier museum is closed until the year 2000. The museum will then reopen at its new home in the Royal Exhibition Building in Carlton. The pride of place is still likely to be occupied by Phar Lap, the famous racehorse of the 1930s, believed to have be poisoned while in California.

►►► **National Gallery of Victoria**   95B4
180 St Kilda Road
This sombre bluestone building makes a striking contrast to the other edifices making up the Victorian Arts Centre. Completed in 1968, the gallery houses some of the finest artworks to be seen in Australia. The collection of Australian art is possibly the most comprehensive in the country, from John Glover's charming scenes of colonial Tasmania, to the story pictures of the later 19th century and the works of Sidney Nolan and Jeffrey Smart. In addition, there is a good selection of European Old Masters, pre-Columbian, Aboriginal and American art, and the courtyards contain a number of fine modern sculptures.

▶▶ Old Melbourne Gaol   94E3
Russell Street
Of all the countless gaols that are such a feature of Australian townscapes, this grim bluestone building is one not to be missed. Its chilling interior seems to sum up the harshness of 19th-century concepts of justice and punishment. Here you can see the death mask of Ned Kelly who was hanged in 1880. Kelly was a horse-thief who became the most notorious and defiant of Australia's bushrangers. He seems peaceful enough, his wayward spirit expressed perhaps more strongly by the home-made suit of armour displayed alongside.

▶ Parliament House   95E4
Spring Street
Begun in 1856, this great neo-Grecian palace of government was planned on such an ambitious scale that it has never been completed. The state government was moved from its grandiose home here in 1901 to make way for the newly established Federal Parliament, which sat in Melbourne until finally persuaded to make the move to Canberra in 1927. There are guided tours of the splendid interior when parliament is not in session; the Legislative Council Chamber was described by poet and connoisseur of Victorian architecture, John Betjeman (1906–84), as 'the best Corinthian room in the world'.

▶ Polly Woodside Maritime Museum   94A1
South Wharf Road, South Melbourne
Built in Belfast in 1885, the sailing barque *Polly Woodside* ended her working days as a rusty, filthy coal hulk in the Port of Melbourne. Immaculately restored and moored in an old dock basin in South Melbourne, she is now the proud centrepiece of this maritime museum, which has numerous other exhibits evoking the age of sail.

▶▶ Queen Victoria Market   94E1
Victoria Street
Melbourne's sole surviving 19th-century market is an exciting place to either shop for bargains or just wander around. Trading has been carried on here since 1859, and there are now more than a thousand stalls selling everything imaginable at affordable prices.

▶▶ Rialto Towers Observation Deck   94C2
525 Collins Street
From this viewing area on the 55th level of Melbourne's highest building, the views are simply stupendous. The panorama takes in the city, Port Phillip Bay, and many of the city's outlying regions.

▶▶ Rippon Lea   95A4
192 Hotham Street, Elsternwick
Begun in 1868 by the Walworth (London) born Frederick Thomas Sargood, this polychrome brick house is perhaps the most splendid late-Victorian mansion to have survived in the Melbourne suburbs. On completion in 1887, its interior had no fewer than 33 rooms. The gardens are opulent and extensive.

Continued on page 103.

Dream on Elm Street
Some of the prestige of the top end of Collins Street in early days was due to the fact that it was one of the few places to have any street trees. Early photographs of Melbourne show the young city, once the bush had been cleared to build it, to have been a virtually treeless town. This was eventually remedied, and today's city enjoys the benefit of the countless trees, now fully mature, that were planted towards the end of the 19th century. Scorning the rich array of native trees, city fathers planted to remind themselves of 'home', and as a result, streets and parks are graced with wonderful specimens of oaks, elms and poplars. Now that disease has removed elms from the European landscape, this is one of the few places left where it is still possible to see these fine trees in all their glory.

101

The Botanic Gardens: a fine example of 19th-century English landscaping

■ **Early European Australia was not distinguished by its architecture. No architect sailed with the First Fleet, and the very first structures erected were primitive affairs of wattle and daub, bark or whatever materials came quickly and easily to hand. Some prefabricated structures were shipped out from England and reassembled on site, sometimes by guesswork.** ■

The first proper edifice in Sydney was Government House, a two-storey brick dwelling that amazed the Aborigines when they found people walking around above their heads. A sense of restraint and emphasis on good proportion contributed towards simple but effective structures like Elizabeth Farm at Parramatta, built in 1793. Its veranda, destined to become a persistent motif in Australian building, was derived from British practice in India. But architecture capable of making some kind of civic statement had to await the rule of Governor Macquarie and his forger-turned-architect, Francis Greenway. Thanks to buildings like **Hyde Park Barracks** and **St James' Church**, Sydney began to take on the airs of a real city for the first time.

The development of the terrace Gold was the making of Melbourne, and of many architects too. Melbourne is still one of the world's great 19th-century cities in terms of building, with grand self-confident edifices in a variety of revived styles – Gothic for churches, Romanesque and Venetian for offices and banks, and classical for public buildings. This was the period when terrace houses reached a high point of development, their elegance and cast-iron decoration helping to make the inner suburbs of both Melbourne and Sydney some of the most liveable of their kind in the world.

An Aussie style The terrace was replaced after the turn of the century by the detached villa, built for a decade or so in 'Federation' style, with a wealth of varied forms and features like terracotta kangaroos on the roof line and eucalyptus leaves in the barge boards.

The later, 20th-century suburbs are undistinguished. The interwar Californian bungalow has given way to brick veneer dwellings and bizarre neo-Grecian palaces. Similarly, the redeveloped city centres do not seem to have a particularly Australian style either.

Australia's own
What has been described as the most original local contribution to Australian architecture is the tropical house of Queensland. Raised above ground for ventilation, it is liberally provided with verandas and with a roof of corrugated iron – handsome, cheap and durable, albeit noisy!

Right: renovated Victorian building in downtown Melbourne

Continued from page 101.

► ► ► **Royal Botanic Gardens**   *95A6*

The jewel in the crown of parkland extending along the Yarra from the city centre, these superb gardens are some of the finest of their kind in the world.

The site was chosen as early as 1845 by La Trobe, and the gardens were laid out and stocked with an incredible range of plants by successive directors, each of whom made their own contribution to the development of the gardens. Ferdinand von Mueller (Director, 1852–73) preferred a formal layout, while his successor, William Guilfoyle, redesigned the gardens in a more romantic, English style with sweeping lawns, informal lakes and curving pathways.

Plants from many parts of the world thrive here in Melbourne's kind climate; there are more than 6,000 tree species, from cool temperate regions through to subtropical areas. English elms and oaks contrast with grass trees and river red gums. The Australian Lawn is planted with eucalyptus from all over the country, and the Australian Border is the place to enjoy other native flora; it features a fine modern rockery, designed by the aptly named landscaper Ellis Stones. There is also the Oak Lawn, the Rose Garden, a cactus and succulent garden and a bulb garden. There are a number of buildings in the gardens which complement the plantings; they include the classical Temple of the Winds and the 1930s Visitor Centre and Herbarium with its excellent modern extension. A good way to get to know at least some of the riches of these wonderful gardens is to take one of the free guided walks that start at the visitor centre (10am and 11am daily except Monday and Saturday).

► **St Patrick's Cathedral**   *95E4*

Cathedral Place, East Melbourne

Less hemmed in by modern buildings than the Anglican Cathedral, the 103m central spire of the great Roman Catholic cathedral features in many city views. It was designed by William Wardell, the state's official architect, who also built the fabulous Venetian-style ANZ Bank.

An inhabitant of the highly acclaimed Melbourne Zoo

The Separation Tree
This is the name given to one of the fine river red gums in the Royal Botanic Gardens, since it was beneath its branches that the grand public celebration took place in 1851 to mark the independence of Victoria from New South Wales.

Inside St Patrick's
St Patrick's has a splendidly soaring interior, with magnificent stained-glass windows. Long regarded as an Irish stronghold, it also has a statue of Daniel O'Connell – the great 19th-century Irish patriot known as 'the Liberator' – in the churchyard.

On guard at the impressive Shrine of Remembrance

Arts tour
The Victorian Arts Centre complex is adorned inside and out with numerous works of art, many of them specially commissioned. These can best be experienced in the course of the centre's guided tours.

Melba's Melbourne Memorial
Born in the Melbourne suburb of Richmond in 1861, world-famous soprano Helen Mitchell changed her name to Nellie Melba to honour her native city. Like so many Australian artists of the period, she made her reputation abroad, her association with London's Covent Garden lasting for three decades. The Performing Arts Museum has much Melba memorabilia.

► **St Paul's Cathedral**   94C3

Corner of Swanston and Flinders streets
No longer the dominant element in the cityscape, this fine church in Gothic Revival style still has a commanding presence. Standing on the site where the first official church service in Melbourne took place in 1836, the cathedral was built in 1880–91 to a design by the British architect William Butterfield, also responsible for the Chapter House and Diocesan Offices in the cathedral complex.

►► **Shrine of Remembrance**   95A5

Off St Kilda Road
This huge temple to the dead forms a dramatic terminal feature down the long vista which starts in the city centre. Modelled on the Parthenon, the shrine sits massively on top of a rise in the ground in Kings Domain. It was completed in 1934 to honour the 114,000 Victorians who served in World War I, of whom 19,000 died. Its central chamber has a Stone of Remembrance illuminated by a shaft of light at 11am every 11 November. Deep below is the crypt, displaying regimental colours, and high above is a gallery with fine panoramas over the city and its environs. The immaculate surroundings of the shrine have been laid out to commemorate those who fell in other wars.

►►► **Victorian Arts Centre**   94B3

100 St Kilda Road
Although the modern Arts Centre is no cultural ghetto, it, is still a vibrant part of city life, comprising a complex of exciting buildings on the south bank of the Yarra.

Next to the National Gallery is the **Theatres** building, topped by a stunning 115m-high spire. The three theatres themselves are built below ground: the State Theatre is the home of the Australian Ballet; the Melbourne Theatre Company performs in the Playhouse; and the third is a highly adaptable studio space. The great drum of the **Concert Hall** has a spectacular interior whose mineral colours reflect the geology of the Australian continent. The centre also embraces two restaurants, the Arts Centre shop, a Sunday Market, the entertaining Performing Arts Museum and, in Kings Domain, the Sidney Myer Music Bowl.

Walk — Melbourne's city streets

See map on pages 94–5.

From the traditional meeting place of Melburnians – 'under the clocks' at Flinders Street station – to grandiose Parliament House, this walk of about 3km conveys the feeling of civic and commercial Melbourne.

The station steps open on to the bustle of the city centre. Freed from motor traffic, Swanston Walk is a calm setting for the Gothic grandeur of **St Paul's Cathedral**. Modern City Square, with its elaborate water features, marks the junction with Collins Street, dominated by the splendid Town Hall. Commercial dynamism has taken many shapes along this prestigious artery, from American deco of the 1930s to Victorian Gothic.

In Queen Street the elaborate Safe Deposit Building (nos 88–92) is dwarfed by the **ANZ Tower**. Trams and shoppers throng Bourke Street Mall, off which runs the city's oldest shopping gallery, Royal Arcade, with its 1870 figures of Gog and Magog. Colourful archways signal the entry to Chinatown.

The grid of city streets ends where Little Bourke Street emerges into Spring Street, overlooked by the imposing colonnade of Victoria's **Parliament House**, and the Windsor Hotel of 1883. Near by, the **Old Treasury Building** (1857) contains the Melbourne Exhibition on the city's social and architectural history.

You can call a halt here, or return to Flinders Street station via the eastern 'Paris' end of Collins Street.

Walk — Along the Yarra

See map on pages 94–5.

A 5km walk along Melbourne's River Yarra into the green spaces of Kings Domain and the Botanic Gardens.

Downstream from Princes Bridge, the Yarra is crossed by a sprightly new footbridge. Avoiding the temptation of the riverside cafés of the Southgate Centre, you are rewarded with one of the best views of the city skyline from Southbank Promenade on the far side of Princes Bridge.

Negotiate the crossing of Alexandra Avenue with care and enjoy the calm of **Kings Domain**, with its various focal points like the Sidney Myer Music Bowl and the Pioneer Women's Memorial Garden. The far bank of the lake in the **Royal Botanic Gardens** marks the outermost point of the walk, excuse enough for a pause at the lakeside café. Beyond the Herbarium and Visitor Centre is the **Shrine of Remembrance**, whose outside gallery gives a wonderful vista back to the city centre.

The return to Flinders Street station can be made on foot or by tram along St Kilda Road.

The Yarra River: locals' playground

The birds of Wyperfeld
Much of the park is alive with great flocks of birds: white and pink cockatoos, galahs and regent parrots. The most curious bird, though, is the mallee-fowl, builder of underground nests in which its young are hatched in meticulously controlled incubation conditions.

Peaks and beaches
Although Victoria cannot lay claim to any of Australia's World Heritage regions, this small state encompasses an extraordinary variety of national parks and wilderness areas. Apart from the alpine regions, which are particularly popular with skiers, Victoria's favourite park is probably the superb coastal region of Wilsons Promontory – see page 121.

From high alps to rolling downlands, from luxuriant rain forests to desert scrub and from the spreading floodplains of the Murray River in the north to some of the country's most dramatic coastline in the south, Victoria's landscape is as varied as its climate. A relatively high rainfall over much of the state contributes to the luxuriance of the forest cover as well as to the productivity of grasslands and other farmed areas; by contrast, the far northwest is extremely arid.

Victorian Alps The dominating physical feature of the state is its mountain backbone, the southernmost stretch of Australia's Great Dividing Range. Majestic alpine summits rise to almost 2,000m, while foothills and lower ranges stretch southwards and westwards to form a hilly backdrop to the metropolitan area of Melbourne. Many of the highest and most spectacular parts of the Victorian Alps are protected as national parks; they include **Mount Buffalo** (1,721m), whose characteristic hump-backed shape was first seen by the explorers Hume and Hovell in 1824. Beneath the summit stretches a vast upland plateau bounded by cliffs falling abruptly to the plains below. Used for skiing in winter, the plateau becomes an elaborate embroidery of wildflowers in spring.

As in the highlands generally, the vegetation cover varies with altitude, the dense wet forest of the valleys becoming more open further up the slope, with peppermint gums giving way to alpine ash and finally to snow gums. In the early days of white settlement, cattlemen drove their beasts high into the uplands to feed off the summer pastures, building stone huts for shelter. Many of the huts remain, but grazing has been forbidden because of erosion. A number of physically separate national parks – the strangely named Bogong, Cobberas-Tingaringy and Wonnangatta-Moroka parks – have since been grouped together to form the exhilarating **Alpine National Park** which is Victoria's largest at 646,000 hectares.

At Point Nepean on the Mornington Peninsula – the entrance to Port Phillip Bay

Southeastern Victoria Along the border with New South Wales lies some of the most unspoiled scenery in the state. Inland are a number of national parks. **Errinundra National Park** encompasses a large tract of cool, temperate woodland, and there are other pockets of rain forest at **Lind** and **Alfred National Parks**. The splendid gorges along the course of the **Snowy River** offer exciting whitewater canoeing; this park is also the habitat of the rare brush-tailed rock wallaby. Running from Sydenham Inlet to the NSW boundary is one of the country's finest coastal reserves, the **Croajingolong National Park**, with savage cliffs and headlands protecting pristine beaches and tranquil inlets. In complete contrast are **The Lakes** to the west, where the seemingly infinite Ninety Mile Beach is backed by lagoons and waterways.

As well as the Dandenongs, day trips from Melbourne can take in **Point Nepean** at the tip of the Mornington Peninsula, the **Brisbane Ranges**, the forests and fern gullies of **Kinglake National Park** to the northeast, and the strange basalt columns of **Organ Pipes National Park** to the northwest. The **Grampians (Gariwerd) National Park** in the west of the state is one of Victoria's highlights. This reserve, with its stunning mountain scenery, important Aboriginal sites and abundant native wildlife, is just about reachable in a day, but merits a longer stay.

Victoria's southwestern coastline The best can be seen in two contrasting parks: between Lorne and Cape Otway the high ranges of the **Otways**, still covered in glorious rain forest, rise steeply from the sea; further west, the breakers are constantly resculpting the cliffs of the **Port Campbell National Park**, creating some of the most spectacular coastal scenery to be seen anywhere in the world. Inland, volcanic activity has given rise to fertile farmland interspersed with crater lakes and worn-down volcanic cones, as at **Mount Eccles**.

Far from the coast and the wooded uplands is **Wyperfeld National Park**, a complex system of normally dry lakes and lagoons, with mallee (see panel) stretching to the horizon.

The basalt columns of the aptly named Organ Pipes National Park

Mastering the mallee
Much of northwestern Victoria was once covered in mallee, 'a blue and level sea stretching to the horizon'. Mallee is an Aboriginal word describing the fire-resistant scrub composed of 20 or so species of low-growing eucalyptus. The mallee burns fiercely, but quickly regenerates from the surviving roots, making it difficult for farmers to clear. Its demise came about with the invention of mullenisation; a heavy roller was dragged through the scrub by oxen, followed by an ingenious 'stump-jump' plough. Years of burning and cropping finally eradicated the troublesome mallee, except in areas like Wyperfeld, itself threatened with clearance as late as the 1960s.

How to travel

Victoria's relatively small size and excellent roads make driving the ideal way to explore the state

The Great Ocean Road
Australia's most famous drive is perhaps the 300km journey along the Great Ocean Road. Stretching from south of Geelong towards the South Australian border, this extraordinarily scenic route takes in beaches, charming ports and villages, forested hillsides and a dramatically eroded coastline around the town of Port Campbell.

The unpredictable state
The weather in Victoria is notoriously changeable; desert influences may be felt one moment, with searing dry winds and high temperatures, giving way suddenly to cold and wet air from the ocean to the south. If you don't like our weather, say Melburnians, just hold on – it's bound to change!

By air Melbourne's Tullamarine Airport is 22km northwest of the city centre and is connected to many overseas destinations as well as to all major cities in Australia. Domestic and international flights share the same terminal. Frequent buses link the airport to Spencer Street station downtown, from where a shuttle distributes passengers to city centre hotels.

By bus and coach Express coaches travel to major destinations in Australia and within Victoria. Because of the (relatively!) small size of the state, public transport is a reasonable proposition for most journeys. Many places in Victoria are accessible in a day's outing from Melbourne. There is the usual excellent range of organised coach tours – remember that it is worth shopping around for the one that suits your requirements exactly.

By rail Greater Melbourne's comprehensive public transport network is marketed under the name of **The Met**. Electric suburban railways that travel as far afield as the Dardenorg Ranges and Mornington Peninsula are supplemented by one of the world's most extensive systems of tramways and by urban buses. Through-ticketing is based on a zoning system, and there are a number of special deals like day tickets or weekly passes that are worth considering. The principal station is Flinders Street, and most trains travel round the underground loop which circles the city centre with useful stops at Flagstaff, Museum, Parliament and Spencer Street.

Apart from the extensive mileage served by The Met, there are quite a number of towns in Victoria which can be reached by **V-Line train** (sometimes supplemented by a V-Line coach). There are interstate services to Adelaide and Sydney as well as to Perth (changing at Adelaide or Port Pirie).

By car Highway conditions in Victoria are generally good. The grandiose freeway plan for Melbourne was only partly implemented, but traffic still seems to flow more freely than in Sydney. If you wish to visit the more inaccessible national parks, or explore the state thoroughly, hiring a vehicle is recommended, however.

►► **Apollo Bay** 90A2

This little fishing port about 120km to the west of Port Phillip Bay has magnificent beaches and makes an excellent base for exploring the superb forests of the Otway Ranges. The hills reach the sea at Cape Otway, the 'fearful coastline' described by the explorer Matthew Flinders, with a lighthouse rising from 100m-high cliffs.

► **Ararat** 90B2

The town (200km northwest of Melbourne) owes its foundation to the gold strike of 1857, when 3,000oz of alluvial gold were found in the space of three weeks. Then Ararat's population was more than double its present total; now sheep outnumber people by about 150 to one. To the north is the world-famous **Seppelt Great Western Winery**, where the champagne is stored in underground galleries originally dug out by the gold miners.

► **Avoca** 90B2

On the Pyrenees Highway between Ararat and Castlemaine, Avoca was once a gold town and is now the centre of an agricultural area. Since the 1960s, vineyards have been replanted on the north-facing slopes of the foothills, making this one of the state's newer wine districts. The solid Court House complex with bluestone gaol, powder magazine and police residence date from the mid-19th century.

►►► **Ballarat** 90B2

No bigger than in its gold-rush heyday, Ballarat has preserved much of its 19th-century townscape and still exudes the atmosphere of those heady times.

Gold was first found in 1851, and within a few months thousands of ill-assorted diggers were frantically prospecting in spite of mud, cold and frequent bitter disappointment. Surface deposits were soon exhausted, and individual miners were succeeded by companies with sufficient clout to dig deep mines and buy the machinery to run them. Gold may have made Melbourne, but it made Ballarat too; profits seem not to have been gambled or drunk away, but to have been invested respectably in bricks and mortar, giving the town as splendid an array of fine 19th-century building as can be seen anywhere in the country. Banks, churches, a synagogue, clubs, a mining exchange, a splendid town hall and an art gallery all demonstrate how quickly the raw life of the diggings was transmuted into civic respectability.

Ballarat's botanics
By the side of beautiful Lake Wendouree, the Botanic Gardens in Ballarat are a perfect example of High Victorian taste, with white marble statuary among the pretty pavilions and bedding plants. On plinths beneath the trees stand the busts of former prime ministers, some, like Gough Whitlam and Malcolm Fraser, none too comfortable at seeing each other in such close proximity again.

The gold-rush town of Ballarat contains many grand buildings that date from the 19th century

Eureka!
By 1854, passions were running high in Ballarat's goldfields. Grim working and living conditions and encroachment by bigger mining companies were compounded by high licence fees, extracted from resentful diggers by heavy-handed and much hated special police. Eventually, a band of Irish-led miners staged the only major revolt by whites in Australian history. Licences were burnt in a joyous conflagration, and the rebels, armed with pikes, assembled in the Eureka Stockade under the banner of the Southern Cross. But in a savage example of overkill, they were swiftly overcome by government soldiers, who left 30 dead. Australia's 'Civil War' had lasted 15 minutes; it is convincingly re-created, using advanced *son et lumière* techniques, at Sovereign Hill.

Bred in Ballarat
Ballarat Wildlife Park has a wonderful selection of mostly Antipodean animals in its park-like setting. It is one of the few places where Tasmanian Devils are successfully bred; if you are so inclined, you can see these thugs of the animal world being fed their daily ration of white mice.

Sovereign Hill►►► is a superb re-creation of life and work on the goldfields in the 1850s. It is justifiably popular with its many visitors, who can pan for gold, ride Cobb & Co's stagecoach, shop in the emporia of Main Street, savour the strangely distinct world of the Chinese Village, or even spend the night in 1850s-style accommodation at the Sovereign Hill Lodge. Other major features include the Mine Museum, with 600m of underground workings, and the Gold Museum, with exciting displays on the history of the precious metal.

►► Beechworth   91B4
This exceptionally well-preserved 1850s gold town in the foothills of the Australian Alps, 270km northeast of Melbourne, has a fine array of old buildings, many of them constructed from warm, honey-coloured stone. As well as the post office with its imposing tower and the survivors of the 61 hotels of gold-rush times (the carriage house of one is home to a coach museum), there is also the Burke Museum. Named after the ill-fated explorer, the museum is packed with memorabilia, including mementoes of Ned Kelly who spent a night in the cell beneath the town hall.

►► Bellarine Peninsula   90A3
Stretching eastwards into Port Phillip Bay, this broad peninsula, with its fine surf beaches and popular resorts like Ocean Grove and Barwon Heads, has become the summer playground for the inhabitants of Geelong. One of the peninsula's greatest attractions is the charming resort town of Queenscliff (see page 119), with its fort, lighthouse and grand old hotels.

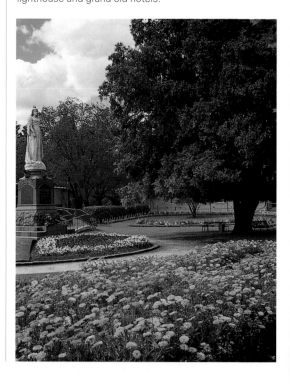

A statue of Queen Victoria presiding over a formal garden in Bendigo

▶▶ **Bendigo** *90B2*

Like Ballarat, Bendigo began as a gold-rush town, expanding rapidly from 1851 onwards to become one of the state's largest inland towns. Many of its fine late 19th-century buildings which were erected with the wealth won from the ground remain in peak condition. These include the vast Shamrock Hotel, a number of imposing churches and a fine group of public buildings. The work that paid for all this architectural splendour is celebrated in the completely preserved **Central Deborah Goldmine**▶▶, with its impressive underground galleries, while the special contribution of Chinese miners is recalled in the delightful **Joss House** at Emu Point. The best way to get acquainted with this fascinating town is to take the 'Talking Tram', which runs along an 8km route and gives a full commentary on all the sights.

▶ **Brisbane Ranges National Park** *90A2*

This extensive block of slate and sandstone has been eroded in places to form deep defiles like Anakie Gorge, a favoured spot for not-too-demanding bush walks. Gold was once mined in quantity at the ghost town of Steiglitz, now an historic park.

▶ **Camperdown** *90A2*

This township is located on the sweeping plains formed from lava and ash which run from the South Australian border to Port Phillip Bay and which have long been the basis of a prosperous grazing industry. Now silent, the volcanic cones responsible for all this fertility are scattered over the area. Mount Leura and Mount Sugarloaf are to the southeast of town, while to the west there are two examples of crater lakes – Lake Bullen Merri (fresh water) and Lake Gnotuk (salt water).

▶▶ **Castlemaine** *90B2*

Once gold had been discovered here in Specimen Gully by a shepherd, 25,000 diggers joined the rush, although Castlemaine declined fairly quickly because of the lack of reef gold. Today it is an attractive township, popular with folk seeking refuge from the metropolitan stresses of Melbourne to the south, and full of interesting old buildings. Most striking is the classical market hall, an almost exact reproduction of a Greek temple which now contains the local museum. Castlemaine is also home to an excellent art gallery, some fine botanic gardens and the mansion known as Buda, begun in 1857.

The Castlemaine and Maldon Railway is a steam train ride which proves popular with children. It is based at Maldon station, 18km west along Highway 122 (see also page 117).

▶▶ **Coal Creek Historical Village, Korumburra** *90A3*

The railways of Victoria used to run on Korumburra coal, and after the last mine had been closed down in the late 1950s it was decided that the days of coal and steam should be re-created at Coal Creek Mine just outside town (about 100km southeast of Melbourne). As well as the gallery of the mine, the popular 40-hectare site has a railway station, tradesmen plying their crafts, old stores and settlers' cottages.

The Gippsland whopper
Of the 100 or so species of Australian worms, *Megascolides australis* is easily the biggest, measuring up to 3.7m long and 2.5cm thick. This extraordinary creature has its own museum, in a predictably worm-shaped building, near the turn-off for Phillip Island on the Bass Highway.

111

Castlemaine is a former mining town about 40km north of Daylesford

■ **For much of its 2,600km length, the mighty Murray forms the boundary between Victoria and New South Wales. The longest river in Australia rises in the Great Dividing Range near Mount Kosciuszko, flowing past stands of red gums and irrigating the semi-arid country around Mildura before entering the sea at Encounter Bay.** ■

For thousands of years the rich wildlife of the Murray and its tributaries gave sustenance to the Aborigines who lived along its banks. It was discovered by Hume and Hovell in 1824, and explored more thoroughly by Charles Sturt in the course of his expedition of 1829–30. As settlers moved in, in the beginning strongly opposed by the Aborigines, the river took on great importance as a transport route. A spirited contest took place in 1853 between the *Mary Ann* and the *Lady Augusta*, to see which would be the first steamboat to make it up the Murray as far as Swan Hill. With the prize money of £4,000, the master of the winning steamboat founded the Murray River Navigation Co, whose sternwheelers dominated river traffic for many years until the coming of the railway rendered them obsolete.

The greatest handicap to navigation was the irregularity of the Murray's flow; for many months of the year there would not be enough water to float a boat of any size, and the risk of running aground was constant. A number of proud vessels survive to carry cargoes of nostalgic tourists rather than the bales of wool which filled their holds in their 19th-century heyday.

Attractions Upstream from the twin towns of Albury (NSW) and Wodonga (Victoria) is **Lake Hume**, several times the size of Sydney Harbour. Built to regulate river flow, it is now an ideal location for watersports. Downstream are the wineries around **Rutherglen**, while **Yarrawonga**, thanks to Lake Mulwala, has become a major inland water recreation area. Around **Cobram** are dozens of surprisingly fine sandy beaches.

Echuca was once Australia's busiest inland port, with a truly magnificent wharf more than a kilometre long built from the timber of red gums. The people of the town are very proud of its heritage, and have taken pains to preserve it for the pleasure of visitors. The port area has been fully restored and has a whole series of visitor attractions, including the Cargo Shed with life-like dioramas. The Bridge Hotel is full of period furniture,

Barmah Forest
Spreading for 300sq km over the floodplain of the Murray upstream from Echuca is this magnificent forest of river red gum trees, some of them 500 years old. Australia was largely built on the extraordinarily durable timber of these majestic trees, which was used for railway construction, bridges, mines, fences, wharves and so on. When the river spills over its banks during exceptionally rainy spells, the forest comes alive with the calls of more than 200 species of migrating birds.

A journey to the past aboard a paddle steamer...

...stopping at Echuca, Swan Hill, Mildura and other places along the Murray

113

The Chaffeys

Canadians George and William Chaffey pioneered artificially irrigated settlements in California before being invited to bring their expertise to the Murray. They both succeeded and failed; from the 1880s on, thousands of new settlers flocked to the newly irrigated areas around Mildura, and the town itself prospered, but there were floods, problems with leaching and salinity, and the great slump of the 1890s. By 1896 George had had enough and borrowed his fare home, but William stayed on, helping to put the area's economy on a firmer footing once the railway arrived in 1903. The water pumps George had designed continued to work into the 1950s.

and the old Customs House has been put to use as the information centre. It is rare to see so many steamboats, either under restoration or in action.

To the northwest of the Kerang lakes is another river port, **Swan Hill**, named by explorer Thomas Mitchell who was kept awake at night by the swans on a nearby lagoon. The town's outstanding attraction is the **Swan Hill Pioneer Settlement**, a painstaking riverside recreation put together using original buildings as well as accurate replicas, and brought alive by the presence of craftspeople practising traditional trades. In addition to its daytime attractions, the Pioneer Settlement offers an illuminating sound and lightshow that concentrates on the early pioneers. A strong sense of the past can also be experienced in two fine old properties, the **Tyntynder Homestead** to the north, and **Murray Downs** to the east, the latter designed to repel attack by Aborigines.

Red to green At the heart of the irrigated area, **Mildura** was originally laid out on the American pattern, with streets given numbers rather than names. In the language of the Kulkyne Aborigines, Mildura meant 'dry red earth', but here red has been turned to green ever since the Chaffey brothers arrived in 1885 from North America to apply their advanced irrigation engineering techniques (see panel). Avocados, melons, oranges and grapes – both for the table and for wine-making – are all grown here, as is a whole range of fruit for drying. A number of establishments are happy to share their production secrets with you, among them Orange World and Sultana Sam Vineyard. Alternatively, you could take a trip on the river as paddle steamers also operate from here.

The lovely Rhododendron Gardens at Olinda in the Dandenong Ranges

A feathered philanderer
The forests and gullies of the Dandenongs provide a habitat for *Menura novae-hollandiae*, the superb lyrebird, a wonderful singer and mimic of the calls of other birds. The rather ordinary looking male of the species comes into his own in winter, when he senses that female lyrebirds are ready to respond to his advances. Having built a series of mounds through-out his territory, the male mounts one and undergoes an extraordinary transfor-mation, fanning out his lyre-shaped tail-feathers so that his body disappears in a froth of plumage, at the same time pouring forth a cascade of song. The more impressive the display, the greater the bird's chances of winning his way with a succession of females.

► **Colac** *90A2*

Colac is the market town for the agricultural wealth of the surrounding basalt plains. This southwestern area incor-porates a lake district of some 50 to 60 water bodies. Those that have formed in deep craters contain fresh water, while the shallower lakes contain salty water as the rate of evaporation from them exceeds the rate of replenishment; Lake Corangamite is a saline lake, and is also Victoria's largest.

►► **The Dandenong Ranges** *90A3*

Melbourne is fortunate to have these magnificently wooded hills on the eastern edge of the metropolitan area, a wonderful destination for a day's outing. The high-est point is **Mount Dandenong**►► (633m), with fantastic views over the sprawling city to the west and the further hills to the east.

Because of their accessibility, the Dandenongs have long been a favourite residential area, and there are pretty townships and many fine mansions, some of which have been converted into hotels and restaurants. There are lush gardens, too, like the **Rhododendron Gardens** at Olinda►, whose exotic shrubs contrast with the native vegetation of towering mountain ash trees, massive tree ferns and rampant creepers. At Belgrave is the terminus of 'Puffing Billy'►►, the vintage narrow-gauge steam locomotive which pulls trainloads of tourists on a scenic 13km railway line through the forest.

►► **Daylesford** *90B2*

Between them, Daylesford (100km northwest of Melbourne) and Hepburn Springs contain half of Aust-ralia's mineral springs. The supposedly therapeutic waters were discovered in the course of gold mining in the 1850s and 1860s, and by the turn of the century the place had taken on the character of the spa resorts so common in Europe, perhaps because many of the early inhabitants were originally immigrants from the Swiss canton of Ticino. At the Hepburn Spa Complex, the old spa building is still intact; you can acquire bottled water, take various treatments and enjoy relaxing walks. The excellent **Daylesford Historical Society Museum**▶ is housed in the old School of Mines, and there are attractive botanical gardens. To the north is the old volcanic cone of Mount Franklin with a fine view from its summit.

▶ Dunolly 90B2

The area around Dunolly, 200km northwest of Melbourne, yielded more nuggets than any other Australian goldfield, including the Welcome Stranger, weighing in at 2,505oz. Reproductions of this and other mega-nuggets can be seen in the quiet little town's Goldfields Museum.

▶ Geelong 90A2

This industrial port city, Victoria's second largest, once saw itself as a rival to Melbourne, but has long since given up the struggle, though its harbour still exports the rich produce of its agricultural hinterland. In spite of much redevelopment, there is plenty of evidence of 19th-century grandeur; imposing public buildings adorn the city centre and the prosperity of Geelong's merchant class is reflected in the many elegant properties, such as Barwon Grange overlooking the Barwon River. Corio Villa above Eastern Beach was prefabricated in Scotland and re-assembled here by guesswork after the plans and instructions had been destroyed. One of the fine old bluestone woolstores has been splendidly restored to house the excellent **National Wool Museum**▶▶. This is the place to come if you want to understand how Australia 'rode to prosperity on the sheep's back'.

▶▶ Gippsland 91A4

Named in the 1840s by Polish explorer Count Strzelecki after the Governor of NSW, Gippsland is the loosely defined region comprising most of southeastern Victoria between the highlands of the Great Dividing Range and the coastline of Bass Strait. The superb temperate rain forest which once blanketed the area has mostly been cut down to yield rich dairying and fruit growing land, though fine tracts of woodland remain in the state forests and national parks along the NSW border in the far east. This is one of the areas where protest action by conservationists has focused public attention on the fact that the glories of Australia's natural heritage are not inexhaustible. The La Trobe Valley in the heart of Gippsland has the world's biggest deposits of brown coal, burnt here in power stations to provide something like 90 per cent of the state's electric power, while oil and gas is extracted in quantity from offshore wells in Bass Strait.

The scale of contemporary opencast mining can be appreciated in the course of tours from the **Morwell Visitor Centre**▶, while more traditional activities can be contemplated in the **Gippsland Heritage Centre**▶ at Moe, with its collection of old buildings from many parts of Gippsland. Inland is some of Victoria's most attractive countryside, running up into the alpine foothills of the Great Dividing Range, while the Gippsland Lakes (see panel) lie landward of Ninety Mile Beach.

Gippsland Lakes
Sometimes described as 'the best example of a coastal lagoon in the world', and with a near-Mediterranean climate, this area offers unrivalled opportunites for sailing, cruising, fishing or just taking it easy. Both beach and lakes are protected as national parks.

Rich dairylands make for fine Gippsland cheeses

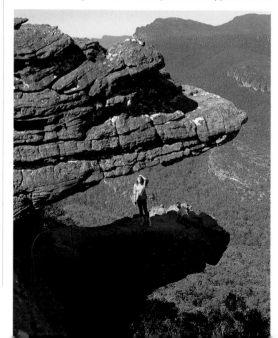

Native Australians maintain a sophisticated ecological and spiritual balance amid a changing environment

Our people
Following the 1988 Bicentenary, Australia's indigenous people decided to try to replace the overall term 'Aborigine' with names from their own languages. 'Koori', meaning 'our people', is now widely in use in southeastern Australia.

The Grampians are an outdoor gallery of Koori art, to be seen in the Billimina, Larngibunja and Ngamadjidj shelters and at Flat Rock.

▶ **Goulburn Valley** 90B3

The Goulburn River runs northwest from artificial Lake Eildon in the foothills of the Victorian Alps through a rich fruit- and vine-growing area to join the Murray River near Echuca. With an indented shoreline more than 500km long, Lake Elidon is an immensely popular place for water-sports of all kinds. There is also some good walking in this area. The lake is fringed by Eildon State Park and Fraser National Park – forested environments that are also rich in wildlife. To the west of the river, Rushworth is a fine example of a gold-rush town of the 1850s.

▶▶ **Grampians (Gariwerd) National Park** 90B1

The Aborigines, who left many traces of their rock art here, knew the Grampians as Gariwerd. Forming the largest national park in Victoria, the region consists of a succession of sandstone ridges sloping gently to the west, ending in sheer cliffs and jagged rock formations to the east. The area is rich in wildlife and is carpeted with wildflowers in summer.

The park has an excellent network of trails and paths, and can also be appreciated by car thanks to a network of scenic roads. There are any number of spectacular view-points; Boroka Lookout▶▶ gives a fine panorama over the tourist centre of Halls Gap, where there is a visitor centre and the **Brambuk Living Cultural Centre**▶ which is intended to bring the history and culture of local Aborigines to life. To the west are two of the most spectacular sights of the ranges; the rock formation known as the **Balconies** and the grandiose water staircase of the **Mackenzie Falls**.

▶ **Hamilton** 90A1

Focal point of much of the prosperous agricultural plains of central western Victoria, Hamilton likes to style itself the 'Wool Capital of the World'. Its outstanding attraction is the **City of Hamilton Art Gallery**▶, with a large and varied collection including wonderful examples of the applied arts of

The huge over-hanging rocks in the Grampians National Park known as the Balconies

Maldon's wide main street slopes gently downhill and features some typically Australian country architecture

many countries, plus a splendid array of the watercolours and etchings of the British topographical artist Paul Sandby.

►► Healesville 90B3

Nestling among its green hills in the Yarra Valley, this attractive township is a good place for walks and picnics, but it is mostly visited now for the **Healesville Sanctuary►►**. A visit to this world-class wildlife park is an excellent way to appreciate the strange and wonderful fauna of the Antipodes, in a range of cleverly re-created habitats and walk-through enclosures. The new Aboriginal cultural centre, **Galeena Beek►**, includes displays of artefacts and ritual dances and offers various walking tours.

►► Lorne 90A2

Protected from the north by the steep and beautifully forested slopes of the Otways, this charming little place facing on to the curving beach of Loutit Bay has enjoyed a high reputation as a seaside resort for over a century. There are also delightful walks in the forest park.

►► Maldon 90B2

Among the many old gold-rush townships of central Victoria, Maldon is outstanding – 'the best preserved town in Australia of the gold-mining era', according to the National Trust. It is certainly full of charm; the scale of the place is modest and the tone is set by delightful cottages, many of them with pretty gardens.

► Marysville 90B3

Pleasantly located in the foothills of the Victorian Alps, the township of Marysville has long been favoured by weekending Melburnians. In summer there is wonderful bushwalking to the Steavenson Falls, some of the highest in Victoria, or to the Cumberland Valley where the state's tallest trees grow. In winter, there is good cross-country skiing to be enjoyed, particularly on the popular snowfields of Lake Mountain.

Duckbilled denizen
Even the normally bashful platypus can be observed going about its daily life at Healesville. The sanctuary has the distinction of being the first place to successfully breed this normally diffident creature in captivity.

VICTORIA

Penguins on parade
The endearing little fairy penguins which live along the coasts of southern Australia are the smallest of the species in the world, being under a metre in length. They spend their days feeding and frolicking at sea, then as evening falls they gather in groups to waddle to their burrows at the back of the beach. On Philip Island they maintain this routine with apparent complete indifference to the floodlighting and to the countless tourists huddled in the viewing stands watching what is justifiably one of Australia's most popular wildlife spectacles.

The dramatic Twelve Apostles near Port Campbell, on the Great Ocean Road

►► **Mornington Peninsula**   90A3

Melbourne's favourite weekend and holiday area embraces Port Phillip Bay in a great curve of sheltered beaches before ending at Point Nepean, overlooking the dangerous currents of the narrow entrance to the bay known as The Rip.

Much of the peninsula is suburban in character, with dwellings crowding along the main road and spreading out from the residential and resort towns like Frankston and Mornington. In the season, the foreshore is crowded with campers and caravanners. Towards the tip, refined Sorrento and exclusive Portsea have retained more of the feeling of early days, when paddlesteamers brought holidaymakers across the bay from Melbourne. Once off limits as a naval base, Point Nepean is now part of the Mornington Peninsula National Park, reached from the visitor centre by shuttle. The 'front' beaches facing the bay tend to be calm but busy, while the 'back' beaches looking out on to the Bass Strait are wild – no place for inexperienced swimmers.

The peninsula's importance in Victoria's history is recalled by the graves of the 'early settlers' at **Sorrento**, and by the 1844 **McCrae Homestead►**, the home of the first permanent settler family. The best overall view is from 305m high **Arthur's Seat►**, reached by road or, more excitingly, by chairlift.

►► **Phillip Island**   90A3

Bounded to the west by the Mornington Peninsula, the great tidal estuary of Westernport Bay is broken up by a number of islands. French Island and Little Churchill Island are rich in wildlife, but the most famous of the islands is Phillip Island, whose irresistible **Fairy Penguin**

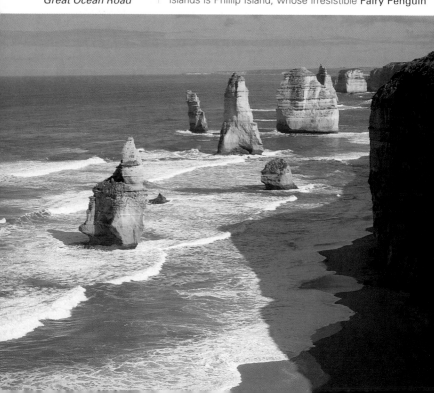

Parade pulls in hundreds of thousands of onlookers.

Reached by bridge and about 128km from Melbourne, Phillip Island is generally flat, but has a splendidly varied coastline which includes rugged cliffs, rock outcrops and long surf beaches. Muttonbirds nest on Cape Woolamai, the highest point on the island, thousands of seals can be seen off the basalt cliffs of Point Grant, and a number of sanctuaries harbour koalas which were introduced to the island in the 1870s. Cowes is the main resort, with boat trips to the seals and to French Island, and a ferry to Stony Point on the Mornington Peninsula.

▶▶▶ Port Campbell National Park 90A2

Backed by the Great Ocean Road running west from Geelong, this park comprises 30km of some of the world's most spectacular coastal scenery, a succession of high cliffs, headlands and strange rock formations standing out to sea. Biscuit-like beds of limestone, sand, mud and seashells formed beneath the sea and then uplifted 25 million years ago are now being eaten away by the breakers rolling in from the Southern Ocean. Because the rock varies in strength and texture, the sea advances more rapidly in some places than others, leaving behind isolated features which have been given evocative names like the Twelve Apostles (at Port Campbell). In a dramatic demonstration of the rate of erosion, the arch of 'London Bridge' collapsed into the surf in 1990, stranding the walkers who had ventured out on to it. Quickly rescued, they were luckier than the many passengers and crewmen who perished along what was named the 'Shipwreck Coast' in the days of sail (see pages 242–3).

▶▶ Port Fairy 90A1

This delightful little fishing port and seaside resort at the mouth of the Moyne River is one of the oldest settlements in Victoria, having been home to sealers and whalers in the early years of the 19th century. There are 50 buildings classified as historic by the National Trust, including Mott's Cottage and a wooden house erected by a whaling skipper in the 1830s.

▶ Portland 90A1

Founded a year earlier than Port Fairy, in 1834, this busy deep-water port is the oldest permanent settlement in Victoria. To the southwest are the spectacular seascapes of Cape Nelson and the blowholes and petrified forest of Cape Bridgewater.

▶▶ Queenscliff 90A3

Separated from Point Nepean on the Mornington Peninsula only by the treacherous waters of The Rip, Queenscliff is a splendidly old-fashioned kind of place, with a harbour, a fort (1882), grand hotels and the Black Lighthouse, prefabricated in Scotland and shipped here in 1863.

▶▶ Strzelecki Ranges 91A3

The best way to see these ridges is to follow the Grand Ridge Road from Nyora, southeast of Melbourne, to Carrajung (about 130km), passing through some of Victoria's finest upland scenery and numerous pretty towns and villages.

Queenscliff on the Bellarine Peninsula where Melburnians come to get away from it all

Count the consonants
His name unpronounceable to Anglo-Saxons, the Pole Paul Edmund de Strzelecki styled himself 'Count', a claim with little apparent substance. Although it was Angus McMillan who had first blazed a trail through the almost impenetrable rain forest jungle of southeast Victoria, it was not his name for the area ('New South Caledonia') that was adopted, but Strzelecki's 'Gippsland'. Strzelecki's own venture into Gippsland was only saved from disaster by the skill of his Aboriginal guide, Tarra, after whom the Tarra Bulga National Park has been named.

■ **Gum trees, or to give them their more dignified name, eucalyptus, are the trees most closely identified with Australia. They comprise more than 500 different species, and grow in most parts of the country; some three-quarters of all Australian trees are eucalyptus, many of them with wonderfully descriptive names like peppermint, ironbark, lemon-scented, bloodwood or blackbutt.** ■

Eucalyptus leaves
All eucalyptus leaves contain a fragrant oil which is used in medicines and flavourings. Their indigestible look doesn't deter the koala either, which in fact depends entirely on one eucalyptus species for its food source.

World-beater
The confusingly named mountain ash (*Eucalyptus regnans*) is the tallest flowering plant in the world, reaching an extraordinary height of up to 100m in the forests of Victoria and Tasmania.

The great river red gum forest at Yarrawonga

Early settlers didn't much like the look of the unfamiliar eucalyptus, with their pale greyish-green or peeling, untidy bark hanging in strips and tatters, and the unseasonal failure of their dull grey leaves to fall at the proper time of year. Many farmers and graziers made haste to plant up their properties with trees from home, and elm, oak, willow and poplar grace many a rural scene. The same was true of townsfolk, who preferred the more orderly European trees for their parks.

Forests and felling But eucalyptus have their own distinct allure, individually or in mass, forming magnificent forests or growing with other trees, shrubs and grasses to form the surprisingly park-like landscapes of many parts of the interior. Over the millenia, eucalyptus have also learned to live with fire, regenerating almost miraculously after an all-too-common bushfire from buds concealed within their bark. Many species, like jarrah and messmate, yield first-rate timber and in consequence were felled ruthlessly until quite recently. Others are logged, somewhat demeaningly, to be turned into woodchip for foreign pulp mills.

Varieties There are many types of eucalyptus, from the Tasmanian blue gum which provided timber for railway sleepers, to the river red gum of semi-arid areas, the ghost gum of deserts and the hardy, cold-resistant snow gum, symbol of the Australian Alps.

▶ **Walhalla**   *91A4*

Tucked away in the deep wooded valleys north of Moe, isolated Walhalla boomed in the late 19th century when more gold was extracted here than from any other area in Victoria. By the time the railway reached here in 1910 via a series of spectacular tunnels and trestle bridges the gold had more or less run out. A stroll along the crooked main street recalls some of the atmosphere of former days, and you can visit the Long Tunnel Extended Mine. Another attraction is taking a ride on the restored Walhalla Goldfields Railway through this magnificent upland scenery.

▶ **Wangaratta**   *90B3*

The Hume Highway is the main route north from Melbourne to Sydney. About 240km from Melbourne is flourishing Wangaratta, a service centre for the surrounding agricultural area. The body of the notorious bushranger Mad Dan Morgan is buried here minus his head, the latter having been sent to Melbourne in order to establish whether he really was mad, or just plain bad. The town's other attraction is the Airworld Museum▶▶, with a splendid collection of vintage aircraft.

▶ **Warrnambool**   *90A1*

The biggest town on Victoria's southwest coast, Warrnambool benefits from superb beaches. Founded by whalers in the 1840s, it is still frequented by southern right whales which come here in winter to calve (see panel). Flagstaff Hill Maritime Museum▶▶ is a conscientiously re-created port village with several historic vessels and other fascinating displays.

▶▶ **Wilsons Promontory National Park**   *91A4*

The southernmost point of mainland Australia, this wild and mountainous granite peninsula protruding into Bass Strait is perhaps Victoria's favourite national park. Many of its rocky headlands, splendid beaches and dense forests are only accessible on foot, and in spite of its popularity it is always possible to find whatever degree of isolation you want (though you may have kangaroos for company). The only settlement is at Tidal River, where the road ends and a network of wonderful walking tracks begins.

Southern right whales playing off Warrnambool

121

'The Prom'
Discovered by maritime explorer George Bass in 1798 and named after a friend of Bass's colleague Matthew Flinders, Wilsons Promontory attracts nature lovers of all types. In summer the area is great for scuba diving and snorkelling; there are some wonderful walks; and the diverse flora makes the park a botanist's dream.

The Warrnambool whales
Between May and August southern right whales gather off Logan's Beach to bear their young. A special viewing platform has been built from which you can observe these magnificent creatures, once hunted to near-extinction, as they dive and play, making spectacular fountains from their blowholes or leaping bodily from the waves.

Drive The Dandenong Ranges

Less than an hour from the centre of Melbourne, the 'Blue Dandenongs' are a favourite recreation area and summer retreat for the inhabitants of the city.

Canterbury Road leads to Montrose at the northern end of the Dandenong Tourist Road. Those with time to spare could continue another 30km to **Healesville Sanctuary**, one of the best places in which to see Australian wildlife at close quarters.

Mount Dandenong, at 633m the highest point of the range, and the sculptures of the **William Ricketts Sanctuary** are accessible from the Tourist Road. The route to the village of Kallista passes the Nicholas Memorial Gardens and **Sherbrooke Forest Park**, where you can see the tree-ferns and the magnificent mountain ash trees for which the area is famous. **Belgrave** is the terminus for the irresistible 'Puffing Billy', a restored steam train which hauls delighted passengers through the forest along its narrow-gauge track.

Drive Mornington Peninsula

The 100km drive to Point Nepean National Park at the far tip of the Mornington Peninsula passes residential areas and resorts enjoying the beaches of Port Phillip Bay.

Frankston marks the end of the commuter railway line from Melbourne.

Beyond **Dromana** with its excellent Tourist Information Centre the coast is lined with holiday homes and campsites, while above the town **Arthur's Seat** rises 305m to give a fine panorama over bay and ocean. On its northern slope is the little **McCrae Homestead**, built in 1844 and still evocative of pioneer days, in spite of its suburban neighbours. Listed as an historic site by the National Trust, the original furniture is on display and guides give tours of the property.

With its broad main street, **Sorrento**, bearing little resemblance to its Italian namesake, has a charm all of its own, while posh **Portsea** does its best to maintain its exclusivity. On the outer rim of the peninsula, the 'back beaches' face the ocean surf of Bass Strait. For a long time off limits as defence land, **Point Nepean** can now be explored, if not by car, then by the transporter based at the National Park Orientation Centre.

The Peninsula Freeway and South Eastern Arterial can be used to speed your return to Melbourne.

Right: Port Phillip Bay begins at the tip of the Mornington Peninsula

VICTORIA DRIVES

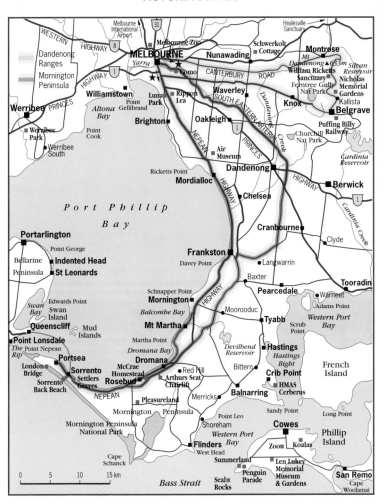

Melbourne International Airport
Melbourne Zoo
31
8
WESTERN HIGHWAY
Healesville Sanctuary
Schwerkolt Cottage
MELBOURNE
Yarra
Nunawading
Montrose
Mt Dandenong ▲633m
Silvan Reservoir
William Ricketts Sanctuary
Ferntree Gully Nat Park
Nicholas Memorial Gardens
Kallista
Knox
Belgrave
Puffing Billy Railway
Churchill Nat Park
Como
Waverley
CANTERBURY ROAD
SOUTH EASTERN ARTERIAL
Dandenong Creek
1
HIGHWAY
PRINCES
Williamstown
Point Gellibrand
Luna Park
Rippon Lea
Oakleigh
Altona Bay
Brighton
Point Cook
Air Museum
Werribee
Werribee Park
Werribee South
Cardinia Reservoir
Cardinia Creek
Dandenong Ranges
Mornington Peninsula
Ricketts Point
Mordialloc
Dandenong
Berwick
HIGHWAY
1
Chelsea
Port Phillip Bay
Cranbourne
Clyde
Portarlington
Point George
Bellarine Peninsula
Indented Head
St Leonards
Frankston
Davey Point
Langwarrin
Baxter
Tooradin
Warneet
Adams Point
Pearcedale
Schnapper Point
Mornington
Balcombe Bay
Edwards Point
Swan Bay
Swan Island
Queenscliff
Mud Islands
Mt Martha
Moorooduc
Tyabb
Scrub Point
Western Port Bay
Devilbend Reservoir
Martha Point
Point Nepean
The Rip
Point Lonsdale
London Bridge
Portsea
Sorrento
Settlers
Graves
Sorrento Back Beach
Dromana Bay
Dromana
McCrae Homestead
Rosebud
Red Hill
Arthurs Seat Chairlift
Bittern
Hastings
Hastings Bight
Crib Point
HMAS Cerberus
French Island
NEPEAN
Pleasureland
Merricks
Balnarring
Sandy Point
Long Point
Mornington Peninsula
Point Leo
Shoreham
Western Port Bay
Cowes
Phillip Island
Zoo
Koalas
Mornington Peninsula National Park
Flinders
West Head
Summerland
Len Lukey Memorial Museum & Gardens
San Remo
Cape Woolamai
Cape Schanck
Bass Strait
Seal Rocks
Penguin Parade

0   5   10   15 km

SOUTH AUSTRALIA

NORTHERN TERRITORY

Stevenson Creek

Witjira National Park

▲ 1231m
Amata
1440m
Mt Woodroffe ▲
● Pukatja

Musgrave Ranges

Granite Downs

Alberga

Fregon ●

Everard Range

● Marla

Neales

Macumba ●

87

Oodnadatta

Roadhouse

OODNADATTA TRACK

Great Victoria Desert

WESTERN

AUSTRALIA

Stuart

Ranges

● Coober Pedy

STUART HIGHWAY

● Dey-Dey Lake

● Lake Maurice

Maralinga ●

Cook

Trans-Australian Railway

Tarcoola

Glendam

Kingoonya

Lake Harris

Lake Gairdr

Koonalda Cave

Nullarbor Plain

Nullarbor

EYRE HIGHWAY

1

Yalata

Lake Everard

Lake Acraman

Nundroo

Penong

Lake Gairdr

Nullarbor National Park

Head of Bight

Coorabie

Cactus Beach

Ceduna

Yardea

Gawler Range

Streaky Bay

1

EYRE HIGHW

Port Kenny

FLINDERS HIGHWAY

Kyancutta

Ey

Venus Bay

Elliston

Lock

Penir

Flinders Island

FLINDERS HIGHWAY

Mount Hope

Tur
Ba

Coffin Bay Nat Park

Port Lincoln

Cape Carnot

Linc
Nat P

Great Australian Bight

0   100   200   300 km

1   2   3

REGION HIGHLIGHTS ◄◄◄◄◄

SOUTH AUSTRALIA

Two claims to fame
South Australia, Australia's driest state, covers an eighth of the continent's total area, but has a population of less than 1.5 million. South Australia also has the distinction of being the only state established without the aid of convict labour – a fact of which it is particularly proud.

Wowsers no more
A wowser originally meant someone who didn't know how to enjoy himself. The epithet was maliciously applied to the good citizens of Adelaide because of their supposed piety and apparent aversion to letting their hair down. The visitor to South Australia is unlikely to see much trace of this today, least of all in Adelaide. It may still be a city of churches, but it is now also a city of restaurants, watered by the products of its wineries. And it was in South Australia that the country's first nudist beach was opened, at Maslins on the coast south of Adelaide.

South Australia Virtually all the inhabitants of Australia's third largest state live along the fertile coasts of its gulf lands and southeastern plains, three-quarters of them in Greater Adelaide. Northwards from this tamed littoral with its almost Mediterranean climate stretches an immense and arid area of Outback and desert, some of it bearing the traces of failed European settlement, and huge tracts of it returned to the Aborigines. This is a land of sharp differences, with a capital that is the most elegant and obviously cultured of all Australian cities.

In the beginning South Australia was not a prison colony but a 'province', settled by free people (mostly from the south of England, but many also from Germany) under the auspices of the South Australia Company. The first group landed from the *Buffalo* in 1836, but the true founding father was Colonel William Light, a brilliant and unorthodox character whose visionary plan for Adelaide has shaped the city to the present day. The development of the colony was erratic. Within a few years of its foundation it was only saved from economic collapse by the discovery of copper at Kapunda and Burra. Attempts to push the frontier of agriculture north were defeated by long years of drought, although the peninsula corn lands flourished.

For many years Adelaide remained simply the centre of a vast agricultural and mining area, its affairs conducted by merchants who lived sober lives ('wowsers' to other Australians). Much of the tone of South Australian life was indeed set by the seriousness with which its Nonconformist (British) or Lutheran (German) citizens took their religion; not for nothing was Adelaide known as the city of churches.

The vulnerability of what was an almost entirely rural economy became apparent in the years of the great Depression, and following World War II the state underwent an industrial transformation, with shipyards at Whyalla and motor vehicle manufacture at Adelaide's satellite town of Elizabeth. In the 1970s, these activities showed themselves to be vulnerable in their turn, and South Australia, along with much of the rest of the country, has its share of economic and financial troubles.

Given the state's range of landscapes, it is not surprising that tourism is of increasing importance. Adelaide attracts visitors with its biennial Arts Festival (even-numbered years), as well as by the elegance of its townscape and its reputation for good living. A new attraction is the Womadelaide festival – a biennial (odd-numbered years) celebration of world music. It is no longer possible to take a luxury cruise from Port Adelaide around the two great inlets, Spencer Gulf and Gulf St Vincent, but an immensely long coastline offers endless opportunites for water-based activities of all kinds at unspoilt towns such as **Robe**, south of the spectacular Coorong National Park. Coastal landscapes vary from the wild isolation of rugged headlands to delightful little fishing ports and resorts. Offshore islands invite those with a taste for escapism, the biggest of them, Kangaroo Island, having a superb range of (accessible) wildlife.

South Australia is the starting point for many of the country's great tourist itineraries. Tarcoola is the junction for two trains of almost legendary reputation – the *Ghan*, on its way north to Alice Springs in the Red Centre, and the *Indian Pacific*, pausing here on its transcontinental run westward across the Nullarbor.

Bethany's Lutheran church and hall in the Barossa Valley

Dashing Don's derring-do
South Australia's Premier from 1967–8 and again from 1970–9, Don Dunstan not only cultivated a progressive and dynamic image, but was instrumental in dragging his state into the late 20th century. Under his leadership, South Australia passed legislation outlawing racial and sexual discrimination. Pastor Sir Douglas Nicholls, a distinguished Aborigine, became Governor, while a police chief who refused to reveal who had instructed him to keep secret files on MPs and other potential subversives was dismissed. The ex-Premier now runs a popular restaurant, Don's Table, in the Adelaide suburb of Norwood.

It is possible to tour some of the World Heritage-listed Naracoorte Caves

'The reasons that led me to fix Adelaide where it is I do not expect to be generally understood or calmly judged at the present. My enemies, however, by disputing their validity in particular, have done me the good service of fixing the whole of the responsibility upon me. I am perfectly willing to bear it; and I leave it to posterity, and not to them, to decide whether I am entitled to praise or to blame.'

Adelaide

Australia's fifth largest city likes to be known for its biennial Festival of the Arts, its restaurants and its generally high cultural tone. Many of its early citizens were religious dissenters escaping from persecution in their home countries; without the 'convict stain', people pursued both work and recreation with what seemed from the outside to be a kind of earnest dullness, in rationally planned surroundings of dignified elegance.

These surroundings were the vision of one man, Colonel William Light, who, as South Australia's Surveyor-General, drew up a brilliant plan in 1836, to which the city has adhered ever since. Having found a suitable site on the banks of the little River Torrens, he set out a square-mile grid of streets on the south bank. The

Shop 'til you drop

Adelaide is fast becoming a shopper's paradise. The Central Markets are excellent for food and produce, while the Lion Arts Centre and the Jam Factory Craft and Design Centre sell fine contemporary art and crafts. North Adelaide is the place for antiques and quality clothing.

Son of a gun

Although 19th-century Britain produced a number of plans for ideal towns, most Australian cities developed in a totally chaotic way. It was left to an army officer, illegitimate offspring of the English founder of Penang in Malaysia and a Eurasian woman, to conceive and implement the ambitious plan for Adelaide. William Light had served as an intelligence officer with the Duke of Wellington, gaining his rank of colonel during secondment to the army of Spain; he revelled in the commission to survey and plan not only the site of Adelaide but much of the rest of the new province. Married to the daughter (also illegitimate) of the Duke of Richmond, he left his wife at home in England, and when he died (probably from overwork) in 1839, was refused the last rites because he was living in open sin with another lady.

central thoroughfare was impressively wide, and the whole was enlivened with a series of squares. A green belt around the city was to remain parkland in perpetuity, a fit setting for public buildings such as Government House; on the far bank of the river was the fine suburb of North Adelaide. In spite of opposition at the time, in spite of the building boom of the 1970s and 1980s, and in spite of the motor car, all these elements are in place today, helping make Adelaide the most agreeable of cities.

It is rare in a metropolis to be able to live in a Victorian villa looking on to parkland, walk or cycle to work in the city centre, spend the evening at the theatre, then walk home again, but here people can. The majority however, inhabit the suburbs that have spread across the coastal plain between the magnificent beaches along the gulf and the Adelaide Hills to the east.

Sailing is a popular pursuit at Port Adelaide, the city's harbour town

Festive season
They say in Adelaide that the Adelaide Festival Centre cost less to build than it did to carpet Sydney's Opera House. The centre is busy all year round, with two major theatres and two outdoor performance areas. Its plaza, designed by the German environmental sculptor Otto Hajek, has been described as Australia's biggest outdoor art work.
Adelaide's Festival of the Arts is held in even-numbered years for a period of three weeks in February/March. Warm days and mild nights help create the right atmosphere for a wonderful choice of events – opera, ballet, concerts, theatre, exhibitions, children's activities and a literary festival – all within walking distance of each other in this compact city.

▶▶ **Adelaide Botanic Gardens**   *129C4*
North Terrace
Founded in 1855, these 20 hectares of trees, shrubs, lawns and lakes glitter with an array of heritage buildings. As well as the Museum of Economic Botany, there is the Simpson Shade House, the 1868 Victoria House with its giant waterlily, and the wonderful Palm House, brought out from Germany in the 1870s and completely restored in 1996. But most extraordinary of all is the soaring **Bicentennial Conservatory**, an environmental capsule of great sophistication, within whose hi-tech skin there flourishes a profusion of plants from the tropical rain forests of North Australia and its neighbours.

▶▶▶ **Art Gallery of South Australia**   *128C3*
North Terrace
Behind its classical portico this refined building houses one of the country's most important collections of Australian, European and Asian art. Some of the paintings by Australian artists are familiar, seeming to encapsulate key aspects of the country's character, like the stampeding sheep in Tom Roberts' *The Breakaway* of 1891 or the subtle beach flirtation depicted in Charles Conder's *Holiday at Mentone* (1888). The Aboriginal section is particularly good, and the gallery also features a large collection of Rodin's works.

▶ **Glenelg**   *128A1*
Once Adelaide's most popular seaside centre, with splendid sandy beaches stretching far in either direction, suburban Glenelg still has plenty of charm, epitomised by the 1920s trams that link it to the city's Victoria Square (a 30-minute trip). It was here that Governor Hindmarsh and the first band of settlers landed in 1836.

▶▶ **Migration Museum**   *128C3*
82 Kintore Avenue
Housed in the restored buildings of the city's Destitute Asylum, this innovative institution presents the story of the immigrant groups who founded South Australia. The museum tells stories of courage and hope – such as the successful adaptation to life in a new country – as well as disappointment and difficulty. This is an essential visit for anyone trying to get to grips with how Australia has evolved.

► North Adelaide 128D3

Adelaide's classiest and oldest suburb has many fine houses. Melbourne Street has the kind of shops, restaurants and boutiques you might expect, while O'Connel Street is famous for its excellent restaurants and al fresco wining and dining. St Peter's Cathedral boasts the heaviest bells in the southern hemisphere, and at Light's Vision Lookout, a statue of the good colonel surveys the city he created.

►► Port Adelaide 128C1

Some 10km northwest of the landlocked city centre, Adelaide's harbour town has been deserted by most of its maritime traffic, leaving it free to concentrate on its fascinating past; it has South Australia's largest collection of distinguished 19th-century buildings. Among the long quayside sheds is the bright red 1869 lighthouse, overlooking a number of historic ships when they are in dock. A short distance inland on Lipson Street are a couple of first-rate museums, each on its own well worth the bus or train trip out from the city centre. The main building of the fascinating **South Australian Maritime Museum►►** is an old bond store, while the **Port Dock Station Museum►►**, featuring 26 locomotives and steam train rides, is the biggest of its kind in the country.

►►► South Australian Museum 128C3
North Terrace

This is the state's museum of natural history with all the geological and zoological displays one would expect, but its main attraction is probably its outstanding collection of Aboriginal artefacts. These are presented in an imaginative and accessible fashion, making the museum the best such place in the country to study the past life of the original Australians.

►► Tandanya National Aboriginal 129B4
Cultural Institute
253 Grenfell Street

This exciting addition to Adelaide's developing East End offers an exceptional opportunity to learn about contemporary Aboriginal culture. There are dance and theatre performances, meetings, talks and celebrations, constantly changing exhibitions, and demonstrations and sales of arts and crafts.

Other Adelaide sights
The 19th-century Ayers House with its curving bays is perhaps the most elegant structure in North Terrace. Seven times premier of South Australia, Sir Henry Ayers used his home for state functions; the hub of city life, its ballroom was washed down with milk to give it a smooth and fast surface.

Not to be confused with Parliament House up the street (still lacking the dome planned for it), the Tudor-style Old Parliament House in North Terrace was home to South Australia's first parliament.

Ngurunderi's dreaming track
An extensive display in the South Australian Museum tells the story of Ngurunderi, one of the great ancestral dreaming figures of the Ngarrindjeri people. His travels from high up the Murray River to Kangaroo Island in pursuit of his miscreant wives explain many of the features of the river and coastal landscape. The bends and meanders of the Murray were made by the giant cod Ponde sweeping his tail, while Long Island near Murray Bridge is Ngurunderi's spear, which missed its target. At Middleton he killed a seal, whose dying gasps can still be heard among the rocks today. As his wives fled west along the causeway which then connected Kangaroo Island to the mainland, Ngurunderi caused the waters to rise and drown them. They turned into the rocky Pages Islands, while Ngurunderi rose to become a star in the Milky Way.

Impressive Ayers House, now open to the public

The Tandanya National Aboriginal Cultural Institute in the East End

Walk Green spaces and old buildings

See map on page 128.

Linking some of Adelaide's splendid green spaces with North Terrace, the city's boulevard, this walk passes through the central shopping mall before ending in Victoria Square, the geographical heart of the city.

A walkway leads to North Terrace from the controversial **Adelaide Festival Centre** complex overlooking parkland along the River Torrens. Stay on the leafy north side of North Terrace to admire the sequence of historic buildings and monuments revealed as you walk eastwards. The post-modern forecourt of the Hyatt Hotel contrasts with the grandiose railway station building now housing the city's Casino. The **Old Parliament House** of 1855 seems very modest compared with its successor, the latter ultra-conservative in design though it was only completed in 1939. **Government House** behind its garden wall gives way to the State

Library (1884), the **South Australian Museum** (1895), and the **Art Gallery of South Australia** (opened in 1881). The south side of the Terrace presents a more or less continuous wall of imposing edifices, ending with the fine colonial mansion of **Ayers House** and the exuberant Botanic Hotel with its tiers of verandas.

The detour into the **Botanic Gardens** should take in the elegant old Palm House and the truly remarkable Bicentennial Conservatory. In Rundle Street are the East End Market Buildings, but you should not miss the **Tandanya National Aboriginal Cultural Institute** in Grenfell Street just to the south. Rundle Mall is a cheerful pedestrian precinct, the main focus of city shopping. It leads into King William Street, Adelaide's main north–south routeway. The General Post Office and Town Hall stand at the northern end of Victoria Square, where the city's last surviving original tramway waits to take its passengers down to the sea at **Glenelg**.

Dry as dust The interminable flatness of the interior is broken only by two mountain ranges worthy of the name. Part of the vast Pitjantjatjara Aboriginal Lands, the Musgrave Ranges in the far northwest parallel the other ridges of the Red Centre just over the boundary with the Northern Territory. The ancient Flinders Ranges run some 500km from near the head of Spencer Gulf towards Lake Eyre, their most spectacular single feature being the magnificent natural fortress of **Wilpena Pound**, an 80sq km natural amphitheatre. Northward are the interminable sand ridges of the **Simpson Desert**, laid down by winds that ceased to blow in prehistoric times. In the rare bouts of rain, its sparse cover of spinifex is supplemented by a sudden tapestry of wildflowers, while its inhabitants include unique creatures like hopping mice and marsupial moles. The Sturt Stony Desert is a virtually impassable plain of wind-polished stones known as gibbers, while , much further south, **Mount Remarkable** has deep gorges.

The wildlife-rich south Towards the sea, the near-total aridity of South Australia's interior gives way to a Mediterranean-type climate, whose hot summers are relieved by relatively cool and moist winters. A century and a half of settlement has converted much of the area into productive farmland. However, there is still plenty of wildness left, particularly along the coast from Coffin Bay and Lincoln national parks at the tip of the Eyre Peninsula in the west to **Coorong National Park** in the far southeast. In between are the dunes and cliffs of **Innes National Park** on the toe of Yorke Peninsula and the scenic and wildlife wonders of **Kangaroo Island**. The extraordinary Coorong begins at the mouth of the Murray where the great river has broken through to the sea. A 100km beach stretches eastward, backed by superb sand dunes and a long, shallow lagoon. The haunt of a multitude of birds, this is one of the best places for observing the habits of the pelican.

Australia's dead sea
Much of the huge expanse of Lake Eyre is below sea level. When filled with water, an event that has only occurred three times in living memory, the lake becomes alive with birds. On the map it appears to be fed by rivers 1,000km long, but their waters usually run dry long before they reach the lake. Its salty surface, flat and featureless, made it ideal for Donald Campbell's successful attempt on the world land-speed record in 1964.

133

The Remarkable Rocks on Kangaroo Island are famous for their strangely weathered granite shapes

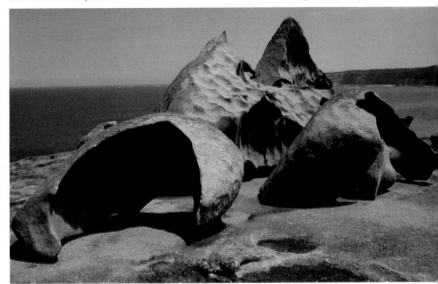

How to travel

The Ghan
One of Australia's most famous railway lines runs from Adelaide to Alice Springs in the Northern Territory. The route is named after the Afghan (and other) camel drivers and trains that the railway superseded in the late 19th century (also see page 189).

By car
Roads in the relatively densely populated coastal area are good and the main interstate highways are all surfaced. In the Outback, roads are of variable quality; check conditions first and take adequate provisions (see page 143).

By water
You can take the car ferry to Kangaroo Island from Cape Jervis, or a passenger ferry from either here, or the Adelaide suburb of Glenelg.

A diesel commuter bus on Adelaide's 'O-Bahn' line, the world's longest guided busway

By air Only 6km from the city centre, Adelaide's airport is served by both international and domestic flights, linking it to all important destinations in Australia and many overseas ones too. The size and geography of South Australia make flights within the state an attractive proposition. There are frequent or at least daily flights between Adelaide and places on the Eyre Peninsula like Port Lincoln and Ceduna, or to Kangaroo Island. Other flights serve Coober Pedy and Oodnadatta, Broken Hill in NSW and Birdsville in Queensland, though most people heading into the Outback get there by road.

By bus and coach Adelaide has a comprehensive metropolitan transport system with integrated ticketing, mostly based on buses, but also deploying suburban trains. A free bus service runs frequently between the main railway station and the Glenelg tram terminus in Victoria Square. The Transadelaide office in King William Street is helpful in planning trips around Greater Adelaide. The Glenelg Tram (a vintage 1929 model) and the replica Adelaide Explorer Tram, which tours the principal attractions on a two-and-a-half-hour circuit, are excellent as an introduction to Adelaide's sights. Long-distance coaches operate express services to all major destinations, and even quite remote places in the Outback may have a bus service of some kind, albeit an infrequent one. If you have a little time to spare, a fun way to travel between Adelaide and Melbourne or Alice Springs and take in many of the good things *en route* is by the very reasonably priced **Wayward Bus** (three days to Melbourne and eight to Alice).

By rail Long-distance trains leave the modern Keswick terminus at the southwestern edge of Adelaide city centre for Perth, Alice Springs, Melbourne, Broken Hill and Sydney. There are also services to Port Pirie and Mount Gambier. Adelaide's suburban network based at the main station on North Terrace is quite extensive, with services to places of interest like Port Adelaide and Belair in the Adelaide Hills.

Sprawling over the coastal plain, Greater Adelaide is defined to the west by the beaches of Gulf St Vincent and to the east by the gorges and steep slopes of these beautiful hills. Laced with scenic drives and walking trails through wild bushland, this is an area of richly varied landscapes, with some of the oldest settlements in South Australia. The forest has regrown since 'Black Sunday' of 2 January 1955, when an uncontrollable bush fire raged for days. As well as many vinyards, there are market gardens, orchards and any number of recreational attractions. The latter include the **Toy Factory**, its emblem the biggest rocking-horse in the world, the animals of the **Cleland Conservation Park** on the slopes of Mount Lofty, 20km southeast of Adelaide, the National Motor Museum at Birdwood (see below), and the Warrawong Wildlife Sanctuary at the village of Mylor.

►► **Arkaroola** 125D4

Formerly a vast sheep station, the Outback resort and wildlife sanctuary of Arkaroola is now the centre for exploring the northern parts of the spectacular Flinders Ranges. The ridges of the **Gammon Ranges National Park►►** glitter in the piercing light with quartz, fluorspar, haematites and other minerals. There are hot springs, a vast salt lake, Aboriginal history, and abundant wildlife.

►► **Birdwood** 125B4

The National Motor Museum is a good excuse for a 50km leisurely drive through the Adelaide Hills. Australia's biggest collection of vintage, veteran and classic cars is housed in the stone-built Birdwood Mill of 1852.

►► **Burra** 125B4

In the 1840s, the discovery of rich copper deposits in Kapunda and Burra rescued the ailing South Australian economy from its doldrums. Miners flocked to Burra, 155km north of Adelaide, from Britain's Celtic fringe, and within ten years had created the Monster Mine, 13km long and 6km across. Today, an 11km heritage trail includes a Cornish engine house, a mine captain's cottage, the inevitable jail, and the extraordinary riverbed dug-outs in which as many as 2,000 miners once lived.

Visitors and cuddly inmate at Cleland Conservation Park

Deutschland Down Under
Germans sailed into Sydney Harbour with the First Fleet, and many thousands have come since. South Australia was the destination in the 1830s and 1840s for whole communities from Brandenburg and Silesia suffering religious intolerance at the hands of the Prussian authorities. The first settlements were Klemzig, now overwhelmed by Adelaide's suburbia, Hahndorf and Lobethal in the Adelaide Hills, then in the Barossa Valley, originally called Neuschlesien (New Silesia).

Holden's heroes
Australia became one of the world's great car-owning nations from early on; by the beginning of the 1960s there was one car per family. Sir Edward Holden's car body firm merged with General Motors in 1931, initially assembling British and American vehicles. 'Australia's Own Car', the first Holden rolled off the production line in 1948, the millionth in 1962. With the advent of the cheap and reliable Japanese cars that now dominate whole sectors of the Australian market, Holden faltered, but in recent years has made something of a comeback.

The lives of the first
'opal gougers' on
display at Coober
Pedy's Old Timer's
opal mine

The Aussie Wave
When you're watching an
Australian game of cricket
on TV, why do the specta-
tors always seem to be
waving casual greetings to
unseen friends? It's not
friends, but the persistent
flies – as noted by Dutch
Commander Pelsaert in
1629: 'Such a host of flies
came to sit in the mouth
and eyes that they could
not be beaten off'. This
early observation would
seem to disprove the theo-
ry that the plague is due to
the dung dropped in quan-
tity by all those cattle in
the Outback. Australians
protect themselves from
this nuisance with door
and window screens at
home and, outside, with
insect repellent and as
nonchalant a wave as pos-
sible, since frantic swat-
ting seems only to
encourage the fly. No one,
but no one (except gullible
tourists) wears a Ned Kelly
hat with dangling corks to
keep the brutes away.

► ► **Coober Pedy** 124D3
The search for opals has created a landscape of mounds
and holes in the ground which greets travellers on the
Stuart Highway some 900km northwest of Adelaide. The
name Coober Pedy comes from the Aboriginal *kupa piti*,
meaning something like 'white fellow's burrow'; ever
since opals were first discovered here in 1915, enterprising folk from all over the world have been hacking away in
the hope of making their fortune, living underground in
order to escape the intolerable conditions on the surface,
which include temperatures in excess of 40°C. As well as
comfortable troglodyte homes, there are underground
shops, restaurants, hotels and even a couple of churches.
Several working mines in the area can be visited.

► **Eyre Peninsula** 124B3
This vast triangle faces the breakers of the Great
Australian Bight to the west and the sheltered waters of
the Spencer Gulf to the east. The northern base of the triangle is formed by the uninhabited Gawler Ranges, while
its southern apex is near the deep-water harbour of Port
Lincoln. The sandy soils of the peninsula support wheat
and sheep, while the subsoil yields iron ore, which is converted into steel in the coke ovens and rolling mills of
Whyalla, South Australia's second city. The Eyre Highway
runs in a great loop from the communications centre of
Port Augusta at the head of the Gulf towards the township of Ceduna, then on towards the Western Australian
border. The trip southwards along the Flinders and
Lincoln Highways takes in any number of fishing villages,
wild seascapes and unspoiled beaches. Both sea lions
and great white sharks may be seen at **Dangerous
Reef►**, some 20km off the cliffs and sand dunes that support the rich wildlife of **Lincoln National Park►**.

► ► **Fleurieu Peninsula** 125B4
Rolling countryside, attractive vineyards and a superb
coastline of wild cliffs and fine beaches provide a
wonderful holiday region right on Adelaide's doorstep.
Within half an hour's drive south of the city is the
McLaren Vale Wine District► ►, centred on the township of McLaren Vale in a setting of delightful hills. Further
south, around Willunga, the crop changes to almonds, a
froth of blossom in July. Studded with sandy beaches,
including the country's first official nudist one, Maslins,
the coast runs southwestward along the gulf to terminate
in rugged terrain around Cape Jervis. The far shore of
Backstairs Passage belongs to Kangaroo Island, reached
from here by ferry.
   Around the corner of the Cape the scenery is no less
spectacular, particularly at **Deep Creek Conservation
Park►** where the land falls sheer into the ocean. The
pleasant resort of **Victor Harbor** (see page 142) is guarded by the massive lump of rock known as Rosetta Head.
From here the vintage Cockle Train chuffs eastward past
the breakers crashing on the beaches of Port Elliot to the
charming town of Goolwa near the mouth of the Murray
River (see page 139). The story of the Murray, its history
and its current problems, are told at the impressive
interpretive centre at Signal Point (see page 138).

▶▶▶ Flinders Ranges 125C4

These ranges are made up of some of the world's most ancient rocks, marking the landscape northeast of Port Augusta with steep ridges and rugged gorges. Of no great height, the ranges owe their popularity to their vivid mineral colouring, dramatic landforms, fascinating plant and animal life, and the incredibly clear sunlight that reveals everything with visionary intensity. One of the gateways to the main part of the ranges is the township of Quorn, once an important railway junction, but now a small town of 1,500 or so people; here is the terminus of the **Pichi Richi steam railway▶**, part of the old Ghan line. Beyond Quorn, the road to Hawker passes close to the ruins of the old **Kanyaka Homestead**, constructed in the 1850s but long since abandoned, as well as the **Yourambulla Caves** with their Aboriginal wall-paintings.

The road to one of the country's great geological curiosities, the mighty natural stronghold of **Wilpena Pound▶▶▶**, turns off at Hawker. The Pound is a great oval, 20km long by about 8km wide, protected from the outside world by sheer 1,000m high walls, sloping steeply to a park-like interior where the flat floor is rich in sugar gums and, in spring, wildflowers. Like any great fortress, the Pound has only one way in, a narrow gorge cut by the Wilpena Creek, sometimes a torrent but usually just a trickle. A number of signposted trails of varying difficulty lead from the tourist centre near this entrance; anyone capable of walking 20km lengthwise and 500m vertically should consider the trek across the Pound and up to its highest point, St Mary's Peak. The reward is a stunning panorama over the whole area, including the dazzling white surface of salty Lake Torrens.

Beyond Wilpena on unsurfaced roads is the main part of the Flinders Ranges National Park, less spectacular perhaps but equally rewarding. Its wildlife includes hosts of birds and two types of kangaroo, as well as the rare yellow-footed rock wallaby.

Reptilian ramparts
Like so many features of the Aboriginal landscape, the walls of Wilpena Pound are perceived to be the petrified forms of the animal ancestors who assisted at their creation. Two giant serpents were lying in wait here for those who gathered to celebrate the very first ceremony of initiation of a young man into adulthood by circumcision. The serpents devoured them all, save for Wala the wild turkey, Yulu the kingfisher, and the young man himself, who all escaped and founded new tribes. The serpents expired, their bodies curling round to enclose the Pound for ever.

137

Typically dry, rugged scenery in the Flinders Ranges

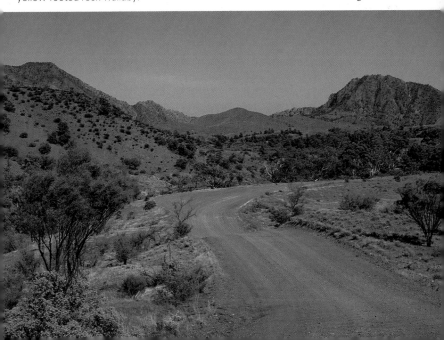

SOUTH AUSTRALIA

Take time for a trip up the broad Murray River...

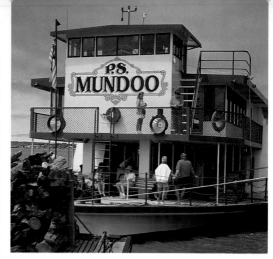

Sir Hans Heysen
Young Hans came to South Australia in 1884 at the age of seven. He is one of the best loved painters of the Australian landscape, whose natural features, particularly its trees and the play of light on them, he studied with great meticulousness. His charming works grace many an Australian gallery, and several can be seen at Hahndorf (where he lived for 60 years – his house and his studio can be visited) in the gallery of the Academy. Sir Hans is honoured by having the long-distance walking trail from the Fleurieu Peninsula to the Flinders Ranges named after him as well as part of the ranges themselves.

Australian seals
Of the three species of seal that inhabit Australian waters, two live around Kangaroo Island: the New Zealand fur seal and the Australian sea lion. The former were almost hunted to extinction in the 19th century; now protected, their numbers are recovering. Sea lions had a rather easier time, largely because they lack the warm coat of the fur seal.

►   **Goolwa**   *125B4*

This little riverport on the lower reaches of the mighty Murray River is the terminus for two trips in time: the old-timer Cockle Train which runs along the coast, and the paddlesteamer *Mundoo* which heads upriver. The **Signal Point Interpretive Centre►**, a model of its kind, has comprehensive displays on the theme of the Murray River yesterday and today.

►   **Hahndorf**   *125B4*

South Australia's second oldest German settlement (1839) can be found in a pretty location in the Adelaide Hills. Conveniently close to the South Eastern Freeway, Hahndorf makes the most of Teutonic tradition, with sausages, a Schutzenfest and waitresses in dirndls. Other attractions are the fine artworks of the Hahndorf Academy, an antique clock museum, and a strawberry farm. You can still see how the first settlers laid out their homes in orderly fashion along the main street.

►►► **Kangaroo Island**   *125B4*

Separated from the Fleurieu Peninsula by the deep straits known as Backstairs Passage, this is Australia's third largest island, a paradise for lovers of nature, with wild coastal landscapes and a particularly rich animal life. The island was named by the redoubtable Matthew Flinders; when the *Investigator* called here in 1802, his crew bagged a few of the locals, members of the sub-species of grey kangaroo still present in large numbers.

Most visitors arrive by ferry from the mainland at the little fishing port of Penneshaw on the Dudley Peninsula at the eastern end of the island. Fairy penguins frequent Christmas Cove just to the west of the harbour. Situated on Nepean Bay, Kingscote conserves some traces of its past in its oldest building, Hope Cottage of 1858. A surfaced main road heads past the airport into the interior, but the island's unique sights lie on the south coast.

Seal Bay►► is home to the country's largest colony of sea lions, seemingly indifferent to their many human visitors. Inland is the spectacular underground world of **Kelly Hill Caves**, discovered by a horse of that name which disappeared for ever into their still unexplored depths (Kelly's rider was saved). The surging waters around Cape du Couedic at the southwestern tip of the island are often visited by another marine mammal, the New Zealand fur seal. At the cape itself is awesome **Admirals Arch**, a natural bridge hollowed out in the limestone cliffs, while to the east are the aptly named **Remarkable Rocks►►**. Crowning a smoothly planed promontory, great blocks of granite have been eroded into strange shapes as if by the chisel of an abstract sculptor at his most imaginative.

Flinders Chase National Park► in the west is a reminder of how most of the island once looked – a wilderness of low-growing eucalyptus and shrubs. The headquarters of the park is at Rocky River, where friendly kangaroos, wallabies and emus are likely to pester you for your sandwiches. Koalas can be seen in the trees near by, and platypuses sometimes reveal themselves to the patient observer. The northwestern tip of the island is marked by the isolated lighthouse at Cape Borda. To the east, accessible by a rough road, stretches a spectacular coastline of cliffs sometimes rising to 200m and relieved by the occasional sandy bay.

►   Mount Gambier   125A5

The most important town in the southeast of South Australia had a turbulent volcanic past which only came to an end in relatively recent times, and which has left a legacy of cones and craters, one water-filled hole being in the very centre of town. Blue Lake, just outside town, changes colour mysteriously according to the season.

►   Murray River   125B5

The sluggish Murray meanders into South Australia near Renmark. From here to where it meets the sea at Lake Alexandrina, the river has become a mecca for those seeking lazy water-based holidays. Houseboats are particularly popular and these can be hired at Renmark, Berri, Loxton, Murray Bridge and several other towns.

Along the mighty Murray
Massive irrigation schemes have transformed the area into a vast orchard and vineyard, producing oranges, apples, pears and some 40 per cent of the state's grape harvest. Loxton Historical Village re-creates life as it was in the difficult early days of settlement. Many of the places along the river have a poignant feel about them, now that the great days of river trade have gone. There is another evocation of bygone times at the Old Tailem Bend Pioneer Village, and the paddlesteamer *Marion* moored at Mannum has been transformed into a floating museum.

139

...it's a wonderfully relaxing way to travel and view the striking scenery

■ **Vine cuttings were among the plants imported with the First Fleet, though it seems that the very first attempts to produce an Australian wine met with failure. However, persistence paid off, and today Australian wines enjoy a high reputation at home and abroad.** ■

Amber fluid in ice-cold tubes
Despite the rise in wine consumption, Australians remain some of the most committed beer drinkers in the world. A century ago, most beers tended to be top-fermented on the model of British ales and stouts, but these have steadily been displaced by bottom-fermented, lager types. More suited to the local climate, these were first brewed by Melbourne Germans as well as by the Foster brothers, originally from New York, who gave their name to what is probably the country's best-known beer.

A winery at Nuriootpa in the Barossa Valley

140

In the early days, the colonists seem to have preferred rum; later it was the country's excellent beer that was rated highly, in contrast to its wines which foreigners wrote off as crude imitations utterly failing to fulfil the promise of their labels.

Since the 1960s, however, things have changed – a result of increased prosperity, greater sophistication and, not least, the wine-drinking habits of many of the country's recent immigrants. A visit to a well-stocked wine merchant reveals a whole world of home-grown wine waiting to be discovered; like other great wine countries, Australia has no real need to import.

New South Wales This state has the most venerable vineyards, in the highly reputed Hunter Valley only a short journey north of Sydney. Wine has been produced in this area since the 1830s, and the valley's 50 or 60 wineries include some of Australia's best. Quality is the keynote here, whereas far to the southwest, in the irrigated valley of the Murrumbidgee River, producers concentrate on making as great a quantity as possible for distilling or fortifying.

Victoria Here there were once as many vineyards as NSW and SA had put together, but most were wiped out by phylloxera in the last century and have never been replanted. But Victorian wines could now be described as up and coming; there are many 'boutique' wines, some of the best from the **Yarra Valley** near Melbourne. The Great Western area is famous for sparkling wine.

Western Australia This state has its old vineyards too, planted along the Swan Valley in the early days of settlement. Perhaps the most interesting wines produced since the 1980s come from the **Margaret River** area.

Tasmania Lying closer to the South Pole, Tasmania is benefiting from a fashion for growing vines over a long ripening period in a cool climate, and there is an increasing number of vineyards (mostly around Hobart and Launceston) producing wines of fine quality.

South Australia This perhaps is the heartland of Australian wine, contributing about two-thirds of the country's total production. Most of the original vineyards of the Adelaide Plains have disappeared, and the huge quantities of grapes grown along the Murray are mostly turned into spirits, but other districts make wines of the highest reputation. Far off **Coonawarra** in the southeast produces wonderful reds on a tiny band of ultra-fertile volcanic soil, while **Adelaide Hills** is the most successful of the newer, cool climate regions. The boutique wines made among the rolling hills of the **McLaren Vale Wine District** are much in vogue and the Clare Valley's cool-climate vintages are excellent, but perhaps the best of all wine districts is the **Barossa Valley**, north of Adelaide. The combination of suitable soils, summer sun and reliable winter rain makes for an excellent product, grown amid a delightful landscape of old-established towns and villages and well-ordered countryside.

Tastings Australian vintners welcome visitors to their wineries. Though choosing can be difficult, the name of a reputable maker is generally reckoned to be a good starting point.

A rum corps
In the early days of New South Wales, the colony seems to have been kept afloat on an ocean of Bengal rum. Coinage was short, and in its absence rum took over many of the functions of the currency. Its sale was controlled by the officers of the New South Wales Corps, perhaps the least prestigious of the British regiments of the time. With little to occupy them in the way of genuine military activity, these gentlemen devoted their time to enriching themselves by all possible means, only stirring into martial action when their monopoly on rum was threatened by Governor Bligh. Their march on Government House on 26 January 1808 and arrest of the governor has become known disparagingly as the 'Rum Rebellion'.

141

SEPPELT

SEPPELT

HERMITAGE

~ GREAT WESTERN VINEYARD ~

750 mL WINE MADE IN AUSTRALIA 11.0% Alc

Petrel Cove at Victor Harbor

► **Naracoorte**   125A5

This southeastern town celebrates the prosperity of its pastoral surroundings in the excellent Sheep's Back wool museum. But most visitors come to marvel at the beauty of the World Heritage-listed **Naracoorte Caves►**. Only a few of the 60 or so known caves are accessible; there are guided tours into Blanche Cave and Alexandra Cave. In 1969, the bones of hitherto unknown marsupials, giant kangaroos and wombats were found in Victoria Cave. To the south, Bool Lagoon forms an important wetland region that attracts many thousands of waterbirds and other wildlife.

► **Strathalbyn**   125B4

Strathalbyn, at the neck of the Fleurieu Peninsula, has something indefinably Scottish about its dignified public buildings and neat public gardens on the banks of the Angas River. The town's past has been tidily gathered up and presented by the National Trust in two buildings, the 1858 police station and the 1867 court house.

► **Victor Harbor**   125B4

Victor Harbor's setting on Encounter Bay is superb, protected as it is from the ocean by both Rosetta Head ('the Bluff') and Granite Island, the latter reached across a causeway by horse-drawn tram and then by chairlift to its highest point. The island's colony of fairy penguins generally puts in an appearance in the evening.

► **Yorke Peninsula**   125B4

Some 240km long, this boot-shaped peninsula projects southwards, bounded by Spencer Gulf on the west and Gulf St Vincent to the east. South Australians come here for quiet holidays, fishing, boating and all kinds of water activities. Because there were few good roads in the past, little ports and landing places were dotted all along the coast, and you are sure to find a place that appeals. Towards the tip of the peninsula the coastline becomes more rugged, though there are still splendid beaches for swimming, surfing and diving.

■ **Strangely compelling, South Australia's 600,000sq km of Outback includes some of the least hospitable parts of the earth's surface. Distances are vast, water is sparse and summer temperatures are almost unbearable. Human life is spread thinly over cattle stations the size of small European states and 'towns' no bigger than hamlets. But the Outback exerts its own fascination; its arid beauty is liable to sudden and miraculous change when rain falls, as salt lakes fill with water and wildflowers carpet the surface of the land.** ■

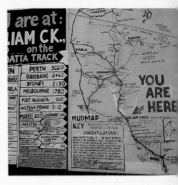

The great vastness of the South Australian Outback is penetrated by a small number of roads, tying together the isolated stations and settlements. Some are surfaced throughout, while others are still rightly referred to as 'tracks' and set a challenge for the more adventurous.

The Oodnadatta Track This track is part of a route north from Adelaide to Alice Springs, an alternative to the Stuart Highway. Beginning at Marree near the southern end of Lake Eyre, it follows the route taken by the explorer John McDouall Stuart and subsequently by the Overland Telegraph and the original Ghan railway line. Before the line was completed to the Alice, Oodnadatta was the railhead, goods being carried on from here on the backs of camels. The old station, now a museum, still stands.

The Strzelecki Track Named in honour of the Polish explorer Count Paul Strzelecki, this track runs northeast from Lyndhurst towards the Queensland border, following the trail used by the notorious Captain Starlight to drive stolen cattle down to southern markets. The track fringes the northern Flinders Ranges before crossing the interminable sandhills of the Strzelecki Desert and ending at Innamincka where the unfortunate Burke and Wills finally expired.

The Birdsville Track Also a droving route, this track was traced out by stockmen possibly more law-abiding than Captain Starlight but equally tough. Like the Oodnadatta Track it begins at Marree, but this track ends up in Queensland's Birdsville some 520km later.

Above: sign at William Creek, on the Oodnadatta Track

143

Birdsville Track sights
Along the track's course are hot springs, deserted homesteads, 9m-high sandhills and the wind-polished pebbles of the Sturt Stony Desert stretching to the horizon. The old frontier post of Birdsville with its famous pub comes alive when its annual horse races are held, an event yielding up to 50,000 empty beer cans!

BAROSSA VALLEY DRIVE

Drive **Barossa Valley**

The world-famous wine-growing district of the Barossa Valley is reached by an indirect but rewarding route through the varied countryside of the northern Adelaide Hills.

Adelaide's Payneham Road, then Gorge Road, lead to the rocky defile followed by the River Torrens, and so into the orchard country around **Gumeracha**. Among the many dams built to take advantage of the relatively high rainfall of these uplands, the **Barossa Reservoir** is a popular stopping point because of the curious sound effects produced by its 'Whispering Wall'. The little town of Lyndoch is the gateway to the Barossa Valley, while **Tanunda**, with its Historical Museum, is the cultural centre of what was Australia's most important German-settled area. All around are inviting wineries. **Bethany**, founded in 1842, sits beneath Mengler's Hill Lookout which offers a splendid panorama over the neatly ordered countryside. It is worth taking a detour to Angaston's **Collingrove Homestead**, now managed by the National Trust but once the centre of the million-acre estate belonging to the Angas family, founders of South Australia.

The route back to Adelaide passes through **Nuriootpa**, the commercial heart of the Barossa, the prosperous agricultural centre of **Gawler** and the satellite town of **Elizabeth**, home to many British immigrants in the post-war years.

MCLAREN VALE WINE REGION AND FLEURIEU PENINSULA

Bird attracting banksias

145

$\mathcal{D}rive$ McLaren Vale Wine Region and Fleurieu Peninsula

This drive leads through the attractive wine-growing countryside of the McLaren Vale Wine Region, across the rolling farmland of the Fleurieu Peninsula to the mouth of the Murray River and the dramatic ocean setting of Victor Harbor.

From Adelaide, Unley Road soon reaches the surrounding hills and climbs to the **Windy Point Lookout**, from where there is a fine panorama of city and suburbs sprawling over the coastal plain. The uplands are a favoured residential area for the city's more affluent commuters, but sub-urban housing soon gives way to farmland and forest, and to the vine-yards and welcoming wineries around McLaren Flat and McLaren Vale.

A beautifully engineered highway speeds you towards the coast through the broad 'waist' of the **Fleurieu Peninsula** to the small town of Goolwa. Here the excellent **Signal Point Interpretive Centre** tells all you could possibly want to know about the longest river in Australia, the Murray, whose waters flow through the bird-thronged barrage to the east of the town.

A short drive along the shore of Encounter Bay leads to **Victor Harbor** with its causeway linking the resort to Granite Island. The view of town and ocean is well worth the 100m climb up **the Bluff**, just to the west of the town.

Return to Adelaide by the direct route to complete a 200km drive.

146

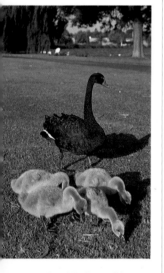

Perth's Swan River was named after the black swans that live here

WESTERN AUSTRALIA

REGION HIGHLIGHTS ◄◄◄◄◄

Virgin karri forests at Warren National Park, southwest of Pemberton

148

Western Australia Devotees of this state, the largest in Australia, are fond of producing maps showing how much of Europe or the USA could fit into its 2.5 million sq km. Western Australia is undoubtedly *big*. It is also very empty, much of it consisting of variations on the theme of desert – voids of various kinds extend from the desert beaches of the Indian Ocean in the far northwest to the cliffs of the Nullarbor being eaten away by the Southern Ocean. A further factor is its isolation. Perth is generally reckoned to be the most remote city on earth; its nearest neighbour, Adelaide, is 2,700km away and Sydney is 4,200km away. For all this, the West provides some of Australia's great holiday destinations.

Friendly, sunny **Perth** is every Australian's second favourite city next to Sydney; until recently, this was the place other Australians migrated to in search of the good life at an affordable price. It certainly ranks high in the hierarchy of Australian cities, not least because of its stunning site on the beautiful Swan River just inland from its port of **Fremantle**, one of the country's most atmospheric historic towns.

Perth and its metropolitan region dominate the coastal plain spreading westward from the **Darling Range**, Western Australia's modest equivalent of the Great Dividing Range. With a Mediterranean climate, an often spectacularly rugged coastline, fine forests and the lion's share of fertile farmland, this is the most densely inhabited part of the state. Inland stretches the Wheat Belt, its yields of grain dependent on a variable rainfall, gradually merging into the scrublands which herald the desert itself. Straggling along the desert rim is a line of gold-rush towns, some defunct, some, like **Kalgoorlie-Boulder**, still with plenty of kick in them.

In the rest of the state, people are thinly spread. Towns, none of them of any size, are widely spaced along the immensely long coast. The old pearling base of **Broome** is enjoying a revival as a tourist centre, while **Port Hedland** deals efficiently with the iron ore being extracted in huge quantities from its Pilbara hinterland. Here are strange new settlements of prefabricated buildings, erected quickly to create air-conditioned shelter from the fierce temperatures for miners and prospectors.

But far more than urban amenities, it is the grandeur of Western Australia's natural landscapes that visitors will want to experience. The surfacing of the highways to the north and the northwest of the state has encouraged visitors to explore areas previously considered to be well off the beaten track. Even more than the harsh vastness of the **Hamersley Range** in the Pilbara, the far-off tropical **Kimberley** is attracting tourists to its wealth of natural wonders, sometimes as part of a trip to the adjoining Northern Territory.

History New Holland was the unlikely name bestowed in the early 1600s on the western rim of the unknown continent by Dutch seamen on their way to their country's possessions in the East Indies. They would race eastwards across the Indian Ocean, then sail along the Australian coast towards Java. Sometimes they were travelling too fast, and Western Australia's earliest European history is studded with the names of famous

On top of the state
The Stirling Range is the highest mountain range in southwestern Australia, and is carpeted by wildflowers during the spring (September to October). The area has numerous hiking trails, but don't forget your waterproofs as sudden rainstorms are common.

Tropical north
Parts of the Kimberley are subject to monsoonal rainfall; rivers which may have been reduced to a few pools in the Dry quickly fill and spill over the surrounding plains. In the far north are habitats of such biological value that their national park status, far from opening them up to the public, has led to the banning of all access.

ships such as the *Zeewijk* and *Batavia* wrecked on the reefs and shoals of its treacherous coastline.

The first British impressions were not favourable either; William Dampier's reports in 1688–9 on the barren north-west were distinctly discouraging. It was a (largely imaginary) French threat in the 1820s that impelled the British to add the west of the continent to the Empire; the port of Albany was founded on the south coast in 1826, and in 1829 Lieutenant-Governor Stirling and his band of free settlers established the Swan River colony where Perth now stands. Progress was fitful, and the colony was only saved by a massive infusion of convict labour in the 1850s and 1860s, then in the 1880s and 1890s by the opening up of the Eastern Goldfields, where the combined city of Kalgoorlie-Boulder still thrives on mining today.

In the early 20th century, Western Australia's adherence to the Federation was only secured by a promise to link it to the rest of the country by the construction of the Transcontinental Railway. Even as late as the 1930s, a referendum revealed a majority in favour of secession. Today, in spite of extraordinary financial mismanagement on the part of politicians, and unscrupulous entrepreneurs like the now imprisoned Alan Bond, the west's position seems to be secure, based on massive postwar immigration and seemingly unlimited mineral wealth.

A land apart
Despite modern transport and communication facilities, western Australia is still very much a land apart. Anything east of the south Australian border – be it Adelaide, Melbourne or Sydney – is often referred to under the blanket term 'Eastern States', and West Australians are more likely to holiday in Bali than on the Great Barrier Reef.

The Stirling Range National Park near Albany in the southwest

149

Perth

Perth, like Sydney, is an inspired fusion of fine building in a splendid natural setting. The view eastward from **Kings Park** reveals one of the world's great urban panoramas – to the left the office towers of the city centre glittering in the constant bright sunlight, to the right the glorious stretch of Perth Water alive with pleasure craft.

The city seems to offer its citizens most of the ingredients of the good life: a Californian-style climate unspoiled by smog; attractive homes in every price group in suburbs that range from the merely pleasant to the opulent; and every kind of outdoor playground, from the generous sweeps of the Swan River and superb ocean beaches, to lavish parklands that bring the bush almost into the city centre.

Suburbs

The plush succession of waterside suburbs you pass if you take the ferry to South Perth (see panel opposite) may tempt you to sell up and move here without further ado. This is where the millionaires of the 'Golden West' choose to live, with easy access to their yachts at the marina or yacht club.

Covering a large area of bushland and parks, Kings Park in the centre of Perth is the ideal place to relax and take time out from sightseeing

City of plenty Perth used to be known for its dullness. True or false, this is certainly no longer the case. Contrasting with the historic and lavishly restored His Majesty's Theatre, the home of Western Australian opera and dance, the Concert Hall and the Entertainment Centre have been major recent additions to the city's cultural life. Another new landmark is the white tower of the Burswood Casino, biggest in the southern hemisphere. New buildings of high cultural significance (the Art Gallery and State Library) have been grouped together to form a new urban focal point. The city centre is quite compact. A network of futuristic walk-ways straddles streets and tunnels through buildings, linking transport terminals, shopping arcades, pedestrian precincts and civic plazas. Spectacular sights may be few, but a stroll reveals a host of urban pleasures.

Riverside Perth
True Perth is a synthesis of city and river, and you should make sure that you enjoy this not only from Kings Park but from the river itself. At the very least, take the ferry across to South Perth (and back again!), but better still travel by ferry to Rottnest Island or Fremantle. For much of the latter part of the journey, your eye will return again and again to the unforgettable image of the city's clustering towers rising over the functionally elegant Narrows Bridge.

Perth, viewed from the Kings Park area, is a most attractive city

Sightsee by water
Ferries connect the jetty at Barrack Square in Perth with South Perth, Fremantle and Rottnest Island, and there are trips upstream too, visiting the early colonial landscapes and wineries of the upper reaches of the Swan River. Cruise ships still occasionally call at Fremantle.

Sun, sand and surf
Perth's suburban beaches are the finest in Australia. The white sands and clear blue Indian ocean waters of Cottesloe, Scarborough, Swanbourne and many other beaches are far superior to those of more famous Bondi – Sydney's favourite strip of sand.

▶▶   **Art Gallery of Western Australia**   150C3

Perth Cultural Centre, James Street, Northbridge
Generously housed in a spacious modern building, the gallery has a fine collection of mostly Australian artworks, including an acclaimed array of Aboriginal art. There are also collections of traditional and contemporary crafts, ceramics, textiles, jewellery, woodwork and glass, and the museum extends its influence beyond its doors with sculpture gracing the plaza linking the city centre to Northbridge. Free guided tours happen regularly.

▶   **Aviation Museum**   150A2

Bull Creek
Australia's largest collection of historic aircraft and aviation memorabilia is to be found in the southern suburb of Bull Creek. The aggressive elegance of war winners like the Avro Lancaster and Supermarine Spitfire contrasts with the workaday lines of the famous Dakota, first built in the 1930s and still flying today. The museum contains 23 aircraft and features engines, models, photographs and memorabilia.

▶▶   **Kings Park**   150C1

Few cities in the world enjoy anything like this great swathe of natural landscape on the very edge of the city centre. From the founding of the colony in 1829 it was always intended that this area, known as Mount Eliza, should be kept as an open space. About two-thirds of the park is bushland, glorious with wildflowers in the spring, and accessible by scenic drive as well as on foot. Fraser Avenue, with its monuments, memorials and lines of lemon gums, gives an unequalled panorama of Perth in its Swan River setting, while the **Botanic Gardens** encapsulate the incomparable floral wealth of Western Australia in a series of richly planted gardens.

▶   **Perth Zoo**   150A2

20 Labouchere Road, South Perth
An excellent reason for taking the ferry to South Perth, the city's zoo has a fine collection of exotic animals as

well as Australian creatures like emus, koalas and kangaroos, which you can meet in the Australian Wildlife Park. The zoo is famous for its research and breeding programmes for endangered species, and one resident of Western Australia now on the endangered list, the little termite-eating marsupial, the numbat, is provided with its own quarters. The zoo is constantly developing; there are innovative features like Harmony Farm (which demonstrates earth-friendly techniques for living harmoniously on Planet Earth), the Conservation Discovery Centre, a Nocturnal House, and the African Savannah, a complete reconstruction of an African ecosystem.

▶▶▶ Western Australian Museum   150C3
Francis Street, Northbridge
This fascinating museum complex comprises a cluster of buildings of many different dates and styles contributing in their various ways to the attractive ambience of Perth's Cultural Centre. Half a day spent here is no substitute for a month spent exploring the natural wonders and human heritage of Western Australia, but it will go a long way towards it!

The centrepiece of the complex is the modern Francis Street building, which has a **Marine Gallery** dominated by the awesome 24m skeleton of a blue whale, as well as an **Aboriginal Gallery** which is a magnificent attempt to review in a comprehensive and sympathetic way the art, religion and culture of the first Australians. Traditional displays of mammals and fossils are in the old Beaufort Street building, while the history of white settlement of the west is evoked in the cool spaces of the stone-built **Old Gaol**, Perth's original prison complex, which dates from the 1850s.

All that glitters
Perth is home to several shops that sell precious and semi-precious stones. You can buy pearls from Broome, opals from Coober Pedy and, not least, pink diamonds from the state's own Argyle diamond mines.

Suburban attractions
There is much to see beyond Perth's city centre. In the southern suburb of Canning Vale you can tour the famous Swan Brewery, while the northern coast offers the Underwater World aquarium and Hillary's Boat Harbour at Sorrento. The historic port of Fremantle lies downstream, while a cruise to the Swan Valley wineries is highly recommended.

153

The mock-Tudor London Court, built in 1937, runs between the Hay Street Mall and St George's Terrace

Walk Perth city centre

See map on page 150.

This walk of about 4km takes in many of the contrasts of old and new that make Perth such a stimulating capital city.

A few steps north of Perth's City Railway Station are the buildings and plazas of the **Cultural Centre**. The pedestrian mall south of the station is dominated by the handsome sandstone **General Post Office** (1925). The junction of Hay Street Mall with Barrack Street is overlooked by the tower of the **Town Hall**, behind which is **St George's Cathedral** and the cottage-style **Deanery** (1859) facing on to **St George's Terrace**.

Government House was built in the mid-19th century and enclosed in luxuriant gardens. Following the slope down towards The Esplanade fronting the Swan River are **Stirling Gardens**, laid out as a botanical garden in 1829, and **Supreme Court Gardens**, laid out on reclaimed land. Next to the Supreme Court itself is the city's oldest surviving building, the **Old Court House** (1837).

The mock-Tudor arcade known as **London Court** links St George's Terrace with Hay Street Mall. In spite of its ecclesiastical Gothic appearance, No 139 St George's Terrace is not a church but the National Trust-listed **Old Perth Boy's School**. Further west, next to a splendid Port Jackson fig tree, is **The Cloisters**, founded in 1858 as Perth's first secondary school and now tastefully converted to offices.

You can complete your walk here, or continue on foot or by free City Area Transit (CAT) bus past **Barracks Archway** to the viewpoints in **Kings Park**.

Drive The southwest

This full day's outing from Perth follows the coastline south of Fremantle towards the southwestern tip of Western Australia, an area rich in flowers, splendid forests and vineyards.

Beyond the resort of **Mandurah**, the old coast road passes close to the lakes, swamps and woodland of **Yalgorup National Park**. Bunbury has fine beaches; between here and Busselton on Geographe Bay the highway runs through fine stands of tuart trees, some of the few remaining after the uncontrolled felling that took place in colonial days.

The coastline of the **Leeuwin-Naturaliste National Park** stretches for about 120km between Cape Naturaliste in the north and Augusta in the south. The backbone of the

area is formed by a granite ridge capped by limestone; erosion by water has given rise to hundreds of caves, some of which are open.

Some two dozen vineyards cluster round the little township of Margaret River. To the south are the wonderful karri trees of the **Boranup Forest**, best seen from the forest drive and the **Boranup Lookout**. There are fine coastal views at Prevelly Park at the mouth of the Margaret River.

If time permits, the tour can be extended to **Augusta** and to **Cape Leeuwin**. The return to Perth is faster via the South Western Highway beyond Bunbury.

Drive

Mundaring Weir

This short excursion enters the heavily wooded Darling Range.

The Great Eastern Highway soon leaves the city behind as it winds up the Darling scarp. The **John Forrest National Park** is a popular recreation area, with streams, waterfalls and a pool, while the dam and reservoir of **Mundaring Weir** have an attractive bushland setting. Return via Lesmurdie Falls and Kalamunda.

PERTH DRIVES

The eerie landscape of the Pinnacles, 245km north of Perth and located within Nambung National Park

The immense spaces of Western Australia include great swathes of unvarying country of little obvious interest, but there are also any number of landscapes well deserving of their national park or special interest designation. The state contains just one of Australia's 11 World Heritage registered sites – spectacular Shark Bay on the mid-north coast.

The southwest Facing the meeting point of the Southern and Indian Oceans, the southwest of the state enjoys a reasonably high rainfall which favours the growth of magnificent forests, notably of the karri tree. Its numbers much reduced by the 19th century's insatiable appetite for timber, this forest giant nevertheless survives in substantial patches in a number of national parks. In the southwest, these include the Stirling and Porongurup Ranges, the Boranup Forest in the Margaret River area, and the **Walpole-Nornalup National Park**, a coastal park beautifully sited around the Nornalup Inlet, where deep rivers wind seawards through heath-covered dunes.

Battered by breakers, these southwestern coasts have a rugged quality, well exemplified in the wild cliffs and rocky shoreline of the **Leeuwin-Naturaliste National Park**. On the shoreline further north resorts mix with wildlife-rich lagoons and lakes, as at **Yalgorup National Park**. The backdrop to the coastal plain is formed by the escarpment of the Darling Range, whose jarrah woods and bushland make a useful playground for Perth weekenders. The jarrah (a eucalyptus) is one of the characteristic trees of the southwest, much logged in the past and sawn up for railway sleepers. The range is accessible at any number of points along its 300km length, from the **John Forrest National Park** east of Perth, or **Lane Pool** on the Murray River, to **Marrinup** and **Pinjarra**.

One of the privileges of life in Perth is easy access to unspoiled nature. Only 35km out of the city to the northeast is **Walyunga National Park**, an area of wild bushland where the Swan and Avon Rivers have cut through the Darling Range. Equally near the city, but due north, is

Grass-trees
Among the oddest of Australian plants are the grass-trees. They used to be known as blackboys, from their supposed resemblance to an Aborigine brandishing a spear, but this term has been discarded, at least officially. Resin exudes from the blackened, stubby trunk above which flares a skirt of grass-like leaves and a spectacular flower spike (the 'spear'). Grass-trees depend on fire for their growth, reaching a maximum height of about 5m.

Yanchep National Park where the bush is home to honey possums, kangaroos and bandicoots, and there are a loch and limestone caves to be explored. Few sights are as compelling as the countless limestone pillars known as **The Pinnacles** in the Nambung National Park.

The northwest There is a great contrast of natural landscapes in the vast northwest. Some of the most stunning scenery is on the coast. Among the inlets and peninsulas of the World Heritage-listed **Shark Bay Marine Park** is unique and dazzling white Shell Beach, 60km long and built up of a 10m depth of crushed and compacted shells. The North West Cape has twin parks of outstanding interest. To the east are the parched plateau and deep rocky gorges of the **Cape Range National Park**, descending to the west through fossil reefs and sand dunes to Australia's 'other' barrier reef, the **Ningaloo Marine Park**, 260km of coral reef sheltering a shallow lagoon. Running inland from the tidal flats and mangrove swamps of the coast is the **Pilbara**, a spectacular upland deeply incised by river valleys and culminating in the vividly coloured 100m deep gorges of the **Karijini (Hamersley Range) National Park**.

Between the Pilbara and the Kimberley, the Great Sandy Desert claims part of the coastline. Where it merges with the Little Sandy Desert, far inland, are the salt lakes of the **Rudall River National Park**, accessible only to the well-equipped (contact the Western Australian tourist office for information).

The Kimberley Beyond the desert, dramatic landforms include **Geikie Gorge**, **Windjana Gorge**, the world's second largest meteorite crater at **Wolfe Creek**, and the strange beehive rock formations of the **Bungle Bungles**. Plant life ranges from sparse spinifex to scenes of great luxuriance in spots with a guaranteed water supply.

A possum – part of the myriad wildlife of the state

A rare bird
In 1894 Windjana Gorge was the scene of a gun battle between heavily armed police and a band of Aborigines led by Jundumurra, known to his adversaries as Pigeon. A skilful horseman and tracker, Pigeon had been compelled to work for the police against his own people. Eventually turning against his masters, he shot a constable, set prisoners free, and for years waged a minor guerilla war. He was finally hunted down and killed at Tunnel Creek on 1 April 1897.

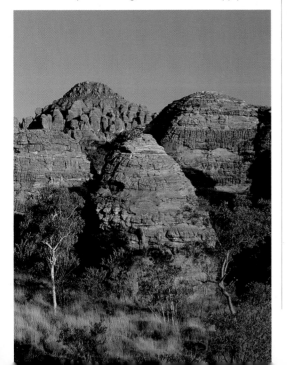

The fragile silica and sandstone forms of the Bungle Bungles are best seen from April to October

The rugged wilderness of Kalbarri National Park can be appreciated by helicopter

Eyre travel
The 2,700km of the Eyre Highway between Adelaide and Perth are less of an obstacle than might be supposed. Plenty of Australians refuse to be deterred by such distances and plan their driving accordingly, settling down to a steady pace and accepting the discipline of distance. At holiday periods it's as well to book ahead if you plan to stay in any of the motels along the route. Your vehicle should be absolutely roadworthy before setting out, since repair facilities are limited. Two hazards to remember: articulated trucks ('semi-trailers') may be difficult to overtake, especially if travelling at speed in convoy or if the road edge breaks away sharply; and when travelling west, you will have the setting sun to reckon with for long and disagreeable periods. One solution (book well in advance!) is to put the car on the train for the westward journey and drive back to the east.

By air The remoteness and sheer size of Western Australia mean that air travel is often used, not only for travelling between major cities but also to reach faraway places of interest or for day and half-day trips. Perth has direct connections to numerous overseas destinations, as well as daily flights to all state capitals and a number of other Australian cities.

By bus and coach Express coaches link Perth to the rest of the state, and to other Australian cities (given time!). The metropolitan area of Perth has a comprehensive network of buses, some of them operating out of the futuristic terminal near the Narrows. The capital also enjoys free services in the central area: City Area Transit (CAT) buses circle the city centre each day at very regular intervals, a great boon once you've got the hang of their routes.

By rail Perth has a three-pronged suburban rail service, connecting City Station with Guildford, Armadale and, usefully for the visitor, Fremantle. Fares are reasonable, and the service is generally efficient. Most of Western Australia's railways now carry freight only, though there are passenger trains from Perth to Bunbury in the south (the Australind) and west to Kalgoorlie (the Prospector). One of the world's great trains runs from Perth Terminal Station, the twice-weekly *Indian Pacific* to Sydney via Adelaide. Linking west and east across the Nullarbor Plain, this train is the railway experience of a lifetime – the journey to Adelaide takes 38 hours, and it is a two-day, three-night trip to Sydney.

By car The alternative routes north from Perth to Port Hedland, the **North West Coastal Highway** and the **Great Northern Highway,** are both sealed, as is their continuation onward to the Kimberley and the Northern Territory. It's a long way, though! The road network around Perth and in much of the southwest is well developed, but many places can only be reached on unsealed roads, in varying states of upkeep. Some particular favourites, like the rough but very scenic **Gibb River Road** through the Kimberley, can definitely only be negotiated by 4WD.

▶▶ Albany 146A2

Albany was the first European settlement in Western Australia, founded on King George Sound in 1826 by Major Edmund Lockyer to pre-empt any possible French interest in this quarter of the continent. It became an important base for whalers, then a coaling station for ships on the India–Sydney run; it is now a popular holiday town. The 19th-century buildings include the **Old Gaol**, built in 1851 as a convict hiring depot; **Patrick Taylor Cottage▶** of 1832, probably the town's oldest building, constructed from wattle and daub and now a folk museum; the **Old Post Office▶**, now the Inter-Colonial Communications Museum; and the excellent **Albany Residency Museum▶**. Near by is the **Amity Replica**, a full-size reproduction of Major Lockyer's brig.

The town nestles between Mount Clarence and Mount Melville. Further inland are the granite domes and karri forests of Porongurup National Park, and further still the high Stirling Range. To east and west lies one of Australia's finest stretches of coastline, and protecting the sound to the south is the rugged peninsula of **Torndirrup National Park▶▶**, with spectacular features like the **Blowholes▶**, **The Gap▶** and **Natural Bridge▶**, a huge granite, bridge-like suspension. The old whaling station on Frenchman Bay is now **Whaleworld▶**, which claims to be the world's largest whaling museum.

▶ Armadale 146A2

Armadale, 30km to the south of Perth, is famous for **Pioneer World▶▶**, a conscientious reproduction of a 19th-century village. Old-timers, including prospectors and blacksmiths, work in authentic-looking old buildings and visitors can join in with a variety of activities.

▶ Augusta 146A2

Overlooking the mouth of the Blackwood River, the attractive holiday town of Augusta has spectacular **Jewel Cave▶**, with strange rock formations, including an enormous straw stalactite, and an underground river.

Diggers on horseback
Australia's Desert Mounted Corps distinguished itself in the Middle East in the course of World War I. Albany was the port of embarkation for many of its troops, and they and their mounts are commemorated by the statue on Mount Clarence. This is a recast of the bronze erected on the banks of the Suez Canal in 1932, which came to grief during the Suez crisis of 1956. The original of the horse's head was recovered, however, and is on view in the Residency Museum.

A lady lion
The map of Australia reveals a number of names of Dutch origin. Perhaps the most famous of these is Cape Leeuwin, with its lighthouse overlooking the meeting point of the Indian and Southern oceans. Its name recalls the Dutch vessel which first put it on the map, the *Leeuwin*, or lioness, which passed this way in 1622, and which is also commemorated in a national park and a winery.

Armadale's Pioneer World

Broome's zero hour
It was not only Darwin that suffered Japanese air raids in World War II. On 3 March 1942, a squadron of Japanese Zero fighter planes spent a leisurely hour attacking a number of Allied flying boats moored off Mangrove Point. At very low tides, the remains of some of these machines can be seen in the bay.

A stairway to the sky
Another effect of Broome's exceptional tidal range is the optical illusion known as 'The Golden Staircase to the Moon', visible only at certain times of the year when the rays of the moon are reflected off the exposed bed of the ocean.

The pleasant town of Bunbury is a major seaport and the centre of the south-west

▶▶ **Broome**   *147D3*

The tourist's southwestern gateway to the Kimberley, Broome makes the most of its colourful past, when divers from all over Asia braved the bends and fierce rivalry to harvest precious mother-of-pearl from the sea bed (see page 161). Although only a few luggers still sail today, cultured pearls are farmed in the vicinity.

The authentic past can best be savoured in the **Broome Historical Society Museum▶**, where the restored Japanese section is particularly impressive. The town overlooks the mud flats and mangroves of Roebuck Bay, a rich haven for birdlife. The tidal range at Broome is exceptional, up to 10m, and at very low tide the footprints of dinosaurs can be seen at Gantheaume Point to the south. From here the white sands of Cable Beach stretch north for 20km.

▶ **Bunbury**   *146A2*

With its population of 25,000 inhabitants making it one of Western Australia's largest settlements, Bunbury serves as the urban centre for much of the southwest of the state. The viewpoint known as Boulter's Heights provides a panorama over the town and its surroundings. As well as a port, Bunbury is a popular resort, with good fishing, a fine string of beaches along the 8km Ocean Drive and, a relatively recent phenomenon, a friendly school of dolphins that enjoy the company of visitors to Koombana Beach on most mornings.

▶▶ **Bungle Bungle (Purnululu)**
      National Park   *147E4*

The soft sandstone of this part of the East Kimberley has been eroded into strangely strange rock formations resembling domes, turrets and beehives. Access to the national park, which was discovered as recently as 1983, is by 4WD only and there are no facilities: the region is closed from January to March to help prevent too much disturbance during the wet season. Most visitors prefer to view the park by plane or helicopter; the aerial perspective reveals clearly nature's weird beauty and striking colours. The park also has numerous examples of the art of the tribes who lived here, plus a number of burial sites.

Pearling

■ **Pearl oysters thrive in the tropical seas from Cape York in northern Queensland right round to Shark Bay in the west of Western Australia, a distance of some 3,000km; but there is a particular concentration between Derby and Cossack in the northwest. From early on, the pearls themselves were a bonus, the mainstay of the industry being mother-of-pearl shell, used for jewellery and in particular for humble buttons. ■**

Commercial exploitation This began in the 1860s, when Aborigines were more or less press-ganged by pearling masters into diving for the shell on the sea bed, an often lethal task; even if drowning was avoided, there were shark attacks, and many boats and their crews were lost in the frequent cyclones. With the expansion of the trade and the introduction of diving suits later in the century, there was an influx of Chinese, Filipinos, Malays, Koepangers from Timor and, above all, the most expert of all pearlers, the Japanese. In the 1920s Broome, one of the world centres of pearling, had a population of about 3,000, some 600 of them of British and 1,200 of Japanese descent. A typical pearling lugger might have had a European master, a pair of Japanese divers, a Japanese engineer and a crew from Timor. The different races lived in sometimes uneasy proximity in Broome, with occasional outbreaks of violence. Each August during the famous Shinju Matsuri (Pearl Festival), Broome remembers its golden days.

Pearling today By the 1930s the shell beds had been seriously depleted and, later, mother-of-pearl was displaced by plastic in the manufacture of buttons. Nowadays a few luggers still set off for the oyster beds some 6km off the coast, but most of Broome's current output comes from cultured pearls, raised in 'farms' away from public view. Pearling's colourful history is explained in the **Broome Historical Society Museum**, while an old pearling lugger can be seen outside the **Maritime Museum** in Fremantle. A real curiosity connected with this exotic trade is the Catholic mission at Beagle Bay, 130km north of Broome, its altar shimmering with mother-of-pearl.

The pearl farmer's year
From December to March there is little to do as this is the region's wet season; from April to August the young oysters are seeded so that they produce pearls; during the remainder of the year the large oysters are removed and their shells used for mother-of-pearl.

161

Until recently, Broome relied on pearling for its livelihood

WESTERN AUSTRALIA

Watering the goldfields
Extracting gold from the fields of Western Australia posed fewer difficulties than finding water in this utterly arid area. The Irish-born engineer Charles Yelverton O'Connor solved the problem. Already responsible for the construction of Fremantle Harbour and the building of much of the state's railway system, this late-Victorian genius built one of the wonders of the age, known as the Goldfields and Agricultural Water Supply Scheme. Beginning at the splendid dam at Mundaring Weir near Perth, O'Connor's great pipe sucked water 550km eastwards in sufficient quantities to quench the miners' thirst and leave some over to irrigate the farms of the Wheat Belt. Attacked by landed interests and ridiculed by critics, O'Connor's morale cracked, and he committed suicide a year before completion of the project.

Coolgardie – model of Ned Kelly

▶   **Busselton**   146A2

Busselton is a pleasant family resort with good beaches, facing north across Geographe Bay and sheltered from the west. Fishermen still frequent the remains of what was – until Cyclone Alby in 1978 – the longest (2km) timber jetty in Australia.

The approach to the town from the north passes through a splendid forest of tuarts, a tree unique to Western Australia. Just off the highway is the long and low tin-roofed 1830s colonial mansion known as **Wonnerup House▶**, furnished in period style and open to the public.

▶   **Carnarvon**   146C1

Only 150km south of the Tropic of Capricorn, Carnarvon wears a tropical air, with palm trees lining its fascine promenade and hibiscus and bougainvillea blooming in its elegantly broad main street. Famous for its fishing industries (you can visit the prawn and scallop processing plant), it is also the centre of a prosperous fruit and vegetable growing area, the Gascoyne district.

The **Bibbawarra Bore▶**, 16km to the north of town, produces a constant gush of water at 65°C. There is another demonstration of the power of water at **The Blowholes▶**, 70km north, where jets of water spout 20m into the air.

▶   **Coolgardie**   147B3

A classic boom-and-bust town 560km east of Perth and 39km from Kalgoorlie-Boulder, Coolgardie was the centre of Australia's most frantic gold rush. With a peak population in the 1890s of 15,000, its needs were catered for by two stock exchanges, three breweries and a couple of dozen hotels. Now a tenth of its former size, the symbols of its former glory remain.

Looking like an exceptionally grand railway terminus, the old Government Buildings are now the home of the **Goldfields Exhibition▶**, with extensive displays including a model of the town at its height. Opposite is the weird **Open Air Museum**, its scrapped machinery and statues of Australian heroes standing out surrealistically in the implacable sun. More abandoned machinery, rolling stock and a locomotive have been preserved in Coolgardie's **Railway Station Museum**, located in the 1896 rail terminus.

▶   **Darling Range** 146A2

The unbroken line of this wooded escarpment stretches far to the north and south of Perth, rising to a height of about 300m and defining the boundary of the coastal plain. Not far from the city are several popular recreation areas, like the bushland and streams of the John Forrest National Park or Mundaring Weir. The reservoir here was built in 1898–1902 to supply the far-off Eastern Goldfields with water; attractively landscaped, it is a favourite picnic spot. The **C. Y. O'Connor Museum▶** at the reservoir is named after the engineer who oversaw this vast project and tells the story of its construction (see panel opposite).

▶　　**Denmark** *146A2*

Rugged coastal scenery contrasting with the tranquil Denmark River and attractive farmlands makes the small town of Denmark in the extreme southwest a popular place for family holidays. Wilson Inlet is one of the largest areas of sheltered water on the south coast, with fine fishing, boating and other aquatic pleasures. To the west, **William Bay National Park▶** has sand dunes and pristine beaches, as well as heathland and karri forest.

▶　　**Derby** *147E3*

On the shores of King Sound to the north of the mouth of the Fitzroy River, and within striking distance of the West Kimberley, Derby likes to describe itself as the 'Gateway to the Gorges'; indeed, Windjana Gorge is only about 140km east of the town. Nearer at hand (8km away) is a famous boab tree, popularly supposed to have served as a lock-up for a small part of its 1,000-year life.

▶　　**Esperance** *147A3*

This deep-water port on the south coast flourished and declined in parallel to the boom and bust in the goldfields to its north. Now tourism has discovered Esperance, not least because of the magnificent beaches and the islands of the Recherche Archipelago. A scenic drive takes in part of the fine coastline and leads to **Pink Lake▶**, an extraordinary salt lake, genuinely pink in colour. Some of the best coastal scenery is some 50km to the east; here is the **Cape Le Grand National Park▶**, with stunning bays of blue water and white sand set between rocky headlands.

▶▶▶　**Fremantle** *146A2*

Now part of the built-up area of Greater Perth, the old harbour town of Fremantle continues to serve as Western Australia's principal port. Founded in 1829, Fremantle owes some of its attractive appearance to the convict craftsmen shipped in to save the colony's faltering fortunes in the gold-rush building boom of the 1890s. These were Fremantle's great days, when the harbour was improved out of all recognition by the great engineer O'Connor (see panel opposite).

The centre of town is compact, its venerable (by Australian standards!) townscape best enjoyed on foot. Good places to get your bearings include the viewing platform on top of the Port Authority Building or the **Round House▶**, erected in 1831 as the new colony's prison. The **Western Australian Maritime Museum▶▶** has a pearling lugger drawn up outside the old Commissariat Store in which it is housed; inside are excellent maritime history displays. The town's other major museum, the **Fremantle Museum▶**, occupies a neo-Gothic edifice on the far side of town. In between are any number of places worth a visit, including the famous **Fremantle Markets**, alive with dealers and (some) bargains.

The fine port and city of Fremantle lies 19km southwest of Perth, where the Swan River meets the Indian Ocean

Howe Fremantle got its name
Fremantle is named after the commander of the British naval force sent here to claim the west before anyone else. Captain Charles Howe Fremantle planted the Union Jack here on 2 May 1829, a month before the first settlers arrived to found the Swan River colony. An optimist, he believed that the colony would become 'in time, a place of consequence', in spite of 'its sandy and uncompromising appearance'.

Unwilling immigrants
It was on the shores of Kalbarri that Australia's first known European settlers made their landfall, albeit an involuntary one. Wouter Loos and Jan Pelgrom had been among the mutineers of the *Batavia*. After their arrest by Commander Pelsaert, they were put ashore at the mouth of the Wittecarra Creek in late 1629, where they are commemorated by a cairn. Their further story is unknown; ordered to look for them in 1644, Abel Tasman could find no trace.

▶▶ **Geikie Gorge National Park** *147D4*

The tiny settlement at **Fitzroy Crossing** has grown up around the point where the Northern Highway traverses the 550km-long Fitzroy River which drains much of the Kimberley. Reduced to a series of pools in the dry season, the Fitzroy rises an extraordinary 16m in the Wet, flooding vast areas. The effects of this phenomenal difference in water level can be observed (in the Dry!) by taking a boat trip up nearby Geikie Gorge in the national park, where the lower parts of the sheer 30–50m cliffs have been dramatically scoured by the annual floodwaters. Cut by the river through the limestone that aeons ago was an ocean reef, the gorge is home to many tropical aquatic lifeforms, including stingrays and freshwater crocodiles, and is fringed by reeds and dense forest supporting a rich range of birdlife.

▶ **Geraldton** *146B2*

This prosperous harbour town to the north of Perth, noted for its export of locally caught lobsters, is popular with visitors all year round, but particularly in winter because of its excellent sunshine record. Some 60km off shore is the archipelago aptly named the Houtman Abrolhos (derived from the Portuguese for 'Keep your eyes open'!) Islands, notorious as a death trap for ships heading eastwards across the Indian Ocean. Relics from famous wrecks are the mainstay of the Maritime Display Building, part of the **Geraldton Museum▶**; the museum's other sections are housed in the nearby Old Railway Building.

▶ **Halls Creek** *147D4*

Half-way through the Kimberley on the Northern Highway, Halls Creek seems the archetypal Outback town, centre of a vast area thinly populated by cattlemen and mineral prospectors. A short distance away is Old Halls Creek, with its evocative remains of an 1880s gold rush. Between the two settlements is a natural curiosity, a vein of white quartz standing clear of its surroundings and inevitably named the China Wall. A 130km drive to the south lies the 800m wide and 50m deep Wolfe Creek Meteorite Crater.

Crumbling sandstone has created rugged cliffs around the resort of Kalbarri

Instead of horses, cars now front Kalgoorlie's often elaborate hotels

Lawlessness
Kalgoorlie always was a rip-roaring kind of place, and even today takes a perverse pride in being labelled the most crime-ridden of Australia's smaller towns. In 1926, gold thieves hacked to death the detectives sent after them, and ten years later anti-immigrant riots raged for two days before a train-load of police could be brought up from Perth. Many of today's misdeeds seem to be the result of enthusiastic weekend drinking getting out of hand rather than anything more serious.

165

►   **Kalbarri**   *146B1*

The gorges in the **Kalbarri National Park►►** are up to 80km long and 170m deep, cut into the vivid red and wonderfully named tumblagooda sandstone. A number of easily accessible viewpoints like Hawk's Head Lookout overlook this landscape in its setting of sandy plains. The coastal scenery has its drama, too, with high red cliffs dropping sheer into the ocean. The national park is also famous for its spring wildflowers.

►►►   **Kalgoorlie-Boulder**   *147B3*

The classic gold-rush towns of Kalgoorlie and Boulder were amalgamated in 1989. Gold was first found at nearby Coolgardie; not long after, on 10 June 1893, Patrick (Paddy) Hannan and two mates made the greatest find of all – known for ever after as Hannan's Reward – and within a year tens of thousands of eager prospectors had swarmed to the 'Golden Mile'. In under a decade, both places had been transformed from ragged settlements to solid-seeming municipalities.

Hannan's slightly bemused statue sits outside the massive 1908 Town Hall on the pavement of the street named after him. This gently sloping roadway is of boulevard dimensions, wide enough to turn a camel train. On either side are monuments to the town's great days: canopied shopfronts; grandiose public edifices like the colonnaded government buildings; and the swaggeringly self-confident hotels, the **Exchange** (1894), the **Palace** (1897), the **Old Australia** (1896) and the **York** (1900).

►►►   **The Kimberley**   *147E4*
See page 173.

►   **Kununurra**   *147E4*

This town in the East Kimberley was created in the 1960s to act as an urban centre for the Ord River Irrigation Scheme (see panel). A solitary relic of the past, the **Argyle Downs Homestead** was rescued when the land on which it stood was flooded, and is now a pioneer museum. Outside town at **Mirima (Hidden Valley) National Park►**, 300 million years of erosion have created spectacular patterns in the red sandstone – the park is often described as a mini Bungle Bungle.

Out of order
Frustrated at seeing the floodwaters of the Ord River in the Kimberley running uselessly into the sea while for the rest of the year the land lay scorched and thirsty, the goverment spent huge sums on the Ord River Irrigation Scheme. Completed in 1972, its dams held back the muddy tide and distributed it among thousands of hectares of irrigated cropland. But the desert, on the whole, failed to bloom. The cotton crop was killed by caterpillars, and other crops have been only partially successful, while DDT-resistant insects seem to enjoy life in the 725sq km of the project's main water body, Lake Argyle.

■ 'We can make this country a quarry to serve the whole world' enthused Henry Bolte, Premier of Victoria 1955–72. With the exception of ACT, the prosperity of Australia's states and territories rest with the abundant mineral resources locked up in their ancient rocks. ■

Visitors can pan for real gold at the Soverign Hill historical park in Victoria

Ironing out the landscape
Long suspected, the existence of unbelievably rich deposits of iron ore in the Pilbara were confirmed almost by accident in the 1950s. Forced by poor weather to fly low over one of the area's many gorges, Lang Hancock noticed that its walls gave off a metallic sheen. Subsequent investigation revealed what proved to be the world's greatest concentration of iron ore. The topography of whole tracts of land has been transformed by its removal, for example at the Mount Whaleback Mine near Newman, the biggest opencast pit in the world.

A wealth of minerals Western Australia really came alive with the discovery of gold in unprecedented abundance in the Eastern Goldfields at the end of the 19th century, but the state also has (or had) reserves of antimony, bismuth, asbestos, coal, tin, copper, iron and nickel, as well as such rarities as tungsten, tantalite and beryl. Exploration and prospecting are very much a matter of the present as well as of history. The world's biggest iron mountain was discovered by accident in the Pilbara in the 1950s (see panel), while the incredibly productive Argyle Diamond Mine, which produces exquisite white, champagne and pink coloured stones, and is the world's largest producing diamond mine, near Kununurra only came on stream in the 1980s.

The first rush But it is the lure of gold that still catches the imagination most. The gold rushes, here as everywhere, were epic events, with their extraordinary mixture of greed, determination and endurance. The first rush in Western Australia was to Halls Creek in the Kimberley, in 1885, when Charlie Hall's Christmas present to himself was a 28oz nugget. Conditions in this utterly remote and harsh area were perhaps the worst anywhere; one devoted 'mate', Russian Jack, carted a sick friend 320km in a wheelbarrow in search of a doctor.

Halls Creek failed to live up to its promise, and the prospectors soon abandoned the Kimberley for the infinitely greater pickings to be found in the Eastern Goldfields. In 1892 Arthur Bayley rode into Southern Cross with 554oz of gold that he and his partner, Bill Ford, had found at Fly Flat 200km to the east; bars emptied as news of their find got around, and within hours the greatest rush in the colony's history had begun. Fly Flat was renamed Coolgardie; within six months thousands were living in a city of tents, having trekked through the water-less waste on foot or horseback, while supplies were brought up by dray or camel train. A year later the biggest find of all was made at Boulder. The rush increased Western Australia's population by leaps and bounds and was an immense stimulus to the colony's development. Terrible conditions endured for a while, with plagues of flies, outbreaks of typhoid, and water that sometimes cost as much as champagne. Before the completion of O'Connor's 550km pipeline from Perth in 1903 (see panel on page 162), traders in water often became richer than prospectors.

Companies move in Within the space of a few years, individual prospectors had scarred most of the Eastern Goldfields area with their shallow diggings ('specking') and extracted most of the alluvial gold. From now on it became necessary to mine more deeply, requiring the use of sophisticated machinery and the outlay of capital. Companies took over from rugged individuals.

Contemporary opencast methods of gold extraction and the extraordinary landscape they are creating can be observed from the viewing platform overlooking Kalgoorlie's **Super Pit**, which will eventually stretch for several kilometres and reach a depth of 500m.

Paddy's patter
A 'living' Paddy Hannan recounts the tale of the Eastern Goldfields at Hannan's North Mine in Boulder, a faithful recon-struction of a mine and its surroundings in its heyday. Here you can drop under-ground in the cramped miners' cage and have the mysteries and miseries of extraction explained to you by a veteran miner. Back on the surface, a railway meanders around the site.

Other mine museums in Kalgoorlie-Boulder are the School of Mines Mineral Museum and the Museum of the Goldfields.

167

Giant trucks, used to transport iron ore, Pilbara

The golden sandy beaches around the resort of Mandurah are always popular

Rails through the forest
In the early part of the century the jarrah forests inland from Mandurah echoed to the hiss of steam and the toot of whistles as narrow-gauge locomotives hauled timber to the mills. One of these forestry railways, the Hotham Valley Tourist Railway, running between Pinjarra and Dwellingup, has been kept alive by enthusiasts, and steam trains meet passengers off the modern Australind train from Perth. The enthusiasm is such that an additional line, the Etmilyn Forest Tramway, was opened in 1986, leading deep into the heart of the atmospheric jarrah woodlands.

▶ **Mandurah** *146A2*

Less than an hour's drive south of Perth, Mandurah is deservedly popular with city holidaymakers. Vast areas of sheltered water along the Murray and Serpentine Rivers and the Peel Inlet, 40km of beaches and an abundance of shady picnic spots help distribute the crowds and keep at least some of the town's tranquil atmosphere.

▶▶ **Margaret River** *146A2*

The township of Margaret River is the centre of the attractive district named after it, where the manicured landscape of prestige wineries contrasts with the savagery of surf pounding a rugged coastline and with a mysterious underground world of limestone caves. Arts and crafts abound in the town itself, while music (of the highest calibre, but only once a year) is performed in the delightful grounds of the Leeuwin Winery.

Among the more sheltered places along the coast, most of which forms part of the Leeuwin-Naturaliste National Park, is **Prevelly Park▶**. This is one of Australia's premier surfing spots, and the Margaret River Classic surf competition is held in the area each November. Only a few of the hundreds of caves are accessible, among them Mammoth Cave▶ (named for its size) and Lake Cave▶. The **Boranup Forest▶** is a good place to see the extraordinary massed ranks of karri trees, standing like cathedral columns.

▶▶ **Monkey Mia** *146C1*

Some of the several hundred dolphins living in Shark Bay mix with humans and accept fresh fish. To stand in the water of Monkey Mia beach and be nuzzled by a dolphin is an experience that few can resist, but do check first with the rangers at the Dolphin Information Centre. (Also see page 174.)

▶ **New Norcia** *146B2*

The Benedictines came to Western Australia as early as 1846, leaving the unmistakable imprint of Mediterranean Catholicism here in the bush 130km north of Perth, where they established a mission for the Aborigines. As well as the Abbey Church and Monastery, there is a museum and an art gallery with fine collections.

Wildflowers

■ **The 'strangeness' of Australian plants – including eucalyptuses in all their glorious variety, wattles and banksias – fascinates visitors from the northern hemisphere. Its vegetation provides a constant and stimulating backdrop, and is a continual reminder that you really are somewhere else.** ■

Early settlers tackled the isolation of this unfamiliar land by manipulating its appearance to recall the landscapes left behind. Planted in uncountable numbers, oaks, elms, willows and poplars transformed whole tracts of countryside – particularly in Tasmania – into a version of lowland England; the occasional eucalyptus looked like an intruder.

A great variety One of the joys of springtime is the abundance of wildflowers, particularly in Western Australia. Here a twofold isolation, not only from the rest of the world but from the rest of the continent, has resulted in flora of extraordinary variety. The state has some 8,000 named species, plus a further 2,000 which are still anonymous, three-quarters of them unique to the area though not necessarily unrelated to plants elsewhere in Australia. Some of Western Australia's most famous plants are the kangaroo paw, with its strangely shaped red or green flowers; a range of banksias, including the scarlet and acorn varieties; and the 60 species of tooth-leafed dryandras.

Springtime spectacular Wildflowers pattern the ground from north to south as springtime advances. At the **Kalbarri National Park**, 600km north of Perth, flowers begin to bloom in July. Some of the most spectacular displays occur in the heathlands of the southwest. In places like the **Stirling** and **Porongurup Ranges**, spring arrives much later than in the north, with November being the most rewarding month. For those unable to leave Perth, **Kings Park** makes a splendid substitute, with its extensive areas of natural bushland and its special section devoted to Australian trees, shrubs and wildflowers.

Below: trailing orchid in bloom

169

Wildflowers in coastal Western Australia

Harold Heights
Named after former Prime Minister Harold E Holt, the joint US/Australian Naval Communications Station keeps in touch with what is going on around the oceans with an extraordinary cluster of tall towers, the central one of which, at 388m, is taller than the Empire State Building. American accents can be heard in the streets of Exmouth, founded in 1964 as the support town for the base, but visitors come here mostly for the excellent fishing; North West Cape is the nearest point in Australia to the teeming marine life of the continental shelf.

The lesser-known rival to the Great Barrier Reef, Ningaloo Reef is home to over 500 varieties of fish

►► **Ningaloo Marine Park and Exmouth Area** *146C1*

A long detour leads off the North West Coastal Highway to far-off North West Cape, whose backbone is formed by the rugged **Cape Range**. This national park is made up of a high limestone plateau cut into by gorges and ravines, some containing deep pools. To the west stretch rarely visited dunes and beaches, protected from the ocean rollers by a barrier reef, 260km long and extending some 16km from the coast. With its 220 species of coral, whale sharks, the world's biggest fish and more than 500 varieties of tropical fish, the reef of Ningaloo Marine Park is one of the great natural wonders of Australia, as yet hardly exploited; there is fishing, camping, diving and swimming, and glass-bottomed boats operate from Coral Bay and **Exmouth**. The best place to begin your exploration of these natural wonders around Exmouth is at the innovative Milyering Visitor Centre in the Cape Range National Park.

► **Northam** *146A2*

An important road and rail junction and depot for the Goldfields Water Scheme, this Wheat Belt town is the regional centre for much of the attractive Avon Valley. The railway up from Perth about 100km away used to terminate here, so Northam was the point at which prospectors would begin their thirsty trek to the Goldfields 450km to the east; the old railway station is now a museum with evocative memorabilia of those days.

► **Northcliffe** *146A2*

This tiny place lost among the magnificent karri forests of the extreme southwest began as one of the townships of the ill-fated Group Settlement Scheme of the 1920s, whose hopes and failures are documented in the excellent **Pioneer Museum►**. A good base for viewing the karris (some of the tallest of them grow in the nearby Forest Park), Northcliffe is also the starting point for a 27km road leading to Windy Harbour, the only readily accessible beach between Augusta and Walpole.

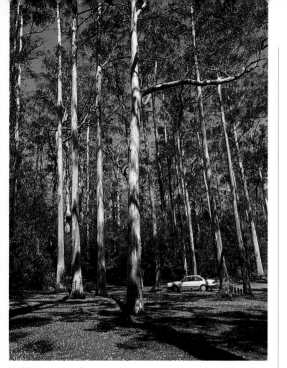

A forest of karris, the tallest of the eucalyptuses which can reach a height of 80m or more

The Gloucester Tree
It was difficult to build fire-watch towers of sufficient height to rise above the canopy of the giant karris. The answer was to wind a peg ladder around the trunk of a suitable tree and make a look-out cabin at the top. Planes perform the look-out function nowadays, but the Gloucester Tree near Pemberton has been kept for fearless tourists to climb its 153 rungs and be rewarded with a stupendous view over the treetops. It's the loftiest fire look-out tree in the world, but at around 60m it is by no means the tallest karri.

Rails across the desert
Passengers aboard a transcontinental train have the dubious distinction of taking part in one of the world's few rail journeys where the view from your sleeping berth in the morning is identical to the one on which you closed the curtain the night before! Imposing-sounding stations turn out to be nothing more than a marker planted in the wilderness, or at the very most a huddle of railway paraphernalia with a section of loop allowing trains to pass. The 478km 'Long Straight' between Ooldea and Watson tests the patience of even the most disciplined driver of the big diesel hauling its train of stainless steel coaches.

► ▓▓▓▓▓ **Nullarbor Plain**   *147B4*

Renowned for its utter desolation, the world's largest flat surface stretches interminably eastward into South Australia, covering an area of more than 250,000sq km. Few plants (other than saltbush) and fewer animals flourish in this unyielding environment – the name Nullarbor means 'no trees'.

The explorer Edward John Eyre survived his terrible journey across the plain from east to west in 1840–1 by keeping close to the coast, where brackish water could occasionally be found beneath patches of sand dunes. The highway named after him also follows a southern route, while the transcontinental railway strikes off boldly from the goldfields far inland. The landscape along the highway, which is entirely bitumen coated, is not entirely without incident, since only a relatively short section traverses the Nullarbor proper, but the 145km continuous straight between the Balladonia Roadhouse and Caiguna tests any driver's ability to stay alert!

►► ▓▓▓▓▓ **Pemberton**   *146A2*

Steeped in timber lore, the township of Pemberton in the southwest corner of the state is the best place to experience the magic of the magnificent karri forest growing all around. Its wonders can be appreciated in a variety of ways – by car, on foot or aboard a 1907 replica tramcar of the Pemberton Tramway, which travels through the forest on a 36km railway line. One tree can be walked through, another, the **Gloucester Tree►** (see panel) can be climbed. You can visit a restored 1865 sawpit, take a guided tour around a huge modern sawmill, or trace the area's history in the nearby **Manjimup Regional Timber Park►**. The beauty of the forest is enhanced by clear streams and pretty cascades, and by a wealth of wildflowers in the spring.

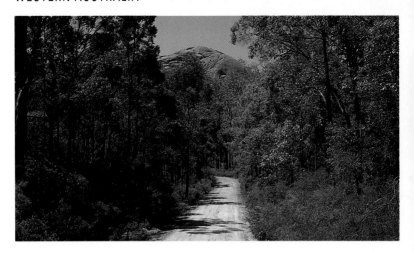

There are several high peaks in Porongurup National Park in the Albany hinterland

Karried to extremes
The tallest of all eucalyptuses is the karri (*Eucalyptus diversicolor*), a magnificent tree reaching a height of 85m and with a lifespan of up to 1,000 years. Growing together in the forest, the soaring stems of the karris create the stately atmosphere of a Gothic church. The finest tracts of karri forest are found in the well-watered south, inland from the coast between Augusta and Albany; much of it was cleared after both world wars to make small-holdings for returned soldiers. Most of these settlements failed, since the deep loamy soil preferred by the karris was good for trees but not for crops.

► **Pilbara** 147C2

Until the 1960s, a few cattlemen were the only inhabitants of this wasteland in the northwest. The accidental discovery in the 1950s of what proved to be the world's largest deposit of iron ore (see page 166) was the stimulus for the construction of mining cities like Tom Price and Newman and of deep-water harbours like Dampier and Port Hedland. Trains 2,000m long haul the ore from the huge opencast pits down hundreds of kilometres of track to the sea. Much of this exported raw material is later returned to Australia in the form of Japanese cars.

Tourists come this way for winter sun and for the stunning landscapes of the **Karijini (Hamersley Range) National Park►►**. The vividly coloured rocks of this ancient plateau have been bitten into deeply by the action of rivers, forming splendid gorges where intensely cold water gathers in pools and where a surprisingly lush vegetation flourishes. Even more luxuriant plants are a feature of the **Millstream-Chichester National Park►** to the north, where there is a large colony of fruit bat and permanently flowing water, nourishing the palm trees of a relict rain forest.

►► **The Pinnacles (Nambung** 146B2
National Park)

The thousands of limestone monoliths scattered around the sandy plain south of the coastal township of Cervantes 250km from Perth were mistaken by Dutch sailors for the remains of an ancient city. Varying in size from 5m giants to finger-thick pieces of piping, they may well be the fossilised roots of long-dead trees and shrubs. Whatever their origin, they remain compelling presences in their desert setting. The Cervantes area boasts several beautiful beaches, and sailboarding and boating are popular activities here.

► **Porongurup National Park** 146A2

The ancient granites of this range of hills in the Albany hinterland have been eroded into domes and curious formations like Balancing Rock. Castle Rock (570m) gives stunning views over karri forest and the country beyond. In spring, the forest floor is brilliant with wildflowers.

The Kimberley

■ **This remote and harsh land in the far north of Western Australia was explored in 1879 by Alexander Forrest, who thought that some of it at least might sustain grazing animals. Million-acre stations still graze their stock on the sparse vegetation, there is diamond mining at Argyle, and now tourism; visitors pass through on round-Australia trips or make the Kimberley their prime destination, drawn by the lure of a 'last frontier'. ■**

East Kimberley The modern township of Kununurra is the gateway to the East Kimberley, a region of ancient volcanic rocks and sandstone ranges. Tropical rainfall fills the rivers in the Wet, supporting a rich pattern of vegetation and wildlife, while mangrove swamps clad the margins of estuaries. The Ord River Irrigation Scheme has attempted to harness the river's summer flow to irrigate vast areas of cropland, with only limited success; remote **Wyndham**, the state's northernmost harbour and a port town since the 1880s, exports cattle as well as whatever crops the project produces. Persistence will lead the determined visitor to natural wonders like the **Mitchell Falls**, or even (with a permit) along the Kalumburu Road to the far off Aboriginal Reserve and Mission near the mouth of the King Edward River. Some areas, like the Drysdale River National Park, of unresearched biological value, may not be visited at all.

West Kimberley Entered via Broome and Derby, the west has spectacular inland gorges, cut through the limestones of an ancient barrier reef, long since hoisted high above sea level. The river running through **Windjana Gorge**, composed of rocks that are part of a 350-million-year-old limestone reef, is reduced to a series of pools in the dry season, while the mighty Fitzroy River manages to maintain an all-year flow through the much longer **Geikie Gorge**.

How to get there
Most traffic takes the long way round from Derby to Kununurra via the main highway. This gives access to Wolfe Creek Crater National Park as well as the magical Bungle Bungles (though both of these extraordinary natural phenomena are better seen from the air). The shorter route is the Gibb River Road, rougher but more rewarding, with well-vegetated creeks, gorges and waterholes.

173

The Argyle Diamond Mine, in the East Kimberley, produces high-quality stones

WESTERN AUSTRALIA

A nest of rats
Rottnest Island, meaning rats' nest island, was named in 1696 by Dutchman Willem de Vlamingh who found the place infested with what he took to be large rodents. The rats were in fact the hare-sized marsupials known as quokkas, a kind of pademelon wallaby, found here on 'Rotto' and on parts of the mainland.

Marine wonderland
Shark Bay Marine Park's Unesco World Heritage status was bestowed for its remarkable natural beauty and significance. The Monkey Mia dolphins are the region's best-known attractions, but the bay also contains stromatolites – some of the world's oldest living things – at Hamelin Pool, and one of the planet's last surviving herds of dugongs, or sea-cows.

Some of the hundreds of dolphins that inhabit the warm waters of Shark Bay

▶ **Rottnest Island** 155E2

Situated 20km off the Fremantle coast, reached by air or ferry from Perth, and measuring a mere 11km long by a maximum of 5km across, Perth's weekend paradise has a special charm, enormously enhanced by the lack of cars; bikes are the main mode of transport for exploring the delightful bays and white beaches along the rugged coastline. The extraordinarily clear turquoise waters are ideal for diving and snorkelling.

▶▶ **Shark Bay Marine Park** 146C1

Divided into a series of inlets by peninsulas and islands, and with 1,500km of coastline, World Heritage listed Shark Bay was named in 1699 by the adventurer William Dampier. The waters of the bay provide excellent swimming, fishing and other watersports, and there are spectacular dunes of red sand, high limestone cliffs, and extraordinary beaches as well. Shell Beach, 60km long, is made up of countless shells to a depth of 10m; naturally compacted at this depth, this strange material can be cut into blocks and used in buildings. The little resort of Denham is the westernmost town in Australia; on the opposite side of the Peron Peninsula are the famous dolphins of Monkey Mia (see page 168).

▶ **Southern Cross** 146B2

The streets of Southern Cross, founded by gold prospectors in 1888, are still wide enough to turn a camel train. There are mementoes of the old days in the 1891 court house.

▶ **Stirling Range National Park** 146A2

A scenic highway threads through this 65km-long range, whose peaks rise abruptly 1,000m above the surrounding country. As well as being southwestern Australia's highest mountains, with occasional snowfall, they are a botanical reserve of first importance and great beauty, with no less than 1,000 wildflower species.

Wave Rock: another ancient geological curiosity

► ► **Wave Rock** 146A2

One of Australia's great tourist attractions, Wave Rock remains forever a surfer's dream turned to stone. More than 100m long and 15m high, the petrified breaker's resemblance to the real thing is emphasized by the colourful vertical streaking, the result of natural chemicals in the granite reacting with rainwater.

Other curiosities near the little Wheat Belt town of Hyden (340km inland from Perth) include further odd rock formations with names like the Humps and the Hippo's Yawn; there are Aboriginal wall paintings in Mulka's Cave.

► **Yanchep** 146A2

Days out from Perth often take in the coastline to the north of the city with its fine beaches, sand dunes and chain of lakes just inland. Yanchep itself is a resort, but around it stretches the **Yanchep National Park►**, with colourful limestone caves, a lake, eucalyptus woods and a wealth of wildflowers in the spring.

► **York** 146A2

With Northam and Toodyay, York is one of a trio of much-visited towns located in the picturesque Avon Valley 100km northeast of Perth. Western Australia's most historic inland town was founded in 1831, and plenty of its lovely old sandstone buildings have survived the ravages of time, which included an earthquake in 1968. The **Residency Museum►** evokes the early days, as does the **Balladong Farm►**, a living museum of agriculture with animals galore. More than 200 vintage cars, motorcycles and even some horse-drawn vehicles are on display in the **York Motor Museum► ►**.

River of the black swans
The Avon is a tributary of the Swan River, given its name in honour of the black swans that made it their home. Both rivers formed a corridor for early settlement, and the old town of Guildford includes many venerable buildings and historic houses like Woodbridge, built in 1885 and now impeccably restored and authentically furnished (open). The Swan Valley is also famous for its wine. A tour of the wineries is a popular excursion, not only for the product but for the attractive setting of many of the vineyards.

Hotel sign in the small, respectable town of York

NORTHERN TERRITORY

176

Map of the Northern Territory showing cities, national parks, highways and geographic features including:

Region F: Cape Van Diemen, Bathurst Island, Melville Island, Clarence Strait, Van Diemen Gulf, Gurig Nat Park, Cobourg Pen, Goulburn Islands, Cape Wessel, Wessel Islands

Region E: Howard Springs, DARWIN, Fogg Dam, Humpty Doo, Jabiru, Berry Springs, Nature Park, Darwin Crocodile Farm, Wildman River Res, Jim Jim Falls, Litchfield Nat Park, Adelaide River, Kakadu National Park, Anson Bay, Daly River Nature Park, Daly River, Pine Creek, Mainoru, Arnhem Land, Arnhem Bay, Melville Bay, Nhulunbuy, Cape Arnhem, Gove Pen, Blue Mud Bay, Groote Eylandt

Region D: Joseph Bonaparte Gulf, Edith Falls, Nitmiluk National Park, Katherine, Katherine Gorge, Upper Roper NP, Elsey NP, Roper Bar, Port Roper, Gulf of Carpentaria, Limmen Bight, Cutta Cutta Caves and Tindal Caves, Matarinka, 'We of the Never Never' Graves, Willeroo, Wingate Mts, Larrimah, Cox, Nathan River, Sir Edward Pellew Group, Keep River Nat Park, Timber Creek, Victoria River, Gregory National Park, Daly Waters, CARPENTARIA HIGHWAY, Dunmarra, Cape Crawford, Borroloola

Region C: Top Springs, Newcastle Waters, Elliott, Wollogorang, BUCHANAN, Kalkaringi, Lake Woods, Renner Springs, Maryville, Barkly Tableland, John Flynn Historical Reserve, Three Ways, McDouall Range, Tennant Creek, Barkly Homestead, Soudan, HIGHWAY, Tanami Desert, Murchison Range, Georgina

Region B: Rabbit Flat Roadhouse, Devils Marbles, Wauchope, Hatches Creek, Lake Nash, 584m Mt Theo, Chilla Well, Lander, Harson, Barrow Creek, 1140m Mt Leichhardt, Ti-Tree, Sandover, Tobermorey, Yuendumu, Ryan Well, Atartinga, Jervois Range, Adam Range, Lake Mackay, Stuart Bluff Range, Simpsons Gap, Hann Range, West MacDonnell National Park, Emily & Jessie Gaps, Arltunga Historical Reserve, Ormiston Gorge, Standley Chasm, Ross River, Plenty

Region A: Gosse Bluff, MacDonnell Ranges, Alice Springs, Kings Canyon, Watarrka National Park, Finke Gorge National Park, Frontier Camel Farm, Lake Neale, Lake Amadeus, Henbury Meteorite Craters, Chambers Pillar, Todd, Hale, Petermann Ranges, Ayers Rock Resort, 1070m Mt Olga, Uluru (Ayers Rock), Uluru-Kata Tjuta National Park, Erldunda, Kulgera, Finke, Simpson Desert

Borders: WESTERN AUSTRALIA, QUEENSLAND, SOUTH AUSTRALIA

Scale: 0, 100, 200, 300 km

A ghost gum, easily recognisable by its white trunk

The Northern Territory With the thin bitumen ribbon of the Stuart Highway as its backbone, the third largest territorial area in Australia stretches from the country's desert heart, the 'Red Centre', to the coast and islands of the tropical north, the 'Top End'. The cattle-rearing which used to form the basis of the territory's economy is still important, but has been overtaken by mining (bauxite, manganese, uranium) and by tourism; more and more visitors are drawn here, not only to the mysterious landforms of the desert, of which **Ayers Rock** is just one, but to Darwin, to the natural riches of the north and, above all, to the incomparable World Heritage wilderness of **Kakadu National Park**.

First settlement The first European sighting of the coast of the Northern Territory seems to have been made in 1623 by the Dutchman Jan Carstenzoon on board the *Arnhem*, but it was not until the 1820s that the British felt the need to deny the remote northern end of the continent to the French and Dutch. First attempts to found settlements came to grief; Port Essington (1824) on the Cobourg Peninsula had no fresh water, Fort Dundas (1824–9) on Melville Island had hostile Aborigines, and Raffles Bay (1827), also on the Cobourg Peninsula, was abandoned after only two years. Victoria (on an inlet of Port Essington) was established in 1838 and, in spite of cyclones and earthquakes, managed to last until 1849, when it too was given up. The splendid natural harbour of Port Darwin was given its name in 1839 by Captain J C Wickham of the *Beagle*, thereby honouring Charles Darwin, a member of an earlier voyage. However, it was not until three decades later, in 1869, that the site of the present capital of the territory was surveyed and a start made on building. The choice was a propitious one, and Darwin, originally named Palmerston, has survived and prospered in spite of cyclones and Japanese air raids.

Conquering the interior The interminable and arid spaces of the centre resisted attempts to cross them until 1862 when, on his sixth attempt and undeterred by five heroic failures, John McDouall Stuart finally blazed a trail from south to north; Stuart's route is followed by the highway named after him. Before the road was built, the famous Overland Telegraph, spanning the unmapped wilderness between Port Augusta on the coast of South Australia and Darwin, had been completed in less than two years. Linked at Darwin to the submarine cable from Java in 1872, the Australian colonies were thus connected with the 'grand electric chain that unites the nations of the earth'. The repeater stations, at Alice Springs, Tennant Creek and other places, constructed along its 2,900km length became focal points for travellers and townships later developed around these isolated outposts. Pastoralists then moved into the territory, and it became part of South Australia in 1863. The telegraph station at Alice Springs still stands, though the town itself has moved south.

Into the 20th century In 1911 the Northern Territory, a drain on the meagre resources of South Australia, became the responsibility of the Commonwealth. Though self-governing since 1978, it has still not acquired full statehood, and some of its affairs (Aboriginal matters and uranium mining) continue to be handled by Canberra. For many years it stayed a backwater; few drivers braved the horrible surface of its unmade roads and there were very few tourists. However, World War II changed all that. In a series of heavy raids, Japanese aircraft inflicted severe damage not only on Darwin but on the Australian psyche. Acutely aware of the country's vulnerability via the empty and remote north, government and armed forces hastily surfaced the road from the railhead at Alice Springs to the coast, and built a chain of depots, bases and airfields, remains of which can still be seen along the highway.

The Northern Territory was hauled bodily into the life of the nation by these events.

Road trains
Taking 51 days on its arduous trip from Adelaide to Darwin, the first car to cross the desert centre signalled the beginning of the end for the horses, camels and buffalo-drawn carts which had served the Northern Territory's needs until then. In the 1930s, a cumbersome AEC diesel and trailer formed what was called the Government Road Train, hauling supplies to isolated communities. After World War II, Kurt Johannsen used an old army tank transporter to pull no less than eight cattle trailers. Today's road trains are limited to a maximum of three 'dogs' or trailers, a formidable sight as they roar along the highways of the Northern Territory and Western Australia.

One of the lovely gorges cut by the Katherine River

National parks

To travel along the Stuart Highway between the arid Red Centre and tropical Top End is to experience some of the most dramatic contrasts nature has to offer in Australia.

The Red Centre Geological processes at their most primeval have shaped the red rocks of the centre, creating an almost abstract world of crater and boulder, jagged ridge and lonely monolith, starkly defined against a background of sandy plain or pebbly desert. Etched into this awesome pattern are the winding beds of watercourses, filled only when rare rainstorms rage. Ancestors of the present rivers were fed more generously, and it is they that carved chasm, gorge and canyon, niches in this hostile world for a surprisingly rich and varied wildlife. The rugged **MacDonnell Ranges** to the west and east of Alice Springs are breached by many a gap filled with ferns, palms and other exotic plants, some of them descendants of the flora that flourished on the shore of the vast sea which once covered much of central Australia. Waterholes may persist here long after rivers have dried up, creating a refuge for both animals and humans.

Experiencing the desert is not difficult (unless you want it that way!). Parks Australia North and the Parks and Wildlife commission of the Northern Territory are improving facilities while conserving the landscapes entrusted to them. Their management of Ayers Rock is a model of its kind.

The more verdant north Towards the northern rim of the centre, permanently flowing rivers are a reminder of a more abundant, monsoon rainfall (up to 1,600mm a year compared with around 120mm in the south). Many rivers have their source on the high plateau of Arnhem Land; the Katherine River has cut a series of spectacular gorges, while the **Kakadu National Park** teems with an almost vulgar profusion of wildlife. The Top End has some of Australia's remotest places, like the Cobourg Peninsula, which closes off Van Diemen Gulf, while Darwin itself enjoys a superabundance of natural areas in its hinterland.

Darwin's territorial waters
At Doctors Gully at the end of the Esplanade, thousands of fish and no small number of tourists come together at Aquascene during every high tide – the former to be fed and the latter to do the feeding.

Another place for seeing fish as well as a re-created coral reef is at the Indo Pacific Marine at the lively Darwin Wharf Precinct. The Precinct is also home to the Australian Pearling Exhibition.

Rainforest and rivers
An easy day's outing from Darwin, Berry Springs has both a nature park with natural swimming pools and the splendid Territory Wildlife Park. This 400ha tract of bushland is aimed at introducing visitors to the Northern Territory's varied wildlife.

Well off the beaten track down the Daly River Road, the Daly River Nature Park is a favourite spot for barramundi fishing and boating, although the large number of salties (saltwater crocodiles) precludes swimming.

The remote Gregory National Park has a spectacular gorge and boat trips along the Victoria River.

Darwin

The capital of the Northern Territory clings precariously to the peninsula protruding into Port Darwin, a superb natural anchorage twice the size of Sydney Harbour. Darwin has almost disappeared from the map no less than four times. Cyclones flattened the place in 1897, 1937 and again with great thoroughness in 1974. In between, the aviators of the Imperial Japanese forces did their best to imitate nature at her most furious in the course of no less than 60 air raids. But Darwin's resilience is legendary; after each disaster, the evacuated population has returned to rebuild. In 1974, Cyclone Tracy destroyed

Getting around
The best way to orientate yourself is to take a trip on the Tour Tub, an open circulating minibus which allows you to get on and off at will at any point along its route.

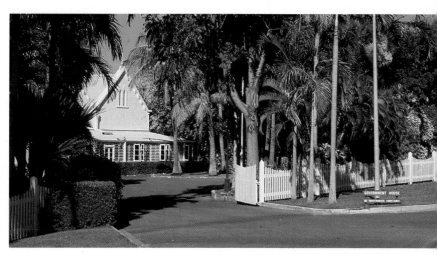

nearly all the town's old buildings, including elegant old stilt houses; their replacements were conceived with cyclone-proofing in mind more than beauty.

Diverse community Advertised as Australia's front door, for much of its life Darwin has looked more like the country's back yard. Its appeal is that it is on the edge, a place in touch with other places. Founded in 1869, it became a base for 'fabulous old-timers – pearlers, buffalo hunters, trepangers, prospectors, cattlemen and overlanders'. The city's population is extraordinarily mixed; the number of ethnic groups varies between 49 and 61 according to who is doing the counting. Many are Asians, and of all Australian cities, Darwin is the most conscious of the lands just to the north; Singapore is no further away than Sydney and Jakarta is closer.

Most visitors pass through Darwin with other destinations in mind, either abroad or in the Northern Territory, many of whose attractions are within easy reach. However, they should beware of the place's insidious allure, one based less on visual appeal than on an utterly relaxed, tropical lifestyle.

City sights and orientation Small enough to walk around, the centre of the city has a number of surviving (or reconstructed) buildings from early days. Some of these front the parkland of the west-facing Esplanade; here is **Government House** of 1883 as well as **Old Admiralty House**, a fine example of a tropical building on stilts dating from the 1920s. Among the grid of streets further inland is the much rebuilt **Victoria Hotel**, the **Chinese Temple** or Joss House and, in the courtyard of the Civic Centre, an ancient banyan, the **'Tree of Knowledge'**, one of Darwin's most resilient landmarks. These venerable structures contrast strongly with the new hugely expensive Northern Territory Parliament House, which can be toured.

Other sights lie further afield, many of them overlooking beautiful Fannie Bay to the north. Here is the MGM Grand Casino, close to Mindil Beach where a famous market is held from May to October.

Tropical-style Government House, Darwin's oldest building (1883)

Ship of brews
The tropical heat provides the people of Darwin with an excellent excuse to drink more beer than anywhere else in what, after all, is not an abstemious country. Discarded beer cans once used to litter the streets and highways, but an ingenious solution has been found for the disposal of the cans in which the amber fluid comes – the Beercan Regatta. Held every August at Mindil Beach, this weird event featuring bizarre craft ingeniously constructed from the humble 'tinnie' has become one of the highlights of Darwin's social calendar, attracting thousands of spectators. Beer consumption during the festivities helps provide the raw material for the following year's event.

Meet the awesome croc Sweetheart at the Museum and Art Gallery

A fast lady
Darwin lies in the path of cyclones, none of which have raged as fiercely as Cyclone Tracy on Christmas Day 1974. In the space of four hours, two-thirds of the city's buildings were destroyed and most of the rest severely damaged. The death toll was put at 66. No one knows exactly how much puff Tracy had in her – the windspeed indicator at the airport broke showing 217kph – but the peak velocity has been estimated at around 300kph. The disaster wasn't totally regretted. Pre-1974 Darwin was no showpiece of urban planning; rebuilding has been carried out along more orderly lines, with the provision of a satellite town, Palmerston, 20km to the southeast.

▶ **Darwin Botanic Gardens** 180C2
Gardens Road
Plants grow rapidly in Darwin's climate, and the damage done to these fine gardens in 1974 has been made good. The opportunity was taken to add new features, including collections of orchids, figs, ferns, and a quite exceptional array of around 400 tropical palms, the largest collection in the southern hemisphere. As much a park as a scientific institution, the gardens are the city's favourite cool retreat.

▶ **East Point Military Museum** 180D2
East Point Road, Fannie Bay
Concrete bunkers and items of military hardware lie scattered around East Point headland. The guns installed here to repel an invader who never came were, ironically, finally removed by a Japanese scrap-metal dealer.

▶ **Fannie Bay Gaol Museum** 180D2
East Point Road, Fannie Bay
With no history of convictism, Darwin nevertheless stresses the importance of its prison, built in 1883 and in use until 1979. The museum features a gallows, used for the territory's last execution in 1952.

▶▶▶ **Museum and Art Gallery** 180C2
of the Northern Territory
Conacher Street, Bullocky Point
This modern complex on Fannie Bay has exhibits emphasising the unique geographical position of the territory and its capital. In addition to an excellent collection of traditional and contemporary Aboriginal art and artefacts, there is a wealth of fascinating objects from Southeast Asia and the Southwest Pacific. A huge shed houses the Maritime Museum with its original seagoing vessels, among them sinister war canoes, dugouts, fantastic outriggers, a lipa-lipa, proas and the last of Darwin's pearling luggers, the *Vivienne*. There is also an interesting cyclone Tracy exhibit, but pride of place should perhaps go to Sweetheart, a monster among crocodiles, now stuffed and harmless.

■ A morbid fascination with crocodiles has no doubt something to do with seeing oneself as the potential prey of a large and aggressive reptile. The crocodiles of the Northern Territory, Western Australia and Queensland have loomed large in the public mind not only because of the film *Crocodile Dundee* but also because of their increasing numbers (a result of effective conservation measures), the opening-up of their habitat to wilderness tourism, and the readiness of the media to make a meal out of any crocodile attack. ■

Two kinds of crocodile live in Australia. Harmless to humans, the relatively small freshwater crocodile frequents rivers and billabongs between the Gulf of Carpentaria and Broome in Western Australia. Double its size (6m specimens are not uncommon), and distinguished by a broader snout, the saltwater or estuarine crocodile prefers the brackish waters of tidal rivers though it is quite capable of penetrating far inland as well as out into the ocean. It occurs from India to the western Pacific, and in Australia from the central Queensland coast around Rockhampton to the Broome area.

Salties prey on fish and animals of all sizes, including human beings. Many victims are taken unawares at the water's edge; the crocodile makes its approach underwater, then uses the massive muscle of its tail to propel itself from the deep like a Polaris missile. The prey is dragged underwater and drowned rather than immediately torn apart; the croc can stay below the surface for up to an hour. Male crocodiles lord it over a territory which they defend from other males. Much of their time is spent lying log-like in the shallows, conserving energy which is rapidly expended in violent manoeuvres to secure dinner.

Look before you dive Darwin's swimming pools and ornamental waters have to be checked before they are opened to the public. Swimming or paddling in areas frequented by crocodiles could well be fatal. Remember, too, that crocodiles are amphibians, capable of reaching high speeds on land. Always obey the signs forbidding swimming (if they haven't been removed as souvenirs!) and seek local advice if in doubt. The best way to see these intimidating creatures is to take a conducted tour in a steel-bottomed boat (one legendary beast – long since dealt with – developed a taste for the more chewy kind of outboard motor, so don't trail your hand in the water!). Craft of this kind ply Yellow Water in Kakadu and, nearer Darwin, the Adelaide River.

Darwin Crocodile Farm
This establishment 40km south of Darwin is home to thousands of crocodiles reared for their skins. Feeding time is always spectacular.

183

Warning
Crocodiles respect neither man nor beast, so take no chances. Just because you can't see them, it doesn't mean they're not there.

CONSERVATION COMMISSION

NORTHERN TERRITORY

Albert Namatjira
Born at Hermannsburg Mission in 1902, this member of the Aranda tribe became a talented watercolourist in the European tradition, his subject the stunning landscapes of his native MacDonnell Ranges. He and his work were acclaimed; he was presented to the Queen during a royal visit, and in 1957 he was given the extraordinary privilege (for the time) of full citizenship. But Namatjira was destroyed by the tension between white and Aboriginal society and by alcohol; imprisoned for supplying drink to a fellow Aborigine, his morale collapsed and he died in 1959 at the age of 57. His wonderfully fresh paintings can be seen in many Australian galleries.

Alice Springs has a number of memorials to...

► ► ►   **Alice Springs**   *176B2*

Bang in the middle of the continent, The Alice (as it is widely known) has transformed itself from a dusty outpost to an indispensable stop on the tourist itinerary. Equipped with all modern amenities, the town makes an excellent base for exploring the Red Centre.

The township began in 1871 as a convenient place for a repeater station on the Overland Telegraph between Adelaide and Darwin – it was named for local waterholes, and after the wife (Alice) of Sir Charles Todd, the Postmaster General of South Australia. Development was slow until the arrival of the railway from Adelaide in 1929, the famous but rickety 'Ghan', named after the Afghan camel drivers it supplanted. In World War II, the railhead acquired enormous strategic value, particularly after the Stuart Highway leading on up to Darwin had been given its first coat of bitumen. But it was the advent of mass tourism from the 1970s onwards that persuaded the town to provide what had previously been lacking: comfortable hotels, sophisticated restaurants and even a tastefully landscaped shopping mall. All this came as something of a surprise to the old-timers, who not so long ago would ride in for an evening's drinking and hitch their horse to the rail in the main street.

The best place to get an overall impression of The Alice in its desert setting is to climb (or drive up) **Anzac Hill** ► with its obelisk memorial. The town centre stretches out on the west bank of the bed of the Todd River. The fact that it rarely contains any water has not stopped the hilarious Henley-on-Todd Regatta becoming a major annual event, with legs rather than oars supplying the motive power for the bottomless craft. For much of the rest of the year the dry river bed serves as a camping ground for some of the Alice's substantial Aboriginal population. To the south are the long ridges of the MacDonnell Ranges, pierced by the Heavitree Gap, through which run road and railway. Beyond is the airport, and then the top-secret US/Australian Pine Gap communications base.

Although visitors come to Alice Springs more because of where it is than for what it is, there are a fair number of attractions in the town and its immediate vicinity. A few older buildings recall its beginnings; the **Old Stuart Town Gaol** is the most venerable of these, dating all the way back to 1907! **Adelaide House** was built in 1920–6 to serve as a hospital and had natural air-conditioning; the building is now an intriguing museum housing memorabilia related to the early days of the Royal Flying Doctor Service. For a short time in the 1920s the administration of the Northern Territory was split between Darwin and Alice Springs. The **Residency**▶ dates from this period, and now houses a small but well-presented museum of local history. The town's main museum is the **Museum of Central Australia**▶ on the upper floor of the modern mall.

Transport and communications are one of the themes of Alice Springs, if not *the* theme. The place's *raison d'être* was the **Old Telegraph Station**▶▶, and its plain but evocative stone buildings still stand just north of the town. Both the **School of the Air** and the **Royal Flying Doctor Service** have bases in town which are open to the public. To the west is the **Museum of Technology, Transport and Communications** which celebrates early flight in the Outback as well as the history of automobile transportation, while off the Stuart Highway beyond the Heavitree Gap is the **Transport Heritage Precinct**, incorporating the Ghan Preservation Society, and dedicated to rehabilitating the rolling stock of the original, narrow-gauge railway line. In pioneering days, the arid interior relied on camel trains for supplies; at the **Frontier Camel Farm** you can ride one of these ships of the desert and find out about them and their Afghan masters.

Alice Springs is one of the places where the overseas visitor cannot fail to become aware of the Aboriginal presence. Part of the town's living comes from money spent by Aborigines, even more from the merchandising of Aboriginal souvenirs, though you are unlikely to be able to buy a painting by Albert Namatjira (see panel opposite). A particularly poignant story about the European/Aboriginal relationship is told in the modern **Strehlow Research Centre** which celebrates the culture of the Aranda people and the German missionary's son who lived and worked among them.

...and reminders of the Royal Flying Doctor Service

185

They both feed and entertain you in The Alice

How to travel

186

The Stuart Highway
This 3,000km road unrolls its thin band of bitumen through the vast and deserted spaces of central Australia between Adelaide and Darwin. Known to all as 'The Track', it follows the route first traced in 1862 by the tough Scotsman John McDouall Stuart. For many years it was a notorious axle-breaker, but nothing was done until Australia's war situation became desperate in 1942 when, with US Forces' help, the road was speedily asphalted from the railhead at Alice Springs to Darwin. Several decades passed before the southern half of the highway was completely surfaced, and the adventure of gravel, rock and bulldust replaced by the predictability of bitumen.

One of the huge road trains that travel across the continent's north and Outback

By air Darwin's international airport acquired a bright new terminal in 1991, less characterful than the tin shed it replaced, but infinitely more convenient. From here there are connections to many overseas destinations, including direct flights to Japan, Singapore, Indonesia and Malaysia, and to all major Australian cities. Alice Springs also has a modern airport, again linked to a variety of Australian destinations. Connellan Airport, serving Ayers Rock and its resort, has a more limited range of connections. Light aircraft will take you virtually anywhere you want to go in the territory; the traveller in a hurry will almost certainly make use of some of the services and day tours available. The desert looks at its most dramatic from the air; try the hot-air balloon operation at Alice Springs.

By bus and coach Long-distance coaches link Darwin, Alice Springs, Ayers Rock and other points in the territory with major Australian cities (though it takes time!). Tour operators offer any number of trips, particularly in the Red Centre. Some day trips, like Darwin–Kakadu–Darwin are not recommended for the faint-hearted – it is often better to arrange an overnight stop. Only Darwin has any sort of local bus service.

By rail The rebuilt line north from Tarcoola in South Australia carries the revived 'Ghan' (also see page 189), a luxury train connecting Adelaide and Alice Springs; this is the only railway within the Northern Territory. There are bus and air connections from various towns to the railhead at Mount Isa, terminus for the 'Inlander' train from Townsville, almost 1,000km away on the Queensland coast.

By car From Darwin, the **Stuart Highway** runs south through Alice Springs to Port Augusta and Adelaide (3,067km); at Three Ways the **Barkly Highway** leaves the Stuart for Mount Isa and on to Townsville (2,556km); at Katherine, the **Victoria Highway** branches off towards the Kimberley and thence to Perth (4,081km). Sealed roads reach Ayers Rock and Jabiru in Kakadu National Park, and all-weather roads will take you to most major tourist destinations.

▶ **Arnhem Land** 176E2

Beyond Kakadu a rugged sandstone escarpment seems to bar the way to this mysterious and inaccessible area. Given the name of the Dutch ship whose crew were the first Europeans to sight it, Arnhem Land stretches spectacularly eastward to form the western coastline of the Gulf of Carpentaria. Now in the hands of its Aboriginal owners, most of it can only be entered by permit, though a limited number of guided tours do take place from Darwin and Kakadu, and you can also fly into the remote resort of Seven Spirit Bay on the Cobourg Peninsula.

▶▶▶ **Ayers Rock (Uluru) and** 176A1
The Olgas (Kata Tjuta)

Reproduced a million times on film, tape and glossy brochure, the great red monolith of Ayers Rock has become one of the world's tourist clichés, yet it still retains the power to stir the spirits of all those who visit it. Not surprisingly, Uluru (to give the Rock its Aboriginal name) occupied a central place in the spiritual lives of local tribespeople whose ancestors may have frequented the area for at least 20,000 years. A number of sacred sites around the base are protected, and must not be entered or photographed.

The Rock was first sighted by the surveyor Ernest Giles in 1872. In 1985 the land, which includes the World Heritage-listed Uluru-Kata Tjuta National Park, was ceremonially handed back to an Aboriginal trust on behalf of the traditional owners, then immediately leased for 99 years to the Northern Territory's parks service. The resort which had grown up in a haphazard way near the base of the Rock was supposed to be demolished, but this too passed into the hands of the Aborigines. Its replacement is the **Ayers Rock Resort▶**, a respectful distance away at 18km from the Rock itself.

The sediments making up Ayers Rock and the neighbouring Olgas were laid down some 500–600 million years ago and then tilted almost vertically by earth movements. Ayers Rock rises 348m above the plain and Mount Olga rises 546m, but their foundations go far deeper.

Continued on page 190.

The domes of the Olgas, or Kata Tjuta, just waiting to be explored

187

Aboriginal place-names
While many Australian place-names were borrowed from the 'old country', the early settlers were also happy to use Aboriginal names. Parramatta was the first town to be designated in this way, and others can be seen all over the map, often sounding more appropriate than names recalling the villages, suburbs or shire towns of faraway England. Who could resist Woolloomooloo? A trend nowadays is to replace an English name with an Aboriginal one; the Olgas (named after a 19th-century queen of Spain) are now officially Kata Tjuta ('many heads') and Ayers Rock is called Uluru, though one suspects that these English names will prove difficult to eradicate, such is their resonance world wide.

■ **Railways helped shape Australia. In such a vast country, the battle to overcome 'the tyranny of distance' was a long and difficult one, and the role of the railway in helping the country to both grow economically and grow together politically was of outstanding importance.** ■

A long short cut
Once the Transcontinental Railway had linked west to east, travellers from Europe who were in a hurry to get to Melbourne or Sydney would leave their ship at Fremantle and continue their journey by rail. In spite of having to change trains each time there was a break of gauge (at Kalgoorlie, Port Augusta, and again at Albury), the advantage was that a day or two would be saved. The fare, just as on the ocean liner, included all meals – as it still does – but today you no longer need to change trains as the standard gauge stretches right across the continent from Perth to Sydney.

There is plenty of time to study the route

Gauging success The first iron road in Australia was a short line in Adelaide for horse-drawn traffic. The earliest steam railways were those linking Melbourne to its port (September 1854) and Sydney to Parramatta (a year later). But already there was trouble. What track gauge should be adopted?

The colonies initially agreed among themselves that the gauge should be George Stephenson's standard of 4ft 8½in (1,435mm), then a preference was expressed for a broader gap between the rails of 5ft 3in (1,600mm) as used in Ireland. In the end each colony went its own way, Victoria and South Australia adopting the broad gauge and New South Wales adopting the standard gauge. South Australia fell for the comfort and spaciousness implied by the broad gauge, while Queensland and Western Australia came up with a different idea altogether, that of systems built entirely on the narrow gauge of 3ft 6in (1,067mm). Tasmania began with standard gauge, then converted to narrow gauge.

This was fine as long as each system remained self-contained, but eventually the tracks reached out to connect (or rather not connect) with those of the neighbouring network. Through-passengers had to disembark, goods had to be unloaded and re-loaded, and the most hated three words in all Australia at the time were supposed to have been 'All change! Albury!', the name of the station on the border between New South Wales and Victoria. In 1897, Mark Twain was more than vexed to have to change trains here, not least because it involved a tedious walk along a lengthy platform.

Natural hazards Railways were often difficult and expensive to build in Australia, because of the distances that had to be covered, the variety of natural obstacles that had to be overcome, and the high cost of importing rails and other materials from England. The capricious nature of the landscape didn't help, and flooding often occurred in places where no rain had fallen for years, washing the track away.

To keep costs down, many country lines were built to a low standard, resulting in irksome speed restrictions. Bridges remained unbuilt; the train ferry which for years carried the coaches and wagons of Sydney–Brisbane trains over the Clarence River was only replaced by a bridge in 1932. Secondary lines were built not only to the 3ft 6in gauge but to an even narrower 2ft 6in standard, virtually a miniature railway of the kind that still chuffs between Ferntree Gully and Belgrave in the Dandenongs today (the famous *Puffing Billy*). Narrower still – a mere

2ft (600mm) – are the sugarcane railways that wander through the plantations of Queensland.

From time to time some parts of Australia have toyed with the idea of going their own way. Such a stance was taken up by Western Australia at the end of the 19th century, when it only joined the Federation on condition that it was physically linked to the rest of the country by a transcontinental railway (paid for by the Federation). It took years to lay the rails across the 479km of the waterless Nullarbor, but the line was ready for traffic in 1917 and is now traversed by the world-famous *Indian Pacific*.

The Ghan A still incomplete but nevertheless fascinating railway project was the South Australia–Northern Territory link. Shakily built narrow-gauge tracks snaked out from Port Augusta in the south and from Darwin in the north. The southern section was called the Ghan because it replaced the Afghan camel trains which had hitherto been the most effective means of transport along the route. Reaching Oodnadatta in 1890, it took another 39 years to get as far as Alice Springs, and the top section only went as far as Birdum, 500km south of Darwin. Both lines were ripped up in the 1970s, the northern section disappearing altogether and the southern section being rebuilt along a less flood-prone alignment which now carries a luxury train. Also called the Ghan, this train provides one of the world's classic train journeys, in standards of comfort that would have been quite alien to Wilfred Thomas's travelling companions (see panel).

Afghan nights
An early traveller on the Ghan, Wilfred Thomas, settled down to try to get some sleep, but was amazed when his fellow-travellers – a tough-looking bunch of miners and stockmen – cleared the seats away brusquely, brought out the drink and some bagpipes, and then danced the night away together.

The luxury Ghan connects Adelaide and The Alice

189

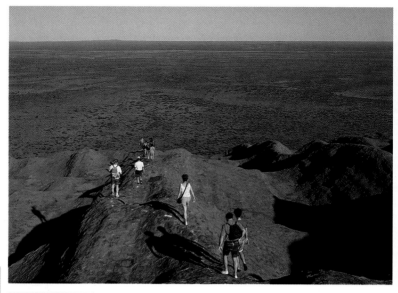

An Outback dragon
The fearsome-looking
thorny devil is one of the
most astonishing denizens
of the desert, well deserving of its zoological name
Moloch horridus. In spite
of its bulbous spine-
covered body and multi-
coloured blotches, it is an
inoffensive creature, rely-
ing on its unappetising
appearance to deter any
predator.

AYERS
ROCK
RESORT
CENTRAL
AUSTRALIA

The spectacular view from the top of Ayers Rock

Continued from page 187.

Much is made of the mysterious responsiveness of both
Ayers Rock and The Olgas to lighting conditions, and few
visitors will want to miss the uncanny changes produced
by dawn and sunset; the basic red colour is due to the
presence of iron.

Most visitors rush to climb the Rock, but the expedition
should not be undertaken lightly, least of all by the elderly
or by those with a medical condition. Take the advice of
rangers and tour guides concerning timing, water supplies and the route (the only one) that must be followed.
You might even bow to the Aborigines' expressed preference that the Rock should not be climbed, but experienced in a more respectful way by a circular walk or tour
around its 10km base. This is worth doing in any case,
revealing as it does a wealth of fascinating detail, the
strange, biscuit-like texture of the stone, or the way in
which the almost vertical lower slopes have been eroded
into deep furrows. If you are really lucky, you could experience a storm and the subsequent spectacle of myriad
waterfalls standing out against a black background.

Of geologically related origin, the 30 or so domes of **the
Olgas** offer a quite different but no less fascinating experience, not least because of the rich vegetation and
wildlife which flourish in the sheltered gorges between
the individual summits. All those able to undertake one of
the somewhat stony walks through the area should
certainly do so, though perhaps the most spectacular way
to view these sleeping dinosaurs (as they have been
called) is aboard a light plane on one of the short flights
that also takes in the Rock. As well as revealing the isolated table mountain known as Mount Conner, perfectly
aligned with the Rock and Olgas, this aerial perspective is
also a good way to appreciate the layout of the Ayers

Rock Resort (see panel). Designed in 1981, its architecture, planning and landscaping represent a remarkably sensitive response to its desert environment.

The visitor to Ayers Rock will find an array of organised tours on offer, ranging from double-deck bus trips to a personalised commentary given while riding pillion on a Harley-Davidson. The **Uluru Experience►** aims to bring small groups of participants into more intimate contact with the plants and animals of the desert, as well as with Aboriginal life and lore.

► **Bathurst and Melville Islands**   *176E1*

Lying off the coast to the north of Darwin and separated from each other by the narrow Apsley Strait, these two large islands are the home of the Tiwi people. Lacking contact with the Aborigines of the mainland, they developed their own very distinct culture, including the making of the extraordinary and highly decorated Pukamani burial poles. The British settlement at Fort Dundas, the first to be attempted on the north Australian coast (1824–9), was a failure. A Catholic mission was set up in the early 1900s, but the islands have now been returned to their traditional owners and can only be visited on an organised tour.

► **Chambers Pillar**   *176A2*

This 50m high red and yellow sandstone monolith rises abruptly from its spreading foundation to make one of the desert's most striking landmarks. Located on the fringes of the bleak Simpson Desert, the pillar, now protected in a historical reserve, was long used as a navigational aid by intrepid explorers, some of whom left inscriptions.

► **Cutta Cutta Caves**   *176D2*

South of Katherine on the Stuart Highway, these ancient limestone chambers linked by narrow passages are the home of the orange horseshoe bat, once believed to be extinct. Near by are the recently opened Tindal Caves, which feature unusual sponge formations.

Green on red
Deserts are fragile environments, whose ecological balance and visual appeal can easily be degraded when visitors arrive in large numbers. The collection of motels and other facilities that had accumulated at the base of Ayers Rock was no triumph of design. Its replacement, the Ayers Rock Resort, is distinguished both architecturally and ecologically. Sited 20km away from the Rock, its visual impact on its unique surroundings is minimal, partly because of skilful landscaping using the characteristic landforms and plants of the desert. The hotel and other buildings of the resort have thick masonry walls for insulation, while bull-nose verandas and eaves shield windows and walkways from the sun. The huge shade sails rising over the main hotel have become the emblem of the place, but they too play a role in energy conservation.

191

Barramundi
This fine tropical fresh-water fish is Australia's favourite catch, making an excellent meal as well as providing good sport. Barramundi can grow to huge sizes; specimens 1.8m long weighing up to 50kg are not uncommon. They live in most northern aquatic environments, travelling to river estuaries to breed. A big barramundi will fiercely resist being taken. Barramundi are still plentiful but there are Northern Territory restrictions on how many may be caught.

The rare orange horseshoe bat can be found in the Cutta Cutta Caves

The rounded granite forms of the Devils Marbles, 90km south of Tennant Creek

Castles of clay
In a land of minimal moisture, there are no earthworms to turn the soil. This role is taken over in the Northern Territory and other arid lands by termites, which pattern whole landscapes with their extraordinary mounds (see below). Sometimes rising to a height of 3m, these insect fortresses are built from a mixture of soil, spit and dung. However hostile conditions outside may be, behind the rock-hard walls the interior of the mound is a climate-controlled environment of 100 per cent humidity and a constant temperature of 30°C.

▶▶   **Devils Marbles**   *176C2*

Hundreds of granite boulders lie scattered across the plain beside the Stuart Highway just north of the village of Wauchope, some huge, some tiny and some perched in impossible positions. To the geologist they are all that remains of the ancient mountains that once rose here, but to the Aborigines they are the eggs of the Rainbow Serpent, Wanambi. They are best seen in the early morning.

▶▶   **Finke Gorge National Park**   *176A2*

Access to the famous gorge in the Western MacDonnell Ranges known as Palm Valley is along the rocky bed of the Finke River, normally dry but impassable after rain. In utter contrast to the desert is the lush vegetation thriving in the protected environment of the gorge. The 46,000 hectare national park's 3,000 or so cabbage palms are unique to the area, the descendants of prehistoric trees which grew on the shore of what was then a tropical sea. A good way to get a general view of the rugged sandstone gorge is to climb up to **Initiation Rock**, where youths of the Aranda people were once introduced to the mysteries of manhood.

▶▶   **Gurig National Park**   *176F2*

Now returned to its traditional Aboriginal owners, this national park covers the whole of the remote Cobourg Peninsula protruding westwards from Arnhem Land. There is splendid sailing and fishing, as well as the experience of utter isolation, since the number of visitor permits issued is strictly limited (permits are obtainable from the Parks and Wildlife Commission of the Northern Territory). The superb natural harbour of **Port Essington** was the site of Victoria, one of the early British settlements later replaced by Darwin.

▶   **Henbury Meteorite Craters
        Conservation Reserve**   *176A2*

At the end of a dirt road off the Stuart Highway 130km south of Alice Springs is a genuine curiosity: a swarm of craters formed about 5,000 years ago when a big meteorite split into pieces on entering the earth's atmosphere.

▶▶▶ **Kakadu National Park** 176E2

Some 250km east of Darwin, Australia's largest national park joined Unesco's World Heritage Area list in 1987 on account of the Aboriginal art sites it contains and its almost unbelievably rich and varied wildlife.

Kakadu extends over a number of very distinct landscapes. The tidal zone along the shore of Van Diemen's Gulf is pierced by the estuaries of four great rivers, the East, West and South Alligator Rivers and the Wildman River. Here the grey of tidal mudflats contrasts with the bright green of mangrove swamps, breeding grounds for the well-known barramundi (see panel on page 191). The floodplains of the rivers become a vast freshwater sea in the Wet, teeming with migratory birds and other waterfowl, including magpie geese, kites, egrets, brolgas, pelicans, cormorants, ibises and the handsome jabiru. Salt and freshwater crocodiles lurk in creek and billabong. As the land rises gradually southwards, eucalyptus woodland develops, interspersed with myriad termite mounds or dramatically interrupted by massive rock outcrops, isolated fragments of the formidable sandstone escarpment marking the western edge of Arnhem Land. This rugged north–south barrier runs for 500km, broken by gorges cut by the streams draining the vast interior, the scene of spectacular waterfalls in the wet season. Two of the best known of these are **Jim Jim Falls▶** and **Twin Falls▶**, in the south of the park, both with abundant tropical wildlife.

Scores of natural galleries in the escarpment sandstone contain some of the country's choicest examples of early Aboriginal art. The most visited are those at **Ubirr▶▶**, and at **Nourlangie Rock▶**. The **Bowali Visitor Centre** for the park is near the main town of Jabiru, but there is also an excellent new complex, the **Warradjan Aboriginal Cultural Centre**, which provides more insight into the area's history and culture. It is just possible to get some idea of Kakadu in the course of a day visit by air from Darwin (there are coach trips too, in spite of the distance).

Art of the Outback
Aboriginal art is traditionally connected to ritual and ceremony rather than self-expression, and is ephemeral or renewable. Much of the art of central Australia is abstract and symbolic. The artist's canvas could be a rock wall or the ground itself, with sand paintings executed in coloured earths, pebbles, feathers and so on. The wall paintings at Kakadu are representational. Some of them, depicting hunting scenes, are incredibly old, dating from the pre-estuarine period up to 23,000 years ago. The x-ray style, showing the internal organs and bone structure of fish and animals, dates from the estuarine period, which followed a rise in sea level some 7,000–9,000 years ago. More recent depictions of Europeans and their accoutrements belong to the so-called contact period.

193

Dawn over Kakadu – a sight to remember

■ In the early part of the 20th century, it seemed as if the Aborigines of Australia were doomed as a race. Their numbers had diminished drastically from an estimated population of half a million at the onset of European colonisation to perhaps 60,000 in the 1920s; and many of these were of mixed blood. ■

Good grub
While Aboriginal men hunted game with boomerang and fire, women and children foraged for smaller animals, lizards, insects, seeds and fruit. A particular delicacy is the witchetty grub. With a buttery taste when cold, the grubs are said to resemble pork scratchings when cooked in hot ashes. Initiation into the delights of 'bush tucker' can be a fascinating experience.

These children live near a school; for those too far away there is always the radio-transmitted School of the Air

Christian missions established in the Outback destroyed the Aborigines' ancient religious links with the land, government 'Protectors' moved them around at will, and half-caste children were removed from their parents and brought up in homes or by foster parents. Devastated by alcoholism, wasted by disease, seldom in steady employment and consistently discriminated against, it seemed to some as if it would only be a matter of time before mainland Aborigines suffered the fate of the Tasmanians.

A genius not extinguished As the end of the century approaches, however, the situation has become more hopeful. A voice has been found, one moreover which is listened to and sometimes acted on by those in positions of power. The Aboriginal plight has been noticed by the white majority, thanks to protests like the 'tent embassy' established for years in front of the Canberra Parliament, or the march of 30,000 people through the streets of Sydney, part of a boycott of the 1988 Bicentennial (or 'Invasion') celebrations. On a small scale, Aboriginal voices are heard on Aboriginal-owned radio and television stations.

In the realm of politics, reforms have been carried out and, in part, implemented. The almost incredible situation in which Aborigines were not classed as citizens or even counted in the official census of population was rectified

by the 1967 referendum which gave the Federal Government overall responsibility for Aboriginal affairs. One outcome was the drafting and passing of the Aboriginal Land Rights Act of 1976 that enabled Crown lands to be handed back to the 'traditional owners'. A dramatic illustration of the effect of this took place in 1985, when **Ayers Rock** and the **Uluru National Park** formally became the property of the Uluru-Kata Tjuta Land Trust on behalf of the traditional owners. Entry to such lands is now only possible by means of a permit. In the case of a world-famous national park, this is obtained both instantly and easily; in the case of less well-known places it is by no means automatic, a fact resented by many white Australians.

As seen by others White attitudes have undergone change, even transformation. In an age of environmental devastation and loss of religious direction, the way in which Aborigines lived for thousands of years in material and religious harmony with their surroundings has earned respect and even wonder. Aboriginal art, both traditional and contemporary, is widely admired. There is a widespread wish, expressed by politicians as well as by ordinary people, to make restitution for the injustices perpetrated over 200 years. But problems remain, even if they no longer seem so insurmountable. While some younger people of Aboriginal descent try to combine old ways of living with some of the benefits of European civilisation, others fail to find a place anywhere and continue to live on the margins of society. In the face of widespread petty criminality and drink-related offences, a repressive police culture persists; a shameful number of young blacks have died while in police custody. Rejection and contempt live on in many white hearts.

It may be that a certain degree of separation must take place before the races can come together again in harmony, and the right of refusal of entry to Aboriginal lands should be seen in this light, rather than denounced as incipient apartheid. In any case, there is a wish on the part of many Aborigines to share their growing pride in themselves and their heritage with their fellow Australians and with visitors. Contemporary Aboriginal art, of variable quality, is available everywhere, while traditional rock paintings are best experienced in the company of an Aboriginal ranger. Music, dance and ritual are performed in many places, but the high point of many people's experience of Australia could be a visit to an Aboriginal community (arranged through the Australian Tourist Commision – see page 266).

A right to land
Since 1976, Northern Territory Aborigines have owned the land in what were formerly reserves and in addition have been able to lay claim to vacant Crown Land. Many of these claims have been opposed, and even when successful do not necessarily inhibit mining and quarrying. But royalties have to be paid to the owners, and quite a few communities in areas like Arnhem Land now have no shortage of funds.

195

Some communities are willing to share and explain their traditions

■ **The total number of sheep in Australia today amounts to over 160 million, more than three-quarters of them the resilient merino with a fleece of up to 10kg in weight. Australia accounts for about a quarter of the world's wool and is the biggest exporter of lamb and mutton. In some places the sheep/people ratio begs belief: one million sheep roam South Australia's Kangaroo Island, for example, compared with only 4,000 humans.** ■

A tough breed One of the animals most closely identified with Australia, sheep were among the passengers of the first fleet, though 59 of Governor Phillip's 90 beasts soon perished. A certain Captain John Macarthur had better luck; he cannily bred Bengal ewes with English rams, then crossed them with Spanish merinos. This mixed breed flourished in the new environment, yielding a fleece of fine quality and good weight – making Macarthur a rich man and providing the foundation of Australia's wool industry, a mainstay of the national economy even today. In the 19th century, it was sheep as much as people that colonised the vast spaces of the new country; by 1900 there were nearly 100 million of them.

Sheep shearers Watching sheep shearers at their highly skilled work is quite a spectacle. The sheep is driven into the shearing shed, thrown to the ground by the shearer and held fast between his or her legs. The electric clippers, which long ago replaced the more laborious hand shears, run swiftly through the fleece, this being removed in one piece if possible. The heaps of wool are sorted according to quality and are then dispatched in huge bales.

Record shearing
Traditionally working in teams that moved from station to station during the shearing season, shearers honed their skills to an almost incredible pitch; in 1892 a Queensland man, Jackie Howe, set the record for hand-shearing, having shorn 321 sheep in 7 hours 40 minutes. Even with electric clippers, today's shearers find this difficult to match.

196

Will this be a new sheep-shearing record?

▶ Katherine 176E2

This township is the centre of the vast and remote territory described by Jeannie Gunn in her classic 1908 novel of the Outback *We of the Never Never*. The area derives its name from the saying that those who live there can 'never never' leave. You can visit the Northern Territory's oldest surviving homestead, Springvale, but most of the town's 250,000 annual visitors come for the spectacular Katherine Gorge at **Nitmiluk National Park▶▶**, about 30km to the east. Rising in Arnhem Land, the Katherine River has cut a series of stunning gorges through the sandstone plateau, providing a refuge for a surprising variety of flora and fauna. The first two gorges can be seen aboard tourist boats, the defiles further upstream in your own canoe. There are a number of walks from the information centre to points along the gorge.

▶▶ Kings Canyon 176A1

One of the most spectacular natural landscapes of Central Australia, this deep canyon (officially called Watarrka National Park and located some 350km southwest from Alice), with its rugged sandstone cliffs rising 200m above the dry river bed, has only recently become well frequented by visitors. A short walk leads up the floor of the canyon to a lookout point, but anyone with proper walking shoes who is reasonably fit should not miss the more challenging (6km) walk up on to the plateau and around the rim of the canyon. Steep to start with, it gives panoramic views over the canyon and a distant glimpse of Ayers Rock.

▶▶ Litchfield National Park 176E1

This 650sq km tract of sandstone plateau and lush rain forest, until relatively recently part of a private farming property, is becoming increasingly popular with both tourists and local people from the Darwin area, not least because of the excellent swimming in the clear pools at the foot of its numerous waterfalls. The park also features many tall termite mounds and the free-standing sandstone pillars of the 'Lost City'. Access is via the pleasant tree-shaded township of Batchelor.

Kings Canyon, rugged, but good walking country

197

A living tradition
As a result of both increasing interest in indigenous Australian history and culture, and the initiative of Aboriginal people, several new cultural centres have sprung up in the Territory. There is an excellent new establishment in Kakadu (see page 193), as well as the Uluru-Kata Tjuta Cultural Centre, near the base of Ayers Rock and featuring traditional dance, art and crafts.

Spinifex
Early explorers cursed the spiky tussocks of spinifex as its spear-like blades impeded their progress through the deserts. Spinifex grasses are great survivors, often the only plants able to withstand the extreme heat and aridity of the centre thanks to their deep tap root. Growing outwards into hollow clumps, the plants provide a habitat for other forms of desert life – insects, lizards, skinks and even a species of pigeon.

The Larapinta Trail
This long-distance trail leads from Alice Springs Telegraph Station right into the West MacDonnells. Hikers can either walk its entire length or undertake shorter sections with an overnight camp. Full details can be obtained from the Northern Territory's Parks and Wildlife Commission.

The blue lagoon of the Glen Helen Gorge

►►► MacDonnell Ranges   *176A2*

These parallel ridges of red quartzite and sandstone extend their corrugations hundreds of kilometres across Central Australia, an almost frightening panorama of total desolation when seen from the air. But this was home to the Aranda people until well after the arrival of the white man, and in the gorges cut long ago by the now infrequently flowing rivers there flourishes a lush vegetation of palms and ferns, descendants of the flora which grew on the shore of an ancient tropical sea.

Some of the most spectacular landscapes of the **West MacDonnell National Park** are easily accessible from Alice Springs via Namatjira Drive. Overlooking The Alice itself from a height of 940m is the distinctive peak of Mount Gillen. Only a little further out at 17km from Alice Springs is **Simpsons Gap►►**, where the steep-sided gorge, pale sands and fine specimens of river red gums and ghost gums make an excellent introduction to the landscape of the ranges. The reserve is accessible by vehicle but, as always, the best way to explore is on foot, using one of several signposted walking tracks, and there is even a sealed bicycle path. Among the wildlife of the gorge is a colony of black-footed rock wallabies.

In dramatic contrast to the impressively wide gorge at Simpsons Gap is **Standley Chasm►►**, an incredibly narrow cleft between 100m quartzite cliffs. For a short period around midday the sun fills the red walls of the gorge with vibrant light, a popular spectacle for visitors who have walked the kilometre or so along the bed of the creek. At **Ellery Creek Big Hole►►**, high red cliffs frame the water-filled gorge which is a favourite spot for swimming and fishing. **Serpentine Gorge►** consists of a narrow winding defile with semi-permanent water holes and ghost gums, and has been left deliberately undeveloped. **Ormiston Gorge and Pound►►** is the largest of the reserves in West MacDonnell National Park, with perma-

Not a mirage
Right up to the 1930s, camels played an indispensable part in opening up the centre of the continent. Explorers, surveyors, miners and pastoralists all used camel trains to transport food, equipment, building materials, barbed wire and metal ores. Their equally tough attendants all acquired the epithet 'Afghan', though many of them were from India. Turned loose when lorries, jeeps and planes took over their work, the camels adapted easily to the wild and today are numbered in their thousands. In captivity, they are successfully bred for export to Arabia, as well as giving many visitors the thrill of a humpback ride. The Frontier Camel Farm 8km south of Alice Springs is one of the best known of such establishments.

nent water holes and magical ghost gums, while **Glen Helen Gorge▶▶** has rugged rust-coloured cliffs contrasting with the blue of the water which forms a deep lagoon in the bed of the Finke River. Further west is **Redbank Gorge▶** with its chilly rockpools. Further on still, Tylers Pass leads to Gosses Bluff, then back towards Alice Springs via the old Hermannsburg Mission; a possible short diversion is to spectacular **Palm Valley▶**.

In the MacDonnells east of Alice Springs, **Emily and Jessie Gaps Nature Park▶** has semi-permanent waterholes and Aboriginal paintings, while in **Trephina Gorge Nature Park▶▶** the pale stems of splendid ghost gums stand out starkly against the rugged cliffs. High above **John Hayes Rockhole▶** is a vista of spectacular scenery and Aboriginal rock art. **Ross River**, where there is a resort, makes a good base for further exploration, to **Arltunga Historical Reserve** for example.

▶   **Mataranka**   *176D2*
Just off the Stuart Highway 100km southeast of Katherine is the Mataranka Homestead and the nearby thermal pool, a popular stop-off. Every minute, 16,500 litres of water at a constant temperature of 34°C gush into a crystal-clear water hole fringed by palm trees.

▶▶▶   **The Olgas/Kata Tjuta**   *176A1*
See pages 187 and 190.

▶   **Pine Creek**   *176E1*
Ah Toy's shop in this tiny Stuart Highway township is a reminder of the gold-rush days of the 1870s, when the Chinese population outnumbered Europeans 15 to 1. The old times are recalled in the **Pine Creek Miners' Park**.

▶   **Tennant Creek**   *176C2*
Legend has it that Tennant Creek came into existence in the 1930s when the axle broke on a wagon carting beer and building materials for a new hotel further north. Moving on seemed too much bother, so once the beer had been drunk the building was put up here. Then gold was found and Tennant Creek became one of the roughest places along the track. Relatively calm now, the town has plenty of amenities for the passer-by. The **Gold Stamp Battery** still crushes the region's gold and has an interesting mining museum, and the 1874 **Overland Telegraph Station** is open to the public.

QUEENSLAND

Idyllic Green Island

REGION HIGHLIGHTS ◄◄◄◄◄

QUEENSLAND

Queensland Second only to Western Australia in area, the Sunshine State straddles the Tropic of Capricorn between the New South Wales border and the Torres Strait separating Australia from Papua New Guinea. The immensely long and fertile coastline, with its succession of incomparable beaches and island paradises, is mostly within sight of the hills and mountains of the **Great Dividing Range**. To the east, across the transparent waters of a broad lagoon, is the **Great Barrier Reef**, the largest structure in the world to have been built by living creatures. To the west, the subtropical rain forest cladding the seaward slopes of the mountains gives way to plateau farmlands of gradually diminishing quality; here, where cattle stations sometimes provide the only names on the map, is some of the country's most authentic Outback, merging in the end with the sands, stones and spinifex of true desert. In the far north, the **Cape York Peninsula** remains one of the continent's strangest and most remote places.

Almost over-endowed with natural beauty and a smiling climate, Queensland has become a favourite destination with visitors from abroad as well as with Australians on holiday or in retirement. Together with a superabundance of mineral wealth, mined in such areas as **Mount Isa** (the world's largest city in terms of area), the growth of tourism has helped Queensland prosper when the economy of other states has languished. Agriculture maintains its importance; along the coastal plain it has created richly textured landscapes of tropical crops including sugar cane, which is delivered to mills by a network of narrow-gauge agricultural railways.

Convict roots Queensland's recent history began with the establishment of a convict settlement at Moreton Bay in 1824. This dumping ground for particularly recalcitrant offenders was soon transferred to an upriver site near by which was named Brisbane after the Governor of New South Wales at the time. In 1859 independence from New South Wales was granted, and the new colony was given its name in honour of Queen Victoria.

The population increased and settlement spread; timber workers took the best trees from the rain forest, leaving farmers to clear the resulting scrub. Gold and other mineral finds helped open up the country; Queensland's richest goldfield was the remote and disease-ridden Palmer River, scene of a rush in the 1870s. Migrant labour has played a relatively minor role in Queensland's history, but at one point the gold-digging Chinese on the Palmer outnumbered the rest of the Far North's population. Tradition has it that the local Aborigines killed and ate these Chinese with more relish than they did Europeans. Another migrant group were the Kanakas, shipped in in their thousands from the South Pacific and New Guinea to work in the canefields (see panel).

A high proportion of Australia's Aborigines lived in Queensland, perhaps more than 200,000 at the beginning of white settlement. Of a fiercer and more warlike disposition than their fellows elsewhere, they put up a spirited resistance to their dispossession. To little avail, however; by the turn of the century their numbers had been reduced to no more than 15,000.

Sugar cane
One of the spectacles of Queensland are the fires that rage through the cane plantations in winter near towns such as Mossman (70km from Cairns), when the dry stalks are burned off to get rid of debris, snakes and insects. At other times the tall green crop presents a peaceful sight, often combined on the coastal plain with tropical fruits like pineapples, mangoes, paw-paws and guavas. Sugar production goes back to the mid-19th century, when South Sea Islanders were brought in in large numbers as indentured labourers (called 'Kanakas'). Many of Queensland's sugar mills can now be visited.

Politics and people For a generation, Queensland was governed by the Ultra-Conservative National Party, formerly known as the Country Party and representing rural interests. This organisation was led from 1968 by the robust peanut farmer Sir Joh Bjelke-Petersen, a sworn opponent of moral permissiveness, conservation or anything that stood in the way of 'development'. Under his authoritarian rule, demonstrations were banned, books censored, homosexuals harrassed and protected buildings demolished. Building speculators prospered and foreign capital was encouraged to share in the state's wealth, with few strings attached or questions asked. Sir Joh's demise came with revelations of police misconduct and corruption.

The typical Queenslander is popularly supposed to be the most Australian of Australians. A frontier mentality lasted longer here than in the southern states; the metropolitan refinements of Sydney and Melbourne were looked down on, as was anything that smacked of 'culture'. Until quite recently, Brisbane took a positive pride in its decidedly provincial character. Much of this has now changed, but enough remains to make the state quite distinct.

View from the world-famous Cairns–Kuranda train

203

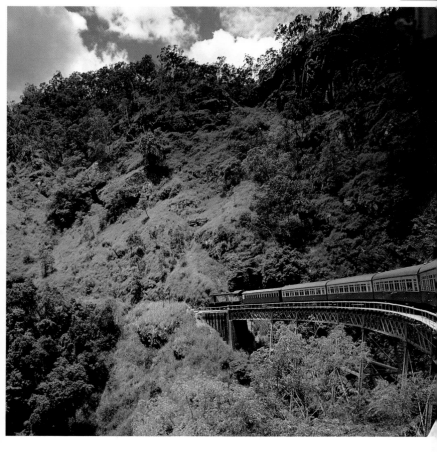

Victoria
Park

SPRING
HILL

FORTITUDE
VALLEY

Brisbane
Tramway
Museum

Mieganyah Folk Museum Brunswick St Sta
and Bowya Park

Newstead
House and
Airport

KELVIN GROVE ROAD
GILCHRIST AVENUE
GREGORY TERRACE
ITHACA ST
MUSGRAVE ROAD
COLLEGE ROAD
BRUNSWICK STREET
WICKHAM STREET
CHINA TOWN

KEMP
PLACE

Mt Coot-tha
Botanic
Gardens

PETRIE
TERRACE

Albert
Park

BOUNDARY STREET
BOUNDARY STREET
WICKHAM STREET
LEICHHARDT STREET
LITTLE EDWARD STREET
BARRY PARADE
WICKHAM STREET
IVORY STREET

Centenary
Park

Cathedral
Square Plaza
St John's
Cathedral

Petrie Bight

STORY BRIDGE

Victoria
Barracks
Military
Museum

Lone Pine
Koala Sanctuary
and University
of Queensland

COUNTESS STREET
CAXTON STREET
PETRIE TERRACE
UPPER ROMA STREET

Roma Street
Station

Brisbane
Transit
Centre

Police
HQ

Wickham
Park

Old
Windmill

Central
Station

Kangaroo Point
Captain John
Burke Park

BRADFIELD HIGHWAY

MERIVALE STREET
WILLIAM STREET
JOLLY BRIDGE
ROMA STREET
NORTH QUAY
RIVERSIDE
GEORGE STREET
TURBOT STREET
ANN STREET
WICKHAM TERRACE
ALBERT STREET
TURBOT STREET
CREEK STREET
WHARF STREET
ALBERT STREET

Anzac
Square

Riverside
Centre

King
George
Square

GPO

Golden
Mile Ferry

City
Hall

MALL

St Stephen's
Cathedral

CT White
Park

QUEEN STREET
EAGLE STREET
EAGLE STREET

State
Library

Law
Courts

Treasury
Casino

City
Plaza

Myer
Centre

ELIZABETH STREET
CHARLOTTE STREET

Eagle St
Pier

QE II
Park

Queens
Gdns

MARY STREET

Town Reach

VICTORIA BRIDGE
EXPRESSWAY
WILLIAM STREET
GEORGE STREET
ALICE STREET
MARGARET STREET

City

Edward St
Ferry

KANGAROO
POINT

Queensland
Art Gallery
& Museum

Queensland
Cultural
Centre

Marine
Wharf

City
Botanic
Gardens

Music Bowl

SHAFSTON AVENUE

Performing Arts
Centre

South
Brisbane
Station

Heliport

The
Mansions

Queensland
Club

SOUTH
BRISBANE

Brisbane Convention
and Exhibition Centre

Gondwana Wildlife
Sanctuary

South

Parliament
House

Queensland
Institute
of Technology

Conservatorium
of Music

MAIN STREET

Earlystreet
Historical
Village

Brisbane Reach
South Reach

Musgrave
Park

Bank

Domain

Gardens
Point

MELBOURNE STREET
CORDELIA STREET
ERNEST STREET
GREY STREET
PEEL STREET

Parklands

Queensland
Maritime
Museum

Raymond
Park

CAPTAIN COOK BRIDGE
SOUTH EAST FREEWAY
STANLEY STREET
MAIN STREET

N

0   200   400 m

HIGHGATE HILL

GLADSTONE ROAD
VULTURE STREET

Vulture
Street
Station

VULTURE STREET

Brisbane
Cricket
Ground

WOOLLOONGABBA

1   2   3

Brisbane

Australia's third largest city stands on the banks of the winding Brisbane River just inland from Moreton Bay. For long it was regarded as a provincial backwater, a kind of agricultural town which as recently as 1961 had hundreds of kilometres of unmade streets. Perhaps to combat this image, Brisbane has recently embraced the idea of progress with an enthusiasm that some people find altogether regrettable.

Old-town sights Not all traces of an older charm have been erased in a misguided pursuit of modernity, however, and enough older buildings remain to tantalise the visitor with thoughts of the stylish tropical metropolis Brisbane perhaps never was but might have become. One such example is the corner of George and Alice Streets where the **Botanic Gardens** help frame the white stuccoed fronts of the **Queensland Club** and **Old Parliament House**. A more positive face of modernisation than the new high-rise parliamentary annexe can be seen on the south bank of the river at South Bank Parklands. **Expo 88** was held here, leaving behind a legacy of parkland and a number of cultural and recreational buildings of the very highest standard.

Suburban splendour The suburbs are among the best places in which to savour the city's special quality. Spread over a vast and largely hilly area, they consist almost entirely of detached houses, and in areas like Red Hill, Paddington and Bardon, the Queensland stilt house can be studied in all its variety.

City centre orientation Brisbane's city centre is surprisingly small and easily explored on foot, although a nice idea is to take the City Sights Trambus which wanders round most of the sights, allowing you to jump on and off when you wish for a flat fare. A boat cruise to historic **Newstead House** makes a pleasant excursion, too, while ferries link a number of destinations along the river bank.

The handsome 1868 Parliament House has been carefully restored

---

W̶a̶l̶k̶ **Brisbane's buildings and Botanic Gardens**

See map opposite.

Allow a half-day for this long exploration of the peninsula on which the city of Brisbane is built.

Extending almost an entire city block, the **Central Railway Station** of 1901 faces **Anzac Square** with its **Shrine of Remembrance**. At the corner of Ann and Edward Streets stands the extraordinary **People's Palace** with its elaborate verandas and cast-iron balustrades. The **General Post Office** is an imposing building, and the GPO arcade leads to Elizabeth Street, to **Old St Stephen's Church** and to **St Stephen's Cathedral**.

The riverside walk extends beyond the Edward Street gates of the **Botanic Gardens**, and the **University of Technology** flanks the gardens.

An intimation of the tropical paradise Brisbane might have been is given by the lovely building of the **Queensland Club** in its impeccably gardened setting. Opposite are **The Mansions**, striking terrace houses now housing shops and restaurants. Just off Queens Gardens in William Street are the 1829 **Commissariat Stores**, one of only two convict era buildings remaining intact in the city. The nearby Lands Building and old Treasury have been meticulously restored to become the Conrad International Hotel and Treasury Casino respectively.

On the far side of Victoria Bridge are the **Queensland Cultural Centre** and the **South Bank Parklands**. A visit here could easily last a whole day, though a quick tour could be made using the Brisbane Transport ferry to return to the city centre.

Queen Street Mall is more commercial, though there are some fine late 19th-century and interwar buildings. The walk ends in **King George Square**.

QUEENSLAND

One of Earlystreet's authentic exhibits

206

South of the river
South Brisbane and the South Bank Parklands have become the city's most appealing precinct. The Parklands include a man-made beach and the Butterfly and Insect House, and many shops and restaurants, while the neighbouring Queensland Maritime Museum is also worth visiting. Also in this area is the vast new Convention and Exhibition Centre.

Parks and gardens
Brisbane is extremely fortunate in the number of green spaces in its centre and immediate environs. The **Brisbane Forest Park** comprises 265sq km of forests, hills and reservoirs, while the **City Botanic Gardens** occupy the tip of the peninsula formed by the great bend in the Brisbane River. There is a riverside walk, and the gardens form an ideal setting for the buildings of the Queensland University of Technology, among them the Old Government House of 1860. At the foot of **Mount Coot-tha** (229m), 6km from the city, there are more splendid botanic gardens. This is one of the best places in Australia to enjoy native plants, and there are stunning tropical glasshouses and a planetarium.

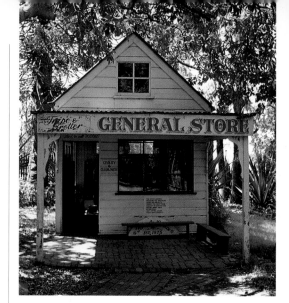

▶ **City Hall** 204C2
King George Square
In the late 1920s, a determined attempt was made to overcome Brisbane's provincial image by the erection of this colossal edifice, whose 91m tower shoots up behind the array of columns facing King George Square. The gallery at the top gives *the* view of the city centre. Inside, there is an art gallery and museum, with plenty of exhibits celebrating the city's importance. Starting from City Hall, Brisbane's Heritage Trail takes in the city's most important historic sites and buildings.

▶ **Earlystreet Historical Village** 204B3
McIlwraith Avenue, Norman Park
This open-air museum to the east of the city centre offers a chance to see some of Queensland's characteristic architecture. A number of buildings from all over the state have been rescued from demolition and re-erected here.

▶ **Miegunyah Folk Museum** 204D2
Jordan Terrace, Bowen Hills
Housed in a fine example of a stilt house dating from 1886, this museum takes as its theme the life led by women in colonial times.

▶ **Newstead House** 204D3
Breakfast Creek Road, Newstead
Built in 1846, this white mansion (4km north of the centre) with its elegant verandas is the oldest surviving house in Brisbane. Now a museum of colonial days, it was once owned by Captain John Wickham, commander of the *Beagle* during its survey of Australia's coastline, who made Newstead the centre of the city's social life.

▶ **Old Windmill** 204C2
Wickham Terrace
This is Brisbane's oldest structure, convict-built and overlooking the city from the pleasant heights of Wickham Terrace. What if its sails failed to work? No worries! Put in

a treadmill! Plenty of convict feet to keep it turning, and more reliable too! It was later used as an observatory.

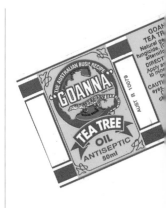

▶▶ Queensland Cultural Centre 204B1

Melbourne Street, South Brisbane

'Culture' seems to have been something that Brisbane was for many years content to leave to the fancy folk down in Sydney. But times change and, having decided that it was a good thing after all, Brisbane set about accommodating culture in as lavish a way as possible. The result is the impressive complex of buildings on the south bank. Completed in 1985, it includes the Queensland Art Gallery, Queensland Museum, State Library and Performing Arts Complex, the latter with a 2,000-seater theatre and an equally large concert hall.

The **Queensland Art Gallery▶▶** has a good selection of Australian art, and a beginner's collection of European painting, some of it interestingly arranged by theme rather than by artist or country. But the pictures have little chance of competing with the architecture, which is on a huge scale and very concrete.

The exhibits in the **Queensland Museum▶▶**, particularly the dinosaurs and the aircraft, are more of a match for their surroundings and there is a major display on the history, art and culture of the Aborigines.

Koala capital
Brisbane styles itself the 'koala capital', and the Bunya Park Wildlife Sanctuary and Lone Pine Koala Sanctuary are both good places to see these friendly marsupials.

▶▶ South Bank Parklands

South Brisbane 204B2

Once the international crowds have gone, Expo sites often become forlorn places. But many of the pavilions and facilities erected for Brisbane's 1988 bonanza are still here, bringing life to this extensive area of parkland stretching along the river opposite the city centre. Its **Gondwana Wildlife Sanctuary▶** is an ambitious and imaginative re-creation of the Queensland jungle, featuring koalas, wombats, colourful birds and a superb rain forest environment. See panel on page 206.

Modern Brisbane is Australia's third largest city

Glass House Mountains scenery

The Sunshine Coast and hinterland

This full day's drive along Queensland's Sunshine Coast goes into the hinterland of farming and hill country along the Bruce Highway.

About 60km north of Brisbane, the **Glass House Mountains** interrupt the monotony of the coastal plain. These old volcanic hills are best viewed from the old main road north of Caboolture as well as from the Mary Cairncross Park near Maleny. The **Blackall Range** panoramic drive gives access to this superb upland country of undulating hills and verdant valleys, tea shops and craft studios. Just north of the little highland resort of Montville is the **Kondalilla National Park**, where splendid 100m waterfalls crash down through the rain forest. Equally spectacular falls can be experienced at **Mapleton Falls National Park**.

In **Nambour**, centre of tropical fruit production, a narrow-gauge sugarcane train trundles nonchalantly through the streets. A sequence of splendid beaches unravels along the Sunshine Coast north of Coolum to the multi-centred and highly fashionable community of Noosa Heads,

QUEENSLAND DRIVE 1

while **Tewantin** boasts a couple of curiosities – a house built of bottles and the Big Shell. Back inland, the charming village of **Eumundi** makes a good stopping place, though it will be packed if you visit on market day (Saturday).

The Bruce Highway should ensure a swift return to Brisbane.

As may be expected in a state of its vast size, Queensland's landscapes are of an extraordinary variety, many of them protected by designation as national or environmental parks.

Tropical coastline to desert heartlands Most visitors will become familiar with the reef and rain forest parks of the tropical and subtropical coastline, but the spectacular and often unique parks of the interior demand attention too. More than 1,200km to the west of the coast are the monotonous sandhills of the **Simpson Desert**, 'stretching interminably like waves of the sea' according to the explorer Charles Sturt, who gave up his attempt to conquer them. First crossed on foot in 1973, they still offer a challenge to anyone venturing into them today.

Further east, the sparse vegetation of the desert gives way to country characterised by grasslands, wattle scrub, eucalyptus woodland, or by scattered individuals of the strange Queensland bottle tree. Among the spinifex and rugged hills of the **Lark Quarry Environmental Park**, the footprints of dinosaurs that perished in a stampede 100 million years ago are preserved in mud that has long since turned to rock.

Further east still, a broad belt of sandstone gives rise to spectacular scenery. This is where many of Queensland's major rivers have their origin; their erosive action has formed deep gorges in which a rich flora thrives, including the cabbage palms of **Carnarvon National Park**, also well known for its strange rock formations. As the land rises and rainfall increases, the blue-green of eucalypts gives way to the dark green of tropical rain forest, with its incredible wealth of species including ferns, climbers and other epiphytes. In parts of far north Queensland the rain forest descends to the beaches fringing the Great Barrier Reef, whose cays and islands are now conserved as part of the **Great Barrier Reef Marine Park**.

Wild north to friendly south Cape York has some of the finest but least accessible of Queensland's national parks, where nature displays herself in all her savage unpredictability. In the wet season, rivers fill with fierce-flowing, silt-rich water, closing fords and cutting off communications for weeks on end, only to dry up into a series of isolated pools when the rain has stopped. Strange termite mounds stud the inland landscape, while mangrove swamps grow from the mud of the coastal plain. In the southeast of the state, nature wears a kindlier air. Brisbane must be one of the world's best endowed capital cities in terms of grand scenery that is easily accessible to city dwellers; a crescent of gloriously wooded highlands extends from close to the city boundary, south to **Lamington National Park** on the border between Queensland and New South Wales.

Brisbane's Lone Pine Koala Sanctuary is the state's best-known animal park, where kangaroos, Tasmanian devils and other creatures can also be seen

In the south
Near the market centre of Warwick, at Cunningham's Gap in the Main Range National Park, there are fine views and a number of trails through rain forest and eucalyptus woodland.

Keep an eye out for the beautiful crimson rosella

How to travel

The Pacific Highway to the south of Brisbane runs through eucalyptus country

A Queensland highland line
Although there is now an alternative form of transport (see page 220), half a million people travel the Cairns–Kuranda railway line every year. Few are disappointed by the spectacular 34km ride from coast to mountain rainforest. The long train of period coaches climbs from sea level to a summit at 328m via a series of tunnels and sharp bends, stopping for a breather at the spectacularly tall Barron Falls. The railway was built in 1886–91 to link the agricultural Atherton Tableland with the port at Cairns; it immediately put paid to Port Douglas as a harbour of any significance. The terminus at Kuranda, planted with palms and shady with ferns, would win any international best-kept station award.

By air Uniquely among Australian states, Queensland has three international airports – Brisbane, Townsville and Cairns – all with regular connections to many overseas airports. A variety of airlines links cities elsewhere in Australia with many places in Queensland, for example with the airports serving the Gold Coast (Coolangatta) and Sunshine Coast (Maroochydore). Given the large size of the state, internal travel by air is well developed, and may sometimes be the only way of reaching remote northern destinations during the wet season. Smaller aircraft, including helicopters and seaplanes, spin a web of services spanning mainland and islands; some islands can only be reached in this way.

By water Visitors are bound to find themselves afloat at some point in their Queensland holiday, even if it is only for a day trip to part of the Great Barrier Reef aboard a high-speed wave piercer or a more humble craft hired locally. Most, but not all the islands are accessible by ferry or launch, with vehicles carried if there are roads when you get there. For short stays it may make sense to leave your car on the mainland. The best way of getting the feel of reef and islands might be to cruise; there are any number of operators competing for your custom, some captaining liner-like vessels calling at luxury resorts, others offering a more adventurous experience involving camping on uninhabited islands. Do not forget to take a cruise or ferry trip up the Brisbane River.

By bus Coach services link Brisbane with other Australian cities as well as with major destinations within Queensland. Local services are variable, though quite well developed on the Gold Coast.

By rail Queensland has the longest rail network in the country, narrow-gauge but much of it electrified, with several well-promoted, named tourist services. These include: the luxury *Queenslander* (weekly Brisbane–Cairns); the *Sunlander* (more frequently Brisbane–Cairns); the *Inlander* (Townsville–Mount Isa); the *Spirit of the Outback* (Brisbane–Longreach via Rockhampton); the *Westlander* (Brisbane–Charleville), and the *Spirit of Capricorn* (Brisbane–Rockhampton). Australia's most popular tourist train labours up from Cairns to Kuranda (see panel), and there are two rail curiosities to attract the adventurous: the weekly run from Cairns to Forsayth in the deep interior, and the strange *Gulflander* running on an isolated section of line near the Gulf of Carpentaria. The only interstate rail link is with Sydney.

By car The road system in the densely populated coastal strip is well developed, and the bitumen now reaches east–west across Queensland and into the Northern Territory via Mount Isa, but many places in the state are only accessible on unsurfaced roads. Cape York and other far northern places may be cut off in the wet season when fords become impassable and roads are swept away. Your own car or 4WD will be an almost indispensable asset if you want to visit many national parks, though if you persevere some sort of guided tour can be found for almost any destination.

▶ **Atherton Tableland** *200D2*

From Cairns south for 150km to near Innisfail, high table-lands rise steeply from the coastal plain. There are remnants of the once dense rain forest, but the area's rich volcanic soils now mostly support tobacco, maize and a whole range of exotic fruits. Southeast of Atherton on the Gillies Highway is **Yungaburra▶▶**, with extinct volcanoes and crater lakes.

▶▶▶ **Cairns** *201D3*

Stretched out in the subtropical sun, Cairns, the key to far north Queensland, breathes in the balmy air of Trinity Bay as if there was no tomorrow. It helped open up the gold-fields and tin mines of the interior, then became a major outlet for the booming agriculture of the area, particularly for sugar-cane. But tomorrow seems to promise even more expansive times; because of the proximity of the Barrier Reef, superb beaches and the rivers and forests of the Daintree and the Atherton Tableland, tourism flourishes. Cairns International Airport, only relatively recently opened, is already fifth among Australian ports of entry in the amount of traffic it handles.

The town's founders laid out a generous grid of streets, whose width and relative absence of traffic contribute to the relaxed atmosphere. The waterfront complex housing boutiques, shops, the Reef Casino, opened in 1996, cruise boat wharves and a luxury hotel adds a sophisticated note, as do the ocean-going vessels of the super-rich in the adjacent marina.

Cairns Museum and Art Gallery▶ gives a fascinating insight into a colourful past populated by Aborigines, railway navvies, goldminers and Chinese labourers. For a different experience, journey just outside town to the **Flecker Botanic Gardens▶**, with more than 200 varieties of palm trees and the tranquil Centenary Lakes. Also on the edge of town is the excellent Tjapukai Aboriginal Cultural Park, which offers a re-created Aboriginal camp, traditional dance performances and much more.

Rum Bundaberg

The name of this substantial town about 300km north of Brisbane at the end of Hervey Bay is synonymous with its principal product – rum, distilled from the canefields of the coastal plain. Bundaberg is also the main gateway to the southern Barrier Reef. Mon Repos Environmental Park, a beach to the north, is a spot favoured by turtles during their egg-laying season (November–February).

Birds and beaches

The wildfowl enjoying the muddy flats of Trinity Bay in Cairns have won their battle against proposals to turn the flats into an artificial beach, but swimmers and sun-worshippers are more than well provided for in the string of beaches stretching along the 26km 'Marlin Coast' to the north, each of them more paradisical than the last.

211

The Esplanade and pier at sunny, tropical Cairns

Drive The Daintree and Cape Tribulation

If you can resist the temptation of the glorious beaches along the way, this full day's drive from Cairns will take you over the Daintree River to tropical rain forest and coral reef.

The **Captain Cook Highway** is without doubt one of the world's finest coastal roads. Rarely overburdened with traffic, it runs inland at first from Cairns, rejoining the shore north of the exclusive resort of Palm Cove. **Port Douglas**, the coastline's northernmost resort of any consequence, is home to the **Rain forest Habitat**, an ambitious re-creation of the tropical rain forest environment.

The canefields around **Mossman** feed the town's sugar mill via miles of narrow-gauge railway. A short diversion leads to the rain forest of the Mossman River Gorge in **Daintree National Park**, with its graded walking track, rapids and delightful swimming holes. At the turn leading to the ferry over the Daintree River the bitumen comes to a (temporary) end; non-4WD vehicles proceed with caution or not at all in the wet season. The wide river is lined with mangrove swamp and crocodiles.

Beyond the ferry begins the tropical paradise of the **Cape Tribulation**

The goanna, or monitor lizard

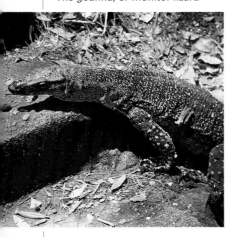

National Park, a remnant of the forests in which flowering plants first appeared on earth. The unmade road lurches crazily through the forest and across dry river beds, pale dust from vehicles coating the luxuriant vegetation. The **Heights of Alexandra Lookout** gives a superb view over the forest tumbling down to the sea. The best initiation into the complex ecology and sheer beauty of the World Heritage Area is at the **Daintree Forest Environmental Centre** with its boardwalk leading deep into this mysterious realm.

Even if noxious stingers inhibit swimming, you should at least walk along one of the incomparable beaches of **Cape Tribulation**, several of which are easily accessible from the road. Beyond the cape itself, the 32km Bloomfield Track begins; it is only negotiable by 4WD.

QUEENSLAND DRIVE 2

The bottlebrush is native to Queensland

Ancient home
Mount Moffat in Carnarvon National Park has strange sandstone formations as well as Kenniff Cave, lived in by Aboriginal people nearly 20,000 years ago and containing Aboriginal rock paintings.

213

▶▶ Cape York Peninsula   200E2

Often described as one of the world's last wildernesses, this great peninsula tapers northwards for hundreds of kilometres to its tip at Cape York itself, overlooking the island-studded Torres Straits separating Australia from Papua New Guinea. A total of perhaps 10,000 people are thinly distributed over this vast area, most of them Aborigines whose ancestors left a legacy of remarkable rock painting, best seen around **Laura**. This little town-ship straddles the lower end of the Peninsula Developmental Road, a less developed highway than its name implies, especially in the Wet when river crossings become impassable even for the most rugged of 4WDs.

In the Dry, the Cape becomes a fascinating destination for the more adventurous type of tourist. The rain forest along the Pacific coast gives way to savannah-like country further inland, punctuated by the surreal turrets of termite mounds, some of them reaching an extraordinary 3m high. The peninsula is studded with some remarkable national parks – including Lakefield, coastal Cape Melville, and the remote crocodile habitat of Archer Bend. The future of the peninsula probably lies in wilderness tourism; civilisation's other activities have left little mark on the land, apart from bauxite mining at Weipa.

Upland architecture
Following the discovery of gold in 1872 at Charters Towers, the town fitted itself out with some fine buildings. Some of these can still be seen today, including banks, the stock exchange, the School of Mines, the city hall and the court house.

▶▶ Carnarvon National Park   201B3

Much of this spectacular park is difficult to get to, but the extraordinary gorges cut by the Carnarvon Creek and its tributaries into the soft sandstone of the plateau can be reached from the Carnarvon Developmental Road between Roma and Rolleston. Here 200m-high cliffs tower over cabbage palms, ferns, mosses and orchids, a shady world quite different from the exposed plateau far above. A number of caves shelter Aboriginal rock paintings. A 10km footpath leads up the gorge from the ranger station, with side tracks giving access to all the park's delights.

▶ Charters Towers   201C3

In contrast to the sweltering heat at Townsville, 135km away, this modest-sized upland town enjoys an invigorating climate. It is a favoured spot for boarding schools and has some of the best early Australian architecture to be seen anywhere (see panel).

If doctors could fly
Set up in 1927–8 by the Reverend John Flynn, the Royal Flying Doctor Service (RFDS) began operations in Cloncurry with a plane supplied by the Queensland and Northern Territory Aerial Service (QANTAS). The event is recalled in a memorial to Flynn, its missionary founder, and in the RFDS Museum in Cloncurry.

Saving the wilderness
Destruction of the Daintree by volcanic explosions and lava flows may have been avoided in the remote geological past; more recent threats have involved the parcelling out of the rain forest into handy packages for 'development' and the construction of the controversial Bloomfield Track. World Heritage designation may have come just in time to save this irreplaceable tract of wild nature.

► ▓ **Chillagoe–Mungana Caves National Park**   200D2

Around the old mining township of Chillagoe are extensive and spectacular caves eroded in the local limestone by the headwaters of the Mitchell River. Not all are accessible, but the Donna and Trezkinn caves are artificially lit to enhance the drama and strangeness of the limestone formations. On the surface, the same rock has been weathered into equally peculiar shapes – turrets, pinnacles and forms resembling animals.

► ▓ **Cloncurry**   200C1

Once a bustling gold and copper town, Cloncurry sits astride the main road and railway line from Mount Isa to the coast, earning its living nowadays from sheep and cattle grazing. It was here in 1928 that the Royal Flying Doctor Service began operating (see panel).

► ▓ **Cooktown**   200D2

A late 19th-century boomtown in the rip-roaring days of gold strikes on the Palmer River, Cooktown was named for Captain James Cook. The great navigator beached the *Endeavour* here after she had been badly holed on the Barrier Reef. Though the peak population of 30,000 or more has shrunk to less than 1,000, enough traces of the past remain to make Cooktown an attractive tourist destination. The Captain's enforced stay is recalled in the Victorian villa housing the **Historical Museum,** as well as by his statue and by the annual re-enactment in June of his landing. Cooktown is easily reached from Cairns by the inland road or, more picturesquely, by the mostly unsurfaced Cape Tribulation coast road. The town is also a useful base for expeditions into the Cape York interior.

►►► **Daintree National Park**   200D2

The outstanding international significance of the Queensland rain forest has been recognised by the designation of the Daintree and Cape Tribulation region as a World Heritage Area. A relic of Cretaceous times over 100 million years ago, the jungle of far north Queensland escaped the volcanic eruptions that destroyed other primitive forests in the region, and consequently has a unique ecological value.

The tiny settlement of Daintree is located on the banks of the Daintree River, famous for its mangroves and crocodiles. The rain forest is penetrable only by the most experienced of bushwalkers; the best place for novices to appreciate its wonders is at the **Daintree Forest Environmental Centre►►**.

►► **Fraser Island**   201B4

This is the largest sand island in the world, stretching 144km along the south Queensland coast and partly enclosing Hervey Bay. With wonderful beaches, some dunes rising to an extraordinary 240m, heathland, rain forest, mangroves and dozens of freshwater lakes, this World Heritage island attracts many visitors, though formal facilities are few and access is only by 4WD (there are no roads). A drive along the east coast takes you past the wreck of the *Maheno* and cliffs of coloured sandstone to the resort villages of Eurong Beach and Happy Valley.

Fraser Island is easily reached by ferry from a number of points on the mainland (Inskip Point, Urangan and River Heads), or by air.

▶ **Glass House Mountains** *201A4*

Inland from the Bruce Highway north of Brisbane rises a group of steep and strangely shaped peaks, the cores of old volcanoes. Given their enigmatic name by Captain Cook, they are a favourite with climbers; the inexperienced can best view them from the Old Gympie Road or from Mary Cairncross Park.

▶▶▶ **Gold Coast** *201A4*

Between Tweed Heads on the New South Wales border and Paradise Point in the north stretches a 40km chain of glorious sandy beaches blessed by regular rolling surf and basking in equally regular sunshine. Everyone is catered for here. Swimming, surfing and sunbathing all have their place, but so do many other activities – there are many excellent golf courses, for example. There are any number of theme parks and similar establishments, among them the incredibly successful **Sea World** at Main Beach and the popular Warner Bros Movie World theme park.

Surfers Paradise, with its lavish malls, excellent restaurants and good nightlife, Cascade Gardens and Jupiters Casino, is where the full flavour of this seaside Arcadia can be relished. A somewhat quieter (and cheaper) ambience can be enjoyed to the south, around Currumbin or at wooded Burleigh Heads, where a discreet national park visitor centre introduces what is left of the coast's natural environment.

Sand for sale
The sands of Fraser Island have a high mineral content which makes them very valuable in certain industrial processes. A notable victory was won here in 1977 by conservationists who succeeded in stopping sand mining and the consequent gradual export overseas of the very substance of the island.

215

Unplanned Utopia
The sprawling Gold Coast is a textbook example of how not to plan an urban environment. The approach from Brisbane, an hour away, is reminiscent of the outskirts of Moscow, save that the high-rise blocks are slightly more varied in shape and decorated in tasteful pastel shades. They jostle each other for a glimpse of the beach, which, because it is to the east and they are too close, is plunged into shade in the course of the afternoon. Through the wire fencing festooning the main highway an array of signs, each more lurid than the last, calls for your custom; Charcoal Chicken competes with Korean Cooking, Cocktail Academy with Coastal Chiropracters, and Jesus is The Answer with the Drive-Thru Bottle Shop.

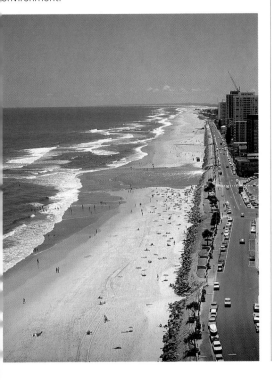

High-rise buildings loom over the beautiful beach at Surfers Paradise

The Great Barrier Reef

■ **The reef, often called the eighth wonder of the world, is Australia's greatest tourist attraction, stretching for more than 2,000km along the east coast from the Gulf of Papua to a point near Gladstone.** ■

Reef fish
The reef is home to thousands of species of fish, from the greedy potato cod (see picture below), to colourful parrot fish, graceful rays and poisonous lion fish. It also harbours many types of shark – attacks are rare, however, and the sharks will probably be more scared of you than you are of them!

216

Giant potato cod expect to be fed and stroked at Cod Hole, 20km off Lizard Island and one of the world's best diving sites

The coral of the reef's outer rim forms a steep submarine escarpment, dropping abruptly into the abyss of the Pacific; only some 30km out from Cairns, this Outer Reef gradually extends further away from the mainland until, opposite Mackay, it is some 260km off shore. To landward is warm and shallow water forming a kind of lagoon broken up by more reefs and hundreds of islands, some of them true coral cays, most of them detached fragments of the mainland, separated from it when sea levels rose. They vary enormously in character, from exposed and unvegetated cays of sand and coral barely rising out of the water at low tide, to reef-fringed mountain ranges covered in splendid rain forest.

Creatures of the deep Hardly another ecosystem on earth can surpass the reef for sheer beauty or variety. Responsible for its formation are humble polyps, tiny organisms with limestone outer skeletons that form a coral reef's basic building blocks. With wildly differing shapes recalling trees, plates, fungi and even brains, the still living polyps paint the underwater scene with vivid colour, to which is added a kaleidoscope of other living creatures. These include not only tropical fish of brilliant hue and intriguing personality, but also sponges, starfish, crabs, sharks, turtles, giant clams and an occasional dugong, a large and harmless creature also known as the sea-cow.

Another creature drawn to this watery paradise in large numbers is *Homo sapiens*, tourist variety. This medium-sized, sometimes amphibious mammal can be observed gazing at the wonders of the reef from aircraft, wave piercers and vessels of all kinds, including flat-bottomed boats and semi-submersibles, or socialising with its other inhabitants while wearing a snorkel or wetsuit. Large numbers stay on the mainland, venturing out on to the Reef on day trips from the main tourist centres such as Port Douglas, Cairns, Townsville and the Whitsunday region; others stay on the islands themselves, in exclusive resorts, and crowded hotels and apartments, or the more adventurous camp on tranquil uninhabited isles with no resources whatever.

Problems of conservation The reef is now a World Heritage Area, controlled and managed since 1976 by the Great Barrier Reef Marine Park Authority. Conservation problems arise not only through the influx of tourists and pressure from developers (who by 1989 had applied for permission to build no less than 250 new resorts along the Queensland coast), but because of agricultural and other pollutants washed into the sea from the rivers draining the interior. Exploratory drilling in the ocean may have been halted, but the petrochemical industry continues to keep a ready eye on the reef's potential as an offshore oilfield.

A more immediate threat comes from a natural phenomenon. The crown-of-thorns starfish has a voracious appetite for the coral polyp, which it easily sucks out of its protective skeleton, and in recent years has devastated huge areas of coral. It is thought by some that over-fishing of the starfish's natural predators, which once kept the numbers under control, may have caused its population to explode; scientists are at a loss for a cure.

The reef is a great place to learn how to snorkel

Butterfly fish: one of the natives of the world's largest living organism

Blue semicircle angel fish seen around Heron Island

▶▶▶ Great Barrier Reef Islands   *201C3*

The following information does not cover all the islands of the reef, but gives details of those that are more popular or accessible, dealing with them from south to north.

Southern Reef At the southernmost end of the reef, Lady Elliot Island▶▶ and uninhabited **Lady Musgrave Island▶▶** are both small coral cays right on the reef with excellent diving and snorkelling. The former is accessible by air from Bundaberg (80km) or Hervey Bay, while the latter, a national park island with the most basic facilities and no resort, is reached on a day trip by launch from Bundaberg (also 80km distant).

Heron Island▶▶ is part resort and part national park, famed for its teeming wildlife, with optimal diving and snorkelling, semi-submersibles and reef-walking. Access is by helicopter or launch from Gladstone (72km).

Large, wooded **Great Keppel Island▶▶** is popular with young people and has glass-bottomed boats, a coral submarine, an underwater observatory, aqua-bikes and water-skiing, plus bush-walking and nightlife. It has some beautiful secluded beaches and is accessible by air from Rockhampton (56km) or by ferry from Rosslyn Bay.

Finally, **Brampton Island▶▶** (a national park and part of the Cumberland group) is a favourite with honeymooners and other couples for its romantic setting. It has good facilities, including golf and walking tracks, and is accessible by air and launch from Mackay (32km).

Whitsunday Islands These hilly, wooded islands, usually fringed with reefs, once formed the tips of ancient mountains and lie scattered to either side of the Whitsunday Passage. Only seven of the 70-plus islands have been developed for tourism, the rest remaining uninhabited.

Numerous high-rise hotels and apartments characterise popular, medium-sized **Hamilton Island▶▶**. It has an international airport with flights from some southern Australian cities and Cairns; alternatively, access is by aircraft from Proserpine or Mackay, and by boat from Shute Harbour (16km).

Great Barrier Reef

Of the six other developed Whitsunday Islands, **Hayman Island** is luxurious and expensive, **Lindeman Island**, although a national park, is now a popular Club Med resort, while **South Molle** and **Daydream Island** cater particularly for families. **Hook Island** (with a splendid underwater observatory) and **Long Island** are casual and their less expensive resorts are popular with the young. All offer day trips to the Outer Reef.

North Islands Large **Magnetic Island▶▶** (just off Townsville) has 500m granite hills, superb sandy beaches, an abundance of koalas, and a large national park. Access is by helicopter or ferry from Townsville (9km) and the island has a bus service. Further north, **Orpheus Island▶▶** is of volcanic origin and is densely wooded. It has fine beaches, exceptional coral and a biological research station. Access is by air or launch from Townsville (80km).

Largest and perhaps wildest of the Queensland islands, national park **Hinchinbrook Island▶▶** has peaks rising through rain forest to 1,142m. The Coastal Walk along the east coast takes experienced walkers several days to complete; access to the island is by launch from Cardwell or seaplane from Townsville (150km).

Medium-sized **Dunk Island▶▶** and smaller **Fitzroy Island▶▶** both have rain forest-clad hills. The former has wonderful beaches and rich wildlife, and is accessible by air from Townsville (160km) and Cairns (120km), and by launch from Clump Point. Fitzroy Island has excellent diving and snorkelling as well as superb views from its lighthouse, and is accessible by launch from Cairns (19km).

Green Island▶ can easily be reached from Cairns (27km) by boat and is therefore popular for a day trip, although the island now has a luxury resort. It has the reef's longest-established underwater observatory.

Northernmost of the resort islands, **Lizard Island▶▶** is sometimes called 'the jewel of the Barrier Reef'. Accessible by air from Cairns (241km), it has wonderful bays and fringing coral, and a superb view from Cook's Lookout.

Island accommodation
Basic and budget Lady Elliot Island (safari cabins and tents), Lady Musgrave Island (self-sufficient camping with permit from the National Parks and Wildlife Service), Great Keppel Island (youth resort and camping), Magnetic Island (backpackers' accommodation), Hinchinbrook Island (camping), Dunk Island (camping with permit) and Fitzroy Island (hostel).
Mid-range and moderate Great Keppel Island (resort and cabins), Brampton Island (resort), Hamilton Island (resorts), Magnetic Island (resorts), Hinchinbrook Island (resort), Dunk Island (resort) and Fitzroy Island (villas).
Exclusive and expensive Luxury resorts are located on Heron, Hayman, Orpheus, Bedarra, Green and Lizard islands.

219

Heron Island becomes a breeding ground for green and loggerhead turtles in October and November

Through the tropics by duck
Equally happy climbing a steep jungle track or crossing a turtle-thronged pool, the Kuranda ducks are really 'DUKWs', the code name for a rugged amphibious vehicle developed for army use in World War II.

Above the rain forest
Although the Cairns-Kuranda Railway is still the most delightful way to reach this charming village, the Skyrail Rain forest Cableway offers a spectacular new option. Opened in late 1995, the cars of this cableway provide a stunning view of the scenery on their 7.5km route up the escarpment.

Lamington National Park, a paradise for hikers and bird-watchers

▶ Innisfail 201D3

A useful gateway to far north Queensland with good access to the Barrier Reef and the Atherton Tableland, the high rainfall area of Innisfail is also well known as a sugar town – there is a sugar museum just out of town. Cane was first planted in the 1880s, and the industry was boosted by a wave of Italian immigrants after World War II. Innisfail's Chinese community is of much longer standing; their joss-house is one of only two still in use in Australia.

▶▶ Kuranda 200D2

High up in the Atherton Tableland, this 'village in the rain forest' is enormously popular with visitors, most of whom have taken the spectacular train ride up from Cairns (see panel). Kuranda is a full-blooded tourist paradise, with rides in amphibious ex-army 'ducks' through the rain forest, a butterfly sanctuary, a noctarium, a huge open-air market, even bungy jumping – everything has been accommodated without damaging the town's character too much. Other attractions are a rain forest interpretation centre, walking tours, Aboriginal dance presentations and a wildlife park. Kuranda is also the ideal base for exploring other areas of the Atherton Tableland.

▶▶ Lamington National Park 201A4

In utter contrast to the glitz and concrete of the Gold Coast is its lush hinterland of upland farms and forests. Rising to 1,204m on the New South Wales border, the green mountains of Lamington National Park are remarkable for their superb stands of Antarctic beech trees, some of them thousands of years old. The forest, of which they form a part, is best experienced by braving the spectacular treetop walk near O'Reilly's Guesthouse. Between here and Binna Burra Lodge, the other main focal point of the park, there runs another famous walk, this one of 22km and with stupendous views out over the New South Wales border country.

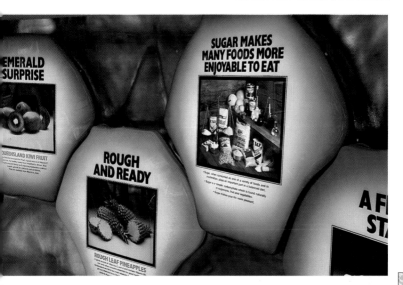

► **Longreach** *200B2*

Far inland on the Capricorn Highway and railway from Rockhampton, Longreach is the centre for a vast pastoral area of the Outback. It was here that QANTAS made its base in the 1920s and here that Australia's first aircraft factory was established. Tourists come here now mostly to visit the splendid **Stockman's Hall of Fame►►**; opened for the Bicentenary in 1988, this large and lavish modern building houses every conceivable kind of display on Outback life.

► **Mackay** *201C3*

This city of nearly 40,000 people prides itself on its important sugar industry, shipping something like a third of Australia's total production from its deep-water harbour. But tourism is of growing significance, with good access to the adjacent Barrier Reef, mainland beaches and the wonderful **Eungella National Park►►** to the northwest. This tract of rain forest-covered upland ('land of the clouds' to the Aborigines) offers a cool contrast to the torrid coast, and has unusual – and sometimes unique – plants, animals and birds like the Eungella honey-eater. You may also catch sight of the normally elusive platypus.

► **Maryborough** *201A4*

Near the mouth of the Mary River, Maryborough serves a rich agricultural hinterland. Founded in 1843, it has a good number of surviving 19th-century buildings as well as parks and gardens of subtropical splendour.

► **Millaa Millaa** *200D2*

This tiny place is famous for the **Millaa Millaa Falls**, one of several picturesque waterfalls along the unsurfaced scenic route known as the Waterfall Circuit. West of the township is the **Millaa Millaa Lookout**, 1,100m up, with fantastic views over the Atherton Tableland, one of the most densely vegetated areas in Australia.

Quite an experience – inside the 'Big Pineapple'

Flamboyant fruit
One of Australia's most convincing examples of emphatic kitsch is the 'Big Pineapple'. Almost 15m high, this fibreglass fruit cannot fail to catch your attention as you drive up the Bruce Highway inland from the Sunshine Coast. Advertising the attractions of an extensive pineapple plantation, it has become something of an unofficial emblem of the tropical fruit country centred on the town of Nambour.

■ **Having been logged for its timber, cleared to make way for cane plantations, and threatened by roads, airports, reservoirs and tourist developments, Australia's magnificent rain forest is at last being recognised as a unique habitat, not only worthy of conservation for its own sake but also for its immense appeal to visitors.** ■

Although it is both shy and rare, the cassowary, Australia's second largest bird, is very powerful

222

Animal life
Rain forest is as abundant in animals as it is in plants. Some of the animals, like the tree kangaroo, the ring-tail possum or the tiny musky rat kangaroo, are unique to this habitat. One endangered species is the cassowary, a flightless bird related to the emu, whose thuggish habits include a grunting cry, kicking to kill with its sharp toe, and an ability to head-butt its way through the densest undergrowth.

Subtropical rain forest in Bunya Mountains National Park

Remnants from the past Scattered along the east coast from Cape York to Tasmania, today's rain forest is a mere fragment of the ancient mosaic of vegetation which covered the whole of the continent millions of years ago. Rain forest flourishes in sheltered, moist conditions, and gradually perished as ancient Australia's climate became drier and drier. But splendid remnants still grace the surface of the land where the complex equation of rainfall, evaporation, soil and temperature balances out. The eastward-facing slopes of north Queensland's coastal mountains, for example, are sheltered by the high ridges of the Great Dividing Range from the parching winds of the interior and enjoy the benefit of moisture-rich onshore breezes. Here are the country's most luxuriant, and perhaps most spectacular rain forests.

Variety A variant, littoral rain forest occurs in unexpected locations close to the sea where sand dunes offer shelter from the scorching effects of salt spray, as on a number of Barrier Reef islands. Further south, into New South Wales and Victoria, the composition of the rain forest changes; its structure becomes simpler and there are fewer species. Nevertheless, the appearance is still one of great luxuriance, and a number of the New South Wales temperate and subtropical rain forests stretching from the Queensland border to the Newcastle area have been grouped together to form one of the country's World Heritage Areas. This type of forest merges imperceptibly with cool-temperate rain forest, characterised by the trees known as southern beech and Antarctic beech. These trees flourish in the cooler climate of Tasmania, although they can also be seen at high altitude in Queensland's **Lamington National Park**.

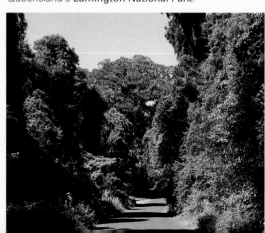

▶ Mission Beach   201C3

The fine beaches between Tully and Innisfail, known collectively as the Mission Beach area, stretch 14km along the coast within sight of Dunk Island. Cassowaries frequent the nearby forest, and there is spectacular whitewater rafting on the upper reaches of the Tully River.

▶▶ Noosa Heads   201A4

Many-centred Noosa Heads (Noosaville, Noosa, Tewantin and Sunshine Beach) at the northern tip of the Sunshine Coast 150km from Brisbane (also see page 225) is the place to come if you crave sophistication but are repelled by the brazen style of the Gold Coast. Stylish Noosa offers low-rise hotels and resorts, some excellent restaurants, and beautiful sandy beaches. It is the starting point for boat trips up the Noosa River and its lagoons or across the river into **Cooloola National Park▶▶**, where there is a 65km beach and the largest sand dune system in the world. Inland, in the Blackall Range area, is the charming village of **Eumundi▶** whose Saturday market is justly famous.

▶ Port Douglas   200D2

This little harbour town and resort 70km north of Cairns exudes a charm all of its own, especially on a tropical evening when only the occasional car disturbs the calm of the broad streets, still lined with old colonial buildings. You can ride through the cane fields on the little Bally Hooley train or visit the fascinating **Rain Forest Habitat**, and near by is a Shipwreck Museum and a Gothic chapel with a view of the Pacific from behind the altar.

▶ Rockhampton   201B4

Australia's 'Beef Capital' lies well inland up the Fitzroy River astride the Tropic of Capricorn. A note of distinction is struck by the elegant late 19th-century buildings and many tropical trees and shrubs; the Botanical Gardens are among the finest in the country. Near by is the **Dreamtime Cultural Centre▶**, with excellent displays on the life of Torres Strait Islanders as well as mainland Aborigines.

223

Coal from the tropics
Queensland makes an important contribution to Australia's coal production. In the Bowen Basin and adjoining country inland from Rockhampton, the coal is extracted on the opencast system from huge pits and exported world wide through Gladstone and special coal ports like Hay Point. Several of the mines (Blackwater, Blair Athol, Goonyella and Peak Downs) welcome visitors.

Cruising home to Port Douglas harbour

■ **Today, steak-happy Australians bite into about half the 1.5 million tonnes of the beef their country produces. The rest is exported, mostly to Canada, the USA and Japan.** ■

The roundup
At muster time the cattle are rounded up by a handful of cattlemen on horseback or, more likely these days, by men on motorbikes or in 4WD vehicles. On the vast stations of the far north helicopters are often used to locate the more wily creatures and drive them from their hiding places.

There is some prime cattle country in New South Wales

The convicts and soldiers landed from the First Fleet seem to have subsisted on Bengal beef, meat from cattle brought out from India. Later, English breeds were introduced, and the colony became first self-sufficient, then embarrassed by the production of a surplus of beef that could not be consumed locally. Canning and refrigeration eventually solved this problem, enabling Australia to become a major exporter of beef; until the advent of the European Community, a good proportion of the roast beef of Olde England started life in the Outback.

Together with sheep, beef cattle were the companions of the white settlers in their conquest of the continent's vast interior spaces. Some treks were epic; in 1870 cattle thief Harry Redford drove 1,000 stolen animals from Longreach in Queensland to outback South Australia, and in 1883–5 the Durack family overlanded 10,000 head of stock 5,000km from Queensland to the Ord River in the Kimberley, a journey lasting more than two years.

Farming on a grand scale Most of Australia's beef cattle are Herefords or Shorthorns, though there has been cross-breeding with Brahmans in an attempt to increase resistance to extreme heat and pests. Numbers peaked in the 1970s at some 33.4 million, but they have declined and today's total is about 18 million.

The majority of animals graze the arid lands of the centre and north of the country, their thirst slaked by the water pumped up from artesian wells. Because of the poverty of the pasture, stocking rates are incredibly low and cattle stations are huge, some of them the size of European states. There are few fences to stop the beasts roaming freely until the time comes for mustering. From the stockyard they are taken by mammoth cattle trucks for the rest cure, which puts flesh on their often meagre bones before they are finally slaughtered.

▶▶ Sunshine Coast   *201A4*

This fabled strip of fine beaches stretches some 100km north of Brisbane from Bribie Island to Rainbow Beach and is much favoured by those who enjoy a quieter alternative to the Gold Coast. Should you tire of sun and sand, there is the garden-like hinterland to explore, including the green world of the Blackall Range.

▶ Toowoomba   *201A4*

High up among the grainfields and pastures of the fertile Darling Downs, Toowoomba is Queensland's largest inland city, distinguished by wide, tree-shaded streets and attractive parks and gardens. Near by is the **Ravensbourne National Park▶**, rich in birdlife, and **Crows Nest Falls▶**, whose waters crash into a deep granite gorge.

▶ Townsville   *201C3*

Overlooked by its Castle Hill, Australia's largest tropical city is the outlet for an awesomely vast region stretching inland to Mount Isa and to the distant Gulf of Carpentaria. As well as a university city and a defence centre, it is an important stop-off for tourists heading north or embarking for the Barrier Reef. Townsville has botanic gardens dating from the late 19th century and a number of buildings from the same period, but visitors are likely to be drawn first and foremost to the complex known as the **Great Barrier Reef Wonderland▶▶**. Here, the glass tunnel of the world's largest coral reef aquarium enables you to marvel at the wonders of the reef without donning wetsuit or snorkel, an experience not to be missed. Almost equally vivid are the films shown on the 360° screen of the **Omnimax Theatre▶**, while a branch of the **Queensland Museum▶** has displays on natural history, history and technology. As if this weren't enough, there is also the **Visitor Centre of the Marine Park Authority**, the body responsible for the management of the reef.

▶ Warwick   *201A4*

A thriving market centre for the southern Darling Downs, Warwick is Queensland's second oldest town (after Brisbane), dating back to 1848.

The Sunshine Coast encompasses dozens of sandy beaches and clear blue waters, like these at the popular resort town of Caloundra

Cane toads
Not far behind the rabbit in nuisance value, these unlovely creatures are an example of an introduced animal that has become more of a menace than the pest it was supposed to control. The toad was originally imported from Hawaii in 1935 in the hope that it would eliminate the beetles attacking the cane fields. Unfortunately it has proved highly successful in reducing the numbers of many kinds of native animals, exuding toxins poisonous enough to kill most of its predators, apart from road vehicles; squashed toads are a common sight along Queensland highways.

King Island

Cape Wickham
Egg Lagoon
Lavinia Nature Reserve
Naracoopa
Currie
Grassy
Stokes Point

B a s s
S t r a i t

Cur
Gro

Hunter Island
Three Hummock Island
Cape Grim
Robbins Island
Stanley
Rocky Cape Nat Park
Montagu
Smithton
Boat Harbour Beach
Wynyard
Burnie
Asbe
Ran
Nat
Marrawah
Irishtown
Somerset
Penguin
Arthur
Calder
Ulverstone
Yolla
Devonport
Ridgley
Temma
Gunns Plains
Sprent
Latrobe
Ra
Leven Canyon
Sheffield
Arthur Pieman Protected Area
Savage
Waratah
1339m ▲
Black Bluff
Mole Creek
Sandy Cape
Savage River
Marakoo Cave
Lake Dove
1545m
▲ *Cradle Mt*
Walls of Jerusalem Nat Park
Pieman
Tullah
Rosebery
Cradle Mt
Lake St Clair
1617m
▲ *Mt Ossa*
Lake Augus
Zeehan
Mt Lyell Copper Mines
Nat Park
Lake St Clair
1447m Lake
Mt Olympus ▲ *St Clair*
Queenstown
Derwent Bridge
Strahan
West Coast Range
L King William
Cape Sorell
Franklin-Gordon
Tarraleah
1443m ▲
Macquarie Harbour
Frenchmans Cap
Wayatinah
Wild Rivers Nat Park
Sarah Island
Frankton
Mt I
Nat
Point Hibbs
Gordon
Lake Gordon
Strathgordon
Mayc
Lake Pedder
Frankland Range
See Drive page 246
Low Rocky Point
Southwest
Arthur Range
National
Port Davey
Park
South West Cape
0   20   40   60   80   100 km
Maatsuyker Group

1   **2**   **3**

227

Tasmania This green and mountainous island's intimate links with mainland Australia are celebrated each summer by one of the world's great spectacles of sail, the Sydney to Hobart race, an exciting sprint down the coast of New South Wales and across the often turbulent waters of Bass Strait. Early explorers assumed Van Diemen's Land (Tasmania's name until 1856) to be part of the mainland, but this error was rectified by George Bass and Matthew Flinders in 1798, and by 1804 Hobart in the southeast corner had become the capital of the second British colony to be founded in Australia.

Small is beautiful 'Tassie' certainly is different. Although a fully functioning state of the Australian Commonwealth, everything else about it conspires to distinguish it from the rest of the country. Australia's smallest state, about the size of Scotland, Bavaria or West Virginia, it revels in a temperate climate which nourishes its forests with an abundant rainfall while providing blue skies in sufficient quantity for all but the most fanatical of sun-worshippers. In the interior, stone-built bridges, villages, townships and Georgian mansions are set among neat farmlands where hedgerows and deciduous trees recall the early settlers' British origin. Beyond the pastures and orchards rise rugged uplands, with clear lakes, rushing rivers and the continent's most magnificent mountain scenery, some of it still hardly explored. The three great national parks of Tasmania's southwest have been declared a World Heritage Area, a wilderness of high peaks, deep gorges and dense rain forest of unequalled grandeur.

Visitors welcome Tasmania's relatively long history has left an exceptional wealth of old settlements and historic buildings, including what for many people is the most

Conflict
In recent decades bitter conflict has arisen between narrowly conceived economic interests and the environment. Unique Lake Pedder was destroyed by the construction of a dam, but public opinion saved the Franklin and Gordon Rivers from going the same way. The environment seems to be winning at the moment.

228

compellingly poignant of all Australia's monuments to convict days, the Port Arthur complex in its evocative setting of sea inlet and parkland. Hobart, Tasmania's capital, is a city of European style and dignity, its deep-water harbour opening on to the broad Derwent River against a backcloth of splendid green hills and mountains.

Perhaps it is the island's small size and relative isolation that have made it a welcoming place, even by the exceptional standards of Australian friendliness. The pace of life is slow, the locals are usually happy to pass the time of day with a stranger; 'no worries' is even more applicable here than in the rest of the country. (This openness has not stopped Tassie's 470,000 or so inhabitants becoming the butt of jokes for other Australians.)

All this, together with generally lower prices, has helped tourism become an important bastion of the local economy, though surprisingly few foreigners make the short journey (240km) from the mainland. Visitors' dollars are particularly welcome; the island faces the perennial problems of an economy based mostly on primary products, and its unemployment rating has remained consistently higher than that of the mainland.

Agriculture thrives in the Midlands, the southeast and along river valleys, though orcharding was dealt a devastating blow when the European Common Market began to exclude its products. Mining of metal ores continues in the thinly populated west, and around Queenstown midway along the coast has left a severely denuded landscape. Forestry is a major industry, though its scope is increasingly restricted by awareness that trees have an ecological and scenic value as well as a short-term financial one. Despite some recent environmental destruction (see panel opposite and page 238), much wild nature survives to attract the visitor.

It is easy to find historic corners in Launceston

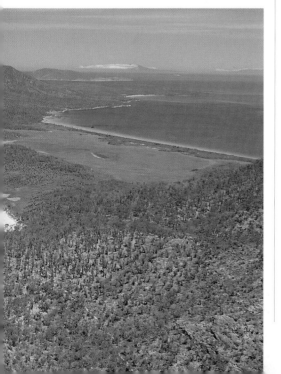

Lovely Freycinet National Park, on the east coast

Hobart

Second oldest city in Australia (after Sydney), Hobart is the country's smallest state capital. It stretches out along both shores of the broad estuary of the River Derwent, one of the deepest harbours in the world and a sporting paradise, linked by the 1,025m span of the Tasman Bridge. The old city centre, with its wealth of colonial buildings, clusters compactly around **Sullivans Cove** on the west bank, backed by wooded slopes rising to the often snow-capped peak of 1,270-m high Mount Wellington. Its rich architectural heritage and incomparable setting make Hobart a delight to explore.

History The city was founded in 1804 by Lieutenant-Governor David Collins, after the first attempt at settlement, the previous year at Risdon Cove just upstream, had failed. For many years the population consisted mostly of convicts and their overseers, though the splendid harbour soon became a base for the whalers and sealers pursuing their prey in the Antarctic and South Pacific.

The city spread inland along the grid of streets leading uphill from the wharves and warehouses of Sullivans Cove, leaving a legacy of fine building; individual monuments abound, but it is the almost European quality of the townscape as a whole that makes Hobart virtually unique in Australia. Streets dominated by splendid Victorian structures like the town hall or the Theatre Royal of 1837 contrast with the delightful informality of the village suburb of **Battery Point**.

Laid-back lifestyle Life in Hobart proceeds at an easy pace, leavened by the good temper of its inhabitants, who seem perfectly content to live in this least metropolitan of capital cities. This is not to say that amenities are lacking; once decried as dozy, today's Hobart has a full range of facilities to keep both locals and visitors stimulated and entertained. Its hotels and eating places equal those found elsewhere, while the casino complex at Wrest Point (Australia's first) has introduced a note of sophistication previously lacking. Every Saturday the dignified sandstone warehouses of **Salamanca Place** look down on what is one of the country's liveliest and most colourful open-air markets, while 31 December and the first week in January are enlivened by the excitement of the Sydney–Hobart yacht race, when thousands of spectators line the shore. This is also the time of the lively Hobart Summer Festival, a month-long event which features Tasmania's gourmet foods.

Tasmania discovered
Dutch mariner Abel Tasman caught sight of an uncharted shore on 24 November 1642 and named it Van Diemen's Land after Anthony van Diemen, Governor-General of the East Indies. Mounts Heemskerk and Zeehan in the west of the island recall the name of his expedition's two ships. Unaware that his discovery was not part of the mainland, much less that it would eventually bear his name, he sailed off, leaving George Bass and Matthew Flinders to circumnavigate the island more than a century and a half later, in 1798. Evidence of French interest was provided by the scientific voyage of Nicolas Baudin in 1800, and it was partly in order to forestall any French designs on the island that Lieutenant John Bowen was sent to plant the Union Jack on the shores of Risdon Cove in 1803.

231

Hobart's spectacular harbour

▶ Anglesea Barracks 230B2

Davey Street

Well sited on rising ground to the west of the city centre, the barracks are outstanding examples of early 19th-century military architecture, a stern assemblage of buildings including drill hall, messes and officers' quarters.

▶▶ Battery Point 230B3

This is the name given to the promontory separating Sullivans Cove on the north from Sandy Bay to the south. Its commanding position made it a natural site for the battery of guns placed here in 1818 to protect the approach to the harbour. Battery Point's interest today is in its delightfully domesticated 19th-century townscape. There are cottages and villas, and little terrace houses looking (apart from their tin roofs) as if they have just been transplanted from late-Georgian England. Grander altogether is 'Narryna', a solid, pilastered stone-fronted home of 1836, protected from the street by fine iron railings. Housing the **Van Diemen's Land Folk Museum**, the interior has been authentically refurnished to evoke the more elegant side of life in 19th-century Hobart, and the gardens and outbuildings are being restored in the same spirit. Battery Point is also the home of the state's interesting Maritime Museum (see next page), some excellent restaurants, and many art and craft shops.

▶▶ Harbour area 230B3

The true spirit of Hobart can still be sensed along the wharves and quaysides of the harbour fronting Sullivans Cove, although the whalers have long since sailed away.

Church landmarks
Hobart's churches were mostly built on prominent sites to act as city landmarks. With its commanding octagonal tower, St George's Church at Battery Point is no exception, although its Egyptian-style stonework, fashionable during the early 19th century when the church was built, is most unusual.

Hobart's Botanical Gardens feature a wide range of native and exotic plants, including ferns and the native Huon pine

Fishing boats and pleasure craft tie up in the twin basins known as Victoria Dock and Constitution Dock, the name of the latter a reminder of the great day in 1853 when the granting of a constitution marked the end of convictism in Tasmania. A venerable Sydney ferry contrasts with trim trawlers and with the spick and span survey ship of the Commonwealth Scientific and Industrial Research Organisation (CSIRO) tied up at Battery Point to the west. The buildings around the harbour are some of the best in Hobart; they include the **Customs House**, now part of the museum, and the restored warehouses along Hunter Street. You will have to make your own mind up about the controversial Hotel Grand Chancellor.

► **Maritime Museum of Tasmania** *230B3*
Secheron Road, Battery Point
This delightfully old-fashioned museum is housed in 'Secheron', a fine Battery Point residence dating back to the 1830s, and has a comprehensive collection of maritime memorabilia showing how intimately Tasmania's history has been linked with the sea.

► **Royal Tasmanian Botanical Gardens** *230D3*
Sloping steeply down to the Derwent near the Tasman Bridge, these superlative gardens are studded with fine specimen trees as well as with structures like the timber Fernery or the Conservatory with its changing floral displays, each more dazzling than the last. It is not just botanists who will be fascinated by the carefully maintained array of specifically Tasmanian plants, some still awaiting classification and some under threat of extinction.

►► **Salamanca Place** *230B3*
In the 1830s the stony slopes of Battery Point were quarried away to build the wharf to the south of Sullivans Cove, and warehouses of magnificently solid appearance were erected to serve the ships docked there. Long since redundant, these superb sandstone structures have happily found new users: boutiques, craft studios, galleries, restaurants, antique dealers and booksellers. Every Saturday morning the place is transformed by the arrival of an army of stallholders offering wares of incredible variety, a must for every visitor.

►► **Tasmanian Museum and Art Gallery** *230C3*
40 Macquarie Street
Tasmania's principal museum is housed in a complex of buildings of various dates, including 40 Macquarie Street, erected in 1808 and supposedly the oldest continuously occupied building in Australia. Within, the Natural History section has displays on Tasmanian creatures (and their ancestors, the megafauna of Pleistocene times which included 3m kangaroos and giant wombats); Ethnography tells the sad story of the island's Aborigines; and Colonial's exhibits, guarded by a redcoat, bring to life the part-epic, part-sordid decades dominated by convictism. The gallery naturally enough features colonial art; of more than passing interest are John Glover's depictions of Tasmania as a paradise populated by Aborigines, and the famous *Conciliation* by Benjamin Duterrau, marking the fateful meeting which led to their exile and death.

The 1837 Theatre Royal has been carefully restored

233

Hobart's mountains
In clear weather both Mount Nelson and Mount Wellington give sensational views of Hobart in its incomparable setting. Mount Nelson (340m), the residences of the privileged cladding its slopes, rises over Sandy Bay; a little signal station still stands at the summit, though the signalman's house has become a tea-room. Mount Wellington (1,270m) is reached via the panoramic road built in 1937 to enable the lazy to enjoy the views which were previously only accessible to determined walkers. At the summit is a boardwalk as well as a shelter with notices explaining exactly what it is you are looking at, though most visitors will probably be quite content to gaze in mindless wonder at the glorious prospect before them.

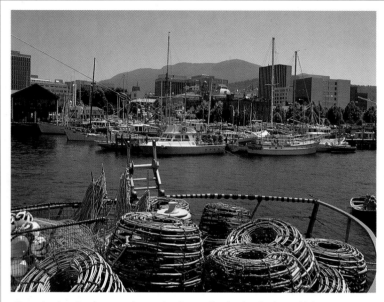

Constitution Dock, mooring point for yachts in the Sydney–Hobart race

Walk Sullivans Cove to Battery Point

This walk from Sullivans Cove begins at the north end of the harbour by the memorial commemorating the city's foundation in 1804 and links Hobart's waterfront to the charming old quarter of Battery Point.

The handsome old warehouses flanking Hunter Street contrast with the modern hotel overlooking Victoria Dock. Take time to enjoy the activity around the **harbour**.

Inland from the harbour are the old buildings of the **Tasmanian Museum and Art Gallery** whose new entrance is just round the corner in Macquarie Street, where you will also find the 1864 Town Hall and the tall-towered **General Post Office** of 1905. Now planted with fine trees and with a fountain at its centre, **Franklin Square** was once a parade ground fronting the first Government House. The crossroads formed by Murray Street and Macquarie Street is unique in Australia in having retained all its early buildings: **St David's Cathedral**, the old **Law Courts**, and a number of mid-19th-century terrace houses.

Opposite St David's Park is a real curiosity, a royal-tennis court, still in use by players of what has become a very exclusive indoor game. The park itself, with its sweeping lawns and fine native and exotic trees, was once the city's cemetery. A memorial recalls John Woodcock Graves, author of the song 'Do ye ken John Peel?', who visited Tasmania in 1886.

Beyond Harrington Street is **Hampden Road**, the artery of Battery Point, with a pleasingly variegated collection of 19th- and early 20th-century buildings. Princes Park descends abruptly to the 1818 **Signal Station**. Beyond Castray Esplanade, the modern CSIRO laboratories occupy the headland, but it is still possible to find a way through and enjoy views across the Derwent.

The Esplanade leads back towards the city centre. Inland from Princes Wharf is the magnificent set of 19th-century warehouses fronting **Salamanca Place**, a fine conclusion to your walk.

How to travel

By air Tasmania is linked to the mainland by a variety of air services from airports at Hobart, Launceston, Burnie/Wynyard and Devonport, and there are more limited services to airfields at Queenstown, Smithton and Strahan, as well as to Flinders and King Islands in Bass Strait. The only direct international link is with Christchurch in New Zealand, and this does not operate in winter. Regular internal flights between all these airfields are supplemented by any number of local firms operating tourist flights; of these, the seaplane trip which takes off from Strahan to fly over Macquarie Harbour and Frenchman's Cap to land in the gorge of the Lower Gordon River cannot be recommended too highly.

By sea Bringing passengers and their vehicles to Tasmania: the *Spirit of Tasmania* takes 15 hours on alternate days between Melbourne (departs Monday, Wednesday and Friday) and Devonport (departs Saturday, Tuesday, Thursday). This modern, luxurious ship offers a wide range of accommodation in its 467 cabins, and can carry more than 300 vehicles.

By car Most visitors bring their own vehicle with them or hire a car once here. Distances are relatively short and roads mostly good, though timber lorries in a hurry to deliver their load can slow traffic down on occasions. The freedom you get from your own car is particularly useful in Tasmania where there is really only the skeleton of a public transport system.

By rail Although a narrow-gauge network still exists, passenger trains (except for enthusiasts' specials) stopped running many years ago.

By bus or coach Every settlement of any size has its bus service, though its frequency may be strictly limited. There are two main operators – **Tasmanian Redline Coaches**, who issue 'Tassie Passes' valid for varying periods, and **Tigerline**. A vital link to the wilderness is maintained by **Tasmanian Wilderness Transport and Tours**, whose robust minibuses will get you into the heart of the major national parks and out again.

Travelling on foot
Anyone who comes to Tasmania should be prepared to walk, even if it is only for a short distance along the numerous well-signposted boardwalks and nature trails. The adventurous will want to climb the more accessible peaks like Cradle Mountain, walk the five- to ten-day Overland Track, or enjoy a conducted adventure rafting down the Franklin River.

Prime bushwalking country

National parks

Over a fifth of Tasmania's land is designated as national parks or state reserves.

World Heritage Area The largest tract of protected land (c 14,000sq km) was declared a World Heritage Area in the 1980s, and stretches from Cradle Mountain to South West Cape taking in several parks and reserves. One of the world's last great temperate wildernesses, its pristine rivers, rain forest and rugged mountain ranges can be appreciated from the Lyell Highway or by flights and cruises from Strahan, but its deepest secrets will only be revealed to the dedicated bushwalker or whitewater rafter. Cradle Mountain-Lake St Clair, the Franklin-Gordon Wild Rivers and the Southwest national parks are all described separately below, but the wild heart of the island also includes the great natural amphitheatre of the **Walls of Jerusalem** as well as the 'land of a thousand lakes', as the Central Plateau area is sometimes known. Through it passes the Lake Highway linking Deloraine with Melton Mowbray, a fascinating and unhurried alternative to the Heritage Highway for north–south journeys.

Beautiful and protected National park or reserve designation applies to many more of Tasmania's outstanding natural landscapes: beaches, caves, lakes and forests. Together with the granite hills of the Freycinet Peninsula, the alpine moorlands, tree ferns and waterfalls of Mount Field were the first to be listed as a national park. In the northeast of Tasmania rise the bare ridges of Ben Lomond, its ski slopes reached by a twisting mountain road. The eucalyptuses of the island's last major tract of dry sclerophyll forest are protected within the **Douglas-Apsley National Park**. Most of the smaller islands have important conservation areas: King Island's **Lavinia Nature Reserve** is the abode of the endangered orange-bellied parrot, while Wybalenna Historic Site on Flinders Island preserves what is left of the ill-fated attempt to re-settle the last of Tasmania's Aborigines between 1833 and 1847.

236

The Franklin River is the ideal location for exciting whitewater rafting

The lush rain forest of the Wild Rivers National Park

The spectacular alpine scenery of Cradle Mountain

▶ **Bicheno** *227C5*

Pronounced Bee-sheno, this little place on the east coast was once a base for sealers and whalers as well as a port for exporting coal from the nearby mines. Nowadays its boats bring in crayfish and abalone, and the township is popular with fishermen, artists and beach-lovers, the latter attracted by the area's mild climate, beautiful beaches and superb scenery. The nearby Douglas-Apsley National Park is excellent for walking.

▶ **Bothwell** *227B4*

Pleasantly set in the beautiful Clyde Valley, Bothwell is of considerable historic interest in its own right, containing numerous colonial buildings, as well as acting as the southern gateway to Tasmania's mountainous Central Highlands.

▶ **Burnie** *226D3*

Most visitors hurry through Tasmania's fourth largest town, but workaday Burnie makes an interesting contrast to the rather self-conscious rusticity of much of the island. There are industrial plants, a huge paper mill ('The Pulp') and a cheese factory, and great trainloads of ore.

▶▶▶ **Cradle Mountain-Lake St Clair National Park** *226C3*

Part of Tasmania's World Heritage Area, this national park of rugged mountain peaks and high moorlands is one of the great landscapes of Australia. The gateways to the park are **Cradle Valley**▶▶▶ to the north and Lake St Clair near the Lyell Highway in the south. At Cradle Valley the spacious visitor centre introduces the national park to its public with displays, talks and events; a boardwalk penetrates the depths of the rain forest and gives a fine view of the Pencil Pine Creek waterfall. A number of shorter or longer walks radiate from the centre, but most visitors will want to press on up the gravel road to the north shore of **Lake Dove**▶▶▶. Bearing in mind that the park generally receives no less than 2,600mm of rain per annum and that most days will bring at least some, let us hope that you will see the unforgettable outline of Cradle Mountain reflected in the clear waters of the lake.

Source of the River Derwent, **Lake St Clair**▶▶▶ is the deepest (200m) body of freshwater in Australia. It is easy to escape into wild nature, even if it is only as far as Watersmeet, confluence of the Cuvier and Hugel rivers.

Weindorfer's 'Home in the Woods'
In 1912, deep in the primeval woodland, an Austrian called Gustav Weindorfer built himself a chalet of King Billy pine and named it 'Waldheim' (Forest Home). It was Weindorfer's enthusiasm that was largely responsible for the area's designation, first in 1922 as a scenic reserve, then later as a national park. Waldheim still stands, albeit rebuilt, but it has been joined by other forms of accommodation ranging from the comfort of Cradle Mountain Lodge to the more basic amenities of a campsite, all designed to harmonise with their incomparable surroundings.

The Overland Track
The route from Cradle Valley to Cynthia Bay on Lake St Clair is 85km long. Walking it is perhaps the best way to savour to the full the varied landscapes of the national park – wild open heaths, forested valleys, deep gorges, lakes and tarns, and rocky peaks, among them Mount Ossa (1,617m), Tasmania's highest point. The trek takes a minimum of five days, but it is better to allow longer to avoid rushing and to be able to explore a little at will. There are huts along the way, but their capacity is limited and you should be prepared to camp. Always check with a ranger before setting off into the wilderness.

■ **With its abundant rainfall and mountainous terrain, Tasmania's potential for the generation of hydroelectricity is easily the greatest of all the Australian states.** ■

GORDON DAM

238

One of the many Tasmanian dams

Water power

Tasmania developed its hydroelectric power supplies partly so that it could expand its aluminium processing industry. It takes huge quantities of electricity to turn aluminium ore (bauxite) into the metal. Hydroelectric power is economical, so it must have seemed the ideal solution. Bell Bay in northern Tasmania was selected as a suitable site for an aluminium plant in the 1950s, lying as it does between the cheap power produced in Tasmania's interior and Queensland's large deposits of bauxite.

Early developments The first projects were built before World War I, but it was in the interwar period that grandiose visions were expounded of Tasmania becoming Australia's Ruhr, whose new industries would feed off cut-price electricity and solve the island's economic problems forever. Founded in 1930, the **Hydro-Electric Commission (HEC)** became a kind of state-within-a-state, Tasmania's biggest employer, capable of overcoming whatever technical challenges might be involved in wresting power from the trackless wilderness.

By the late 1960s the HEC had its eye on glacial **Lake Pedder**, and was able to flood this unique ecosystem in the face of gathering protests from a growing minority of people concerned about the impact of hydro-power on the environment. The destruction of Lake Pedder was described by Unesco as 'the greatest ecological tragedy since European settlement in Tasmania'.

Power or greenery The HEC's next major proposal was the transformation of the Franklin and Lower Gordon Rivers and the surrounding temperate rain forest.

Tasmanian society was bitterly divided, but opposition was better organised this time in the shape of the **Tasmanian Wilderness Society**. A referendum showed the extent of concern, the construction site was blockaded, 1,500 arrests were made, and the project was finally halted in 1983 by a newly elected Federal Labor government anxious to cultivate the 'Green vote'. The wild rivers of the southwest, once described by Premier Gray as 'brown and leech-ridden', were saved; in the end it may well be that Tasmania will gain more from tourists drawn to one of the world's great wildernesses than from any extra wattage that might have been generated.

▶ **Deloraine**   227C4

Now bypassed, but well worth the detour, this attractive and somewhat self-conscious old township lies in fertile country on the Meander River halfway between Launceston and Devonport. In and around the town are any number of interesting colonial buildings, including Bonney's Inn (1831).

▶ **Devonport**   226D3

Devonport is one of the principal gateways into Tasmania. It is here that the overnight *Spirit of Tasmania* vehicle ferry ties up after crossing Bass Strait from Melbourne; and there is an airfield too. Just inland from the 1889 lighthouse, on the rocky promontory of Mersey Bluff, is the **Tiagarra Aboriginal Cultural and Arts Centre**▶, with excellent displays on the life led by the first Tasmanians as well as a guided walk around the enigmatic collection of over 250 carvings which are a feature of the area. Other places to visit include the Maritime Museum and excellent Devonport Gallery and Arts Centre, as well as National Trust-listed 1916 **Home Hill**▶, the white house which belonged to Joseph Lyons, the only Australian to have been both State Premier and Prime Minister. Outside the town to the west is the terminus of the **Don River Railway**▶ where you will find Tasmania's largest collection of veteran locomotives and rolling stock. Vintage trains run regularly, and the museum is quite fascinating.

▶▶ **Flinders Island**   227E5

Guarding the eastern end of Bass Strait, Flinders is the largest island of the Furneaux Group. Once the abode of sealers, then the site of G A Robinson's ill-fated Aboriginal refuge (see page 241), it is a lonely place, with an agricultural and fishing population of barely 1,000. But there is an abundance of wildlife (including the famed muttonbirds – see panel), as well as splendid white beaches contrasting with the rugged granite outcrops of the Strzelecki National Park▶▶.

Muttonbirds
The islands of Bass Strait are the breeding ground of the short-tailed shearwater, a rather nondescript brown bird which migrates in a clockwise direction around the Pacific. The nestlings, chubby creatures rich in fat and oil, are bred in metre-long burrows, then left to their own devices by their careless parents. This made them easy prey for the Aborigines, who would harvest them in huge numbers.

239

The beautiful Liffey Falls to the south of Deloraine are well worth a visit

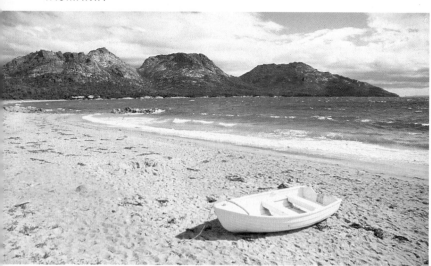

The beautiful beaches of the unspoilt Freycinet Peninsula are some of Tasmania's best

Huon pines
Easily identified because of its feathery foliage and trailing branches, this is a uniquely Tasmanian conifer, occurring mainly in the wetter areas of the far southwest. Extraordinarily slow-growing, it is also extraordinarily long-lived – some specimens still alive may go back to the pre-Christian era. Respect for age meant little in colonial days, when the 'piners' prized the Huon for its exceptionally resilient timber. Today it is valued more for its beauty when converted into ornamental objects such as fruitbowls, and has become a mainstay of the Tasmanian souvenir industry.

▶▶▶ Franklin-Gordon Wild Rivers National Park   226B3

This glorious tract of rain forest, wild rivers and rugged uplands extends from the sheltered waters of Macquarie Harbour to the Lyell Highway, forming the central portion of Tasmania's World Heritage Area. Its highest point (1,443m) is the spectacular quartzite monolith known as **Frenchmans Cap▶▶▶**, whose sheer eastern face drops an alarming 300m. Experienced bushwalkers can make the round trip to Frenchmans Cap in four days; others must content themselves with views from the highway. The adventurous can go whitewater rafting on the Franklin River, an immensely rewarding trip through gorges and over rapids which takes more than a week to reach the little jetty near the mouth of the Gordon. This point is also accessible by launch from Strahan or, more excitingly, by seaplane which drifts down the gorge to land gracefully on the limpid, tea-coloured stream. A boardwalk leads deep into the damp and mossy forest where, among the tree ferns, Huon pines and Antarctic beeches, a waterfall crashes into its pool.

▶▶ Freycinet National Park   227B5

Approached via the fishing township of Coles Bay, the Freycinet Peninsula extends southwards into the azure waters of the Tasman Sea towards little Schouten Island. With its backbone of red granite peaks, immaculate beaches of white sand, forests of eucalyptus and wealth of wildflowers, this was one of Tasmania's very first national parks and has long been popular with locals.

▶ Geeveston   227A4

At the old timber town of Geeveston, dating from 1842 and 70km southwest of Hobart, is the **Esperance Forest and Heritage Centre▶**, an unmissable starting point for explorations of the woodland area. The **Arve Road▶▶** has picnic areas and lookouts, and a little further inland is **Hartz Mountains National Park▶▶**, a rugged alpine region that is part of the state's World Heritage Area.

Tasmanian Aborigines

■ In December 1642, the crew of Abel Tasman's *Heemskerk* heard human voices calling in the forest fringing their landing place near Cape Sorell on the west coast, but the owners of the voices failed to show themselves. Perhaps they had premonitions about the fate of their descendants at the hands of later colonisers. ■

Early conflict Tasmanian Aborigines were quite distinct in character from their mainland counterparts. Thinly spread around the island, they totalled an estimated 4,000–5,000 at the start of white settlement in 1803. The usual complicated relationships arose between the two races. There was plenty of co-operation; Aboriginal women in particular gave freely of their skills in the seal hunts which formed such a staple of Tasmania's early economy. But conflict inevitably grew, in spite of earnest professions of concern on the part of white officialdom; the natives' living patterns were disrupted as their hunting grounds were turned into fenced-off farmland. In the face of the destruction of their way of life, some resisted violently, to be met with more effective violence by the settlers. Within 20 years Aboriginal numbers had been halved.

The end of a race The most fateful episode was reconciliation. The undoubtedly well-meaning George Augustus Robinson travelled the island, making contact with all remaining Aborigines, winning their trust and persuading them to settle in a kind of Christian protectorate on Flinders Island. Here, religion, drink, disease and the loss of their land and culture put paid to those who had survived thus far. The last full-blooded Tasmanian Aborigine, a woman called Truganini, died in 1876.

Above: Aboriginal rock carving in Devonport

Lost but not forgotten
The disappearance of Tasmania's Aborigines is often characterised as genocide, though the processes involved were essentially the same as those at work on the mainland. Though full-blooded Tasmanian Aborigines are no more, many people of mixed blood remain.

241

John Glover's 1836 painting, The Last Muster

■ **Hazards aplenty presented themselves to early mariners negotiating the uncharted coastal waters of the great southern continent: vicious storms, unexpected islands, hidden reefs and no hope of succour from land. Even the careful Captain Cook ran aground on the coral of the Barrier Reef, though his disciplined crew was able to refloat the stranded *Endeavour* on the next high tide.** ■

Captain Bligh

Often called 'Bligh of the Bounty', the naval officer William Bligh (1754–1817) was also known to his contemporaries as 'Breadfruit Bligh', since one of his tasks had been to introduce that fruit to the West Indies. Strict to the point of harshness and beyond, he had the misfortune to suffer not one, but two mutinies. The first, aboard the *Bounty*, is part of popular history. The second rebellion against his rule, in 1808, was led by the officers of the 'Rum Corps', as the New South Wales Corps was disparagingly known. Bligh, as Governor of the colony, had attempted to curb what he saw as the Corps' excessive influence over the colony's commercial life (including a monopoly on the sale of spirits). A *coup d'état* was staged, and Bligh was arrested by his own guards. Undaunted, he refused to return to London as a prisoner, and was later completely cleared by the British government of any misconduct.

A Dutch disaster The first to experience the inhospitable aspect of Australia were the Dutch, who favoured an indirect but rapid route to their possessions in the East Indies. This led them round the Cape of Good Hope, then swiftly eastwards with the winds of the Roaring Forties filling their sails, turning north before reaching the coast of Western Australia (which they named Nova Hollandia – New Holland).

However, not every captain made the turn in time, among them Commandant Pelsaert; his vessel the *Batavia* was named after the chief town of a Dutch colony (now Jakarta) and her cargo included the carefully chiselled stones for the town's main gate. On a fateful morning of 1629, the *Batavia* ran aground on one of the low coral atolls of the Houtman Abrolhos Islands, some 70km off Geraldton. Crew and passengers struggled ashore, rescuing what provisions they could. Once a degree of organisation had been established, Pelsaert set sail for distant Java in a small boat to fetch help. His departure gave the signal for the mutiny that had long been brewing aboard the *Batavia*. Disaffected sailors and marines set up a reign of terror; rape and casual murder became the order of the day, though some managed to flee to neighbouring islands and hold out against the mutineers. By a miracle, Pelsaert's frail craft survived the ocean voyage, and he returned, arresting the rebels and executing the ringleaders on the spot.

This improbable tale is told in full detail in the **Western Australian Maritime Museum** at Fremantle. Many of the *Batavia's* timbers have been recovered, and enough of them put together again to make up her stern, a most impressive and evocative sight. Here, too, the ready-cut masonry from her hold has been erected to form the classical gateway once intended to adorn the approach to the city of Batavia.

The Shipwreck Coast The *Batavia* was not alone in coming to grief off Western Australia, but it is probably Bass Strait between Victoria and Tasmania that has been responsible for the greatest number of Australian shipwrecks. In the last century, the stormy waters of the Strait formed the principal approach for vessels making for eastern Australia; King Island was only provided with a lighthouse in 1861, and until then ships would hug the rocky coast of the mainland, frequently running aground.

The most famous wreck occurred in 1878, when the iron clipper *Loch Ard* foundered on rocks near Port Campbell in Victoria. Of the 50 or so souls aboard, only two survived. Apprentice-boy Tom Pearce clung to a lifeboat and was swept into a narrow cliff-bound gorge. Badly knocked about, he was nevertheless able to rescue young Eva Carmichael whom the current had also brought into the gorge. Leaving the semi-conscious Eva on the beach, Tom somehow managed to climb the cliff and stagger for help. Only four bodies were recovered from the *Loch Ard*; their graves are in the nearby cemetery, one of several containing the remains of victims of this treacherous shore, which bears the name of the Shipwreck Coast.

Between Princetown in the east and Port Fairy in the west, the Historic Shipwreck Trail has markers and infor-mation boards indicating the locations of 25 wrecks of coasters, cargo boats, ships full of hopeful immigrants. At Warrnambool the re-created port called **Flagstaff Hill Maritime Museum** has many objects recovered from these wrecks, and there are other maritime displays at the **Old Cable Station Museum** at Apollo Bay and the **Blackwood Gully Centre** at Lavers Hill.

The waters around Flinders Island are treacherous

Above: The rugged cliffs of Cape Raoul on the Tasman Peninsula

Above and below: Precious objects have been salvaged from the 17th-century Batavia

Devils...
One of Tasmania's unofficial emblems is *Sarcophilus harrisii*, the stocky little predator known commonly as a devil. Invariably shown with a snarl on its less than endearing features, the black and white devil uses its powerful jaws to make short work of the carrion on which it prefers to feed. Devils genuinely do seem to suffer from bad temper, quarrelling fiercely with each other at meal times and not hesitating to dispatch their young if no other food is available. You may see them in the wild or, more reliably, in somewhere like the beautiful Bonorong Park Wildlife Centre at Brighton, 25 minutes north of Hobart.

An old windmill attracts visitors in Launceston

► **George Town**   *227D4*

A centre for historic sites, unspoiled beaches, and gentle scenery, George Town stands near the mouth of the beautiful Tamar River, the 50km-long combined estuary of the North Esk, South Esk and Macquarie rivers. One of the oldest towns in Australia, it has several early colonial buildings, including the elegant Georgian house known as **The Grove**, built in the early 1830s for port officer and magistrate Mathew Curling Friend.

► **Hamilton**   *227B4*

A useful stopping point on the way to the west from Hobart, this charming little place of sandstone cottages and a few larger buildings never realised the ambitions of those early colonists who predicted a great future for it as a minor metropolis. Even Jackson's Emporium has been reduced from two storeys to one.

►► **King Island**   *226E1*

Far out in the stormy waters of Bass Strait to the north-west of Tasmania, verdant King Island has an enviable reputation for dairy products, though much of the 58km-long island consists of unpopulated bushland teeming with wildlife. In the early 19th century it was one of the great battlefields in what has been called 'Man's War on Animals', when the rough and ready 'Straitsmen' butchered vast numbers of seals for their oil and skins.

►► **Launceston**   *227C4*

Located at the point where the North and South Esk Rivers combine to form the beautiful Tamar, Tasmania's second city is the unofficial capital of the northern part of the island. It has retained much of its Georgian and Victorian heritage and offers continuous pleasures to the urban stroller, even though few buildings are outstanding in themselves.

The city was laid out on the usual grid pattern of streets, some of which, like the Mall and Civic Square, have been given over to pedestrian use. In Civic Square is an intriguing sculpture of Tasmanian wildlife, including tail-biting thylacines (tigers – see panel opposite), as well as **Macquarie House►**, an excellently restored stone, iron and timber structure dating from very early colonial days and now housing the local museum. Near by are other reminders of the past – the red-brick Queen Anne-style post office, the Italianate town hall and St Andrew's Kirk in brilliant white stucco, while the Old Umbrella Shop in George Street, now the National Trust shop and information centre, has retained its authentic 1860s frontage.

Launceston's other major attractions lie to the east of the city centre. In a prettily landscaped setting, the **Queen Victoria Museum and Art Gallery►** rivals Hobart's Tasmanian Museum for the interest of its collections and innovative displays (don't tell Hobart!), reminding us with the title of one gallery that Tasmania is indeed 'A Special Island'. Close to King's Bridge over the South Esk is **Penny Royal World►**, with an array of re-erected and reproduced 19th-century buildings including water mills and windmills, as well as a fully operational gunpowder mill, reached by vintage tramway. Upstream is the most dramatic of Launceston's many parklands, **Cataract**

Gorge Reserve▶▶, a wild and rocky canyon in miniature, crossed by chairlift suspension bridge.

A collection of fine country houses (all open to the public) graces Launceston's hinterland. Finely proportioned **Franklin House**▶ near Kings Meadow would not have been out of place in the countryside of Georgian England, while single-storeyed **Entally House**▶ at Hadspen, with its veranda, seems much more rooted, more 'Tasmanian'. **Clarendon**▶, behind its restored Ionic portico, is on a grander scale altogether, one of the great rural residences of Australia, overlooking its grounds and the South Esk River with a haughty eye.

▶ **Maria Island National Park**   *227B5*

Reached by ferry from Triabunna, this east coast island will appeal to all those seeking undisturbed nature. Though pre-dating Port Arthur as a penal settlement – convicts were first sent to Maria Island in 1825 – and once exploited for various commercial purposes, the island is now an oasis of tranquillity, with an abundant wildlife enjoying total freedom from motor vehicles. Visitors will need to take their own provisions, as there are no shops, or electricity, on the island.

▶ **Mole Creek**   *226C3*

The limestone rock around this tiny township is riddled with caves, most of them inaccessible. But two of the more spectacular can be reached: **King Solomon Cave**▶, where a limestone formation recalls the biblical monarch, and the longer **Marakoopa Cave**▶, watered by two streams and lit by glow-worms.

...and tigers
Devils are not an endangered species, but the thylacine or Tasmanian tiger is officially extinct. What is generally thought to have been the last of the race died in Hobart Zoo in 1936, ironically within three months of tigers being declared a protected species. Thylacines were wolf-like marsupials, with stripy backs and wide-opening jaws; their liking for sheep and lambs didn't endear them to farmers. The question of whether or not the tiger lives on in seclusion somewhere has divided Tasmanians into believers and sceptics; there have been plenty of supposed sightings, but no definite proof.

245

The delights of Cataract Gorge, Launceston's favourite recreation area

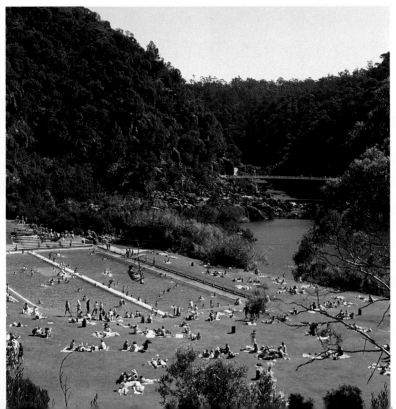

Drive **Through the wilderness on the Lyell Highway**

See map on pages 226–7

Allow a day for this trip from Hobart across the glorious mountain core of Tasmania on the Lyell Highway to the remote fishing port and resort of Strahan.

The first section of the drive runs up the valley of the Derwent, through well-tamed countryside of fields and farms and pleasant towns like English-looking New Norfolk and historic Hamilton. More rugged country follows, with increasing evidence of

The attractively wooded Derwent Valley and its villages lie just a short drive from Hobart

Tasmania's highly developed hydro-electricity industry – signs point down side-roads to dams, there is a surprise of a canal, and huge pipelines snake up and down the slopes. After Lake Binney the forest thins and gives way to featureless button-grass plains.

Some way short of Derwent Bridge, **Mount Olympus** comes into view; this grand mountain overlooks the clear waters of **Lake St Clair** which is reached via a short side-road from Derwent Bridge. The ranger station at Cynthia Bay marks one end of the famous Overland Track between here and Cradle Mountain. The recommended time to complete this famous trek is at least five days, but shorter walks are also available.

One of the world's great mountain roads, the Lyell Highway was only completed in 1932. There are several, mostly well-signposted stopping points along the way between Derwent Bridge and Queenstown: King William Saddle marks the watershed between the Derwent and Franklin-Gordon river systems, while Surprise Valley Lookout has a view of the imposing peak known as **Frenchmans Cap**. A number of short walks can be made from the Franklin River Bridge along part of the Frenchmans Cap Walking Track to the Donaghy's Hill Wilderness Lookout, to the Alma River Crossing or to Nelson Falls.

A new road has been built to circumvent the recently flooded valley bottom at **Lake Burbury**, a mountain scene of incomparable grandeur. Equally extraordinary, albeit in an utterly different way, are the denuded and devastated uplands around the mining centre of Queenstown. The final leg of the journey is along the twisting but otherwise uneventful road through the forest and down into the little port of **Strahan**, one of the best starting points for further exploration of the wild western coast or the rain forest, rivers and mountains of the interior.

► **New Norfolk** 227B4

Upstream from Hobart, the Derwent Valley recalls the landscapes of southern England, with rolling hills as a background to a countryside of big deciduous trees and, in the vicinity of historic New Norfolk, hopfields and their attendant oasthouses, one of which is now a museum.

► **Oatlands** 227B4

Extension of British power into the interior of Tasmania was marked by the construction of highways; one of the most important was the road now known as the Heritage Highway, linking Hobart with Launceston. A small number of strategic settlements were planned along the route, of which Oatlands was one. First surveyed in 1832, the township is no bigger than a modest village, but nevertheless boasts an outstanding number of fine colonial buildings.

►►► **Port Arthur** 227A5

Port Arthur is the most evocative of all the places recalling the days of the convict system, offering an experience that no visitor should miss (see panel on page 248).

The Tasman Peninsula is virtually an island, linked to the rest of Tasmania only by a slender isthmus. The first prisoners were brought here in 1830 to fell the timber which formed the basis of the first of Port Arthur's thriving industries; as more convicts and those sent to guard them arrived, a vast range of activities began to flourish. In time the place became virtually self-sufficient, supporting a population of more than 2,000, housed, working and worshipping in an array of handsome brick and stone structures. To make officials feel more at home, touches of Old England were contrived; oaks and elms were planted and blackbirds released to sing from their branches.

Both extreme cruelty and weird forms of enlightenment were features of life at Port Arthur. Floggings were given for the slightest offence, but it was also here, at Point Puer, that juvenile delinquents received the first compulsory education in the world. By the mid-19th century, the desire to reform rather than punish led to the building of the Model Prison, whose inmates spent their time in total 'solitary'. However, madness rather than rehabilitation was the frequent outcome.

With the end of convictism, Port Arthur was closed down as a penal colony, and in the late 19th century became a tourist attraction. Many of its more substantial structures remain to intrigue the visitor. They include the 1844 penitentiary; guard towers; the sinister Model Prison and, looking down on the site from landward, the fine church with tower and pinnacles.

The Tasman Peninsula has other attractions, including strange coastal rock formations and the Bush Mill, a re-created logging settlement and steam railway.

New Norfolk firsts

The town boasts a number of 'firsts': St Matthew's, the island's oldest surviving church; the Bush Inn, Australia's oldest continuously licensed inn (you are likely to come across several of these); and the nearby salmon ponds, where a batch of ice-packed eggs survived the long trip from England to hatch into the first trout and salmon to swim the streams of the southern hemisphere.

The gentleman bushranger

Filled with 'a deep and concentrated hatred of that power which was undeservedly persecuting me', the Irish convict Martin Cash and two companions braved the sharks in about 1840 by swimming to freedom from the Tasman Peninsula. Recognised in the course of an over-confident visit to a lady friend in Hobart in 1843, Cash shot a police constable while being re-arrested, but avoided execution, and eventually settled down to the life of a farmer.

247

Port Arthur, a legacy of the convict era

Eroded hills behind Queenstown

Tragedy at Port Arthur
A tragic postscript to Port Arthur's strange and often brutal history was added in April 1996, when Hobart resident, 28-year-old Martin Bryant, went on a so far unexplained rampage. In just a few hours, Bryant shot and killed 35 people and injured many more, leaving Tasmania, and indeed the whole of Australia, in shock. Bryant is now serving a life sentence, and Port Arthur is recovering its status as one of the nation's premier tourist attractions.

Leatherwood honey
One of Tasmania's most distinctive trees is *Eucryphia lucida* or leatherwood, a characteristic species of the temperate rain forest. For many years, local bee-keepers have hung hives in the vicinity of leatherwoods in order to take advantage of the bees' liking for the nectar-rich flowers which bloom in spring and early summer.

▶▶ **Queenstown**   *226B2*

Few scenes of industrial devastation are quite as spectacular as the bare highlands surrounding this mining town in western Tasmania. For visitors approaching from the east, the contrast between the vast tracts of luxuriant rain forest to either side of the Lyell Highway and the denuded slopes around Queenstown could not come as more of a surprise.

The miners who came here from the early 1880s onwards were prospecting for gold, but it was not long before copper extraction took precedence. The copper smelters' insatiable demand for fuel was responsible for the wholesale clearance of the rain forest all around, while their emissions poisoned any regrowth that might have occurred. With no vegetative cover to bind it together, the soil was quickly washed away by the abundant rainfall (up to 3,000mm per annum), leaving deep gullies and bare rock faces which are now being slowly revegetated.

Queenstown is not without a certain quiet pride in this horror story, which undoubtedly gave it a distinctive identity, commemorated by the rather odd collection of sculptures at the **Miners Siding**, together with a sturdy little rack and pinion locomotive. The Mount Lyell Mining and Railway Company still processes copper here, and the mine and its museum can be visited in the course of a conducted tour. It is likely that the mine will eventually become a 'living' museum of mining history.

▶▶ **Richmond**   *227B4*

For Tasmanians, tiny Richmond embodies all that is 'historical' about their island. Along the township's main street are a number of fine old buildings from colonial days, some of them dating from the 1820s.

Two attractions in particular capture visitors' imaginations: the 1825 jail, erected to house convicts who were engaged in public works, and the convict-built bridge – Australia's oldest road bridge, which was constructed from local sandstone in 1823–5. The bridge carried the highway which for many years linked Hobart with Port Arthur, and now benefits from its picturesque setting of riverside lawns, trees and ducks.

▶▶ **Ross** 227C4

Driving the Midland (Heritage) Highway is an almost continuous pleasure; the well-engineered road speeds you past a background of blue hills through a countryside that was remade by the early settlers into a facsimile of the England they had left behind.

Ross is one of a number of strategic settlements established along the route in the 1820s to act as staging posts for travellers. Church Street, with its attractive old stone buildings, is nicely shaded by the ubiquitous elms, but it is Ross's famous stone bridge which is quite exceptional. An elegant structure dating from 1836, it is decorated with carvings of such virtuosity that they earned their convict stonemason his freedom.

▶ **St Helens** 227C5

The most populous place on Tasmania's east coast, the fishing port of St Helens is also the most popular, with holidaymakers outnumbering locals five to one in the height of summer. As well as attracting game fishermen, it makes an excellent centre for exploring the magnificent northeastern coast of the island, where there are splendid sand dunes, white sandy beaches and bands of Forester kangaroos.

▶▶▶ **Southwest National Park** 226A3

Forming the southern part of Tasmania's World Heritage Area, this is a vast wilderness of mountain ranges rising from virgin forest of southern beech and Huon pine, with great sweeps of buttongrass, glacial lakes and wild rivers, and a wonderful coastline of deserted sandy beaches.

Until quite recently only the more hardy type of bushwalker, mountaineer or canoeist ventured into this remote and unspoiled world. But in the late 1960s, Tasmania's Hydroelectric Commission drove a road deep into the heart of the area, a harbinger of its plan to drown Lake Pedder beneath an artificial water body 20 times its size.

The outrage this provoked, not only among conservationists but also in a wider public, turned out to be in vain; Lake Pedder, with its unique fauna and beach of brilliant white sand, was duly submerged in the interest of generating marginally cheaper electricity.

The advantage for the visitor is that it is possible to taste, if not fully experience, something of one of the world's last temperate wildernesses by driving up the Strathgordon and Scotts Peak Roads. Both highways give spectacular views of the new Lake Pedder in its rugged setting.

For those wishing to penetrate further, the track from Scotts Peak Dam via the coastal inlet of Port Davey to South East Cape will take up to a fortnight's strenuous trekking; there are several specialist tour operators.

▶ **Stanley** 226D2

On its peninsula protruding into Bass Strait, this historic port and holiday centre nestles beneath its famous landmark, the Nut. Properly known as **Circular Head**, this 143m basalt outcrop is the core of an ancient volcano. It is possible to either walk or take the chairlift to the breezy summit from where terrific views along the northwest coastline can be enjoyed.

Fishing in Tasmania
Fishing is one of Tasmania's main industries and fresh seafood is one of the delights of eating out on the island. There are plenty of opportunities for visiting enthusiasts to go sea fishing, particularly for tuna and marlin from the little ports of the east coast. But it is probably the lure of the trout which will most entice the angler from abroad. Ever since trout spawn from England was successfully hatched in 1864 in the famous Salmon Ponds hatchery near New Norfolk, the island's unpolluted streams and lakes have proved an ideal habitat for both brown and salmon trout.

249

Catching tuna the 'kind' way off the Tasman Peninsula

Railway delights
The West Coast Pioneers Museum in Zeehan is home to a comprehensive array of local exhibits as well as locomotives built long ago in Glasgow, Manchester and Germany. These were shipped across the seas to work the ore trains of one of the most mineralised areas on earth.

Georges Bay at St Helens is still a bustling fishing port, despite an influx of summer visitors

▶▶ Strahan   226B2

A characterful little harbour settlement on the magnificent inland sea of Macquarie Harbour, Strahan (pronounced 'strawn') grew up to export the timber and minerals of the western interior. Its main functions today are fishing, forestry and tourism. The Strahan Wharf Centre on the waterside has displays on the history of the area.

Hell's Gates, as the narrow and dangerous entrance to Macquarie Harbour is known, were so named because they guarded Sarah Island, from 1822 to 1834 one of Britain's most brutally administered penal colonies. Strahan is also the base for exploring the Gordon River – by cruise boat or seaplane.

▶ Swansea   227B5

From the beach here, there is a wonderful prospect across Great Oyster Bay towards the Freycinet Peninsula. One of the best places to stay along Tasmania's Suncoast, Swansea's attractions include the imposing three-storey brick General Store (1838) and the unusual 1885 Bark Mill.

▶ Wynyard   226D3

Linked to the mainland by flights from its own airport, this fishing port at the mouth of the Inglis River is a useful gateway to Tasmania's scenic northwest coast and its fertile farming hinterland. To the east are the wonderful white sands of **Boat Harbour** and **Sisters Beach**, as well as the rugged coastline of the **Rocky Cape National Park▶▶**. The headland at Table Cape has a lighthouse and views.

▶ Zeehan   226C2

Named after one of Abel Tasman's ships, this isolated mining town in Tasmania's far west saw both boom and bust before beginning a modest recovery, brought about by the reopening of a tin mine, in recent years. Legacies of turn-of-the-century prosperity based on silver-lead extraction include the **Gaiety Theatre** and the **West Coast Pioneers Memorial Museum▶** (see panel).

TRAVEL FACTS

Arriving
All visitors to Australia must have a valid passport and, with the exception of New Zealanders, a visa. Visas must be obtained in advance from an Australian High Commission, Embassy, or Consulate; a fee is only charged if you intend to stay more than three months or if you require a multiple-entry visa.

A Working Holiday Maker visa (valid for 12 months) allows you to take employment of a casual nature during your stay, and also carries a charge.

By air
All Australian state capitals (not Canberra) have direct connections with destinations abroad, and there are also international flights from Darwin, Cairns and Townsville. There are many opportunities for combining a visit to Australia with stop-overs at intermediate destinations or by buying a 'round-the-world' flight. Many visitors will want to take advantage of the option of arriving at one point in Australia and departing from another.

Fares vary considerably among the 40 or so international airlines serving Australia and also fluctuate according to the time of year; the cheapest fare may turn out to be a false economy if it involves an exhaustingly long flight with several stops. Check prices and availability well in advance through a travel agent or reputable media outlets; there are some real bargains, particularly in charter flights.

By sea
Those with time to spare can travel to Australia on board the cruise ships of operators such as CTC, Cunard, P & O, and Royal Viking, albeit at a price. Some freighters carry a small number of passengers too, but this is by no means a cheap alternative.

Camping
Discounting the risks of insect nuisance, Australia is a wonderful land in which to camp, not just because of its climate but also because of its exceptionally generous and varied provision of campsites, both on the edge of town and in the bush. Site equipment is generally good, and might include electricity hook-up, hot and cold water, showers, toilets and laundry. Some sites offer pre-erected tents, and many more have caravans and cabins for hire. Operators range from town councils to commercial chains or national park authorities. Some of the national park sites are 'basic'. Camping on your own in the wild is also possible, but discretion is advisable; check that your presence will not annoy a landowner.

Camper-vans and motor-homes are increasingly popular among Australians exploring their own country in a leisurely way. Hiring such a vehicle should be considered by visitors from abroad who intend to spend most or part of their time touring rather than visiting city sights.

Car breakdown
When hiring a car, check with the hire company about breakdown arrangements; they will normally organise help for you. Membership of a motoring club in your own country will in many cases give you access to the facilities of the various state motoring clubs (contact the Australian

The Overland Train runs between Adelaide and Melbourne

Automobile Association for details).

Breaking down in the Outback is potentially fatal and should be avoided by making sensible preparations for your journey (see Driving tips on pages 257–8).

● **National Roads and Motorists Association**, 151 Clarence Street, Sydney, NSW 2000 (tel: 132132).

Car rental

Car rental is well developed in Australia, with vehicles available from a range of agencies (both international and local) at most airports as well as from town and city centres. To hire a car you will need to have a valid driving licence and normally be more than 21 years old. One-way rentals between major cities are possible, but they are not cheap. The total cost of the hire will consist of the basic daily or weekly rate plus various additions like collision damage waiver and possibly a kilometrage charge. Choice of vehicle is very much an individual matter; 4WDs and camper-vans are available, and you might find a six-cylinder home-grown saloon more restful for long trips than a zippy hatchback.

There may be restrictions on taking a vehicle over a state boundary, into 'country' or 'remote' areas, or driving it on unsealed roads.

Climate

As befits a country which is also a continent, Australia has a variety of climates. Visitors from the northern hemisphere will, of course, need to get used to the seasons being reversed (summer is from December to February, and winter is from June to August). In very general terms, the best time to visit the southwest and southeast is between September and April, and the north and centre between May and October.

The southwest and southeast (southwest Western Australia, much of South Australia, Victoria, much of New South Wales, Australian Capital Territory and Tasmania) are at their best in spring and summer, although midsummer temperatures can get very high. Winters here can be dull and rainy, though frost is rare except at high altitudes where snow can be expected – as in the Snowy Mountains.

Many Australians enjoy a winter holiday in the Red Centre or northwestern Western Australia, where there is likely to be an endless succession of bright sunny days with temperatures around the 20°–25°C mark, although nights will be cold in the centre. Summer in these areas can be unbearably hot, with temperatures of 45°C not uncommon.

The subtropical and tropical parts of the country (much of Queensland, Western Australia and the Northern Territory) are at their least comfortable in the Wet (usually November to April), when heavy rainfall and high humidity prevail. This is also the season when box jellyfish make the sea unsafe for swimmers, and when roads may be washed away. In the

Dry (May to October) conditions are much more pleasant, with warm (but not too hot) and sunny days.

Crime
Political and business scandals of sometimes spectacular dimensions, and the activities of a well-organised criminal underworld dominate the headlines in Australia more than casual offences against the person. Thieves and muggers do exist, but Australian cities are still among the safest in the world, and no more than the normal precautions against pickpockets, muggers and car thieves are necessary.

Customs regulations
Personal effects can be brought into Australia without payment of duty, as can 250 cigarettes and 1,125mls of

CONVERSION CHARTS

FROM	TO	MULTIPLY BY
Inches	Centimetres	2.54
Centimetres	Inches	0.3937
Feet	Metres	0.3048
Metres	Feet	3.2810
Yards	Metres	0.9144
Metres	Yards	1.0940
Miles	Kilometres	1.6090
Kilometres	Miles	0.6214
Acres	Hectares	0.4047
Hectares	Acres	2.4710
Gallons	Litres	4.5460
Litres	Gallons	0.2200
Ounces	Grams	28.35
Grams	Ounces	0.0353
Pounds	Grams	453.6
Grams	Pounds	0.0022
Pounds	Kilograms	0.4536
Kilograms	Pounds	2.205
Tons	Tonnes	1.0160
Tonnes	Tons	0.9842

MEN'S SUITS

UK	36	38	40	42	44	46	48
Europe	46	48	50	52	54	56	58
US	36	38	40	42	44	46	48
Australia	92	97	102	107	112	117	122

DRESS SIZES

UK	8	10	12	14	16	18
France	36	38	40	42	44	46
Rest of Europe	34	36	38	40	42	44
US	6	8	10	12	14	16
Australia	8	10	12	14	16	18

MEN'S SHIRTS

UK	14	14.5	15	15.5	16	16.5	17
Europe	36	37	38	39/40	41	42	43
US	14	14.5	15	15.5	16	16.5	17
Australia	36	37	38	39	41	42	43

MEN'S SHOES

UK	7	7.5	8.5	9.5	10.5	11
Europe	41	42	43	44	45	46
US	8	8.5	9.5	10.5	11.5	12
Australia	7	7.5	8.5	9.5	10.5	11

WOMEN'S SHOES

UK	4.5	5	5.5	6	6.5	7
Europe	38	38	39	39	40	41
US	6	6.5	7	7.5	8	8.5
Australia	6.5	7	7.5	8	8.5	9

alcohol (beer, wine, or spirits), and gifts up to a value of A$400. There are tough penalties for importing weapons, drugs (soft or hard), and for attempting to bring in quarantinable articles, particularly plants which may be disease-carriers.

Disabled visitors
Conscientious efforts are made by public bodies and by the tourist industry to make life easier for people with disabilities. Modern buildings and facilities are designed to high standards of accessibility for wheelchairs, pedestrian crossings have audible signals when the way is clear, and many national parks have specially laid out trails for people with disabilities. They will find Australia one of the most helpful countries to visit in this respect, although it would be wise to give advance notice when planning your itinerary. The **Australian Council for Rehabilitation of the Disabled,** (PO Box 29, Garran, ACT 2605 (tel: 02 6282 4333) will provide detailed information about facilities.

Hiring a 4WD is sensible if you wish to journey into the Outback

Domestic travel

By air As you would expect in such a huge country, Australia is very air-minded, with more than three-quarters of all long-distance journeys made by plane. There are few places that cannot be reached by aircraft, whether in the comfortable cabin of a large modern jet or riding the thermals next to the pilot in a single-engine machine of considerable vintage.

Internal airlines are now deregulated, with benefits to passengers in terms of value for money and availability of services. In addition to a number of regional airlines, the main carriers are **Ansett Australia** and **Qantas Airways**, both of which offer visitors from abroad discounts on ordinary fares. Travellers using Qantas to get to Australia can usually make discounted internal flights with that company. Check on what offers are available when planning your journey and bear in mind that flights fill up quickly during the main holiday periods. Student discounts are available, as are stand-by fares. Smoking is not permitted on internal flights, and you will have to have a dollar or two ready if you want a luggage trolley at the larger airports.

- **Ansett Australia** 501 Swanston Street, Melbourne, Victoria (tel: 03 9623 3333 or 131300).
- **Qantas Airways** 203 Coward Street, Mascot, NSW 2020 (tel: 02 9691 3636 or 131313).

By car Australia's roads are of variable quality. In the metropolitan areas around the great cities they compare well with those anywhere in the developed world, while in remote areas they may consist of dirt tracks liable to disappear altogether in the Wet. Motorways are confined to relatively short sections leading out of the major cities. Most main roads have two lanes, although some still consist of a single strip of bitumen with gravel shoulders and others are made entirely of gravel. The recent asphalting of main roads in Western Australia and the Northern Territory has made it possible to drive right round the country 'on the bitumen'.

Having your own vehicle offers the usual flexibility and independence, but you should never forget the great distances likely to be involved in any extensive travelling around Australia. The great majority of the popular tourist areas can be reached in an

Ansett Australia flights are often on offer at discount rates

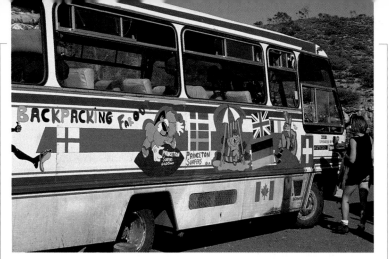

Australia is great for backpackers

ordinary car; a 4WD vehicle will only be necessary if you are contemplating travelling extensively on dirt roads in the Outback – for example, on one of the South Australian 'tracks' (see page 143). A camper-van or similar vehicle offers even more flexibility.

An alternative to hiring a vehicle (see Car rental on page 253) is to buy one, especially if your stay is going to be a long one. Second-hand vehicles can be obtained in the usual ways (dealers, auctions and so on), or from your fellow travellers. Noticeboards in backpackers' lodges may be a useful source of information here, and in some places dusty camper-vans displaying hopeful prices are lined up on the street. The stress of disposing of your vehicle at the end of your stay can be alleviated by purchasing it from a dealer who offers a guaranteed buy-back, although obviously this will not be the cheapest way.

By train A railway map of Australia seems incomplete, with huge areas empty of any trace of tracks. However, the big cities are accessible by train, and some Australian rail journeys count among the great railway experiences of the world. Among them are the three-night transcontinental trip aboard the *Indian Pacific* between Sydney (or Adelaide) and Perth across the aching emptiness of the Nullarbor Plain, or the famous *Ghan*, a 20-hour foray from Adelaide into the centre of the continent at Alice Springs. These, together with trains like the *Sunlander* (Brisbane–Cairns), are a relaxing way of appreciating the vastness and diversity of Australia in great comfort (ingeniously luxurious sleeping compartments, gourmet dining, attentive service and showers). Other railway services are best developed in the east and southeast of the country, with extensive metropolitan networks around Sydney, Melbourne, Brisbane and Adelaide. Europeans, used to frequent services, may be surprised to find that trains may run only once a day. Speeds are less impressive than standards of comfort.

Visitors from abroad can buy an **Austrailpass**, giving unlimited travel for various periods over the whole network (only available outside the country). An Austrail Flexipass is a better option for those who require more flexibility with stopovers without using up the pass's date validity.

Driving tips
The Australian smile sometimes becomes a snarl once its owner is behind the wheel of a vehicle. However, road safety is improving and Australia has a fairly low road fatality rate compared to vehicle numbers and distances travelled. Drinking and driving were once very much part of ordinary life, and may still be so in Outback areas, but police crackdowns (using 'booze buses' to conduct random tests) seem to be having a useful effect in major cities. The legal permitted limit for alcohol is 0.05 per cent blood alcohol level in all states and territories.

In principle, Australians drive on the left and overtake on the right. However, this may not immediately be obvious on a multiple-lane highway where many drivers prefer to stay in the right-hand lane, impervious to the traffic passing them on the left. Driving down the central strip of bitumen on a part-surfaced highway is acceptable, but it can turn into a test of nerves as oncoming traffic approaches. The monstrous 'road trains' to be encountered in Western Australia, Queensland and the Northern Territory expect you to give way to them at all times and have no strategy for coping if you don't. Overtaking a road train which may be 50m or more long and throwing up clouds of dust can be very tricky; if you can't see a long way ahead, it's better to give up altogether.

Driving on unsurfaced roads requires special skills that you are unlikely to have time to acquire. It's best to avoid them or take very special care. At dawn, dusk and at night many animals stray on to the highway; 'roo bars' are not fitted to vehicles just for macho reasons but to minimise the damage that a collision with a large kangaroo can cause. Don't drive in the country at night if you can avoid it.

Road signs in Australia differ from those in other countries, but their meaning is clear!

Speed limits are 50/60kph in urban areas and 100/110kph elsewhere unless indicated; seatbelts must be worn in both front and back seats. Some road signs are peculiar to Australia, but most of these will be immediately understandable to visitors; they may involve tortuous wordage rather than the use of symbols. On some stretches of winding road, long lay-bys are provided which should be used by slow traffic to enable other drivers to overtake, but remember that the overtaking traffic has the right of way.

Visitors from abroad must have a valid driver's licence with a translation if the licence is not in English or, better still, an international driving licence. Petrol is sold (by the litre) in leaded and unleaded varieties. Petrol stations are fairly numerous but tend to have restricted opening hours; there may be problems in some areas with filling up on Saturday afternoons and on Sundays.

Adequate preparations must be made for driving in the Outback. The vehicle must be in good condition and it is sensible to carry a selection of spare parts, including an emergency plastic windscreen. Enough fuel and water (4 litres of drinking water a day) to see you through is essential. On some routes you may be required to complete a police form, giving your itinerary and estimated time of arrival.

In case of breakdown it is vital that you stay in or near your vehicle as it will offer shade and protection, and will also be much more visible than you are on your own.

Electricity
Current emerges at 240/250 volts AC from Australian sockets, these being of a three-pin type unlike those used in most countries. You will either need to bring an adaptor for your appliances or simply fit them with an Australian plug on arrival. Most shaver points are of the universal type.

Embassies and consulates
● **British High Commission**
Commonwealth Avenue, Yarralumla, Canberra (tel: 02 6270 6666).
● **Canadian High Commission**
Commonwealth Avenue, Yarralumla,

The best way to explore Simpsons Gap is on foot, but go prepared

Canberra (tel: 02 6273 3844).
- **New Zealand High Commission** Commonwealth Avenue, Yarralumla, Canberra (tel: 02 6270 4211).
- **United States Embassy** 21 Moonah Place, Yarralumla, Canberra (tel: 02 6270 5000).

There are US consulates in Sydney and Melbourne, and British consulate-generals in Sydney, Melbourne, Perth and Brisbane.

Emergency telephone numbers
For police, ambulance or fire brigade services, dial 000.

Health
No special health precautions are required before visiting Australia. Standards of hygiene are high, and food and drinking water are safe. Sunburn is a common hazard; wear a broad-brimmed hat, a shirt with a collar and apply plenty of sunscreen.

Free hospital medical treatment under the Australian **Medicare** scheme is available to visitors from the United Kingdom and New Zealand, although ambulance charges and the cost of medicines must be met. Medicare also covers the bulk of the cost of a visit to a doctor. Visitors from most other countries will need full medical insurance. Dental treatment has to be paid for in full.

Language
The peculiarities and delights of Australian English are widely known in the English-speaking world, not least through the efforts of the humourist Barry Humphries, creator of Dame Edna Everage, Sir Leslie Patterson and Barry 'Bazza' McKenzie.

Having some affinities with Cockney, the rather nasal Australian accent is, however, quite distinctive and is spoken without any real regional variation – except for the differences between city and country (slow and drawn out) – throughout the whole country. Differences in speech are likely to be more a matter of occasion or class; the types you might meet in the bar on Friday night would probably pour scorn on what is often considered the 'posh' Australian Broadcasting Corporation voice. In turn, their speech would probably present difficulties to a non-native English speaker who has conscientiously learned the 'standard' language. Many Australians speak with a rising intonation which makes their sentences sound like questions.

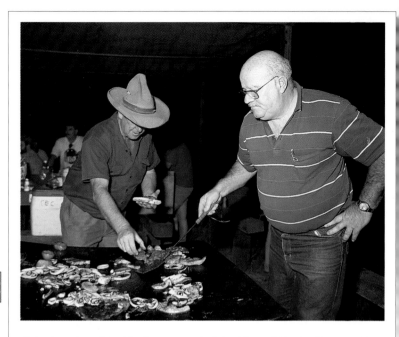

Enjoying a beaut barbie down under with a few mates

The Australian vocabulary contains a number of words of Aboriginal origin (mallee, didgeridoo and kangaroo), as well as plenty of invented terms to describe characteristic Australian phenomena (Outback, bottlebrush and bloodwood), and not a few English words that have changed their original meaning (creek means river, mountain ash is a kind of eucalyptus and mob is a group of people or animals). But the real joy of 'Strine' (Australian) is its slang. Anything that can be reduced to a more or less affectionate diminutive, is ('barbie' means barbecue, 'cossie' is a swimming costume, and 'garbo' is a garbage collector), and there are any number of quirky inventions (dunny is an outside toilet, while bludger is a scrounger) that may be the remnants of the slang of Georgian England. A lot of slang is sexual, scatological, or connected with heavy drinking. Terms evocative of throwing up after a binge are plentiful ('to chunder', 'have a liquid laugh', 'speak into the big white telephone'). Insults are common, sometimes delivered with affectionate intent ('you old bastard'); a recently devised university course instructed 'New Aussies' on how to swear acceptably.

Although Strine is based on British English, the biggest influence on it today is American English – in terms of pronunciation ('quarder' instead of quarter), of vocabulary ('take on board' and 'yuppie'), and in spelling ('program'), although the ALP has been the 'Labor' Party since its foundation in the late 19th century.

The following is a highly selective list of words, phrases and abbreviations a visitor might encounter:

ABC	Australian Broadcasting Corporation
ACT	Australian Capital Territory (Canberra area)
Alice, The	Alice Springs
ALP	Australian Labor Party
ANZAC	Australian and New Zealand Army Corps
arvo	afternoon
barbie	barbecue
beaut	wonderful
billabong	cut-off river bend
billy	tin used for brewing tea

bloke	man
bludger	scrounger
blue	a fight, a redhead
bonzer	wonderful
bottle shop	off licence
bush	countryside
bushranger	outlaw
BYO	bring your own (drink to a restaurant)
cask	wine-box
chook	chicken
chunder	to vomit
crook	ill, no good
dag, daggy	tangled dirty wool at the rear end of a sheep, used abusively (or affectionately) of persons or things
daks	trousers
dinkum	genuine
drongo	a slow-witted person
Dry	the dry season
dunny	outside toilet
fossicking	hunting, as in for precious stones
galah	a kind of parrot, an idiot
garbo	garbage collector
g'day	good morning, good afternoon, hello
greenie	conservationist
hoon	hooligan
international	foreign (as in 'international visitors')
interstate	anything to do with the other Australian states ('he's interstate' means the person referred to is away from his home state)
journo	journalist
larrikin	rogue, hoodlum
mate	universal male greeting
mob	group of persons or animals, for example sheep

mozzie	mosquito
never-never	the far-off outback
new Australian	recent immigrant
ocker	Australian male of crude manners
pokie	poker machine, fruit machine
pom, pommie	English person
property	farm
rort	rowdy party or scam
RSL	Returned Servicemen's League
salties	salt-water crocodiles
semi-trailer	articulated truck
Sheila	female
she'll be right	it'll all be ok
shout	a treat, as in buying a round of drinks
slab	24-pack of beer
smoko	work break
station	extensive farm
stingers	jellyfish
strides	trousers
swag	gear or personal belongings
ta	thank you
tea	evening meal
thongs	flip-flops
tucker	food
uni	university
ute	pickup truck
Wet	rainy season
wowser	puritan, killjoy
yakka	work

261

The best food in town next to the river!

Media
Newspapers and periodicals
A glance inside a newsagent will be enough to convince you that Australians are great readers. The array of publications includes national and regional daily broadsheets, lurid tabloids with screaming headlines, local newspapers, and countless magazines dealing with every conceivable interest.

The Australian was founded in 1964 by media tycoon Rupert Murdoch to perform the role of a national general interest daily paper, supplementing the less popular *Australian Financial Review*. Regionally produced papers like the Melbourne *Age* and *Sydney Morning Herald* are considered superior by many readers, although visitors from abroad may find coverage of non-Australian news rather selective (check how well your favourite home paper covers Australian affairs before judging them too harshly). Australian tabloids, like most such newspapers, are not of the highest standard. Most ethnic groups have dailies or weeklies in their own languages.

Television and radio Radio recalls newspapers in its divisions. The ABC (Australian Broadcasting Corporation) has countrywide coverage and offers by far the best mix of broadcasting, with excellent news coverage and magazine programmes. In contrast are the numerous commercial stations, many of which run on a shoestring, plugging out pop music, phone-ins, traffic reports and similar time-fillers. In addition, there are a number of special interest and community radio stations.

Commercial television, as elsewhere in the world, suffers from a surfeit of advertising and a reliance on imported programmes (though this may enable foreign visitors to catch up on their favourite soap). ABC TV maintains high standards generally and SBS (Special Broadcasting Service, not available over the whole country) is largely devoted to programmes for ethnic minorities in their own languages.

Money matters
The Australian currency was decimalised in 1966, when sterling (pounds, shillings and pence) was replaced by dollars and cents (100¢ = $1). Coins come in 5¢, 10¢, 20¢, 50¢, $1 and $2 denominations, and there are colourful $5, $10, $20, $50 and $100 notes. Most of the notes are made of durable polymer. You can take as much money as you want into and out of the country, although for amounts over A$5,000 you must complete a report form.

Changing money is rarely a problem, with plenty of exchange bureaux at places where tourists congregate, as well as at banks. Bank hours are usually 9:30–4 Monday to Thursday, and 9:30–5 on Friday. Traveller's cheques made out in Australian dollars are likely to be dealt with more speedily. Credit cards are widely in use, but may not

The Abbey Church at New Norcia, Western Australia

Australia Day celebrations, Sydney

be particularly welcome in remote areas or in small shops.

National holidays

- **New Year's Day**   1 January
- **Australia Day**   fourth Monday in January (commemorates the landing of the First Fleet on 26 January 1788)
- **Labour Day**   Varies from state to state (commemorates achievement of the eight-hour day)
- **Good Friday**
- **Easter Monday**
- **Anzac Day**   25 April (commemorates Gallipoli landings on 25 April 1915)
- **Queen's Birthday**   Second Monday in June
- **Christmas Day**   25 December
- **Boxing Day**   26 December (28 December in South Australia)

Opening hours

Shops These are generally open 9–5 (or 5:30) Monday to Friday and 9–4 on Saturday, with late-night shopping on Thursday or Friday until 8 or 9. Corner shops keep longer hours and also open on Sundays.

Offices *Open* Mon–Fri

Museums and galleries Usually closed on Christmas Day and Good Friday, with some also closed on Anzac Day. Major institutions are usually open 10–5 daily, although they may be closed on one day of the week. Many smaller museums open only at weekends or during school or public holidays, so the best advice is to check before you set out.

Pharmacies

Called both pharmacies and 'chemists' (as in the UK), these dispense a range of medicines and products which will probably be familiar to you. Many are open long hours, and you will find a 24-hour service in big cities. Prescriptions must be written by an Australian-registered doctor. Prices of pharmaceuticals are fairly high.

Places of worship

Most religions are represented in Australia, although outside the big cities only the major Christian denominations have places of worship. The Roman Catholic Church and the Anglican Church have roughly the same number of adherents; their cathedrals were once among the dominant buildings of city centres. The Uniting Church was formed in 1977 as a union of Methodists and Congregationalists. Islam was introduced by the Afghan camel drivers in

Fly-fishing on London Lakes in Tasmania

the 19th century and there are now some two dozen mosques throughout the country. Synagogues are concentrated in the state capitals.

Police

Australia has both state and federal police, the latter (the AFP) being responsible for the investigation of major crimes, intelligence work and anti-terrorist activities, as well as for policing the Canberra area (ACT).

The boys in blue are usually extremely helpful to visitors from abroad, but don't expect any special privileges if you break the law (see Driving tips on pages 257–8). In the unlikely event that you are arrested, you must give your name and address, but are then entitled to say nothing until you have contacted a friend or legal representative. In this situation, the best thing to do is to ask to be put in touch with your consul (see Embassies and consulates on pages 258–9).

Post offices

The offices of Australia Post are to be found in city centres, suburban areas and all over the country, often combined with a general store in smaller places. Larger offices have a wide range of services available to the public like fax and electronic post.

Services are reasonably efficient. Airmail letters can arrive in Great Britain or the US after a few days, provided the correct rate has been paid and the letter or postcard is clearly addressed. A parcel sent by surface mail to Europe will undergo an interminable sea voyage. An alternative to paying the full airmail charge in this case is to send it Economy Air which should ensure its arrival in the UK or US after about two weeks. Post offices usually have a good range of stationery and parcel material for sale, and poste restante and telegram facilities are also available. Some post boxes are of the traditional type but most (painted red with a white stripe) resemble litter bins.

Public transport

The sprawl of low-density suburbs surrounding major cities is not conducive to the operation of an effective public transport system, and Australians have become very dependent on cars for work, shopping and recreational trips. However, city public transport services based on bus, rail, tram (Melbourne), and ferry (Sydney) are surprisingly extensive, frequent and efficient, albeit a heavy drain on the public purse. Most systems offer special deals that are likely to be of interest to a tourist (day tickets covering the whole network, reduced fares for travel outside the rush hour and so on). Further details are given in the travel sections headed within each chapter. For long-distance transport, see Domestic travel on pages 256–7.

Student and youth travel

There are relatively few official concessions in Australia for young visitors from abroad, but given the relative cheapness of the country this does not constitute a problem. Accommodation is provided by the countless hostels and backpackers' lodges. Membership of your national Youth Hostels Association may get you the occasional discount and also entitles you to use Australian youth hostels. Long-distance travel by bus is not expensive, and hitch-hiking is easier than in many countries, although not entirely without danger. The noticeboards in lodges and hostels are an invaluable source of information on car-sharing and on what is on offer in terms of meals, excursions and entertainment.

Working holidays, once very popular, have become less feasible in harder economic times. **STA Travel**, a specialist in youth travel, may be able to help here, as well as with other travel arrangements; they have offices in the UK at Priory House, 6 Wrights Lane, London SW8 6TA (tel: 0171 361 6111) as well as in Australia.

Telephones

The public telephones of Telstra are easy to find in most places. Long-distance or STD (Subscriber Trunk Dialling), calls can be made from most telephone boxes and international calls can be made from boxes designated ISD (International Subscriber Dialling). Many machines take phone or credit cards. Local calls have no time limit, while interstate calls are relatively inexpensive given the distances involved. Cheap rates apply between 6pm and 8am on weekdays, and between 8pm on Friday and 8am on Monday. Hotels frequently double the cost of a call made from your room.

To call an Australian number from overseas, dial the international access code, the country code for Australia (61), the local code (minus the initial 0), then finally the subscriber's number. To call an overseas number from Australia, dial the international access code (0011), the country code, the local code (minus its initial 0), then finally the subscriber's number. It is also worth working out the time disparity between home and Australia (see Time below).

Time

The enormous width of Australia has resulted in the creation of three time zones. Eastern Standard Time (EST) applies to New South Wales, ACT, Victoria, Tasmania and Queensland; Central Standard Time (CST) to South Australia and the Northern Territory; and Western Standard Time (WST) to Western Australia. CST is half an hour behind EST, while WST is two hours behind. Daylight saving (Summer Time) is practised in all states except Queensland, the NT and Western Australia from October or November to March, when clocks are advanced one hour. Eastern Standard Time is 10 hours ahead of Greenwich Mean Time.

Paddling on Bondi Beach

Tipping

Tipping is not universal in Australia – for example, tips are not expected by taxi drivers, airport porters and hairdressers. Railway porters have set charges and hotel porters can be tipped at your discretion. Service charges are not normally added to restaurant bills; given exceptionally good service you might leave a tip of 10 per cent.

Toilets

Australian cities are exceptionally well provided with (usually clean) public toilets. In addition, city plans often make a point of identifying their location.

Tourist information

Australia supplies its visitors with an abundance of information from a variety of sources. The **Australian Tourist Commission** provides information on individual states and the country as a whole from its offices abroad (see opposite), while each state has its own Tourism Board with headquarters in the state capital, and offices in some other state capitals. Places of any size in Australia will have one or more infor-

mation centres , with plenty of material on local attractions and booking facilities for accommodation and excursions. The advice given may not always be impartial, however, as the centre may have links with the services it recommends.

Other useful sources of information are the motoring organisations which give out free maps for members of allied organisations abroad, and the visitor centres or offices of the National Parks and Wildlife Service.

Australian Tourist Commission:
- **New Zealand** Level 13, 44–48 Emily Place, Auckland 1 (tel: 09 379 9594).
- **UK** 1st Floor, Gemini House, 10–18 Putney Hill, London SW15 6AA (tel: 0181 780 2229).
- **USA** 2049 Century Park East, Suite 1920, Los Angeles, CA 90067 (tel: 310/229 4870).

Women

Australia is a reasonably safe place for women, and female travellers should encounter no special problems, although the more extreme manifestations of 'ockerism' (see Language on pages 259–61) may be irritating.

The Northern Territory Tourist Commission will provide information on sights of interest such as the Devils Marbles

HOTELS AND RESTAURANTS

HOTELS AND RESTAURANTS

ACCOMMODATION

The wide variety of accommodation available in Australia ranges from some of the world's finest and most luxurious hotels through motels, 'units' (equipped apartments), 'hotels' (which may be the most basic of pubs), to backpackers' hostels of no pretensions whatsoever. You are rarely likely to have difficulty in finding somewhere to stay, though it's advisable to book in advance in the peak season (July to September and December to February). Prices compare very favourably with those in other developed parts of the world, and discounts can often be obtained for longer stays or if you use hotels in a particular chain.

The following recommended hotels have been divided into three price categories:
● budget (£)
● moderate (££)
● expensive (£££)

SYDNEY

Aarons Hotel (£/££) 37 Ultimo Road, Haymarket (tel: 02 9281 5555). Better than average budget accommodation near Darling Harbour and Chinatown.
The Cambridge (££) 212 Riley Street, Surry Hills (tel: 02 9212 1111). This hotel is situated just to the south of the city centre and lies within easy walking distance of Darling Harbour, the Entertainment Centre and Chinatown.
Chateau Sydney (££) 14 Macleay Street, Potts Point (tel: 02 9358 2500). In the Kings Cross area, with a pool, good facilities and harbour views.
Cremorne Point Manor (£–££) 6 Cremorne Road, Cremorne Point (tel: 02 9953 7899). This charming old mansion provides good value accommodation, just a short ferry ride from the city centre.
Double Sir Stamford Bay (£££) 22 Knox Street, Double Bay (tel: 02 9363 0100). This upmarket boutique-style hotel is located in one of the city's most colourful and exclusive inner suburbs.
Grand Hotel (£) 30 Hunter Street (tel: 02 9232 3755). One of Sydney's oldest hotels, situated right in the city centre.
Harbour Rocks Hotel (££) 34 Harrington Street, The Rocks (tel: 02 9251 8944). This medium-sized hotel is situated in an excellent location.
Hotel Inter-Continental Sydney (£££) 117 Macquarie Street (tel: 02 9230 0200). Partly housed in the authentically restored Treasury Buildings dating from 1851, the hotel occupies a landmark site on historic Macquarie Street in the very centre of the city.
Hotel Nikko Darling Harbour (£££) Corner of Sussex and King streets (tel: 02 9299 1231). A glossy modern five-star hotel overlooking Darling Harbour and close to the city centre.

Hyatt Regency Sydney (£££) Kings Cross Road, Kings Cross (tel: 02 9356 1234). The deluxe standards of the Hyatt chain in the heart of Sydney's nightlife area.
Manhattan Hotel (££) 8 Greenknowe Avenue, Elizabeth Bay (tel: 02 9358 1288). The rooms in this reasonably priced art deco hotel feature a TV, fridge and coffee-making facilities. The Manhattan is located close to the heart of lively Kings Cross.
Manly Beach Resort (£) 6 Carlton Street, Manly (tel: 02 9977 4188). This hotel is located a short distance from all the attractions of Manly and its popular beach.
Manly Pacific Parkroyal (£££) 55 North Steyne, Manly (tel: 02 9977 7666). This Pacific Parkroyal hotel has a beachfront location in Sydney's own seaside resort of Manly, which lies only a short and enthralling ferry trip away from the city centre.
Mercantile Hotel (££) 25 George Street, The Rocks (tel: 02 9247 3570). Small, atmospheric pub in a central location.
Oakford Apartments (££) 10 Wylde Street, Potts Point (tel: 02 9358 4544). Comfortable self-contained apartments with water views in the Kings Cross area.
The Observatory Hotel (£££) 89–113 Kent Street (tel: 02 9256 2222). This is one of Sydney's newest and most luxurious boutique hotels, and is situated close to The Rocks area.
Old Sydney Parkroyal (£££) 55 George Street (tel: 02 9252 0524). Right in the middle of The Rocks, this luxurious and characterful hotel has a main section which once served as a warehouse and stables.
Park Hyatt Sydney (£££) 7 Hickson Road, The Rocks (tel: 02 9241 1234). Winding itself elegantly around the edge of the harbour, this hotel could not be better located.
Ravesi's on Bondi Beach (££) Corner of Campbell Parade and Hall Street, Bondi Beach (tel: 02 9365 4422). Small and interesting boutique-style hotel overlooking world-famous Bondi Beach. The restaurant is excellent.
The Regent of Sydney (£££) 199 George Street (tel: 02 9238 0000). Situated near The Rocks, The Regent has terrific views of the harbour and city.
Sebel Town House Hotel Sydney (£££) 23 Elizabeth Bay Road, Elizabeth Bay (tel: 02 9358 3244). Not far from Kings Cross, this intimate hotel is the haunt of the rich and famous when in Sydney, and is a member of the Leading Hotels of the World group.
Sydney Central YHA (£) Corner of Pitt Street and Rawson Place (tel: 02 9281 9111). With 530 beds, this is the world's biggest youth hostel. It is located close to Central Station and offers a licensed café and rooftop pool/barbecue area.
Sydney Hilton (£££) 259 Pitt Street (tel: 02 9266 2000). Recently emerged from a lavish refurbishment programme, the Hilton was

one of the first high-rise buildings in the city centre and is close to all the central attractions.

Thelellen Beach Inn (£) 2 Campbell Parade, Bondi Beach (tel: 02 9130 5333). Recapture the atmosphere of the seaside as it was during the 1930s in this refurbished hotel on the beachfront at Bondi.

Victoria Court Hotel (££) 122 Victoria Street, Potts Point (tel: 02 9357 3200). This delightful Victorian-style guesthouse is located in a leafy street near Kings Cross.

Wynyard Vista Hotel (£££) 7–9 York Street (tel: 02 9290 1840). Aimed at business travellers, this hotel is conveniently close to Circular Quay, Wynyard bus station and the city's business area.

ACT
Canberra

Embassy Motel (££) Hopetoun Circuit, Deakin (tel: 02 6281 1322). Located in the city's diplomatic district.

Hyatt Hotel Canberra (£££) Commonwealth Avenue, Yarralumla (tel: 02 6270 1234). Canberra's best hotel. The service is excellent and the facilities comprehensive in this restored 1920s art deco building.

Macquarie Hotel (£) 18 National Circuit, Barton (tel: 02 6273 2325). Situated in a peaceful suburb within walking distance of Parliament House.

Olims Canberra Hotel (££) Corner of Ainslie and Limestone avenues, Braddon (tel: 02 6248 5511). Good quality accommodation at a reasonable price, and located close to the city centre.

Rydges Canberra (££/£££) London Circuit, Canberra City (tel: 02 6247 6244). Close to central attractions and with great views.

Tall Trees Motel (££) 21 Stephen Street, Ainslie (tel: 02 6247 9200). This motel is but a short distance from the city centre in a quiet and attractively landscaped setting.

NEW SOUTH WALES
Blue Mountains

The Chalet Guesthouse (££) 46 Portland Road, Medlow Bath (tel: 02 4788 1122). This charming guesthouse dates from the 1890s and lies within easy reach of the major attractions of the mountains.

Fairmont Resort (£££) 1 Sublime Point Road, Leura (tel: 02 4782 5222). Excellent accommodation and recre-ation facilities are available in this modern resort, along with some wonderful clifftop views.

Jemby Rinjah Lodge (££) 336 Evans Lookout Road, Blackheath (tel: 02 4787 7622). This environmentally aware lodge is located right next to the Blue Mountains National Park. The accommodation is in timber cabins, some of which are self-catering, and the lodge includes an excellent restaurant.

Jenolan Caves House (£££) Jenolan Caves (tel: 02 6359 3304). A splendidly rambling and comfortable 19th-century survivor in Tudor style from the great days of mountain lodge holidays.

Lilianfels Blue Mountains (£££) Lilianfels Avenue, Echo Point, Katoomba (tel: 02 4780 1200). The most exclusive place to stay in the Blue Mountains. The original 1890s home now houses an award-winning restaurant.

Mountain Heritage Country House Retreat (££) Corner of Apex and Lovel streets, Katoomba (tel: 02 4782 2155). A charming old-style hotel – complete with log fires, comfortable rooms of varied sizes and configurations, and some of the best views in the region.

Hunter Valley

Peppers Guest House (££/£££) Ekerts Road, Pokolbin (tel: 02 4998 7596). Most attractively located among the vineyards, colonial-style Peppers consistently receives awards for its comfort, facilities, hospitality and, not least, for the food in its Chez Pok restaurant.

Pokolbin Village Resort (££) Broke Road, Pokolbin (tel: 02 4998 7596). The Pokolbin is centrally located within the Hunter Valley, and the resort offers a choice of either suite-style accommodation or self-contained villas.

Southern Highlands

Berida Manor (££) 6 David Street, Bowral (tel: 02 4861 1177). English-style manor house accommodation, set in attractive gardens. Antique furnishings and fine dining complete the picture.

Links House Small Hotel (££) 17 Links Road, Bowral (tel: 02 4861 1408). In a quiet position opposite the local golf course, this friendly hotel provides a garden and tennis court, pleasant rooms, two cosy lounge areas with log fires, and a popular restaurant.

Mercure Grand Bowral Heritage Park (££) 9 Kangaloon Road, Bowral (tel: 02 4861 4833). This award-winning accommodation offers full resort facilities, including large gardens, tennis, croquet, golf and billiards.

Milton Park Country House Hotel (£££) Hordern's Road, Bowral (tel: 02 4861 1522). Glorying in its reputation as one of the best places to stay in Australia, this prestigious country hotel is set in splendid grounds and has the full range of modern facilities as well as fine dining.

VICTORIA
Melbourne

Albany Motor Inn (£) Corner Toorak Road and Millswyn Street, South Yarra (tel: 03 9866 4485). Offers budget-priced accommodation in the normally more expensive South Yarra area of the city.

All Seasons Crossley (££/£££) 51 Little Bourke Street (tel: 03 9639 1639). Modern 'boutique' hotel with excellent range of facilities.

HOTELS AND RESTAURANTS

Batmans Hill Hotel (££) 66–70 Spencer Street (tel: 03 9614 6344). Located opposite Spencer Street Station behind a fully restored historic façade.

City Limits Hotel (£) 20–22 Little Bourke Street (tel: 03 9662 2544). In the heart of the city centre, this is a friendly, budget-priced hotel that provides no-frills comfort, including an en-suite bathroom, TV and kitchenette in each room.

City Park Motel (£/££) 308–310 Kingsway, South Melbourne (tel: 03 9699 9811). Reasonably priced accommodation, close to the city's Botanic Gardens and the colourful St Kilda area.

Georgian Court Guest House (£) 21–25 George Street, East Melbourne (tel: 03 9419 6353). This guesthouse is located in the exclusive and attractive area of East Melbourne, and lies within easy walking distance of the city centre.

Grand Hyatt Melbourne (£££) 123 Collins Street (tel: 03 9657 1234). Probably the most luxurious hotel in the heart of the city, the Hyatt offers a full range of leisure and dining facilities.

Hotel Grand Chancellor Melbourne (££) 131 Lonsdale Street (tel: 03 9663 3161). A centrally located hotel that offers good service and facilities at reasonable rates.

Kingsgate Hotel (£) 131 King Street (tel: 03 9629 3049). Offering extremely good value accommodation in the city centre, the Kingsgate Hotel also has a restaurant, a coffee shop and a bar.

Le Meridien at Rialto (£££) 495 Collins Street (tel: 03 9620 9111). Splendidly Gothic late 19th-century hotel with all the usual comforts.

Oakford Gordon Place (££/£££) 24 Little Bourke Street (tel: 03 9663 2888). Between Parliament and Chinatown, the Oakford's luxuriously appointed apartments (there are even books on the shelves!) open on to a vine-clad interior courtyard with a huge palm tree. The historic building which it occupies has a delicatessen, a bar and Places Restaurant, and literally buzzes with big city excitement.

Oakford The Park (££) 631 Punt Road, South Yarra (tel: 03 9820 8544). One of a number of 'Oakford' blocks of excellent serviced apartments that can be rented at locations scattered around the city.

Old Melbourne Hotel (££) 5 Flemington Road, North Melbourne (tel: 03 9329 9344). Has a flagstone courtyard around which are grouped three restaurants and a couple of bars.

Parkroyal on St Kilda Road (££/£££) 562 St Kilda Road, St Kilda (tel: 03 9529 8888). An elegant boutique-style hotel with large rooms and excellent service. Located a short tram ride from the city centre, this Parkroyal can be found in one of Melbourne's most interesting inner suburbs.

Rockman's Regency Hotel (£££) Corner of Exhibition and Lonsdale streets (tel: 03 9662 3900). Melbourne's most luxurious boutique hotel is close to the city centre. There are excellent facilities and the hotel is home to some of the city's most upmarket bars and restaurants.

Rydges Carlton Hotel (£) 701 Swanston Street, Carlton (tel: 03 9347 7811), and **Lygon Lodge Carlton** (£) 220 Lygon Street, Carlton (tel: 03 9663 6633) are two high standard motels in the inner suburb of Carlton.

Rydges on Flinders (££/£££) Corner Flinders Lane and Spencer Street (tel: 03 9629 4111). Located in the heart of the financial district, this establishment prides itself on catering for the discerning visitor.

Sheraton Vista Hotel (££/£££) 13 Spring Street (tel: 03 9205 9999). A reliable city centre hotel, the Sheraton overlooks the Treasury Gardens.

South Yarra Hill Suites (££/£££) 14 Murphy Street, South Yarra (tel: 03 9868 8222). These serviced one- to three-bedroom apartments are situated in exclusive South Yarra. They come complete with fully equipped kitchens and spacious lounges.

St Kilda Road Travelodge (££) Corner of St Kilda Road and Park Street (tel: 03 9699 4833). Opposite the Botanic Gardens and close to the Arts Centre, this 230-room hotel represents good value in a prime location.

Victoria Hotel (££) 215 Little Collins Street (tel: 03 9653 0441). This comfortable turn-of-the-century hotel is located in the city centre and has become a Melbourne institution.

The Windsor (£££) 103 Spring Street (tel: 03 9633 6000). This grand, old-fashioned hotel has been splendidly restored and furnished with antiques. It has an unbeatable location opposite Parliament and has been classified by the National Trust.

Great Ocean Road

Caledonian Inn (£) Corner of Bank and James streets, Port Fairy (tel: 03 5568 1044). With its bar and seafood lounge, the Caledonian Inn is claimed to be the oldest continuously licensed hotel in Victoria. However, no such claim is made for the motel section.

Cumberland Lorne Resort (£££) 150 Mountjoy Parade, Lorne (tel: 03 5289 2400). A recently completed luxury apartment resort in the centre of this well-established seaside resort.

Erskine House (££) 136 Mountjoy Parade, Lorne (tel: 03 5289 1209). Rudyard Kipling stayed in this venerable hotel, situated among immaculately maintained gardens.

Seacombe House Motor Inn (££) 22 Sackville Street, Port Fairy (tel: 03 5568 1082). One of the older buildings in this delightful old harbour town, Seacombe House has been classified by the National Trust. The Inn, however, con-sists of modern motel units.

Northeast Victoria

Eucalpyt Ridge (£££) 564 Skyline Road, Eildon (tel: 03 5774 2033). An upmarket mountain lodge with views of Lake Eildon. Luxurious suites and fine dining are complemented by 100 hectares of bushland and a national park located near by.

Mount Buffalo Chalet (££) Mount Buffalo National Park (tel: 03 5755 1500). A splendidly old-fashioned Alpine-style establishment situated in the exhilarating surroundings of this mountain national park.

Pension Grimus (£££) 149 Breathtaker Road, Mount Buller (tel: 03 5777 6396). This is the finest accommodation in the Mount Buller region: the lodge is ideal for winter skiing or summer alpine walking and features spa baths and an award-winning restaurant.

Rose Cottage (££) 42 Camp Street, Beechworth (tel: 03 5728 1069). Bed and breakfast style accommodation in a charming cottage that is full of old world atmosphere.

Tanswells Commercial Hotel (£) 50 Ford Street, Beechworth (tel: 03 5728 1480). In the middle of this perfectly preserved gold-fields town, the 19th-century Tanswells has fine ironwork and is authentically furnished. The building has been National Trust classified.

Trackers Mountain Lodge (££/£££) 88 Schuss Street, Falls Creek (tel: 03 5758 3346). Luxurious accommodation in the heart of one of Australia's most popular ski resorts. The location is also perfect for a summer walking, horse-riding or fishing holiday.

SOUTH AUSTRALIA

Adelaide

Adelaide's Bed And Breakfast (££) 239 Franklin Street (tel: 08 8231 3124). Homely rooms in an historic sandstone building dating from the 1870s, centrally located in the City Square.

Apartments on the Park (££) 274 South Terrace (tel: 08 8232 0555). Self-contained units at the southern end of town. The apartments are ideal for families or small groups.

Barron Townhouse (££) Corner of Hindley and Morphett streets (tel: 08 8211 8255). Conveniently central apartments.

Earl of Zetland Hotel (£) Corner of Gawler Place and Flinders Street (tel: 08 8223 5500). Comfortable old-fashioned pub-style hotel in a central location.

Festival Lodge Motel (£) 140 North Terrace (tel: 08 8212 7877). Reasonably priced motel-style accommodation in Adelaide's most famous street.

Grosvenor Hotel (££) 125 North Terrace (tel: 08 8407 8888). More or less opposite the Hyatt, this is where up-country farmers and their families would stay when in town. Rooms are available at a variety of rates.

Hilton International (Adelaide) (£££) 233 Victoria Square (tel: 08 8237 0777). The usual good standards of the Hilton group, this time right in the heart of the city.

Hindley Parkroyal (££–£££) 65 Hindley Street (tel: 08 8231 5552). A good quality hotel with a pool, spa and restaurant, located on Adelaide's main restaurant and nightlife street.

Hyatt Regency Adelaide (£££) North Terrace (tel: 08 8231 1234). Decorated with stunning works of art inside and out, the Hyatt is the city's most sumptuous hotel, centrally located near all the major attractions.

The Mansions Apartments (££) 21 Pulteney Street (tel: 08 8232 0033). Well located self-contained apartments in interesting old building.

North Adelaide Heritage Apartments (££) (tel: 08 8272 1355). Self-contained apartments in a variety of North Adelaide locations.

Richmond Hotel on The Mall (££) 128 Rundle Mall (tel: 08 8223 4044). Central business district apartments.

Stamford Grand (£££) Moseley Square, Glenelg (tel: 08 8376 1222). The best hotel in Adelaide's most famous beach suburb – a short and pleasant tram ride from the city centre.

Stamford Plaza (£££) 150 North Terrace (tel: 08 8217 7552). Adelaide's most elegant hotel offers good views, excellent service and tastefully decorated rooms and suites.

Adelaide Hills

Hahndorf Inn Motor Lodge (£/££) 35 Main Road, Hahndorf (tel: 08 8388 1000). Offers reasonably priced motel-style accommodation in the heart of the Hills' most picturesque town.

Mercure Grand Hotel Mount Lofty House (£££) 74 Summit Road, Crafers (tel: 08 8339 6777). Luxury country house living, South Australian style. The hotel is located just below the summit of Mount Lofty in the Adelaide Hills only a short drive from the city itself. There is also a gourmet restaurant.

Thorngrove Country Manor (£££) 2 Glenside Lane, Stirling (tel: 08 8339 6748). Thorngrove lies just 20 minutes from the city centre, but is another world of European-style country grandeur. This elegant hotel features gardens, European antiques and large suites.

Barossa Valley

Blickinstal Hillside (££) Rifle Range Road, Tanunda (tel: 08 8563 2716). With magnificent views over the Barossa, this bed and breakfast establishment has a German name meaning 'valley view'.

Collingrove Homestead (£££) Eden Valley Road, Angaston (tel: 08 8564 2061). Stay comfortably in the servants' quarters of this fine National Trust property on the edge of the Barossa, once the home of one of Australia's greatest landowning families. Dinner is available by arrangement.

The Hermitage of Marananga (£££) Corner of Seppeltsfield and Stonewell roads, Marananga (tel: 08 8562 2722). These colonial-style buildings rising out of the Barossa vineyards offer bed and breakfast accommodation of a highly superior kind. Gourmet dining is also on offer (see page 279).

Tanunda Hotel (£) 51 Murray Street, Tanunda (tel: 08 8563 2030). Budget accommodation in the often expensive Barossa Valley area.

WESTERN AUSTRALIA
Perth
Airways City Hotel (££) 195 Adelaide Terrace (tel: 08 9492 7799). This provides an affordable alternative to the nearby Sheraton.

Baileys Parkside Motel (£) 150 Bennett Street (tel: 08 9325 3788). These budget-priced self-contained units are centrally located: family units and suites are available.

Burswood Resort Hotel and Casino (£££) Great Eastern Highway, Rivervale (tel: 08 9362 7777). On the far bank of the Swan River from the city centre, Burswood is a luxury resort with its own golf course. The casino itself is one of the largest in the southern hemisphere.

Carlton Hotel (£) 248 Hay Street East (tel: 08 9325 2092). Is it really the friendliest pub in town? The price includes your morning paper.

Chateau Commodore Hotel (££) 417 Hay Street (tel: 08 9325 0461). Good quality accommodation at a reasonable price. The hotel has a swimming pool and restaurant and is just a short walk from the city's central business district.

City Waters Lodge (£/££) 118 Terrace Road (tel: 08 9325 1566). This lodge offers self-contained apartments on the Swan River foreshore.

Cottesloe Beach Hotel (£/££) 104 Marine Parade, Cottesloe (tel: 08 9383 1100). Just 15 minutes from the city, this beachside hotel provides good value accommodation, bars and a café.

Hyatt Regency Perth (£££) 99 Adelaide Terrace, East Perth (tel: 08 9225 1234). One of the city's best hotels, the Hyatt Regency is located just to the east of the centre and overlooks the Swan River.

Metro Inn Apartments (£) 22 Nile Street, East Perth (tel: 08 9325 1866). Budget self-contained apartments and hotel rooms, close to the city centre and near the river.

Miss Maud Swedish Hotel (££) 97 Murray Street (tel: 08 9325 3900). Scandinavian chic in city centre location. Good and reasonably priced eating.

Parkroyal Perth (£££) 54 Terrace Road (tel: 08 9325 3811). The Parkroyal offers luxury accommodation in the heart of the city, yet with good views of the Swan River. This is one of the best addresses at which to stay in Perth.

Parmelia Hilton (£££) 14 Mill Street (tel: 08 9322 3622). One of the most characterful of all the hotels in the Hilton chain, the Parmelia is located right in Perth's city centre.

Radisson Observation City Hotel (£££) The Esplanade, Scarborough (tel: 08 9245 1000). A luxurious five-star resort on the front at Scarborough beach, just a 15-minute drive from the city centre.

The Royal Hotel (£) Corner of Wellington and William streets (tel: 08 9481 1000). A renovated pub-style hotel in the city centre with both self-contained and shared facility rooms.

Sheraton Perth Hotel (£££) 207 Adelaide Terrace (tel: 08 9325 0501). Sheraton comforts and conveniences on one of Perth's main arteries.

Sullivans Hotel (££) 166 Mounts Bay Road (tel: 08 9321 8022). A small, friendly hotel that is located at the edge of Kings Park. Some rooms have views of the river.

Fremantle
Esplanade Hotel (£££) Corner of Marine Terrace and Essex Street (tel: 08 9430 4000). This international standard hotel is situated in the heart of historic Fremantle. Rooms, studios and suites are available, and the hotel also has excellent recreation and dining facilities.

Tradewinds Hotel (££) 59 Canning Highway, East Fremantle (tel: 08 9339 8188). In a fine position overlooking the Swan River and just a short walk from central Fremantle, this hotel provides self-contained apartments that are serviced daily.

Kalgoorlie-Boulder
Hannan's View Motel (££) 430 Hannan Street, Kalgoorlie (tel: 08 9021 3333). Recommended central motel.

Mercure Plaza Hotel (££) 45 Egan Street, Kalgoorlie (tel: 08 9021 4544). Claimed to be the finest hotel in town, which is certainly true as far as comfort and facilities are concerned. It is located reasonably close to the centre (unlike most motels in Kalgoorlie).

York Hotel (£/££) 259 Hannan Street, Kalgoorlie (tel: 08 9021 2337). This is a splendid hotel from the early days of the century, with an authentic feel of the gold-rush days including darkly furnished rooms and balcony bathrooms. The restaurant will serve you chops and steak for breakfast – a real gold-miner's feast!

Other historic hotels in Kalgoorlie/Boulder include the **Exchange** on Hannan Street (tel: 08 9021 2833) and the **Palace**, also on Hannan Street (tel: 08 9021 2788).

NORTHERN TERRITORY
Darwin
Beaufort Darwin (£££) The Esplanade (tel: 08 8980 0800). Housed in an intriguing pink and blue post-modern complex in an enviable position on Darwin's Esplanade, the luxury Beaufort is one of the more striking additions to the city's post-Tracy skyline. There are also excellent restaurants here, including the **Siam** (fine Thai cuisine) and sophisticated **Siggi's** (international).

Capricornia Motel (£) 44 East Point Road, Fannie Bay (tel: 08 8981 4055). Comfortable and well priced units, situated just out of the town centre. The motel has a restaurant and a swimming pool.

Cherry Blossom Motel (£) 108 The Esplanade (tel: 08 8981 6734). This motel provides acceptable accommodation in an excellent Esplanade location that is convenient for the city centre.

City Gardens Apartments (££) 93 Woods Street (tel: 08 8941 2888). Centrally located complex that offers apartments and family units, as well as a swimming pool and barbecue area.

Darwin Travelodge (££/£££) 122 The Esplanade (tel: 08 8981 5388). A good quality modern hotel on Darwin's waterfront.

MGM Grand Darwin (£££) Gilruth Avenue, The Gardens (tel: 08 8943 8888). Deluxe hotel that is part of Darwin's casino complex. Located on the beach, just out of the city centre.

Novotel Atrium Hotel Darwin (££/£££) Corner of Peel Street and The Esplanade (tel: 08 8943 0755). This medium-sized modern hotel has good facilities and service. Rooms vary from standard to deluxe suites and the hotel has a great seafront position.

Plaza Hotel Darwin (£££) 32 Mitchell Street (tel: 08 8982 0000). The tallest building in Darwin, the Plaza has a cool and spacious atrium which provides some welcome relief when Darwin's heat and humidity start to become too much for any weary sightseers.

Poinciana Inn (££) Corner of Mitchell and McLachlan streets (tel: 08 8981 8111). Good value single to family rooms, just a 5-minute walk from the city centre.

Alice Springs
Alice Springs Pacific Resort (££/£££) 34 Stott Terrace (tel: 08 8952 6699). Attractive resort-style accommodation with family, standard and deluxe categories. The resort has a restaurant, swimming pool and barbecue area.

Alice Tourist Apartments (£) Corner of Gap Road and Gnoilya Street (tel: 08 8952 2788). Two-bedroom apartments at a very reasonable price. The small complex is just out of town and provides a pool and full cooking facilities.

Diplomat Hotel (££) Corner of Gregory Terrace and Hartley Street (tel: 08 8952 8977). In tasteful two-tone pink, very superior or motel-style accommodation is on offer at two levels in the heart of town. Executive suites with spa baths are also available.

Frontier Oasis Alice Springs (££) 10 Gap Road (tel: 08 8952 1444). Well located motel-style accommodation with good facilities, including a pool and gardens.

Lasseters Hotel Casino (££/£££) 93 Barrett Drive (tel: 08 8952 5066). This is one of the town's most up-market hotels, and is part of the Alice Springs casino development. The hotel offers both rooms and suites.

Melanka Lodge (£) 94 Todd Street (tel: 08 8952 2233). Possibly the best range of inexpensive accommodation in central Australia, from basic rooms to motel-style accommodation with own bathroom and so on. There is a licensed restaurant and two pools, and the lodge lies in a central location.

Plaza Hotel Alice Springs (£££) Barrett Drive (tel: 08 8952 8000). Provides resort-type luxury at the foot of the stark MacDonnell Ranges just a short distance to the south of town.

Ayers Rock
All accommodation and most other facilities at Ayers Rock are provided and managed outside the National Park at Ayers Rock Resort (formerly Yulara). You can stay in luxury at the superbly landscaped **Sails in the Desert** (tel: 08 8956 2200), in comfort at both the **Desert Gardens** (tel: 08 8956 2100) and the somewhat plainer but very affordable **Outback Pioneer Lodge** (tel: 08 8956 2170). Backpackers and campers are also catered for. There are restaurants in each of the hotels, all of approximately the same quality and in the same price range.

QUEENSLAND
Brisbane
Albert Park Hotel (££) 551 Wickham Terrace, Spring Hill (tel: 07 3831 3111). A comfortable hotel located near Albert Park, a short walk from the city centre. The pool and terrace overlook the park and the hotel has full à la carte dining.

Bellevue Hotel (£/££) 103 George Street (tel: 07 3221 6044). This well-priced central-city hotel offers a pool and restaurant, and is close to the casino and South Bank Parklands.

Conrad Treasury Brisbane (£££) Corner of William and George streets (tel: 07 3306 8888). Brisbane's newest luxury hotel is connected with the nearby casino – both are housed in historic sandstone buildings which have been superbly renovated with no expense spared.

Coronation Motel (£) 205 Coronation Drive, Milton (tel: 07 3369 9955). Budget-priced motel rooms situated a short distance from the city centre. The motel isn't anything special, but it does offer good value accommodation.

273

HOTELS AND RESTAURANTS

Gazebo Hotel Brisbane (££) 345 Wickham Terrace (tel: 07 3831 6177). The most prominent among the cluster of hotels on the leafy heights overlooking the city centre (which is within easy walking distance).

The Heritage (£££) Corner of Margaret and Edward streets (tel: 07 3221 1999). A luxurious city centre hotel that makes the best of its location near the waterside and the famous Botanic Gardens.

Kirribilli Apartments (££) 150 Oxlade Drive, New Farm (tel: 07 3358 5622). These serviced apartments are located on the Brisbane River, and lie just minutes from the city by car or ferry. Both one- and two-bedroom apartments are available.

Mercure Hotel Brisbane (££) 85–7 North Quay (tel: 07 3236 3300). Located close to the city centre, the Mercure overlooks the river and South Bank Parklands. This comfortable hotel features some excellent facilities, including bars, restaurants and a swimming pool.

Metro Inn Tower Mill (££) 239 Wickham Terrace (tel: 07 3832 1421). Overlooking the city from high on Wickham Terrace, this comfortable hotel offers balconies, a cocktail bar and 24-hour room service.

Powerhouse Boutique Hotel (££/£££) Corner of Kingsford Smith Drive and Hunt Street, Hamilton (tel: 07 3862 1800). This elegant boutique-style hotel is conveniently close to the airport, yet only a short drive from the city. It has good facilities, including an excellent restaurant and bar.

Sheraton Brisbane Hotel and Towers (£££) 249 Turbot Street (tel: 07 3835 3535). All the luxury of a Sheraton in the heart of the city.

Sunshine Coast

Hyatt Regency Coolum (£££) Warran Road, Coolum Beach (tel: 07 5446 1234). A self-contained and extremely luxurious resort with a wide variety of types of accommodation as well as an extraordinary range of sports and recreational facilities. Located between Mount Coolum National Park and the glorious sands of the Sunshine Coast. Among the places to eat, Petrie's Restaurant is a regular award-winner. Bargains and special offers are available.

Netanya Noosa Resort (££) 75 Hastings Street, Noosa Heads (tel: 07 5447 4722). A delightful resort located right on the beachfront. All suites have a balcony and kitchenette, and the hotel is close to a great selection of restaurants.

Novotel Twin Waters Resort (£££) Ocean Drive, Mudjimba Beach (tel: 07 5448 8000). Another exclusive resort on the Sunshine Coast, Twin Waters has a wide range of facilities and is located near the mouth of the Maroochy River.

Sheraton Noosa Resort (£££) Hastings Street, Noosa Heads (tel: 07 5449 4888). Up-market accommodation in a well-designed, low-rise, resort complex. Rooms are spacious and provide spas and kitchenettes.

Sun Lagoon (££) Quamby Place, Noosa Sound (tel: 07 5447 4833). This waterfront resort is on the Noosa River and provides fully equipped self-contained apartments that can accommodate up to six.

Noosa has a good variety of accommodation, not in brash highrises like the Gold Coast but mostly in pleasing modern buildings of a more human scale. Details can be obtained from: **Accom Noosa**, Hastings Street, Noosa Heads, PO Box 694, Noosa, Qld 4567 (tel: 07 5447 3444).

Gold Coast and Hinterland

Conrad Jupiters (£££) Broadbeach Island (tel: 07 5592 1133). With its 600-plus rooms and 24-hour casino, this is one of the Gold Coast's prime places to see and be seen.

Diamonds Resort (££) 19 Orchid Avenue, Surfers Paradise (tel: 07 5570 1011). Diamonds is situated in the heart of Surfers Paradise and just a block back from the beach. Rooms, apartments and suites are all available at a reasonable price.

Sheraton Mirage (£££) Sea World Drive, Main Beach (tel: 07 5591 1488). Proving that not everything on the Gold Coast is the last word in brashness, the Sheraton is a tasteful and luxurious low-rise complex of buildings with impeccable landscaping. The famous eat at the prestigious Horizons Restaurant.

In the green hills beyond the coast:

Binna Burra Mountain Lodge (££) Beechmont, via Nerang (tel: 07 5533 3622). This is an excellent alternative to O'Reilly's (see below).

O'Reilly's Rainforest Guesthouse (££) Lamington National Park, via Canungra (tel: 07 5544 0644). Still run by a pioneer family, O'Reilly's has been welcoming people into the mountains for over 80 years. The price of your accommodation includes meals and activities.

Springbrook Mountain English Manor (££) Springbrook Road, Springbrook (tel: 07 5533 5344). Rural hotel with lots of the atmosphere of the 'Old Country' as well as fine food.

St Bernard's (£) 101 Alpine Terrace, Tamborine Mountain (tel: 07 5545 1177). Kookaburras make their usual racket in the rain forest around this rambling old hotel near the top of Mount Tamborine.

Cairns and the Far North

Cairns Colonial Club Resort (££) 18–26 Cannon Street, Manunda, Cairns (tel: 07 4053 5111). A popular resort-style complex with extensive gardens, the Colonial Club is located a short drive from the centre of town. Features include tennis courts, swimming pools and two restaurants.

Club Tropical (£££) Corner of Wharf and Macrossan streets, Port Douglas (tel: 07 4099

5885). Club Tropical offers total luxury – it is expensive, but is also one of the most exotic and up-market resorts existing in the area.

Coconut Beach Rainforest Resort (£££) Cape Tribulation (tel: 07 4098 0033). This unique resort is well integrated into its wonderful rainforest and tropical beach surroundings.

Country Comfort Outrigger (££) Corner of Florence and Abbott streets, Cairns (tel: 07 4051 6188). This modern interpretation of traditional north Queensland architecture can be found just back from the waterfront in the centre of Cairns.

Daintree Cape Tribulation Heritage Lodge (££) Turpentine Road, Cooper Creek, via Mossman (tel: 07 4098 9138). Stylish modern units designed to fit into their rain forest surroundings.

Garrick House (££) 11–13 Garrick Street, Port Douglas (tel: 07 4099 5322). High-standard apartment units with all amenities in a quiet street in delightful Port Douglas.

Mercure Hotel Harbourside (££) 209 The Esplanade, Cairns (tel: 07 4051 8999). This impeccable but rather anonymous modern hotel is located along The Esplanade, and is within easy walk of the centre of Cairns.

Radisson Plaza at the Pier (£££) Pierpoint Road, Cairns (tel: 07 4031 1411). The Radisson offers luxury living atop the lively new Pier Marketplace on the Cairns waterfront.

The Reef Hotel Casino (£££) 35–41 Wharf Street, Cairns (tel: 07 4030 8888). This very sophisticated hotel is part of the Cairns casino development, which was completed in 1996. The Reef offers butler service, excellent restaurants, tasteful décor and the ultimate in comfort.

Reef House (£££) 99 Williams Esplanade, Palm Cove (tel: 07 4055 3633). Situated on one of the beaches north of Cairns, this is a tropical-style resort with the best facilities and a high reputation.

Tradewinds Esplanade Hotel (££) 137 The Esplanade, Cairns (tel: 07 4052 1111). An attractive and centrally located hotel with views of Trinity Bay, gardens or the swimming pool.

TASMANIA
Hobart
Balmoral Motor Inn (£) 511 Brooker Highway, Glenorchy (tel: 03 6272 5833). Budget-priced motel units: a few minutes out of town, but good value.

Battery Point Guest House (££) 'Mandalay', 7 McGregor Street (tel: 03 6224 2111). Just up the steps from Salamanca Place are the attractively converted coach house and stables of 'Mandalay'.

Country Comfort Hadley's Hotel (££) 34 Murray Street (tel: 03 6223 4355). Good-value accommodation in a central location, with a licensed restaurant and two bars.

Crabtree House (££) Crabtree Road, 7km north of Huonville (tel: 03 6266 4227). An easy drive from Hobart down the Huon Highway amongst fine countryside is this colonial residence, beautifully furnished, providing bed and breakfast and a sumptuous dinner.

Hobart Pacific Motor Inn (££) Kirby Court, West Hobart (tel: 03 6234 6733). The inn offers comfortable, reasonably priced accommodation but the best feature is its location – just a few minutes from the centre with excellent views over the city.

Lenna of Hobart (££/£££) 20 Runnymede Street, Battery Point (tel: 03 6232 3900). This is a Victorian villa with a modern extension and overlooks the Derwent River.

The Lodge on Elizabeth (££) 249 Elizabeth Street (tel: 03 6231 3830). At the top end of town, but within walking distance of the centre is the oldest residential building in Hobart, tastefully converted. Your courteous hosts serve pre-dinner drinks.

Marquis of Hastings (£) 209 Brisbane Street, West Hobart (tel: 03 6234 3541). This is a somewhat forbidding 1960s red-brick building, but the accommodation is good value.

Regent Park Apartments (££) 17–22 Regent Street, Sandy Bay (tel: 03 6223 3200). Located near the casino, these well-appointed self-catering apartments are ideal for small groups and families.

Salamanca Inn (£££) 10 Gladstone Street (tel: 03 6223 3300). Integrated with unusual sensitivity among the old warehouses of Salamanca Place, the Salamanca is a luxury apartment hotel.

Tantallon Lodge (££) 8 Mona Street (tel: 03 6224 1724) and **Barton Cottage** (££) 72 Hampden Road (tel: 03 6224 1606) are well-established bed and breakfast villas that are conveniently located in Battery Point.

Wrest Point Hotel Casino (£££) 410 Sandy Bay Road, Sandy Bay (tel: 03 6225 0112). The casino's hotel provides some of the best accommodation in Hobart, in an excellent riverside location. As one would expect, there are good dining and entertainment facilities.

Cradle Mountain—Lake St Clair
Accommodation for visitors to the national park ranges from the chic cabins (log fires) of **Cradle Mountain Lodge** (PO Box 153 Sheffield, tel: 03 6492 1303) to a campground and bunkhouses. Further into the park are the **Waldheim Huts** (££) giving wilderness living with some home comforts. The handsome timber-built lodge has bars and an excellent restaurant. Possums and maybe a Tasmanian devil or two are likely to join you by the balcony after dinner.

Launceston
Adina Place Motel Apartments (££) 50 York Street (tel: 03 6331 6866). Fully serviced self-contained apartments located just a few minutes from the city centre.

HOTELS AND RESTAURANTS

Ashton Gate Guest House (£) 32 High Street (tel: 03 6331 6180). This elegantly restored Victorian home is a short walk from the city centre, overlooking St George's Square Park.

Colonial Motor Inn (££) Corner of George and Elizabeth streets (tel: 03 6331 6588). Once an old school, this building has been modernised and accommodation added, to say nothing of the Quill and Cane restaurant.

Country Club Casino (£££) Country Club Avenue, Prospect Vale (tel: 03 6344 8855). Although situated some distance outside Launceston, this pricey international standard resort and casino is a great place to stay. Facilities include an 18-hole golf course, horse-riding and fishing.

Kilmarnock House (££) 66 Elphin Road (tel: 03 6334 1514). With National Trust classification, this splendid large villa has been carefully refurbished and redecorated to evoke the atmosphere of the time (one night in 1904) when it was patronised by the Prince of Wales.

Novotel Launceston (££) 29 Cameron Street (tel: 03 6334 3434). All the services and comforts of a modern luxury hotel which has made some effort to fit in gracefully with its town centre surroundings. Phone up first to check for any special offers that may be available.

The Old Bakery Inn (££) 270 York Street (tel: 03 6331 7900). This well-restored old inn is a member of Historic Hotels of Australia and offers accommodation along traditional lines.

Tamar River Villas (££) 23 Elouera Street, Riverside (tel: 03 6327 1022). This standard but well-priced motel offers comfortable accommodation with views of the river.

RESTAURANTS

Eating out is relatively inexpensive in Australia, with a wide choice of ethnic cuisines and generally excellent ingredients. Costs can be further trimmed if you BYO – bring your own (wine or other liquor), which is allowed by many establishments. The 'counter meals' served in many pubs are usually excellent value, and most places where tourists congregate have a variety of take-away outlets.

The following recommended restaurants have been divided into three price categories:
- budget (£)
- moderate (££)
- expensive (£££)

SYDNEY

Arun Thai (££) 13/39 Elizabeth Bay Road, Elizabeth Bay (tel: 02 9357 7414). One of Sydney's most reliable Thai restaurants with a pleasant outdoor dining area. Close to the Kings Cross area.

Balkan Seafood (££) 215 Oxford Street, Darlinghurst (tel: 02 9331 7670). Excellent seafood at very reasonable prices, in a lively atmosphere on trendy Oxford Street.

Bayswater Brasserie (££/£££) 32 Bayswater Road, Kings Cross (tel: 02 9357 2177). The best and most stylish brasserie in town. A three-course meal tends towards the expensive, but there are cheaper alternatives.

Bennelong (£££) Sydney Opera House, Bennelong Point (tel: 02 9250 7578). This is the best of the Opera House's food and drink outlets, with excellent Modern Australian food served up with wonderful 180-degree views over the harbour.

Borobudur (£) 123–125 Glebe Point Road, Glebe (tel: 02 9660 5611). Good value and friendly service are provided in this BYO restaurant in the inner east suburb of Glebe.

Catalina Rose Bay (£££) 1 Sunderland Avenue, Rose Bay (tel: 02 9371 0555). This establishment is expensive, but worth it for its wonderful harbourside location (particularly entrancing at night) and acclaimed Modern Australian menu, which features many seafood dishes.

Doyle's On the Beach (£££) 11 Marine Parade, Watsons Bay (tel: 02 9337 2007). Classic fish and chips are served in huge quantities to up to 700 enthusiastic diners in this, one of the world's most famous fish restaurants. In its splendid location near South Head, there are great views of the harbour. There is also another branch of Doyle's at Circular Quay West (tel: 02 9252 3400).

Flavour of India Edgecliff (££) 120 New South Head Road, Edgecliff (tel: 02 9326 2659). Sydney is not renowned for its Indian restaurants, but this is one of the best. There are both traditional and South Indian dishes, and some inventive Aussie-Indian concoctions.

Golden Harbour (££) 31 Dixon Street (tel: 02 9211 5160). Among the wealth of inexpensive Chinese eateries that can be found in Chinatown, the Golden Harbour was identified by *The Sydney Morning Herald* as serving the very best value in *yum cha* (also known as *dim sum*).

Hyde Park Barracks Café (£–££) Queens Square, Macquarie Street (tel: 02 9223 1155). Set in the grounds of the historic Hyde Park Barracks, this long-running café is excellent for a city centre lunch or daytime snacks (closed in the evenings).

Imperial Harbourside (£££) 15 Circular Quay West (tel: 02 9247 7073). One of Sydney's very best Chinese restaurants, the Imperial Harbourside has a sensational location opposite the Opera House.

Jordons Seafood Restaurant (££) 197 Harbourside, Darling Harbour (tel: 02 9281 3711). One of the best places to eat at Darling Harbour. Good seafood, an excellent atmosphere and views of the water.

Kable's (£££) The Regent, 199 George Street (tel: 02 9238 0000). Attentive service and a wide-ranging wine list complement the stylish cooking of Kable's, one of the best hotel restaurants in the city.

Kam Fook (££) Market City, 9 Hay Street, Haymarket (tel: 02 9211 8988). One of Sydney's newest restaurants, the bustling 800-seater Kam Fook specialises in seafood, and also offers some unusual options for *yum cha*.

Kamogawa (£££) Corn Exchange Building, corner of Sussex Street and Market Street, Darling Harbour (tel: 02 9299 5533). A relative newcomer, the Kamogawa has already established a reputation equal or superior to the Suntory (see the listing below).

Laurie's (£/££) Corner of Victoria and Burton streets, Darlinghurst (tel: 02 9360 4915). A wonderful, great-value vegetarian eatery situated in the Kings Cross region. BYO and no-smoking area.

Malaya (££) 761 George Street (tel: 02 9211 0946). This old-established restaurant with attractive décor offers good Malaysian food such as *satay* and *sambal* at reasonable prices.

Nelson Bistro (££) The Nelson Hotel, 232 Oxford Street, Bondi Junction (tel: 02 9389 1442). Some of Sydney's best-value modern Australian cuisine in the back of a traditional Aussie pub.

Ravesi's (££/£££) Corner of Campbell Parade and Hall Street, Bondi Beach (tel: 02 9365 4422). Another great brasserie, this restaurant can be found in the boutique-style Ravesi's Hotel overlooking Bondi Beach.

Rossini's Rosticceria (£) Shop W5, Circular Quay (tel: 02 9247 8026). There are harbour views to accompany Rossini's swiftly served and tasty food and drink.

Sailor's Thai (£–£££) 106 George Street, The Rocks (tel: 02 9251 2466). There are two options here – a noodle bar with communal canteen-style seating, or a much more exclusive downstairs restaurant. The food is superb in both venues, however.

Suntory (£££) 529 Kent Street (tel: 02 9267 2900). Something of a Sydney institution, Suntory offers exquisite Japanese food in elegant surroundings.

Sydney Tower Restaurant (£££) Sydney Tower, Centrepoint (tel: 02 9233 3722). There is an unsurpassable panorama over the city and harbour from this revolving restaurant perched more than 300m above ground level. The food's not bad either.

Tetsuya's (£££) 759 Darling Street, Rozelle (tel: 02 9555 1017). One of Sydney's very best restaurants, the acclaimed Tetsuya's blends Australian, French and Japanese cuisines. Both lunch and dinner menus are *dégustation* and set-price.

Thai Flora (£) 46 Hall Street, Bondi Beach (tel: 02 9130 2751). Bangkok comes to Bondi Beach. Although fairly basic, this restaurant serves great food at even better prices and is a local favourite.

Tre Scalini (££) 174 Liverpool Street, East Sydney (tel: 02 9331 4358). Simple and good food, especially fish and pasta. A lunchtime favourite.

ACT
Canberra
Cavalier Carousel Restaurant (£/££) Red Hill Lookout, Red Hill (tel: 02 6273 1808). Modern international cuisine is on offer here, and in the downstairs café, with the bonus of spectacular lake and city views.

The Lobby (££) King George Terrace, Parkes (tel: 02 6273 1563). Contemporary Australian cuisine is served up in an attractive garden setting near the old Parliament House.

Fringe Benefits (££) 54 Marcus Clarke Street, City (tel: 02 6247 4042). Fringe Benefits has been described by patronising Sydneysiders as the nearest thing the capital has to a trendy Sydney brasserie.

The Oak Room (£££) Hyatt Hotel Canberra, Commonwealth Avenue, Yarralumla (tel: 02 6270 8977). The Oak Room provides an elegant setting for equally refined food.

Vivaldi (££) Australian National University, Campus Arts Centre, University Avenue, Acton (tel: 02 6257 2718). This restaurant is usually full of locals, which can't be a bad sign. It serves generous portions and offers BYO.

NEW SOUTH WALES
Blue Mountains
Café Bon Ton (££) 192 The Mall, Leura (tel: 02 4782 4377). At this pleasant café you can dine on anything from snacks to a hearty breakfast or a three-course dinner. There is a fire in winter, and garden seating for the warmer months.

Cleopatra (£££) 118 Cleopatra Street, Blackheath (tel: 02 4787 8456). Marvellous French cooking in one of the best restaurants in New South Wales.

Paragon Café (££) 65 Katoomba Street, Katoomba (tel: 02 4782 2928). A National Trust classified café dating from 1916, The Paragon is worth visiting for its own sake as well as for its delicious chocolates.

Silks Brasserie (££–£££) 128 The Mall, Leura (tel: 02 4784 2534). This nicely decorated brasserie has a deservedly high reputation for its Modern Australian menu, which includes kangaroo fillets and innovative Atlantic salmon dishes.

VICTORIA
Melbourne
Caffe Grossi (££) 199 Toorak Road, South Yarra (tel: 03 9827 6076). A popular Italian restaurant with great food and good service.

Colonial Tramcar Restaurant (£££) (tel: 03 9696 4000). Dine on Australian fare while travelling Melbourne's streets in a beautifully renovated old tramcar.

Fanny's (£££) 243 Lonsdale Street (tel: 03 9663 3017). This Melbourne institution

277

serves award-winning French food in elegant surroundings.

Flower Drum (£££) 17 Market Lane (tel: 03 9662 3655). This is an exceptionally good Cantonese restaurant that has won high praise, particularly for its Peking duck and seafood dishes.

Geppetto (£) 78a Wellington Parade, East Melbourne (tel: 03 9417 4691). A quiet and inexpensive Italian restaurant.

The Last Aussie Fishcaf (£) 256 Park Street, South Melbourne (tel: 03 9699 1900). This jokey fish and chip shop has a 1950s theme.

Madame Joe Joe (££) 9 Fitzroy Street, St Kilda (tel: 03 9534 0000). In the heart of Melbourne's most lively suburb, this popular, fun place serves Modern Australian meals with a Mediterranean emphasis. The char-grills are very good.

Malaysian Delight (£) 1335 Burke Road, East Kew (tel: 03 9817 2459). Everything the name promises at a reasonable price.

Maria Trattoria (£) 122 Peel Street, North Melbourne (tel: 03 9329 9016). A favourite with the academic crowd from the nearby university.

Mount Lebanon Restaurant (££) 177 Toorak Road, South Yarra (tel: 03 9826 9080). The best Lebanese food in town at good prices. Entertainment includes live music and belly dancers. The restaurant is licensed and offers BYO.

Nudel Bar (£) 76 Bourke Street (tel: 03 9662 9100). A bustling city centre café that offers a range of noodles – from pastas to fried Thai varieties with a choice of sauces and cooking styles. Great value.

The Pavilion (£££) 40 Jacka Boulevard, St Kilda (tel: 03 9534 8221). Great seafood is served both inside and outside a splendidly restored bathing pavilion overlooking the bay.

Rogalsky's (£££) 440 Clarendon Street, South Melbourne (tel: 03 9690 1977). An army cook finally able to realise his full culinary potential, Tony R runs one of the city's most sensational French restaurants.

Stella (££–£££) 159 Spring Street (tel: 03 9639 1555). One of Melbourne's favourite Modern Australian restaurants: the food is excellent, the décor stylish, and the service very professional.

Stephanie's (£££) 405 Tooronga Road, East Hawthorn (tel: 03 9822 8944). Consistently the critics' favourite since the 1970s, and a source of culinary wisdom, Stephanie Alexander runs one of Australia's top restaurants in a series of elegant dining rooms in a venerable Victorian mansion.

Sukhothai (£) 234 Johnston Street, Fitzroy (tel: 03 9419 4040). Good Thai cooking is dished up at very reasonable prices. Salads and curries are a specialty and there is a large vegetarian selection. The restaurant offers BYO.

Suntory (££/£££) 74 Queens Road (tel: 03 9525 1231). Fine Japanese food and service in traditional oriental garden surroundings.

Thy Thy (£) First floor, 142 Victoria Street, Richmond (tel: 03 9429 1104). Excellent and very inexpensive Vietnamese food. It is also worth trying **Thy Thy** 116 Victoria Street, Richmond (tel: 03 9428 5914).

SOUTH AUSTRALIA
Adelaide

Bangkok (££) 217 Rundle Street (tel: 08 8223 5406). Adelaide's longest established Thai restaurant offers authentic cooking at very reasonable prices. It is conveniently located in the city centre.

Blake's (£££) Hyatt Regency Hotel, North Terrace (tel: 08 8238 2381). This elegant hotel restaurant serves innovative Modern Australian food, with an emphasis on South Australian produce and wines. The ideal location for a special night out.

Chloe's (££/£££) 36 College Road, Kent Town (tel: 08 8362 2574). In a splendidly restored Victorian villa with veranda and antique furnishings, elegant but friendly gourmet French food is served up.

Earl of Aberdeen (££) 316 Pulteney Street (tel: 08 8223 6433). This stylish old pub has an excellent restaurant – you can enjoy steaks and even sample kangaroo here.

Fishcaf (£) 100 Flinders Street (tel: 08 8232 3660). Value for money fish restaurant in superior surroundings.

Jolleys Boathouse (££) Jolleys Lane (tel: 08 8223 2891). This refurbished old boathouse is right on the River Torrens and serves Modern Australian food. Great views.

Lemongrass Bistro (£–££) 289 Rundle Street (tel: 08 8223 6627). With its excellent contemporary Thai cuisine, an outdoor dining area and lively atmosphere, this is a very popular city centre bistro.

Mona Lisa's Bistro (££) 160 Hutt Street (tel: 08 8223 3733). This bistro describes itself as 'strongly Mediterranean influenced'. It is housed in a heritage-listed former general store.

Nediz Tu (££) 170 Hutt Street (tel: 08 8223 2618). Smart but not pretentious, this relaxed restaurant is run by an Anglo-Chinese couple.

The Oxford North Adelaide (££) 101 O'Connell Street, North Adelaide (tel: 08 8267 2652). Located in trendy North Adelaide, this award-winning restaurant features an outdoor dining area, and an outstanding wine list.

Paul's Seafood Restaurant (££) 79 Gouger Street (tel: 08 8231 9778). The dishes on offer here are basic, but reportedly the 'best fried fish in Australia'. There are generous helpings of whatever you fancy – garfish, whiting, snapper...

Pullman Restaurant (££) North Terrace (tel: 08 8218 4273). Adelaide's casino houses this surprisingly reasonable buffet-style restaurant. The menu includes salads, pastas and a wide variety of hot dishes.

Red Ochre Grill (££) 129 Gouger Street (tel: 08 8212 7266). One of Adelaide's hottest dining spots, this popular place specialises in Aussie 'bush tucker'. The menu might include dishes featuring emu, possum, local seafood, native plants and kangaroo.

Adelaide Hills
The Bistro at Hochstens of Hahndorf (££) 145a Main Road, Hahndorf (tel: 08 8388 1176). One of the best places to dine in the Adelaide Hills, this restaurant in the charming town of Hahndorf offers a great atmosphere, open fires and fine views.

Barossa Valley
The Hermitage of Marananga (££/£££) Corner of Seppeltsfield and Stonewell roads, Marananga (tel: 08 8562 2722). This highly acclaimed Barossa Valley hotel and restaurant offers breakfast, lunch and dinner – either inside, or *al fresco* on the patio.

WESTERN AUSTRALIA
Perth
Belissimo (£/££) 3 Bay View Terrace, Claremont (tel: 08 9385 3588). Serving fine Southern Italian food, particularly wood-fired pizzas, and a good range of pastas, this is a popular suburban restaurant.
Canton Restaurant (££) 532 Hay Street (tel: 08 9325 8865). One of Perth's best and longest-running Chinese restaurants. The Canton is licensed and offers BYO.
Dusit Thai (££) 233 James Street, Northbridge (tel: 08 9328 7647). This popular Northbridge establishment serves excellent and authentic Thai cuisine.
Fraser's (££) Kings Park (tel: 08 9481 7100). Fine Western Australian produce and seafood are the flavours at this Kings Park eatery. There are wonderful city and river views.
Gershwin's (£££) 99 Adelaide Terrace (tel: 08 9225 1234). You'll find good international cuisine in this upmarket restaurant located in the city's Hyatt Regency hotel.
The Loose Box Restaurant (£££) 6825 Great Eastern Highway, Mundaring (tel: 08 9295 1787). This restaurant has one of the best reputations in Western Australia, and is well worth the half-hour drive out of Perth along the highway into the Darling Ranges.
Mamma Maria's (£) Corner of Aberdeen and Lake streets, Northbridge (tel: 08 9328 4532). Both cheap and highly cheerful, Mamma Maria's is a Perth institution *all'Italiana*.
Matilda Bay Restaurant (£££) 3 Hackett Drive, Crawley (tel: 08 9386 5425). Excellent seafood specialities are served in a relaxed setting by the Swan River among the houses of the prosperous citizens of Perth's western suburbs.
The Oyster Bar (££) 20 Roe Street, Northbridge (tel: 08 9328 7888). Described as 'Perth's leading seafood restaurant', this friendly family-run concern has just moved into spacious and stylish new premises amongst its numerous competitors. It pro-

vides good, cheap food in Perth's trendy Northbridge area.
Perugino (££) 77 Outram Street, West Perth (tel: 08 9321 5420). A fully licensed restaurant serving fine Italian cuisine.
Tuscany Grill (£££) Sheraton Perth Hotel, 207 Adelaide Terrace (tel: 08 9325 0501). Excellent Mediterranean-style cooking and elegant surroundings are the hallmark of this hotel restaurant.
Vino Vino (££) 157 James Street, Northbridge (tel: 08 9328 5403). Flavoursome Italian food served with style. Wines include Italian as well as Western Australian vintages.

Freemantle
Café Panache (££/£££) Esplanade Hotel, corner of Marine Terrace and Essex Street (tel: 08 9430 4000). Excellent seafood but not just seafood, imaginatively prepared and presented. At the same address is the much more affordable **Atrium Garden Restaurant**.
Chunagon (£££) 46 Mews Road (tel: 08 9336 1000). With wonderful views of Fremantle's harbour and the ocean, this large Japanese restaurant offers authentic sushi, tempura, sashimi, and many other dishes.
Prickles Café (££) Corner of Douro Road and South Terrace, Fremantle (tel: 08 9336 2194). Western Australia's favourite 'bush tucker' restaurant – sample buffalo, prawns, emu and kangaroo, cooked in an innovative style.

Kalgoorlie-Boulder
Basil's on Hannan (££) 168 Hannan Street (tel: 08 9021 7832). This is a pleasant all-day café, serving snacks, coffees, cakes, lunches and dinner on some nights. The pastas and other Italian dishes are particularly recommended.
Top End Thai (££) 71 Hannan Street (tel: 08 9021 4286). Located in the same building as a skimpie bar, but much more refined, is this excellent Thai restaurant.

NORTHERN TERRITORY
Darwin
Corellas Restaurant (£) The Atrium Hotel, corner of The Esplanade and Peel Street (tel: 08 8941 0755). Inexpensive soups, salads and buffet meals are dished up in a tropical garden setting. Open daily to 10pm. BYO.
Christos on the Wharf (££) Stokes Hill Wharf (tel: 08 8981 8658). In a unique wharfside location, this restaurant is deservedly popular for its seafood.
Genghis Khan Mongolian Barbecue Restaurant (£££) 44 East Point Road, Fannie Bay (tel: 08 8981 3883). As well as steaks derived from more conventional creatures, you may be able to taste crocodile, kangaroo, buffalo...
The Hanuman (££–£££) 28 Mitchell Street (tel: 08 8941 3500). This is arguably Darwin's finest restaurant – the service is

279

admirable and the food consists of Thai and Malaysian Nonya dishes.

The Magic Wok (££) 48 Cavenagh Street (tel: 08 8981 3332). Wok-cooked meals that include such exotic ingredients as buffalo, crocodile, deer and camel. More everyday seafood and vegetables are also available.

Raymond's (££) 21 Cavenagh Street (tel: 08 8981 2909). Locals come here for fine international cuisine. Good ingredients are used in well prepared and presented dishes.

Rock Oyster (££)110 Mitchell Street (tel: 08 8981 3472). This long-running establishment claims to be Darwin's best seafood restaurant.

Scales (££) 56 Marina Boulevard, Cullen Bay (tel: 08 8981 6522). Darwin's Cullen Bay region offers some excellent new restaurants, including this bistro which serves inventive Modern Australian cuisine.

Siam (££) The Esplanade (tel: 08 8941 2555). Thai cooking, including steamboats, in this Beaufort hotel restaurant.

Alice Springs

Alice Springs Bush Restaurant (££) PO Box 1820, Alice Springs (tel: 08 8952 9355). Lies 30km from Alice Springs. Under ownership of the same old Territorian family which runs Bojangles (see below), this is a replica of an Outback stock camp offering a 'total Outback experience', including a bush walk, entertainment, and substantial quantities of typical Australian fare such as beef, billy tea, bread pudding and spotted dog.

Bojangle's Bush Bistro (££) 80 Todd Street (tel: 08 8952 2873). Buffalo and camel feature on the menu of this cheerful establishment with its long bar and live entertainment.

Oriental Gourmet (£) 80 Hartley Street (tel: 08 8953 0888). The menu of this Outback restaurant is traditional Chinese, and fairly predictable, but the food is fresh and good.

Overlander Steakhouse (££) 72 Hartley Street (tel: 08 8952 2159). Rough-cast walls, low timber ceilings and swagman's impedimenta together with huge portions of stockman's tucker create an agreeable Outback atmosphere.

Ristorante Puccini (££) Ansett Building, Todd Mall (tel: 08 8953 0935). Family-owned restaurant with an unusually good Italian menu.

Ayers Rock

See hotel listings on page 273.

QUEENSLAND

Brisbane

City Gardens Café (£/££) Brisbane Botanic Gardens (tel: 07 3229 1554). A delightful surprise in the lush setting of the city's botanical gardens, this cottage with a terrace serves delicious snacks to restore your sightseeing abilities. Full meals are available too at lunchtime.

Coronation Seafood Restaurant (£££) 205 Coronation Drive, Milton (tel: 07 3369 9955). The Coronation enjoys a high reputation for serving the best seafood in town – no mean feat!

Emperor's Palace (££) Chinatown Mall, Fortitude Valley (tel: 07 3252 3368). This is one of the more pretentious of the many eateries which characterise Brisbane's diminutive Chinatown.

Kookaburra Queen (££) Departs from Eagle Street Pier, Eagle Street (tel: 07 3221 1300). As with many 'tourist restaurants', the food isn't sensational, but a dinner cruise (with live entertainment) along the Brisbane River is worth the price alone.

Il Centro (£££) Eagle Street Pier (tel: 07 3221 6090). Modern Italian food is served in this popular and elegant riverside restaurant. The menu changes seasonally.

La Grange (££) 153 Elizabeth Street (tel: 07 3221 5590). French provincial cooking is served in this city centre restaurant.

The Lotus Room (££) Corner of Elizabeth and Edward streets (tel: 07 3221 8546). The service is both fast and efficient in this popular Chinese eatery.

The Malaysian Experience (££) 80 Jephson Street, Toowong (tel: 07 3870 2646). Perhaps the finest Malysian restaurant in town, this establishment serves mouth-watering laksas, noodles and plenty of authentic chilli-inspired dishes.

Michael's Riverside Restaurant (£££) Riverside Centre, 123 Eagle Street (tel: 07 3832 5522). Italian and international cuisine are available in two dining rooms, both of which have excellent views over the river.

Mount Coot-tha Summit Restaurant (££/£££) Sir Samuel Griffith Drive, Mount Coot-tha (tel: 07 3369 9922). Good food and stunning views over the city and out to Moreton Bay are available from this mountaintop restaurant, within the city boundary.

Oshin Japanese Restaurant (££) 1st floor, Koala House, Corner of Adelaide and Creek streets (tel: 07 3229 0410). Serves up Japanese fare, including traditional dishes such as *yakiniku* and many others.

Pier Nine (££/£££) Eagle Street Pier (tel: 07 3229 2194). Here, riverside views and menus reflect the availability of delicious seafood.

Romeo's Italian Restaurant (££) 216 Petrie Terrace (tel: 07 3367 0955). Northen Italian cuisine is the specialty here – the Venetian veal and seafood dishes are particularly good, as is the rich tiramisu for dessert.

Siggi's at The Heritage (£££) Corner of Edward and Margaret streets (tel: 07 3221 4555). *The* place to meet and celebrate in Brisbane, Siggi's is part of the Heritage Hotel.

Sunshine Coast

Artis Café and Bar (££) 8 Noosa Drive, Noosa Heads (tel: 07 5447 2300). Among

Noosa's many restaurants, this stands out for its delicious European-Australian food that exhibits Asian influences.

Chilli Jam Café (£–££) 195 Weyba Road, Noosaville (tel: 07 5449 9755). Just a short drive from the main Sunshine Coast resort of Noosa Heads, this very popular restaurant serves innovative Thai cuisine.

Lindoni's Ristorante (££) Hastings Street, Noosa Heads (tel: 07 5447 5111). Highly recommended Italian food.

Gold Coast and Hinterland

Great Wall (£££) Marina Mirage, Seaworld Drive, Main Beach (tel: 07 5591 0898). Some of the best Chinese food in Australia served in elegant surroundings.

Oskar's on the Beach (£££) Marine Parade, Coolangatta (tel: 07 5536 4621). On Coolangatta Beach just on the border with New South Wales, Oskar's is famous for its refined and delicious food. This reputation is well deserved as it has been voted one of the world's top ten restaurants.

Cairns and the Far North

Barnacle Bills (££) 65 The Esplanade (tel: 07 4051 2241). On the Esplanade in Cairns, this is a popular seafront seafood eating emporium whose fame has spread to the shores of the Inland Sea, and an evening spent here is an essential part of any tourist's stay in Cairns!

Macrossans (£££) Sheraton Mirage, Davidson Street, Port Douglas (tel: 07 4099). Part of the opulent resort set back discreetly from the palm-lined highway leading into Port Douglas, McCrossan's produces fine food that is also presented in a most elegant way.

Marina Connection (£) Marina Mirage, Port Douglas (tel: 07 4099 5258). Food here is served both indoors and outside near the jetty for the Barrier Reef wave-piercers.

TASMANIA
Hobart

Alexander's (£££) 20 Runnymede Street, Battery Point (tel: 03 6232 3900). This excellent, award-winning restaurant serves seafood and international cuisine in the elegant surroundings of the Victorian Lenna of Hobart hotel.

The Asian Restaurant (£££) Wrest Point Hotel Casino, 410 Sandy Bay Road (tel: 03 6225 0112). Serving up dishes that are far above the usual standard of Chinese and other Asian food, this restaurant is presided over by a particularly genial host. Book early for seats if you wish to have a view of the Derwent.

Ball & Chain Grill (££) 87 Salamanca Place (tel: 03 6223 2655). Charcoal-grilled steaks, poultry and seafood are dished out at affordable prices. There is also an outdoor courtyard area in summer.

Battery Point Brasserie (££) 59 Hampden Road, Battery Point (tel: 03 6223 3186).

Serving brasserie-style food, including some delicious desserts, this is one of Hobart's favourite eateries. The prices are very resonable, and it is also BYO.

Blue Skies Dining (£–££) Murray Street Pier (tel: 03 6224 3747). In a superb location right on the Hobart waterfront, this lively brasserie offers a good Modern Australian menu, and outdoor seating.

Dear Friends (£££) 8 Brooke Street (tel: 03 6223 2646). Considered by many to be Hobart's finest restaurant, this award-winning establishment produces international fare and the very best service.

Drunken Admiral Restaurant (££) 17–19 Hunter Street (tel: 03 6234 1903). Well established in one of Victoria's old warehouses and decorated with maritime memorabilia, this popular restaurant naturally specialises in seafood.

Mures Lower Deck (££) Victoria Dock (tel: 03 6231 2121). Long queues form next to the fishmonger's counter for top-value seafood to eat here, on the quayside beyond, or to take away.

Mures Upper Deck (££) Victoria Dock (tel: 03 6231 2121). From its first-floor pavilion between Victoria and Constitution Docks, Mures serves the bounty of the sea with great flair. It is advisable to book.

Sisco's on the Pier (££) Murray Street Pier (tel: 03 6223 2059). Located above Blue Skies Dining on the main pier, Sisco's is famous for its innovative Spanish/ Mediterranean-style cuisine and fine service.

Cradle Mountain
See hotel listing on page 275.

Launceston

Fee and Mee (££–£££) 190 Charles Street (tel: 03 6331 3195). Considered to be one of the best restaurants in Tasmania, this establishment specialises in fine Modern Australian cuisine, and there is an excellent wine list.

The Gorge Restaurant (££) Cliff Grounds (tel: 03 6331 3330). Fine Tasmanian produce and wines in a superb location, overlooking Launceston's famous gorge and its surrounding gardens.

Shrimps (££) 72 George Street (tel: 03 6334 0584). This popular establishment, located in a National Trust-classified building in the town centre, serves excellent seafood – mussels, oysters, Atlantic salmon...

Squires (£) 70 Brisbane Street (tel: 03 6334 1466). Just down the arcade opening off this central street, Squires serves up delicious local seafood and game dishes.

Star Bar Café (£–££) 113 Charles Street (tel: 03 6331 9659). The prices are very reasonable at this casual city centre café, which serves snacks, main meals or just drinks.

Woofies (££) Macquarie House, Civic Square (tel: 03 6334 0695). In another historic building in the heart of town, this restaurant has a good choice of attractively priced dishes.

Index

INDEX

INDEX

287

PICTURE CREDITS AND CONTRIBUTORS

Picture credits

The Automobile Association would like to thank the following photographers, libraries and associations for their assistance in the preparation of this book.

ACT TOURISM 82 Skiing Snowy Mountains. ALLSPORT UK LTD spine Australian cricketer (M. Hewitt), 166 Melbourne Cup. ARDEA LONDON 88a Feather Star (V Taylor), 88c Taipan (C J Mason), 228–9 Freycinet Nat Park (Jon P Ferrero), 236b The Lower Gordon (Jon P Ferrero), 238b Gordon Dam (Jon P Ferrero), 242–3 Tasman Peninsula (Jon P Ferrero). AUSTRALIAN TOURIST COMMISSION back cover Great Barrier Reef. BRIDGEMAN ART LIBRARY 19 *Dog & Duck Hotel* by Sidney Nolan (1917–92) Roy Miles Gallery, 29 Bruton Street, London W1/Bridgeman Art Library, London. DEPARTMENT OF MARITIME ARCHAEOLOGY, WA MARITIME MUSEUM 243a Silver dish with decorations, 243c Astrolabe. MARY EVANS PICTURE LIBRARY 26a Convicts Sydney, 26b Dampier attacked by natives, 27 Governor Phillip Sydney Cove, 28–9 Burke & Wills, 30b Prospectors, 76 Captain Cook, 77 Cook at Botany Bay, 161b Pearl diving. CHRIS FAIRCLOUGH COLOUR LIBRARY 116a Aborigines, 166–7 Diamond mine, 194 Aborigine children at school, 195 Aborigines in the bush. FFOTOGRAFF 24a Cave paintings Nourlangie Rock, 174 Dolphins, Monkey Mia, 241 Aboriginal rock engraving. FOOTPRINTS 216–17 Coral Reef (A Dalton), 216 Feeding potato cod (N Hanna), 217b Butterfly fish (Carlos Lima), 218 Angel fish (A Dalton), 219 Heron Island (N Hanna). RONALD GRANT ARCHIVES 18c Paul Hogan, *Crocodile Dundee*. INTERNATIONAL PHOTOBANK 12a Acacia, 13 Kangaroo, 14a Boat to Great Barrier Reef, 24b Aborigine, 29 Alice Springs, 31 Sovereign Hill, 32 Eucalyptus gum, 34 Caravan park Sydney, 82–3 Lake Blowering, 90 Native plant, 92–3 Great Ocean Road, 97 Trams, 114 Olinda Rhododendron Garden, 114b Grampians, 118 Great Ocean Road, Twelve Apostles, 127 Bethany Church, 134 Commuter bus, 135 Cleland Wildlife Park, 137 Flinders Ranges, 138 Goolwa P S *Mundoo*, 140–1 Barossa Valley grapes, 142 Victor Harbor, 175b York sign, 177 Ghost gum tree, 178 Alice Springs sign, 184 Memorial to Rev John Flynn, 185b Restaurant sign Alice Springs, 200 Green Island, 208 Glass House Mountains, 209b Crimson rosella, 210 Pacific Highway, 211 Cairns, 213 Bottle brush plant, 217a Snorkelling instruction, 252 Australian, 253 Overland train, 257 Backpackers, 267a Standley Chasm. MICHAEL IVORY 8b, 25 Ranger Kakadu National Park. NATURE PHOTOGRAPHERS LTD 121 Southern right whale (R Tidman), 222b Cassowary (S C Bisseroi). NORTHERN TERRITORY TOURIST COMMISSION 181 Government House Darwin, 182 Nat Mus of Arts & Sciences Darwin, 189 The Ghan, 191 Cutta Cutta Caves, 198 Glen Helen Gorge, 255 Jeep, 259 Simpsons Gap. CHRISTINE OSBORNE PICTURES 224b Cowboy. ANDY PRICE 18a Tjapukai Aboriginal dance, 21a Aboriginal art, 178–9 Katherine Gorge, 192b Termite mounds, 193 Kakadu National Park, 194–5 Aboriginal art. QUEEN VICTORIA MUSEUM & ART GALLERY 241b J Glover *Last Muster of Aborigines Brighton*, ROYAL GEOGRAPHICAL SOCIETY 23 map. SPECTRUM COLOUR LIBRARY 99 Melbourne Cricket Ground, 103 Melbourne Zoo, 120 Gum tree 203b Kuranda train, 215 Surfers Paradise, 220 Lamington National Park, 222a Rainforest, 222c Rainforest Bunya Mountains, 223 Yacht Port Douglas, 225 Sunshine Coast, 235 L Dove, 237 Cradle Mountain National Park, 247 Port Arthur Convict Museum, 250 Fishing boats St Helens. TONY STONE IMAGES front cover Kata Tjuta, front cover windsurfer, front cover Aboriginal boy. TOURISM SOUTH AUSTRALIA 130 Port Adelaide, 131 Ayers House, 132 Tandanya Aboriginal Culture Centre, 133 Remarkable Rocks, Kangaroo Island, 139 R Murray. TOURISM TASMANIA 236a Rafting, 240 Boat Freycinet Peninsula, 243 Shipwreck, 246 Derwent Valley, 248 Queenstown, 249 Tuna fishing, 264 Trout fishing. WESTERN AUSTRALIAN TOURISM COMMISSION 148 Warren National Park, 151 Kings Park, Perth, 157b Bungle Bungle National Park, 159 Pioneer World Armadale, 160 Bunbury, 167 Iron ore mine Pilbara, 168 Mandurah, 170 Ningaloo Reef, 173a Gibb River road truck, 173b Argyle Diamond Mine, 175a Wave Rock, 262 New Norcia Abbey Church. ZEFA PICTURES LTD 224a Farmer & bulls.

All remaining pictures are held in the Association's own picture library (AA PHOTO LIBRARY) with contributions from:

ADRIAN BAKER 2, 5b, 5c, 6a, 7a, 7b, 8a, 10–11, 10, 11, 15, 20, 21b, 22–3, 22, 23, 28, 30a, 33a, 35, 47, 48, 49, 52a, 54, 55b, 60, 64–5, 66, 67a, 69, 70, 71, 72, 73, 75, 76–7, 78, 79, 83, 85, 87, 88b, 89, 92, 98, 100a, 100b, 102b, 106, 107, 109, 111, 112–13, 112, 113, 115, 117, 119, 120b, 122, 123, 126–7, 136, 143a, 143b, 145, 146, 149, 152, 153, 154, 156, 157a, 158, 161a, 162, 163, 164, 165, 169a, 169b, 169c, 171, 172, 185a, 186, 187, 188–9, 190a, 190b, 192a, 196a, 196b, 197, 199, 202, 203a, 205, 206, 207, 209a, 212, 221, 228, 229, 231, 232, 233, 234, 238a, 239, 244, 245, 256, 258, 260, 261, 263. PAUL KENWARD 3, 4, 5a, 9b, 12b, 14b, 16a, 17, 33b, 39, 40, 40–1, 42, 43, 45, 46a, 46b, 50, 51, 52b, 53, 55a, 58, 59, 61, 62, 67b, 68, 74, 80–1, 84, 86, 183b, 188, 251a,b, 265, 266, 267b. CHRISTINE OSBORNE 96a, 96b, 101, 102a, 104, 105, 108, 110, 166. KEN PATERSON 183a.

Contributors

Revision copy editor: Rebecca Snelling   **Original copy editor:** Sally Knowles
Revision verifier: Anne Matthews